Population
Growth:

Anthropological
Implications

The MIT Press

Cambridge,
Massachusetts, and
London, England

Proceedings of
a colloquium in
general anthropology
entitled
"Population,
Resources,
and Technology,"
held at
the University of
Pennsylvania,
March 11–14, 1970,
under the combined
auspices of the Near
East Center, the
University Museum,
and the Department
of Anthropology of
the University of
Pennsylvania,
in association with the
Wenner-Gren
Foundation for
Anthropological
Research,
Incorporated.

**Population
Growth:**

edited by
Brian Spooner

**Anthropological
Implications**

This book was designed by The MIT Press Design Department.
It was set in Monotype Baskerville,
printed on Mohawk Neotext Offset
and bound in Interlaken AL3–890 (Brown)
by Halliday Lithograph Corp.
in the United States of America.

Library of Congress Cataloging in Publication Data
Main entry under title:

Population growth.

    "Proceedings of a colloquium in general anthropology entitled 'Population, resources,
and technology,' held at the University of Pennsylvania, March 11–14, 1970, under
the combined auspices of the Near East Center, the University Museum, and the
Department of Anthropology of the University of Pennsylvania, in association with
the Wenner-Gren Foundation for Anthropological Research, Incorporated."
    Bibliography: p.
    1. Population—Congresses. 2. Social change—Congresses. 3. Technological innova-
tions—Congresses.

I. Spooner, Brian, ed. II. Pennsylvania. University. Near East Center. III. Penn-
sylvania. University. University Museum. IV. Pennsylvania. University. Dept. of
Anthropology.
HB849.P67   301.32   72-4209
ISBN 0-262-19102-4

Contents

Contributors

Robert McC. Adams — University of Chicago

Bennet Bronson — Field Museum of Natural History

Robert L. Carneiro — American Museum of Natural History

Don E. Dumond — University of Oregon

John D. Durand — University of Pennsylvania

Robert B. Ekvall — University of Washington

Alfred Harris — University of Rochester

Solomon H. Katz — University of Pennsylvania

Richard B. Lee — University of Toronto

Robert McC. Netting — University of Pennsylvania

David O'Connor — University of Pennsylvania

William T. Sanders — Pennsylvania State University

Philip E. L. Smith — University of Montreal

Brian Spooner — University of Pennsylvania

Bernard Wailes — University of Pennsylvania

T. Cuyler Young, Jr. — Royal Ontario Museum

Preface

This volume is the outcome of a colloquium in general anthropology entitled "Population, Resources, and Technology" which was held at the University of Pennsylvania, March 11–14, 1970, under the combined auspices of the Near East Center, the University Museum, and the Department of Anthropology of the University of Pennsylvania, in association with the Wenner-Gren Foundation for Anthropological Research, Incorporated. The purpose of the colloquium was to provide a forum for the discussion of the relationship between population growth and the traditional interests of anthropology in technology, culture, and social organization. This theme was suggested by the proposition by Ester Boserup in a book entitled *The Conditions of Agricultural Growth: The Economics of Agrarian Change under Population Pressure* (Chicago: Aldine, 1965) of a model of technological and cultural change built on population growth as an independent variable.

Stimulated by the anthropological implications of Boserup's hypotheses (often referred to in the text simply as "the Boserup model"), P. E. L. Smith and T. Cuyler Young, Jr., prehistorians specializing in the Near East, reexamined the archaeological data from their special area of interest. It was their work that led directly to the idea of the colloquium, which was planned so that it should be small enough for there to be real discussion and interaction among all the participants as one group, and at the same time large enough to include specialists from a very broad range of cultural areas and historical periods. Within this framework it was also considered desirable to confine invitations, so far as possible, to established scholars who were still actively occupied in field projects and thus had firsthand data fresh in their minds, as well as being theoretically inclined toward the investigation of the problem that was to be our central theme.

Smith and Young had their paper ready by the summer of 1969, and it was circulated to the other participants so that they would have before them while preparing their own contributions an example of what might be done with the model in one particular area and period. Most of the other papers were finished and circulated during the winter. When we met in March 1970, the first two mornings were devoted to the presentation of the papers, and a little time was left after each for discussion specific to the particular paper. The remainder of the sessions was left open for general discussion of the theoretical problems involved, though an attempt was made to deal first with the technological aspects and later with aspects of social and political organization. Many of the contributions were later revised in the light of the discussions, which as a whole benefited greatly from the active participation of Ester Boserup, who both patiently and continually propounded the details of her hypothesis and acted as economic control in our anthropological speculations.

I would like to record a very real debt of gratitude both in the organization of the colloquium and in the preparation of this volume: most especially to Dr. Thomas Naff, Director of the Near East Center of the University of Pennsylvania, for his personal help and encouragement and for providing the administrative infrastructure without which neither would have been possible; similarly, to the Wenner-Gren Foundation for Anthropological Research and Dr. Froelich G. Rainey and the University Museum for making the colloquium financially possible; to Dr. A. F. C. Wallace and the Department of Anthropology for general backing and administrative assistance; and to the Director and Associate Director of the University of Pennsylvania Libraries for the use of the Henry Charles Lea Library and other facilities. I would also like to thank George Allen and Unwin Ltd. of London for gracious permission to quote extensively from *The Conditions of Agricultural Growth: The Economics of Agrarian Change under Population Pressure* by Ester Boserup (1965).

Many hands have helped invaluably with the myriad editorial chores —some mechanical, some less so—of a volume of this nature. Among these I am particularly grateful to Lee Ann Crawford and Dr. David O'Connor. Joan Naff, Gulbun O'Connor, Mary Voigt, Esther Wroten, Eileen Bliss, Mary Farvar, Catherine Wynkoop, Gabrielle Minai, Elisabeth Rappolt, Caroline S. Toomey, and Carol Dougherty transscribed, typed, advised, and proofread. Maria Miller, Jana Hesser, Matthew Stolper, and John McGinn drew maps and diagrams.

The greatest debt I owe is of course to the participants, for their cooperation and forbearance, and particularly to Drs. P. E. L. Smith and T. Cuyler Young, Jr., who guided me to Boserup and have helped me generously with advice and discussion, and Drs. Ward H. Goodenough, Igor Kopytoff, and Robert McC. Netting for guidance and encouragement throughout. Naturally my few words of introduction and comment owe much, if not all, to discussions with the other contributors to the volume. I have tried not to appear the originator of another's idea, and if I have misrepresented, only I am responsible.

Brian Spooner

Philadelphia
June 1971

Introduction   Brian Spooner

The Boserup Model

The relationship of agricultural development and population growth
has long been debated by social scientists. In 1965 an economist, Ester
Boserup, entered this debate with the proposal that population growth
should be treated as the independent variable in technological and cultural change (*The Conditions of Agricultural Growth: The Economics of
Agrarian Change under Population Pressure* [Chicago: Aldine]). This proposal was not entirely new, although Malthusian respect for the limits
imposed by the inelastic carrying capacity of resources and rigid technologies is still implicitly dominant in the literature. However, Boserup's
thesis had not before been so comprehensively and logically worked out.
In economics—the disciplinary context from which it arose—it has had a
mixed reception, largely according to the ideological inclinations of the
critics; and its implications for other disciplines, including anthropology,
have been slow to percolate.

As an economist Boserup is concerned primarily with agriculture and
the economics of development. Her book is based on the directly anti-
Malthusian assumption that the main line of causation in the relationship
between population growth and agricultural development is from the
former to the latter: she treats "population growth . . . as the independent
variable which in its turn is a major factor determining agricultural
developments" (Boserup 1965: 11). Moreover, she extends her thesis
from the recent decades of agricultural development to a much broader
theoretical and historical context and expresses the hope that "this approach is conducive to a fuller understanding of the actual historical
course of agriculture, including the development of patterns and techniques of cultivation as well as the social structures of agrarian communities" (Boserup 1965: 12).

A central feature of her approach is her rejection of traditional tax-
onomies of land use in favor of the concept of frequency of cropping.
Uncultivated land thus ceases to be a category opposed to land under
cultivation and becomes rather one end of a continuum, of which the
other end is multicropping, where as soon as one crop is reaped another
is sown. All other types of primitive land use take their place between
these two extremes, and population growth is seen as a prime mover in
the evolution (in both pristine and secondary conditions) from one stage

to the next. If this at first sounds simplistic, there is a range of variables to be borne in mind, in particular the effects of capital investment and external political constraints. The exposition is sophisticated in the consideration of these, and the model is meant as an explanation of internal dynamics only.

As population grows, more people per unit of land are faced with the necessity of producing more food per unit of land, and they are able to do this by intensifying their relationship with the land—their technology—moving from hunting and gathering through stages of cultivation with ever shorter fallow periods to the final stage of intensification, which is multicropping with no fallowing. However, according to her thesis there is a penalty: with each increase in output per unit of land, output per unit of labor is more likely to decline than to increase. Therefore, according to the Law of Least Effort, cultivators do not normally intensify, or adopt technological innovations related to intensive agriculture, except when forced by the pressure of population on resources (Boserup 1965: 41). Two of the most essential elements of her thesis, therefore, may be characterized as (1) the elasticity of the limits of the carrying capacity of land, and (2) the Law of Least Effort.

Also implicit in her exposition is the idea that intensification in the use of land is accompanied by parallel processes of intensification in other aspects of culture and society. The effects of growing populations and this resulting process of intensification do not always constitute an unmixed good. The land itself may be spoiled

for a time or forever. But nevertheless, the neo-Malthusian theories [that regard population growth as a variable dependent mainly on potential for food production] . . . are misleading, because they tend to neglect the evidence we have of growing populations which managed to change their methods of production in such a way as to preserve and improve the fertility of their land. Many tribes did not become nomads destroying the land by their herds of herbivorous animals, but used these same animals to cultivate the grass lands in short-fallow rotations with the result that soil fertility was improved by animal manure. Others irrigated the dried-up lands and prevented erosion by terracing of the land. It is true that some regions which previously supported a more or less dense population are barren today, but it is equally true that regions which previously, under forest fallow, could support only a couple of families per square kilometer, today support hundreds of families by means of intensive cultivation. Growing populations may in the past have destroyed more land than they improved, but it makes little sense to project past trends into the future, since we know more and more about methods of land preservation and are able, by means of modern methods, to reclaim much land, which our ancestors have made sterile [Boserup 1965: 22].

In answer to the question whether it is realistic to deal with technical change in primitive communities as a variable dependent on population growth, Boserup asks how many examples can be found of nongrowing primitive populations that advanced in technology. She discusses the "vicious circle of sparse population and primitive techniques" (Boserup 1965: 70–76) and draws attention to those parts of Africa that never pushed ahead in the past, because of low birth rates and high mortality rates, which in turn were caused, not by limited availability of food, but by conditions of slave trade, by tropical disease, and by many other factors. Her model of population as "prime mover in society" is constructed precisely in order to bring out this difference between those primitive societies that are growing and successful and those that are nongrowing and unsuccessful.

Finally, the obverse of her thesis should also be true: population decline should logically result in "extensification" or technological "reversion" to methods that are both less labor-intensive and less land-intensive. And in fact, "in cases where population density was reduced by wars or other catastrophes there often seems to have been a relapse into more extensive systems of cultivation" (Boserup 1965: 62).

The Colloquium and the Following Essays

In converting the contributions to the colloquium into the chapters of this volume, the essays have been arranged according to the type of data they deal with. The first eight chapters are concerned primarily with agriculture as a subsistence base. The first two concern ancient Mesopotamia, though dealing with different geographical units and time ranges and, consequently, with different problems. Chapter 1 offers a survey of the development of attitudes toward population within anthropology before proceeding to a discussion of the origins of food producing in Greater Mesopotamia. Chapter 2 treats the urban revolution in the same area. Chapter 3 is concerned generally with the formation of the state without geographical or temporal referent. Chapter 4 moves from prehistoric to historical archaeology and reconstruction with a discussion based on the analysis of burial populations in ancient Egypt. Chapter 5 presents the Mesoamerican situation. Chapter 6 brings us much closer to the present and into the temperate zone of Europe, and is followed in Chapter 7 by our first ethnographic set of data—from East Africa. Chapter 8, which ends the agricultural half of the volume, is cross-cultur- ally and theoretically oriented and argues (against the Boserup model) for a multilinear model of agricultural evolution with special attention to environment as a variable independent of population.

The second half of the volume, Chapters 9–17, leaves the exclusively agricultural emphasis of the first half of the volume and treats broader problems of intensification in the context of technological diversity, and beyond the technological plane. Thus, Chapter 9, while based on the consideration of primarily agricultural West African societies, looks at the evolution of ritual and political roles, which peacefully articulate potentially competing groups in the context of the pressure of population on resources. Chapter 10 presents a case of demographic interaction and ideological opposition, based on difference in technology (for example, peasant versus nomad) in the "marginal" environment of the deserts of the Iranian plateau, where, generally, no one technology suffices for subsistence. Chapter 11 is concerned with the demography and tech- nology of nomads in Tibet against the background of their interaction with the agricultural majority of the total society. Chapter 12 explores the political implications of population growth without technological or geographical referent and constructs a model, the first stage of which is then tested in Chapter 13 against data from the maritime and terrestrial hunter population of prehistoric Eskimo Alsaka. Chapters 14 and 15 combine the hunter-gatherer interest with analyses of the dynamics of family size and group size in relation to technology among the !Kung Bushmen of Botswana.

The two final chapters take us out of cultural anthropology and ar- chaeology to provide the physical and demographic contexts of our discussions.

The participants reacted in a range of different ways to the basic model—in terms of both their particular types of data and their personal theoretical inclinations. Both the essays and the discussions constituted an exploration of the various processes of intensification of technology, culture, and society that may result from an increase in the pressure of population on resources. Not all the reactions were positive. Apart from Smith and Young, who, in Chapter 1, introduce the model in a specifically anthropological context and advocate its application to the data from their own special field, and Bronson (Chapter 8), who reacts negatively arguing a priori against unilinear models, the contributions tend to be not direct investigations of the model but rather allied theses inspired by its heuristic features. For instance, O'Connor in the necrophilic context of Egyptology is performing the demographic exercises without which an appreciation of the relationship between the Nile as a subsistence resource and the historical society and culture it generated is unapproachable. Sanders is largely in favor of the model but wishes to modify it with particular respect for the geographical variable. Wailes explores Medieval European agricultural technology and demographic data (where available) for patterned relationships but fails to find any. Harris introduces some modifications paying particular attention to what he sees as the internal dynamics of a technological system that comprehends a range of microenvironments. Spooner similarly introduces a range of adaptational and occupational variation within a unitary environmental context. Ekvall describes the situation of long-term population decline in Tibet. Dumond deduces from Alaskan Eskimo data that population growth and subsistence should be treated as equivalent variables. Netting is concerned with the evolution of extrasocietal roles that buffer and referee conflicts resulting from increased contact between groups in situations of population growth. Lee investigates the same problems as Smith and Young but in a modern ethnographic context that allows him to ask the logistical questions about mobility, fertility, and productivity that the archaeologists cannot get at. In his second essay he also investigates the centrifugal and centripetal forces that affect the size of social groups and distinguish large groups from small. Katz explores the interaction of physiological with ecological, demographic, and sociocultural factors in the context of population growth. Carneiro and Dumond propose slightly conflicting extensions of the model into the political sphere.

Many of the disagreements in our discussions derived from the difficulty of making differential evaluations of distinct types of data and then feeding them into one unitary theoretical framework. Among the questions that were posed but not treated in any detail were how to deal with the special case of tree crops—for example, the date, breadfruit, olive, and perhaps the ramon—within this framework; the relationship between knowledge and engineering as different forms of investment in an environment; the significance of the diffusion of certain major cultural values—such as bread-eating and rice-eating—that require a certain crop and therefore have adaptational implications (see Bronson, Chapter 8); and finally, the concept of "overload" and the nonecological and noncultural factors that play a role in determining the size of local groups —forces that make for clustering versus dispersal and vice versa.

Questions Raised

A number of theoretical problems that were explored in the discussions but have not found a place in the revised versions of the papers, nevertheless bear closely on the main theme and require some rehearsal here. Perhaps the most vital of these scarcely became explicit until the final hour of the discussions though it was present from the beginning.

1. This question is how to define the logical unit or universe of study for any given theoretical problem. On the basis of what criteria should such a universe be defined? Little explicit attention has been paid in anthropology to this extremely important question. Implicit difference in its solution lies at the very base of the differences between the contributions of the Near Eastern archaeologists (though difference in their "microregions" of specialization within Greater Mesopotamia is, of course, a factor). The relationship between the Tibetan nomads (described by Ekvall in Chapter 11) and the agricultural areas from which they draw demographic reinforcement raises the same question, as does the similar demographic relationship between ecological areas in the Iranian desert described by Spooner in Chapter 10. Harris's approach in Chapter 7 emphasizes the importance of the problem, and Bronson's argument (Chapter 8) about the role of investment begs the same question in its temporal dimension. In Chapter 3 Carneiro implicitly assumes that the problem is solved with his concept of the "circumscribed area." On the other hand, in Chapter 5 Sanders uses charts to demonstrate a very basic and practical way in which, in the investigation of our particular problem, the appraisal of any "sub-" region is meaningful only when seen in the context of its universe, however that may be defined.

The symbiotic interaction of communities with slightly different histories, each responding to a distinctive localized combination of ecological relationships, has for some time been recognized in the literature; it is mentioned by Smith and Young (Chapter 1), lies at the base of Chapter 5, and was brought out further in the discussions:

Within a region, one community or zone is often catastrophically affected at the same time that another is prospering. Thus the crude average may be a one one-hundredth percent increase for a whole region, with a thousand or five thousand villages or whatever. But the significant units of process are hidden by overall averages. Instead they may consist, for example, of interacting pairs or small groups of communities, where fortunes of one are rising while the other's decline [Adams, discussions].

In many cases the pattern of communications gives rise to settlement clusters whose agricultural or other direct food-producing, subsistence adaptations are not explainable without reference to their role in the communication system, as in the case of Nayband in the Iranian desert (Chapter 10).

With regard to an area such as ancient southern Mesopotamia, these observations lead to the question:

To what extent is a town like Uruk, or even all of the lower alluvial plain, really a significant unit of study in connection with problems like population pressure? There have been many recent straws in the wind suggesting surprisingly far-flung trading or other contacts: tablets with certain striking relationships with early Mesopotamian writing turning up in Romania, representations of Mesopotamian boats found on the Upper Nile, beveled-rim Uruk bowls in Kerman, massive (if highly selective) early third millennium trade networks in materials like steatite that extended across the whole Iranian plateau and all the way down the Persian Gulf. This does not necessarily imply that population movements lay at the root of any of these specific relationships, but we can dimly recognize patterns of interaction that were not confined to local communities and were not even limited to the narrowly defined ecological areas with which we normally deal. How can we continue to assume that the significant causative processes were those that were localized rather than those that ranged for 1,000 or 1,500 miles? If we cannot, then the question of the relationship of population pressure to technology has to be dealt with within a specified geographical frame, and the assumptions that we are making in order to specify that frame ought to be opened up for discussion [Adams, discussion].

2. This brief discussion of the trade factor in the geographical definition of the unit of study leads to the question of the definition of technology and its relation to the other dimensions of our universe of study.

Harris's essay (Chapter 7) deals with this problem with particular reference to an agricultural people in east Africa. In the discussions Adams took up the problem with particular reference to ancient Mesopotamia. Both explicitly based their arguments on Merril (1968):

Let us take as technology the acquisition, processing, storage, distribution and employment of the raw materials needed by a society, especially resources directly or indirectly associated with subsistence. So used, the term obviously includes, but is not limited to, the entire artifactual inventory associated with these activities. In addition, technology must include the planning and regulating techniques required for each activity and for maintaining an ordered pattern of interrelations between them. This makes the social system, at least insofar as it is directed toward production, storage, exchange, and distribution, a part of the technological system as well.

Turning to Mesopotamia to illustrate a few specific aspects of this much broader approach to technology—first of all, systems of redistribution were characteristic of the major, early Mesopotamian institutions (whether they be temples or private estates). Usually we have tended to define these institutions in religious or sociocultural terms, but they can be taken equally well as a necessarily fundamental part of an adaptation to urban life at a new level of complexity, and therefore as an aspect of the technological system as well. What was required in order to maintain a complementary relationship between the various eco-niches of which the alluvial plain was constituted was an institutional framework through which subsistence specialities—the fisherman, the herdsman, the cultivator—could be articulated with one another. In this sense, the accounting capability that permitted the disbursement and recording of rations for participants from a number of eco-niches becomes a part of the technological system. The same obviously applies to weights and measures, for they permit the orderly exchange of the oil being processed by one set of specialists for the fish being dried by another, for the grain being cultivated by a third, and for the wool being produced by a fourth. Similarly, there are textual attestations of massive grain storage, for which—unfortunately but typically—there are as yet few convincing archaeological examples. References to the seizure of granaries said to contain ten thousand and more tons imply a centrally directed, large-scale, fairly sophisticated system of storage, which places the issue of technology right in the center of the political and social system.

Second, there is the military dimension of technology. During what might be called "the urban implosion" in lower Mesopotamia, that is, the growth of major urban centers in an apparently short period after 3000 B.C., the problem of articulating the various components of a complex subsistence system must have reached an unprecedented severity. Military considerations certainly played a part, and probably the crucial one, in the formation of walled cities. Further, if urbanization was a response to increased intergroup hostilities engendered by "population pressure," then the economic and administrative innovations that permitted the subsistence requirements of enormously larger population units to be met have to be understood at least in part as further derivatives of population pressure. The same applies to a more obvious technological category—advances in military equipment.

There are also some less obvious although perhaps equally important links between urbanization/militarization (and hence population pressure) on the one hand and technological or administrative innovations on the other. For example, there is some evidence that one of the purposes of the walls around major urban centers was to provide a place of protection into which the herds of animals could be brought under conditions of long-continuing military insecurity. Such conditions were unprecedented at the village level, as were also the facilities to feed and house large herds of animals that had to be designed to meet them. This interjected the state apparatus into herding operations that earlier may have been the responsibility of small local groups. Again, given the conditions of dense nucleation, populations in the new centers were forced to reside at considerable distances from their fields. Hence an unprecedented need arose for centrally planning the deployment of plow animals. Does this explain the introduction by mid-third millennium times of plows regularly drawn by six draft animals? Do later references to very long and narrow fields suggest that the central control of animal tractive power encouraged cadastral changes that would permit heavy plows to draw long, straight furrows? One of the functions of a symposium of this kind is to raise such questions, but I do not mean to imply that they can yet be answered.

[However,] if we are to deal constructively with the suggestion that population increases or the pressure of population on resources is articulated with technological development, we have to view technology in this far more complex and ramifying sense [Adams, dicussions].

3. Any study of man, insofar as it concerns men in groups, begs demographic questions, and it is unfortunate that there has been so little contact in the past between anthropology and demography. In the colloquium we were fortunate to have the active participation of John D. Durand, whose contributions to the discussions have been edited to appear as a statement of the demographic context of our theme in the final chapter. The penultimate chapter is Katz's essay on the physiological factors that interact with our basically cultural theme. In the discussion the question of the relevance of nutrition to fertility was raised. The following case of the dietary roles of corn and milk provides an interesting example of this:

First, there is evidence that a pure cereal diet—and corn is especially notorious for this—is very deficient in lysine, an essential amino acid. This means that on a corn diet there is a growth retardation effect which, if not supplemented by another source of lysine, can be very serious.

However, it so happens that milk and milk products contain considerable lysine, and therefore the two foods together produce a balanced
diet. In the long run this sort of nutritional balance has a great deal to
do with the survival of a population and must indirectly influence its
fertility.

Furthermore, in order to digest the sugar (lactose) in milk, it is necessary to have the enzyme lactase in the intestinal tract. There is considerable evidence that lactase only occurs in infants and certain adults. It
seems that the adults of some populations can digest lactose, while the
adults of others cannot. This probably indicates the action of a gene
for the synthesis of the enzyme in the adult. The evidence indicates that
most milk-drinking populations and especially the European population
has the adult lactase present and active. If an adult does not have the
enzyme, the lactose is not broken down in the intestine (to galactose and
glucose) and is excreted into the large intestine or colon. Here it is broken
down by the lactobacillus bacteria into lactic acid. Unfortunately, lactic
acid is osmotically active and produces a great deal of secretion into the
colon which results in diarrhea. Over a longer time this continuous irrita-
tion of the colon leads to ulcerative colitis, a more severe disease.

This suggests that since milk and cereals generally are nutritionally
complementary, (1) there is some evolution going on with respect to the
ability or inability to digest lactose, and (2) the treatment of certain
dairy foods by various bacteria outside the gastrointestinal tract into
foods such as cheese and yoghurt is an important adaptation for the lack
of the enzyme in the adult individual. In this way the technology of food
preparation allows the food to be digestible in persons who might not
otherwise be able to consume it [Katz, discussions].

Thus, a physiological barrier—to demographic movements—is thrown
up between populations with different subsistence technologies.

A further nutritional point, with perhaps more direct relevance to
demography, was introduced by Lee, who wished to combat the more
traditional thesis that the agricultural diet is a better diet than the hunting and gathering diet, for his own data suggest that the opposite is the
case—specifically that the hunting and gathering diet is superior in terms
of protein and the range of minerals and nutrients. He has nutritional
assays on forty-five species of Bushman foods that show that some of
these wild foods concentrate certain minerals and vitamins such as vitamin C and carotene in remarkable amounts, and high-quality vegetable
protein comprises 25 percent of the staple nutrients.

The Bushmen may possibly face nutritional problems in terms of gross
overall calories, but they certainly have a very good array of vitamins,
minerals, and proteins, both vegetable and animal. Because of this we

should reexamine the argument that, in the early Neolithic, populations increased because of improvements in the quality of the diet [Lee, discussions].

In Chapter 14 Lee presents the view that the dietary cause of population growth is not a better diet but a softer (that is, more easily digestible) one. Katz was able to append a comment to this to the effect that

in general a baby can survive very well on mother's milk till two and a half years of age. However, if the culture has available to it certain kinds of soft foods that babies can chew and digest, then that supplements the mother's milk. Therefore, the quantity of milk the mother produces is decreased, ovulation can return sooner, and the birth rate is increased [Katz, discussions].

4. The most significant points in the history of population, in the context of this volume, would appear to be four: (1) at the dawn of the Neolithic, sedentarization brought about the first major increase in the rate of population growth; (2) population growth has caused intensification on all planes of culture and society, particularly in the technology of agriculture and subsistence in general, and in political and social organization; (3) natural catastrophes, such as the Black Death in Europe and floods in China, did not reverse or stop the rate of growth, but caused only minor temporary setbacks; (4) the rate of growth was reaching geometrical proportions well before the great improvements in sanitation and medical treatment began to accord it an extra fillip in the nineteenth century (see Marshall and Brown 1971).

Population decrease has not been entirely neglected, but documented cases do not figure very prominently because they are relatively difficult to find. This may be justifiable since, taken in general perspective, the world's population has shown an unbroken upward curve. However, cases of decrease are important for the support of our hypothesis. With this in mind it is well to cite here a contribution to the discussions suggesting that investment and intensification may in some cases lead to disease and a decrease in fertility (though the newly available lands in which the former inhabitants had made an investment might attract enough in-migration to maintain the rate of population increase).

In the country irrigated from the Aswan Dam in Egypt, due to the methods of irrigation in use, the level of parasitic infection—in this case schistosomiasis—runs at about 99 percent of the population, which is severely debilitating and has adverse effects on both productivity and fertility. This disease used to strike in Egypt on a seasonal basis with the flooding of the Nile. With the intensification of the irrigation system (by means of major investment), it has become active throughout the year. Thus, major irrigation systems, whether or not they are as technologically advanced as the Aswan Dam, may introduce secondary variables such as disease that limit not only population growth but also productivity. We have to take into account the biological factors that interact with population change. To take the argument one step further: the rate of schistosomiasis and similar diseases is intimately associated with population. The greater the density, the higher the transmission rate [Katz, discussions].

5. Finally, in this as in all discussions in the social sciences, a basic problem between the participants, which was implicit throughout, was the problem of explanation in anthropology. It was verbalized usefully at one point in the discussions by Carneiro, and I paraphrase and adapt his comments in what follows:

The very identification of a set of variables—which are in the first place selected more or less arbitrarily—as dependent or independent must be recognized as an explanatory device. Linear causation is sought by some for similar reasons. There is obviously reciprocal influence between factors. Dependent on the goal of the explanation, some will be causally more significant than others. Among some of the participants an obvious preference was detectable for stressing all the various factors, an attitude of a democracy of causes where no one should be rated higher than any other. It is an implicit epistemological assumption in works such as that of Boserup and many of the contributors to this volume that there is an advantage to trying to find those causes or that cause which is strongest and to see how far it may be used to explain an entire process. We should not be afraid of such monism, cultural or otherwise, if in fact a pursuit of this type of interpretation really gives us better results than we get otherwise. To the extent that we can explain one principle, or a very economical number of principles, and a very large amount of cultural behavior—to that extent we have progressed. This is a legitimate scientific objective. When we have made our explanation in terms of one (or more) selected principles, the next stage is to introduce auxiliary hypotheses and make modifications in order to explain the residue that is not covered in the first explanation. Gradually the first explanation will be superseded. Such is the dialectical process of scientific explanation. It is not a reason to try from the start to be fair to every cause by giving it equal weight. Instead of one supermodel to answer all questions, we must content ourselves with various types of fairly simple models to answer different questions.

Altogether we have of course made only a small beginning in the investigation of a major series of related problems, but at the very least we may claim to have drawn attention to the importance of a major noncultural factor in cultural change and evolution. The central theme of these essays and the discussions that generated them (as suggested by Smith at one point in the discussion) is that changes in population pressure are not the sole prime mover in history and society, but an ever-present force— sometimes gentle, sometimes compelling.

1

The Evolution of Early Agriculture and Culture in Greater Mesopotamia: A Trial Model

Philip E. L. Smith and T. Cuyler Young, Jr.

Greater Mesopotamia has been the classical area of study for the problem of the origins of agriculture in archaeology and therefore provides a fitting subject for the first chapter of this volume. Smith and Young first explore the history of thought leading up to this explicit choice of population as a primary explanatory factor in anthropology and then assemble the available archaeological data and rearrange them according to the Boserup model. Thus they set the scene for the remainder of the essays by combining the genealogy of anthropological thought on population with their discussion of domestication and the evolution of agricultural technology.

Introduction

Between roughly the end of the Pleistocene and the beginning of the third millennium B.C. a number of apparently related events of far-reaching significance occurred in Southwest Asia. Prominent among these was a substantial increase in the density of population inhabiting the area, involving considerable changes in the distribution of that population and in settlement type, size, and permanency. Associated with these events were the development of food obtaining based on wholly new principles and a new technology, changes in the nature of social and political organizations, and a degree of cultural elaboration and specialization that had important effects on areas far removed from Southwest Asia itself. Some of these changes occurring in this relatively brief period have at times been termed "revolutions" (for example, Childe 1936, 1950, 1952; White 1959) or "transformations" (Redfield 1953; J. G. D. Clark

1967: 12), and even before many substantive data were in hand, numerous attempts were made to explain as well as to describe the processes involved.

The expressions made famous by Childe have served to dramatize concepts that have been advanced, in less precise forms, by anthropologists and others since the nineteenth century. The concepts of Neolithic and Urban "revolutions" are now deeply embedded in the thinking of many anthropologists and archaeologists working in both the Old and New Worlds, as well as in the minds of some scholars in other disciplines. The idea of a thinly scattered, parasitic population of human beings, rapidly increasing in numbers and social complexity as food producing was developed and then experiencing further quantitative and qualitative changes as town and city life developed could hardly fail to grip the imaginations of all who wished to establish long-term trends in prehistory and history.

The consequences of these transformations are well-known and need not be described at length here. Among those consequences some writers have emphasized the expanding population growth from the end of the Pleistocene to the present; thus Childe (1937) correlated the population curve with cultural progress on the premise that, just as in biological evolution, cultural adjustments will be considered progressive if they further the multiplication of the species in the long run. Perhaps in a world faced with the "population explosion" it is not surprising that in recent years much archaeological energy and many resources should have been devoted to the search for a fuller understanding of the conditions under which that explosion began.

Traditionally, Near Eastern archaeologists have tended to be more concerned with what Steward (1955a: 18) calls "the sequential reconstruction of culture" rather than with the discovery of the processes of development; or, at least, this was true until very recent years. In this paper, however, we are attempting what might be considered a study in cultural ecology in Steward's sense, that is, a study of the adaptive reactions of a society to its natural and social environments that create internal processes of change. Specifically, we try to attain another of Steward's objectives: "to ascertain the detailed processes by which hunters and gatherers were converted into farmers or herdsmen and these latter into more 'civilized' people" (Steward 1955a: 25). Our viewpoint is essentially that recently expressed by Spiro, that in the broadest evolutionary perspective economic change is the causal condition for other types of structural change (Spiro 1965: 1117); but whereas he admits that the data he describes "shed no light on the determinants of economic change," we propose to tackle this obstacle directly by presenting a hypothesis and constructing a model that can be tested to some degree by archaeological means. The issue is the evolution of agricultural methods and the interaction between population density, available land resources, and the agricultural techniques available or practicable. The hypothesis leans heavily on the study of land use and of traditional agriculture, a study that, in dealing with a sector of human activity involving the greatest interaction between physical environment and the human cultures growing in and from it, qualifies as one in human ecology (De Schlippe 1956: 25). This approach is not completely novel, of course, and other writers have also studied land-use patterns in the ancient Near East from the viewpoint of agricultural ecology (Whyte 1961; Adams 1965: 133; Flannery 1969). Here we are attempting to demonstrate that land use and agricultural techniques are to be seen, even from the archaeologist's necessarily blurred viewpoint, not only as culturally adaptive adjustments to the natural environment but also as functions of demographic realities. We make no attempt to deal with such matters as political, social, commercial, religious, or military developments per se but only with the demographic changes interacting with the local environmental conditions that initiated this series of developments.

Our geographical focus in this paper is on the area sometimes called Greater Mesopotamia (Flannery 1965: 1247), that is, those parts of Iran, Iraq, Syria, and Anatolia which are in the main drained by the tributaries of the Shatt al-Arab, at the head of the Persian Gulf. We have not included the Levant area in this discussion, in spite of the great potential significance of the Natufian culture and of the possible existence of an original center of cereal domestication, for two reasons: we have no firsthand knowledge of this area, and we do not consider the most recent research to be sufficiently well published to be evaluated at this time. Chronologically we are concerned with the period from the late Pleistocene to the end of the fourth millennium B.C., the period that witnessed the modification in this area of local societies of hunters and gatherers into food producers and eventually brought man to the threshold of urbanism. The focus is admittedly somewhat narrow, but if our assumptions are justified and our premises sound, our interpretations may be applicable to other regions and broader time ranges as well. Certainly if the general assumption that the initial steps toward food production and town life in the Old World were taken in Southwest Asia is justified, then a framework helping to explain the original processes in a pristine context where no influence from other regions was apparently operable would be of some value to all scholars.[1] We begin with a brief summary of the present status of understanding of the processes concerned. There follow a statement of our hypothesis and a description of the mechanisms through which the situation characteristic of each cultural stage might have been produced. This is at present little more than a trial hypothesis, and though we realize that it cannot claim to explain satisfactorily all of the events and changes in question, we hope that it at least helps to make the cultural variations observed intelligible in terms of adaptations to external factors. Next, it will be necessary to summarize our present understanding of the environmental situation in Greater Mesopotamia during the time range in question. Finally, we shall present an archaeological model and attempt to see if the archaeological data at present available in published form from the area are, at least in broad outline, compatible with our fundamental hypothesis. The procedure followed is essentially that advocated by Steward: "The most effective way to further research along these new lines is to devise admittedly tentative hypotheses and to endeavor to specify the kinds of research needed to validate or reverse them" (Steward 1955b: 5).

Historical Review

The history of thought concerning the so-called Neolithic and Urban revolutions has not yet been written, even for Near Eastern developments. Earlier "reconstructions" by nineteenth- and twentieth-century writers such as Sven Nilsson, Lewis Henry Morgan, Max Müller, Theodor Mommsen, Eduard Hahn, Wilhelm Koppers, Wilhelm Schmidt and many others were, for the most part, based on ethnological and philological data, albeit often showing shrewd insight into the problems of origins and developments. While it would be easy to exaggerate and distort the importance given by earlier commentators to the purely technological aspects of the Neolithic, it seems true nevertheless that it was not until the 1920s that the emphasis came down heavily on subsistence as the prime consideration—first in the writing of Elliot Smith, who stressed the role of food producing, and later by Childe (1935, 1936), who emphasized this point and with the term "Neolithic Revolution" gave it wide popularity. Childe's definition of the Neolithic was based primarily on its food-producing aspects; such elements as pottery and polished stone, to which earlier writers had attached so much importance, were treated as subsidiary issues. Later, Braidwood, while essentially adopting Childe's idea, was to add the concepts of settlement pattern and the natural habitat zone as important in determining Neolithic origins (Braidwood 1952).

Clearly the problem of Neolithic and urban origins is a complicated historical and cultural issue. The shift from parasitism to food production is not inevitable, nor does urbanism always follow, and, as Braidwood and Willey (1962: 354) have pointed out, the causal factors concerned, the "elements in the equation of social and cultural behavior," are many and difficult to weigh. Past answers range in value from useless speculation to suggestions of considerable insight; they have involved such factors as chance, the innate spirit of a people, the possession of a superior technology, the availability of superior local natural resources (or inferior ones to activate "challenge and response" mechanisms), the potentiality of diffusion from other centers, and climatic-environmental "shock-stimuli." Their shortcomings are their failure to offer detailed and consistent mechanisms to explain the changes concerned that can be tested both archaeologically and in what we know of analogous situations existing today in groups on the same social and economic levels.

Although there has been no real agreement among anthropologists on the causes of food producing in early Holocene times in Southwest Asia —its beginnings in the "incipient" or supplementary agricultural stage— there is a widely accepted hypothesis that purports to explain the subsequent developments. This might be termed the classic statement and is intimately linked to the concept of economic surplus in food production. Childe has presented this argument in its purest form:

The new economy allowed, and indeed required, the farmer to produce every year more food than was needed to keep him and his family alive. In other words, it made possible the regular production of a social surplus [1950: 6].

Food-producing, even in its simplest form, provides an opportunity and a motive for the accumulation of a surplus. . . . The yield of crops and of herds soon outstrips the immediate needs of the community. . . . The surplus thus gathered will . . . serve to support a growing population. Ultimately it may constitute a basis for rudimentary trade, and so pave the way to a second revolution [1936: 82–83].

The surplus thus accumulated, Childe argued, could then be made available to support new economic classes not directly engaged in producing their own food, and thus class differentiation and specialization were established (1962: 69). (This is a concept that goes back at least as far as 1776, when Adam Smith published *The Wealth of Nations*.) One of the ways in which this surplus could be extracted from otherwise inert groups unenthusiastic about producing above their basic needs might be conquest by outsiders, for example pastoralists establishing themselves as aristocrats over landed peasants; but Childe also saw improved technology as a causal factor. Thus the plow, by permitting more and deeper furrows, would be more productive than the hoe and would encourage an expanding population (1936: 123). Finally, such a surplus of foodstuffs would be a necessity in executing the ambitious works, especially of land reclamation and irrigation, which underlie the Urban Revolution.

This hypothesis of surplus has, explicitly or implicitly, been absorbed by many, if not most, of those attempting to explain the events (Hole 1966: 610; Sauer 1956: 66; but see Adams 1966 for a dissenting view). This paper does not provide the opportunity to discuss in any detail the topic of economic surplus, and indeed a long-standing controversy continues among social scientists about whether, as Wolf says (1966: 110–111), it is possible to arrive at absolute criteria for the definition of surpluses. The anthropological literature in recent years has abounded in examples of this controversy, which was recently summarized by Orans (1966). In this essay we do not wish, even if we were qualified, to enter into the discussion of the methodological validity of the approaches offered by Polanyi and Pearson (in Polanyi, Arensberg, and Pearson 1957) which are essentially attacks on classic economic theory as applied in anthropology by Melville Herskovits, Thorstein Veblen, and V. Gordon Childe. Polanyi's approach has been severely criticized, for example, by Harris (1959), who has attacked both the classic surplus concept and its total rejection by Polanyi and Pearson. Nevertheless, Harris agrees that while there may be *absolute* surpluses in primitive food-producing societies, it is fallacious to assert that primitive societies will produce *superfluous* quantities of food (p. 191) and that apparent surpluses, such as those of the Trobrianders, are the result of faulty ethnographic observation. Basically the conclusion reached by a large number of other anthropologists, economists, and geographers who have discussed the question in recent years (Oberg 1955; Wolf 1966; Carneiro 1960; Sahlins 1958; Erasmus 1965) is that, while an economic surplus is often technologically feasible, it is certainly not inevitable, and indeed the mechanisms by which food producers can be persuaded first to produce surpluses, and then to surrender them to those who are not food producers, are by no means clear (Sahlins 1958; Harris 1959: 198). Economic incentives and political compulsion are certainly among the mechanisms, however. An excellent illustration of this latent surplus in a New Guinea subsistence farming unit, and the changes that provoke an actualized surplus when the unit becomes linked with the outside world, is provided by Fisk (1962).

Intimately related to the surplus explanation of cultural change is the concept of leisure. According to this theory, the security provided by a more certain food supply and the surplus of food possible for lean periods permitted the free time for developing the cultural elaborations characterizing the Neolithic and later periods (Childe 1936: 67). Now it is undoubtedly true, as a number of authors have stated (for example, in Lee and Devore 1968; Harris 1959), that in the past the amount of leisure available to hunting and gathering groups as contrasted with food producers has been grossly underestimated. Erasmus (1965) has similarly criticized the misuse of the concept of leisure (and of surplus food) in swidden agriculture in Mesoamerica. Nevertheless, there *can* be a good deal of leisure time available to primitive food producers (see, for example, Carneiro 1961); the difference is that among food collectors and hunters leisure time will usually come in short, irregular intervals between hunting or collecting, while among food producers there may be longer stretches of free time between such activities as planting, weeding, harvesting, and so on. The point we wish to make here is that this leisure is *not* necessarily a function or result of a food surplus; indeed it may be simply the result of a choice to produce no surplus at all! Again, the aspect of storability and storage of food will be important in considering whether there will be a surplus, or whether, in the event of a fortuitous superfluity, it will be relevant. Thus in areas such as New Guinea the

staple foods deteriorate rapidly after harvesting, and this in itself limits any
tendency toward surplus production (Fisk 1962: 463). Watters (1960: 93)
has also emphasized this point and its relevance in considering surplus
and leisure, and this was underlined even earlier by Chapple and Coon
(1942: 127) in their distinction between societies that can preserve and
accumulate food and those that cannot or will not. Writers such as
Childe (1951: 23) have pointed to the usefulness of pottery in archaeological sites as a valuable clue to the existence of a desire and ability to
store food, while the great advantage of cereals in this respect (their
storability for several years) has been emphasized by many authors from
Adam Smith in 1776 (Smith 1954: 147) to Childe (1936: 67).

Just as it is important to examine the relationship between a possible
surplus and leisure time, so we must consider the relationship between the
creation of a surplus and population growth, for one of the crucial arguments put forth in the hypothesis presented in this paper is that the classic
explanation of surplus causing population growth is inadequate and
oversimplified and that, in fact, it has tended to reverse the cause-and-
effect relationship between these two phenomena.

Birdsell (1957: 47) has remarked that there has been little recognition
by cultural anthropologists (except for some archaeologists) of the nature
of population equilibrium among preagricultural peoples, that is, the
mode and rate of population increase which continue until equilibrium
(determined primarily by environmental variables and secondarily by
cultural factors) is reached. This statement still holds in large measure
for research on preagricultural peoples. There seems, however, to be no
shortage of studies of the role of population growth and density among
agricultural groups. In this section we give a rapid overview of past
opinion concerning the relationship between population density and
growth, on the one hand, and levels of sociocultural development, on the
other.[2] In general, these opinions can be divided into two groups: those
that stress that population growth is a result of increasing technology
and productivity and those that see these last two aspects as functions
of the former.

We have seen that Childe is the classic proponent of the position that
population growth was stimulated by increased food resources, although
similar opinions had been offered, explicitly or implicitly, by some earlier
writers. Childe, like Morgan (1877), saw technological innovations as

the agents responsible for each stage of progress. In Childe's view (1935: 11–12; 1936: 69), the new forms of technology of the food-producing economy removed the limits on population numbers imposed by a food-gathering economy and indeed added a positive incentive to larger groups that had been absent before: the new economic value of children who would be more useful among food producers (1936: 69–70). With the increased efficiency of food producing, its greater security, and its self-sufficiency, this trend would become cumulative, and "a certain size and density of population" (1950: 4) would eventually be an essential feature of civilization as contrasted with village farming communities.[3] This point of view is essentially that adopted by most other writers who have dealt with the topic (for example, White 1959: 289).

In recent years, however, some archaeologists and especially social anthropologists have begun to view the relationship in a different light— a light that may have had its beginnings as early as 1758, when Buffon, in his *Histoire Naturelle*, vol. II, speaks of territorial divisions appearing in his hypothetical primitive society *after* a great increase in population (quoted in Slotkin 1965: 283). Clark, writing from an archaeological viewpoint, has suggested that settlements in late Neolithic Europe became more permanent and conflict increased as a result of increasing population pressure on dwindling land resources (Clark 1952: 97). Ethnographers and social anthropologists have not only discussed this question from the theoretical side but have pointed out many cases where the relationship can be illustrated in recent populations. Thus Steward (1955a) makes numerous references to the role of population size or increase as factors in, or correlates of, social and cultural change in the context of state origins (p. 197), of warfare (pp. 198, 204), and of revolt (p. 204). Oberg (1955) has discussed the relationship between population size, surplus food, and social complexity among lowland tribes of Central and South America. Dobyns (1966: 395) agrees that in a given area there is a relationship between human population and cultural development and that changing population density is to be regarded as a social dynamic. Carneiro (1960, 1967) has also emphasized the causal relationship between increasing population size and increasingly elaborate organization, a position that Fried (1967) essentially shares. Watson (1965) has given a valuable description of the possible changes in social and political organization from patrilocal bands to larger communities in Highland

New Guinea as population density increased after the introduction of a
new food crop (but see Brookfield and White (1968) for criticism of some
of Watson's conclusions). Other writers who have paid some attention to
the role of population increase are Barnett (1953: 56) from the viewpoint
of creativity, Binford (1968) in an early Holocene context, and a large
number of geographers and anthropologists in the context of simple
agricultural systems, especially of shifting cultivation (Brookfield and
Brown 1963: 164; Watters 1960: 90; Nye and Greenland 1960: 84, 123;
Gourou 1956; Ferdon 1959: 15–16; Leach 1959: 64; Carneiro 1961;
Netting 1969). Perhaps the most valuable discussion to date, however,
is by Dumond (1965b), where he says:

When treating matters of cultural change and development, it is common for anthropologists to ignore the factor of population size, or to treat
population size as a simple dependent of culture or some aspect of it;
this seems equally true when they are considering the course of the development of civilization [p. 302].

He suggests that "population growth is not a simple effect of culture
change but is both a cause and effect of that change" (p. 302), and that
"it seems reasonable to hold that through much of the development of
civilization as we know it, the tendency towards population growth has
been chief spur to the improvement of subsistence techniques" (p. 312).

Most of the authors mentioned earlier, however, have tended to regard
population growth as a correlate of cultural changes. Thus Oberg (1965)
sees the consequences of population pressure as territorial expansion, or a
limitation of population growth. Steward (1955b) considers it in its role
in promoting warfare, internal revolt, conquest, and dislocation, with
their consequences for social and cultural changes.

The Boserup Hypothesis

While the role of population change in these directions cannot be denied,
we feel that there is another aspect that most writers up to now have
neglected: the influence of population pressure on the available resources,
bringing about in some cases developments in the technology of the group
concerned, and this in turn influencing the cultural alternatives then
made available. Dumond, in two valuable papers (1961, 1965), perhaps
comes closest to this viewpoint, while White (1959: 289) and Binford
(1968) have discussed the role of population pressure on groups in early

post-Pleistocene times practicing initial or experimental food producing. But in the literature so far examined we have been able to find only one example of a hypothesis that can be applied to archaeological cases to explain at least some of the events in the millennia immediately following the initial stage of food producing: Boserup (1965) considers land use and agricultural techniques as cultural adaptations to the natural environment in relation to the local demographic situation.

Boserup's thesis is an attempt to answer in non-Malthusian terms the question: What is the relationship between agricultural conditions and population size and change? In the classic Malthusian theory the food supply for the human race is inherently inelastic, and it is this lack of elasticity that governs population growth; population growth is the dependent variable and is determined by preceding changes in agricultural activity caused by technical inventions or borrowings. Modern or neo-Malthusians see world population as pressing against a static or even decreasing food supply.

Boserup's argument is that the reverse is true: population growth is itself the autonomous or independent variable and is a major factor in determining agricultural developments and productivity and thus for bringing about economic and social changes. For her, as for C. Clark (1967: 49), the modern population explosion is caused, not by improved conditions of food production, but among other things by the application of medical advances.[4] At the root of her thesis is the claim that an additional input of labor is very important in increasing production per land unit, and that under primitive agricultural conditions such a supply of labor is what finally determines the level of development reached. Boserup asks: Would output per man-hour be likely to rise or fall when a given population in a given territory shortens the fallow period and changes its agricultural methods and tools correspondingly?

The answer that emerges from this discussion is that output per man-hour is more likely to decline than to increase. This means that in typical cases the cultivator would find it profitable to shift to a more intensive system of land use only when a certain density of population has been reached. In a region where this critical level of density has not yet been reached, people may well be aware of the existence of more intensive methods of land use and they may have access to tools of a less primitive kind; still they may prefer not to use such methods until the point is reached where the size of the population is such that they must accept a decline of output per man-hour [Boserup 1965: 41].

Thus famines in rural areas under feudal conditions result from under-population, not overpopulation, when too much of the labor supply is drained away for other purposes, too little food is produced, and too much of it is removed from the villages as taxes. Likewise it is sustained population growth that is often the cause of prosperity in agricultural societies, contrary to Malthus's claim. (It is conceded, however, that this may not be true of communities with a very high rate of population growth which are already densely populated and which are unable to undertake the investment necessary to intensify further their agricultural methods.)

Boserup argues that the classical theories of Western economists are based on the peculiar and, in the worldwide sense, abnormal conditions of European and North American agricultural systems that make a clear distinction between cultivated and uncultivated land. She empha-sizes, instead, not the distinction between "field" and "uncultivated land," but *the frequency with which the land is cropped*. Thus there is a con-tinuum of land use, ranging from the extreme case of truly virgin land never used to land where a new crop is sown as soon as the old one is harvested. She maintains that this is a more realistic and dynamic theory than the fixed and immutable theories of the "traditional" economists which emphasized and exaggerated the distinction between fertile and less fertile land and focused attention on what was happening in the cultivated field while overlooking what took place in the "uncultivated land" being used for pasture, hunting, collecting or fallow.

This is not the place to discuss the merits of Boserup's argument in terms of economic theory. Clearly she subscribes to the body of economic opinion (apparently a minority one today) that maintains that economic productivity and commerce are easier under conditions of population increase and are even stimulated by it. Colin Clark is perhaps the best known of this school, and he appears to agree wholeheartedly with Boserup's thesis, summarizing it approvingly (1967: 133). Less favorable opinions have been expressed by Blitz (1967) and Dovring (1966), al-though Jones (1967) finds her basic argument attractive and reasonable, in spite of what is termed a somewhat single-minded argument in support of one exclusive proposition. However, these criticisms are rather periph-eral in the context of the present article, which is aimed at demonstrating that Boserup's concept of a spectrum or range of land use, though not designed with archaeological problems in mind, can be of great assistance in understanding what was happening in prehistoric times in Southwest Asia.[5]

At the heart of her argument is her typology of land use, divided into five necessarily somewhat arbitrary types in the following order of increasing intensity (see Figure 1.1):

1. Forest-fallow cultivation (often called swidden or slash-and-burn), in which plots are cleared in the forest, cropped for a year or two, and then left fallow for a much longer period, from as few as six to as many as twenty or more years to allow secondary forest to grow up. The ashes add certain nutrients to the soil, while the heat partially sterilizes the soil and temporarily inhibits weed growth (Steensberg 1957).

2. Bush-fallow cultivation. Here the fallow or recovery period between crops is shorter (usually six or seven years), so that only bush and small

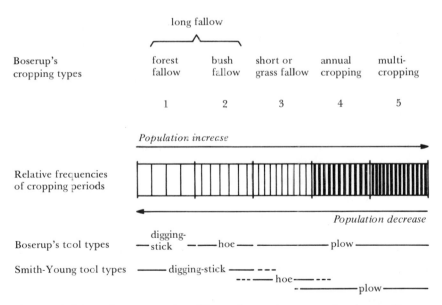

Figure 1.1. Schematic representation of Boserup's cropping types and tool types. Our modified sequence of tool types for Greater Mesopotamia is shown below.

trees can grow up. Cultivation periods vary in length and may be as
short as one or two years or as long as six or eight years.[6]
3. Short-fallow cultivation. The fallow period is only one year or at most
a few years, so that only wild grasses grow; this can also be called "grass
fallow cultivation."
4. Annual cropping. Here the fallow period is only a few months; it
includes systems of annual rotation.
5. Multicropping. This is the most intensive, and two or more successive
crops are obtained each year. The fallow period is short or negligible.
Obviously this is found only in very favored regions.

The actual typology offered by Boserup is not new. Roughly similar
schemes have been outlined by Wolf (1966: 20), Oberg (1965), and
Watters (1960: 65). However, the valuable contribution of her thesis is
her suggestion that movement along this five-type scale of land use is
controlled largely by population pressure. That is, as population grows in
a given region of shifting agriculture, the system becomes restrained by a
lack of sufficient land for rotation. Consequently, land use is ideally
forced in the direction of shorter fallow periods, and along the continuum
from type 1 to type 2 and out of the range of shifting agriculture altogether to types 3, 4, and 5. In other words, Boserup rejects the old idea
that the different fallow systems are to be seen simply as adaptations to
particular types of soils or climates and instead sees them as finely balanced, culturally adaptive adjustments between the natural environment
and population density.

One other important point must be stressed here since it bears directly
on the concepts of surplus and leisure already discussed. As cultivators go
along the continuum from type 1 to type 5, production increases per
unit of land, but individual productivity decreases per unit of labor (that
is, per man-hour), thus necessitating a higher labor input per worker in
almost all cases until draft animals are introduced. With forest- and
bush-fallow cultivation only cutting, burning, and planting are required
before cropping; the forest-fallow system (type 1) is especially easy and
profitable, yielding good crops with comparatively little input of labor as
many writers have pointed out (Conklin 1957; Sauer 1956; Carneiro
1961; Dumond 1961; Clarke 1966). The fire does most of the work, and
complete clearing of the land is not necessary. Bush-fallow cultivation
requires rather more labor input but not a great deal more; however, the

more frequent burning destroys the humus and valuable organic matter in the soil and can lead to invasion by tough grasses (Watters 1960). On the other hand, with short-fallow, annual cropping, and multicropping methods there must usually be fertilizing as well, and in particular intensive weeding. Plowing, if it is practiced, involves hard work for men and animals, and the animals must be taken care of. But, although it involves more man-hours of labor input, plowing does prevent a fall in production and even permits an increase in output per man-hour (Boserup 1965: 33–34). Thus the use of the plow will spread, and new regions of heavy soils and sods can now be exploited provided suitable draft animals and grazing land are available in disease-free environments. The draft animals will be important sources of manure for fertilizer, and visits by nomadic or transhumant pastoralists may also be exploited for this purpose. In some regions, such as parts of southern China, where presumably no alternative was possible, intensive manuring seems to have been the response to population pressure on the land (Ferdon 1959: 15–16). The ultimate in labor intensiveness and low per worker productivity is the stage of "agricultural involution" described by Geertz in Javanese wet-rice cultivation (Geertz 1963).

Again, it should be recalled that this is not necessarily a smooth, orderly progression of cultivation systems and technology. The size of the population can be suddenly decreased by wars, epidemics, famines, and other causes (Malthus's *misery*), and there can be long periods of static conditions or even regression to longer fallow systems such as seems to have occurred in some parts of Latin America, Asia, and Africa since European contacts (Gourou 1956: 345). In addition, at any given time in a single area a whole range of cultivation systems might be found coexisting; indeed, the same group of people in a single village may practice various proportions of several systems at the same time to maintain an equilibrium or to exploit different terrain (Nye and Greenland 1960: 4; Brookfield and Brown 1963: 162).

Boserup assumes that the transition to more intensive systems of land use takes place in response to the increase of population within a given area (see also Dumond 1961: 312 and Carneiro 1958 for somewhat similar suggestions). But would not cultivators deliberately choose a more intensive system of land use if they recognized that it would yield more, regardless of whether the population was increasing, stable, or decreasing?

Boserup's answer is that, in fact, this is not to be expected because the more intensive system yields a lower output per man-hour. Primitive cultivators do not deliberately try to produce additional or surplus food by changing from one cropping system to another. All things being equal, they prefer to use the system that gives them the highest output per man-hour, thus maximizing their leisure periods, which can then be spent in activities such as hunting, warfare, ceremony, or loafing, and to keep the amount of hard labor down to the minimum even if it entails a period of hunger later on in the year. There is considerable ethnographic evidence to support this opinion, for example, De Schlippe (1956) for the Zande of the Sudan, Clarke (1966: 357) for New Guinea groups, Leach (1959) for North Burma, Richards (1939) for the Bemba of Rhodesia, Carneiro (1961) for the Kuikuru of central Brazil. This operation of the "Law of Least Effort" has been noted in the former French Indochina, where groups practicing intensive, permanent agriculture reverted to their traditional shifting cultivation, with a higher return per man-day, once colonial administrative pressure from above was relaxed (Gourou, quoted in Watters 1960: 92). As Nye and Greenland have put it, "But within limits set by custom, the desire to acquire rights over land and so forth, the best general rule to the behavior of primitive farmers is that they work to get the maximum return for the minimum effort" (1960: 129).[7]

The conclusion seems to be that what brings about changes in the cropping systems of independent cultivators is not a voluntary decision to produce more food above the needs of domestic consumption but population pressure, where there are more mouths to feed pushing against a naturally or artificially restricted amount of available land. In such cases the solution is very often to make the fallow period shorter even at the risk of depleting soil fertility, creating artificial grasslands, or producing soil erosion. The transition from one system to another is probably a slow process; a cultivator would likely not change over all his land at once but would modify only part of his total holdings to more frequent croppings and make no change in the rest for the time being. This is not to say that the trend toward shorter fallow periods is an inevitable one. It is obvious that a population may voluntarily find other means of avoiding the choice between harder agricultural work and a lower standard of living. It may be by methods of population limitation such as infanticide, abortion, contraception, or delayed marriage (see Stott 1962), or by predatory activity toward neighbors possessing desirable long-fallow land (Vayda 1961; Rappoport 1962). Another solution, of course, is emigration, and the rapidity with which food producing spread about 6000 B.C. indicates that it was an important, perhaps in many cases even a preferred solution—both literally and figuratively a "way out" of the problem. They may also find an outlet in fishing, as in Polynesia, or in gathering wild foods. Depending on circumstances, a group might opt for a number of these remedies simultaneously. Nevertheless, one of the more important contributions of Boserup's scheme is that it underlines a simple truth often overlooked: that higher mortality rates, lower fertility rates, and emigration are not the only solutions to "chronic overpopulation" among early cultivators, as some writers have suggested (for example, Butzer 1964: 439). The adoption of more intensive systems of land use represents another perfectly feasible choice, although, of course, we do not know if it was always the preferred one or exactly what conditions had to be met to accomplish it.[8] But it provides a more accommodating explanation in many cases than the simple either/or choice suggested by most writers, and the application of Boserup's model permits us to introduce greater determinism into the situation.

Archaeological Implications

We must now consider the relevance of this framework for an understanding of the origins and development of prehistoric agriculture, and in particular for understanding the cultural changes that took place in Greater Mesopotamia during early agricultural and early urban periods.

As many archaeologists have emphasized (for example, Tallgren 1937), artifacts must be studied not only in formal terms but also in the context of their functions within the system of production and the economic development of the society concerned. Fortunately, there seems to be some relationship, though not usually a complete coincidence, between (a) the system of land use, and (b) the kinds of agricultural tools used. Some changes in land use can come about only if they are accompanied by the introduction of new tools. Conversely, some technical changes will come about only if the system of land use is modified at the same time. Since there is some possibility of recovering and identifying agricultural tools in archaeological sites, it is obvious that these will be highly pertinent in interpreting the land-use systems whose evidence is always elusive.

There are three main types of tools used for soil preparation in pre-modern agriculture: digging sticks, hoes, and plows. Each of these is typical (though not exclusively) of a range within Boserup's five types of land use.[9] In the long-fallow systems (forest and bush fallow), after the trees are cut down, the larger trunks are usually left alone, and the planting is done in the ashes between them. For this purpose a digging stick (sometimes more properly called a planting stick or dibble) is sufficient in such loose soil. But when the period of fallow is shortened and the natural vegetation thins out, a grass cover invades the plots to restrict further swidden activities, and at a certain point a hoe becomes the best tool to break up the sod cover that develops. That is, the hoe is not simply a technical perfection of the planting stick but an adaptation to a new situation (see also Oberg 1955: 475; Watters 1960: 88). As the fallow periods become progressively shorter, the dense grass roots make even hoes inefficient. At this point the plow is needed, and true agriculture is developed, though the exact point where it will appear depends upon such natural factors as topography and climate as well as on the availability of draft animals and the kind of plow adopted (see Wolf 1966: 29 for further discussion of this aspect).[10] Animal traction is not wholly necessary for use of the plow, of course, since human energy can be employed, and this may have been the original method. When the plow is introduced, it will require more man-hours of work; but even if the population density is high, it will produce enough food so that some of the traditional long periods of leisure are still available, especially for hunting, gathering, fishing, and other practices which also produce some supplementary food.

Since the introduction of the traction plow may coincide, at least in most tropical areas and in Europe, with the spread of grasslands, herbivorous animals can be supported to pull the plows (and, as a by-product, will supply manure to maintain soil fertility). In cases where draft animals are not practicable or available, as in parts of Africa today and in the aboriginal New World, agriculturalists either avoid short-fallow systems and preserve a bush-fallow system or develop means of intensified agriculture without the use of the drawn plow, for example, chinampas, foot plows.

The final stages (annual cropping and multicropping), which involve regular daily work all year round for many hours each day, are reached only when (climate permitting) population densities and the requirements of other classes force cultivators to give up their periods of seasonal freedom. This is particularly true in areas that can be irrigated, such as the paddy fields of East Asia, the Nile Valley, and, theoretically, Mesopotamia, where, in response to a rising population, agriculture can reach the intensive or "involuted" form described by Geertz in Java (Geertz 1963). The productivity per unit of *land* is high, though the productivity per unit of *labor* is low. Irrigated land produces larger and more frequent crops than ordinary land, so that tax revenues would increase. Thus it is easy to see that a landlord or ruler would realize the advantages of irrigated land and would arrange to have irrigation facilities built by his peasants when the population had increased to the point where the manpower was available and larger and more frequent harvests could be handled than before. This perspective in fact supports the argument of Wolf and Palerm (1955) and Adams (1966) that irrigation is more probably the result of centralized control, rather than the cause, as proponents of the hydraulic school have claimed (Childe 1951; Wittfogel 1957).

The growth toward urbanism—life in sizable towns—can also be examined in the light of population pressure. An instance of this is found in Europe during the eleventh and twelfth centuries A.D. when there was a growth of towns, which is well documented historically. Traditionally this growth has been explained as the result of the preceding technical inventions in agriculture. But some authors believe that it was in fact the consequence of an overall population increase that had resulted from the period of internal peace in Europe after many centuries of war, invasions, and unrest following the decline of the Roman Empire. As the rural population increased, it was now once more possible, especially as the system of three-course rotation of fields and crops spread, to feed the urban concentrations that came into being with their service industries and non-food-producing specialists (see Boserup 1965: 71–72; Pirenne 1956: 57–59; White, Jr., 1962: 69). Slicher Van Bath (1963: 60, 74, 89) also agrees that the consequence of increasing population in twelfth- and thirteenth-century Europe was a changeover from the two-course to three-course rotation as more people had to be fed; this in turn brought about the development of new land and, perhaps, provoked increased technological efficiency as represented by a change from oxen to horses as draft animals. In turn, the advantages of living in larger concentrations, with their social and economic attractions, led to a "balling," or drawing together, of peasants into larger and larger villages and the abandonment of many hamlets, since the peasants were now able to travel longer distances to their fields by using horses (White, Jr., 1962: 67–68).

Thus one of the implications of Boserup's model of cultivation systems for prehistoric archaeology is that the presence of certain implements in archaeological deposits can provide valuable clues as to the type (or types) of agriculture practiced. Obviously there are certain limitations to this approach, as Whyte warns (1961: 60). Wooden digging sticks will rarely be preserved, and stone weights that might in some cases indicate their presence are not always employed. In Neolithic Europe, for instance, there seems to be no example of a digging stick found (Steensberg 1957: 69). Wooden plows present the same limitations, and even hoe blades may be of wood. In addition, since more than one system can be in use in a given community simultaneously, especially in a period of change or transition, the tools are not entirely land-use specific. Thus the presence of stone hoes alone would not be a clear indication of the kind of land use present, though it would at least suggest that it was not exclusively long-fallow types. On the other hand, the absence of hoes and plows in a site believed to be early might be used to argue in favor of a long-fallow system, the wooden digging sticks not having been preserved. It should also be remembered that there are many gradations between digging sticks and hoes, and even between digging sticks and plows, in form as well as in function, and that the divisions are probably less well defined than Boserup suggests. Another problem is that the very earliest type of land use may very well not be detectable by purely archaeological means, for scattering cereals haphazardly on loosely disturbed soils (say, the slope in front of a rock shelter) may have required no special implements, not even digging sticks. Furthermore, agricultural tools are perhaps more likely to have been discarded or lost in the fields than in the habitation areas of the sites excavated by archaeologists. In addition we should bear in mind Watters's statement that some modern shifting cultivators deliberately choose to cultivate former village sites where accumulated refuse and remnants of thatch give superior soil fertility

(Watters 1960: 70). In other words, many of the earliest sites must have been destroyed in this way not long after they were abandoned, thus skewing the available sample from this stage.

But there is another contribution, already mentioned, which Boserup's thesis offers for the reconstruction of cultural history. Although some doubts have been expressed concerning the existence of a single continuum or evolution from shifting to permanent agriculture (Brookfield and Brown 1963: 166), we believe that from an evolutionary viewpoint it is a useful concept. Thus Boserup provides us with a developmental model that helps to explain the evolution of food production from the beginnings of agriculture (in the sense of plant domestication), and to a lesser degree from the beginnings of pastoralism, to the rise of urban centers some millennia later. This model is dynamic and rational, encompassing factors that can to some extent be studied in surviving systems among groups still practicing analogous types of cultivation and in some cases can be tested against archaeological materials in order to understand at least the broad outlines of the processes involved. Further, it permits us to make the archaeological variations intelligible in some cases; that is, it helps explain the differences that are observable in the archaeological sites and assemblages in both time *and* space.

The Environmental Setting

Before attempting any detailed application of our model to the archaeology of agricultural developments in Greater Mesopotamia, we need to consider the environment of the area, past and present, in order to understand the choices in patterns of exploitation available to the cultures with which we are concerned. Greater Mesopotamia may be divided into seven environmental zones (see Figure 1.2). Each of these zones could, of course, be further divided into microenvironmental units, but on the whole the crudeness of the archaeological data available precludes any such description at this time. The one exception to this would be the Southern Mesopotamian Alluvium, given Adams's and Wright's recent survey data (Adams, personal communication). It will be noted that the seven major zones here described vary somewhat from the standard divisions of the area as found, for example, in Zohary (1963) and Flannery (1965). These latter treatments are based almost entirely on

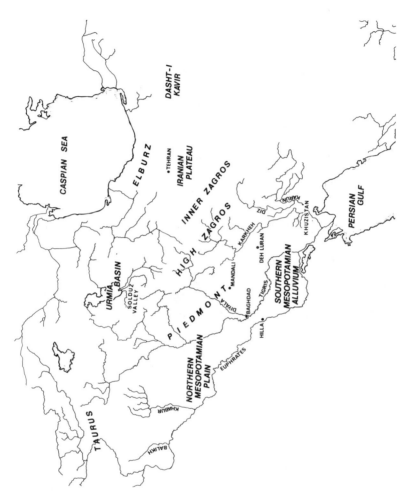

Figure 1.2. Greater Mesopotamia—environmental zones.

the distribution of the flora in the area, combined with somewhat gross mappings of rainfall patterns on the basis of simple altitudinal zonation, and do not fully consider the basic topography of the region.

1. The Southern Mesopotamian Alluvium (Fisher 1950: Fig. 58, Zone IIb): This zone is defined by the lower reaches of the Tigris, Euphrates, Karun, and Karkheh rivers. The basic geology and geography of the area are well known (for example, Buringh 1957; Lees and Falcon 1952). Suffice it here to note that though dry farming is impossible over most of the area (northern Khuzistan being the exception to the rule), the gradient of the rivers is very gradual (1 inch per mile for the lower Euphrates) and hence flooding is extensive, causing considerable alluviation in the central and more northern reaches of the zone, primarily in the form of fans reaching outward from points where the rivers break through their levees. Thus over much of the zone nature herself not only renews annually the fertility of the soil (one should remark at the expense of northern Mesopotamia and the highlands of Anatolia and Iran) but also creates a natural system of primitive irrigation (Adams 1965). As is so often the case under these conditions, however, both extensive marshland and a long-term tendency toward salination are characteristic of the zone (Jacobsen and Adams 1958).

2. The North Mesopotamian Plains, roughly Fisher's Zone IIa (Fisher 1950, Fig. 58): This zone is defined on the east by the Jebel Hamrin and on the north by the Taurus mountains. Rainfall is fairly limited in the zone, with certain marked exceptions; the most important being along the flanks of the Jebel Sinjar, between the Jebel Sinjar and the Taurus range, along most of the east bank of the Tigris between the river and the Piedmont Zone, and within the Assyrian heartland formed by the Tigris and the Greater Zab rivers where dry farming is possible. Were they not now overgrazed, fairly heavy grasslands would be characteristic of these areas. The core of the zone is the Jezireh: fairly inhospitable country deeply etched by wadis and marked with patches of marsh country, suitable primarily for exploitation by pastoralists. Both the Tigris and the Euphrates, as well as the several tributaries entering the Tigris from the east, are here in a stage of down cutting, and any irrigation involves the difficult task of artificially raising the water of the rivers above their banks. Thus, not only is there no alluviation to renew the fertility of the soil, but there is an actual loss of soil through erosion.

3. The Piedmont (Braidwood and Howe 1960: 9–17): This zone is one of rolling foothill country leading east from the North Mesopotamian Plains to the High Zagros. There is abundant rainfall throughout the zone, with precipitation increasing as one moves east toward the mountains. Dry farming is ubiquitous throughout the area, and heavy grasslands spread between stands of oak and pistachio trees that mark the outer limits of the more heavily forested High Zagros. The Piedmont is at its widest in what is now Iraqi Kurdistan, though scattered patches of somewhat similar country can be found further to the south between the Mesopotamian lowland and the first main folds of the High Zagros. In general, however, south of the Diyala the lowlands tend to approach the very base of the mountains, leaving little actual foothill area (the alluvial fans and eastern borderland of Buringh 1957: 35).

4. The High Zagros: Rising immediately east of the Piedmont are the high mountains of the Zagros, of which the major range is technically known as the *chaîne magistrale* (Levine 1969). This zone is sharply divided into southern and northern subzones by the great High Road leading from Baghdad through Kermanshah to Hamadan and the central Iranian plateau; the environment and topography are different in each subzone. In the north (roughly Iranian Kurdistan) precipitation is fairly high, and the slopes of the mountains are comparatively heavily forested with oak and pistachio trees (best preserved today in the area between Baneh and Sar Dasht). The exploitation of this rainfall by agriculturalists, however, is severely limited by the ruggedness of the topography. Small, isolated valleys provide few soil resources, and crude terracing combined with the farming of limited alluvial stream fans hardly suffices to support one or two villages per valley. In the south, in modern western Luristan, precipitation is much lower, and the oak and pistachio are more scattered. The valleys are more open, larger, and less isolated; but lower precipitation and generally high altitudes, causing severe winters, sharply limit the agricultural value of the region. In fact, this area has been traditionally exploited primarily by pastoralists (see also Benet 1960, for perspective on modern exploitation and the implications for past occupation). The Kermanshah and Shahabad valleys are striking exceptions to the basic pattern, for they combine large, open areas and reasonable soil resources with a precipitation pattern similar to the more northern half of the High Zagros zone.

5. The Inner Zagros (Young 1966): This zone is defined on the west by the *chaîne magistrale* and on the east by the Alvand alignment and roughly describes eastern Luristan and the valleys along the High Road east of Kermanshah. North of the High Road there is no Inner Zagros zone, for the Alvand alignment swings gradually to the west until it merges with the *chaîne magistrale*. The Inner Zagros is characterized by fairly open valleys with good soil resources (the valleys of Bisitun, Sahneh, Kangāvar, Asadābād, Tuiserkān, Nehāvand, and Borujerd) but receives less precipitation than the High Zagros zone. Rainfall agriculture is practiced in several areas within the zone, sometimes to excellent effect, but other sections of the zone are difficult to exploit without irrigation.

6. The Iranian Plateau: East of the Alvand alignment lies the Iranian plateau proper. The Hamadan plain is the dominant topographic feature of the western edge of the pleateau, and here precipitation is sharply limited; dry farming is possible only in isolated patches, and the country is essentially more suitable for pastoralism than for agriculture. As one moves still further east and approaches the central salt desert of Iran, the Dasht-i Kavir, the agricultural possibilities become sharply confined to points along the south face of the Alburz mountains and the eastern face of the Zagros range, where water draining toward the central plaeteau breaks out of the mountains.

7. The Lake Urmia Basin: Discussion of this zone has been reserved for last because it is something of an anomaly in a geographical situation that otherwise lends itself well to broad generalization. This fact has its roots in the geological history of the zone (Fisher 1950: 256–258), for the Urmia area is a downthrust basin that tends to break across the main trend lines of the Zagros range. Thus the area cannot properly be included with the High Zagros, the Inner Zagros, or the Iranian plateau. It is a region blessed with both considerable precipitation and an abundance of perennial streams, making rainfall agriculture, supplemented by irrigation, perhaps easier than anywhere else in the whole of western Iran. Oak and pistachio are found on the western slopes of the basin but are not common, at least today, over most of the zone.

Present environmental conditions in Greater Mesopotamia, of course, are not necessarily a reasonable measure of the conditions that existed in prehistoric times. For one thing, man consistently rapes his environment. Overgrazing and deforestation alone have undoubtedly led to increasing erosion in the area causing a general decrease in the available land for cultivation in the Zagros and northern Mesopotamia. Beyond these obvious considerations, however, lies the possibility of actual shifts in climate and hence in environmental conditions within Greater Mesopotamia since the end of the Pleistocene.

Until recently the best evidence available, based primarily on geomorphological studies in the High Zagros and Piedmont zones, indicated that there had been little change in the basic natural environment since around 10,000 B.C., aside from human activity (Wright 1960). Some would have argued that modern conditions were not met until as late as 8000 B.C. (Butzer 1964: 426), but these differences in dating are not significant in archaeological terms. Further, all scholars working in the field seemed to agree that one of the fundamental characteristics of Greater Mesopotamia was its climatic and environmental zonality, based on elevation (Wright 1960: 97; van Zeist 1969). Hence, it was assumed that for the High Zagros and Inner Zagros zones oak and pistachio forests were relatively thick by ca. 10,000 B.C., that the Piedmont zone showed scattered oak and pistachio mixed with grasslands, and the well-watered sections of the North Mesopotamian Plains were characterized by fairly heavy grass. In general, it seemed doubtful that the development of this post-Pleistocene environment could be linked very closely chronologically with the economic and cultural developments observed in the archaeological record, and scholars working in the area tended, with some exceptions (for example, Clark 1961: 64; Solecki 1963), to discount the possibility of environmental change as a major factor causing the observed cultural and economic shifts (Wright 1960: 72).

Recent research, however, based on a limited number of core borings grossly dated by a few radiocarbon samples from fresh water lakes in the Zagros, seems to indicate a more complex picture of events (van Zeist 1967; Wright, McAndrews, and van Zeist 1967; Megard 1967; Wasylikowa 1967; Wright 1968). In sum, a general and gradual shift from cold, dry to warmer, wetter conditions is now seen to have occurred in the Zagros and neighboring areas between the end of the Pleistocene and ca. 3500 B.C. Prior to ca. 12,000 B.C. the Zagros area is characterized by a cold, dry climate and an *Artemisia* or sagebrush steppe environment comparable to that which is found today in a small area southeast of Tabriz and on the high plateau country around Lake Van. About 12,000

B.C. conditions begin to get gradually warmer and wetter. The amount
of *Artemisia* in the pollen rain falls off rather sharply, and we have the
first slight evidence for the movement of oak and pistachio trees into the
area. These trends continue, and around 9000 B.C. three events of some
importance occur in the environmental record. Grass appears on the
landscape in considerable quantity, the amount of oak in the environment begins a sharp increase, and *Plantago*, a peculiar plant, which often
tends to move on to cultivated or recently cultivated land, appears in
quantity. These trends continue for the next two or three millennia: the
amount of grass on the landscape remains high, pistachio trees become
even more common than they are today, and oak becomes an ever more
significant component of the environment. Between 6000 and 3500 B.C.
oak pollen values rise rapidly to modern levels, grass values gradually
decrease, and pistachio values fall to modern levels. Thus it would appear
that not until about the end of the Ubaid Period (ca. 3500 B.C.) did the
climate and the environment of the Zagros, at least, reach modern
conditions.

Several important changes in interpretation have followed from these
new conclusions. First, Wright and van Zeist at least are more inclined
to see a possible connection between cultural and economic developments in the period of the food-producing revolution, on the one hand,
and the general environmental developments traceable in the pollen
record, on the other (Wright 1968: 388; van Zeist 1969). Second, and
perhaps more important, on the basis of core borings from two sites at
different altitudes (Lake Mirivan at 1,400 meters and Lake Mirabad at
800 meters), Wright now tends to reject the movement of vegetation
belts on a basis of altitudinal zonality as the explanation of the history of
environmental changes in the Zagros. Not only does he maintain that the
oak-pistachio zone could not have been depressed on to the Piedmont or
even into the North Mesopotamian Plain in the years prior to 12,000 B.C.,
but he also argues that the main Pleistocene distribution of oak may have
been as far removed from the Zagros as the Mediterranean littoral
(Wright 1968: 336). Others, however, would appear to be less willing to
press this point, emphasizing that the environment in the immediate
vicinity of the lakes from which the samples were taken might vary from
the environment in the foothills (that is, the Piedmont) just as it dose
today, though the general climatic trend would probably have been the

same in both zones (Megard 1967: 188; Bobek, personal communication).

There is not the space here to go into a detailed analysis of these new conclusions. Suffice it to say that as archaeologists we are not yet entirely convinced that a limited number of borings containing so few radio-carbon determinations from widely separated points in as large and environmentally complex a region as the Zagros necessarily tell the whole story of prehistoric environmental change. Altitudinal zonality, on the other hand, has undoubtedly been overstressed in the past. In general it is a useful approach to the study of past and present environments in Greater Mesopotamia. We tend, however, to see a good deal more varia-tion in the environment of the region on north-south lines, influenced primarily by local topographic conditions: variations that have heretofore been partially obscured by an overemphasis on simple east-west zonality. These considerations are reflected in the archaeology and ethnology of the region and are incorporated into the basic description of the environ-mental zones given earlier. For purposes of the present discussion, how-ever, we propose to accept in the main the more recent reconstruction of the environmental history of the area proposed by our colleagues in the natural sciences and based on the palynological and fossil record of the Mirivan and Mirabad cores.

The Archaeological Sequence

In attempting a detailed description of the several developmental stages in the agricultural history of Greater Mesopotamia, we are working under anything but ideal archaeological conditions. In no area of the Near East, for that matter, is it possible to describe with certainty the microevolution of adaptations, as human groups made, probably at varying tempos, the transition from food gathering to urbanism. No single site in Southwest Asia is yet known that convincingly shows the transition from food gathering to food producing, though such sites as Jericho (Jordan), Shanidar Cave (Iraq), and Tepe Guran (Iran) perhaps approximate it. In the earliest stages of the sequence we are not even able to state that Greater Mesopotamia was in advance of such other areas as Palestine; it may have been the reverse (see Kenyon 1959), and indeed there is some evidence suggesting that emmer wheat was first domesticated in Palestine (Harlan and Zohary 1966). Thus the model presented here rests on a body of evidence that is scattered, incomplete, ambiguous, and often frustratingly enigmatic. Nevertheless, we venture to propose the following sequence of stages based on a relationship between population growth and density, on the one hand, and types of land use on the other (see Figures 1.3 and 1.4).

1. Toward the end of Pleistocene times (ca. 12,000–10,000 B.C.) and immediately thereafter a thinly distributed population of hunter/gatherers within the natural habitat zone of Southwest Asia, which had already had considerable experience with broad-spectrum hunting and collecting, began to emphasize more heavily those plants that were later to become domesticates: wheat and barley. Certain animals were probably also being manipulated in the direction of domestication, but we do not yet know whether the same groups of people were doing both.

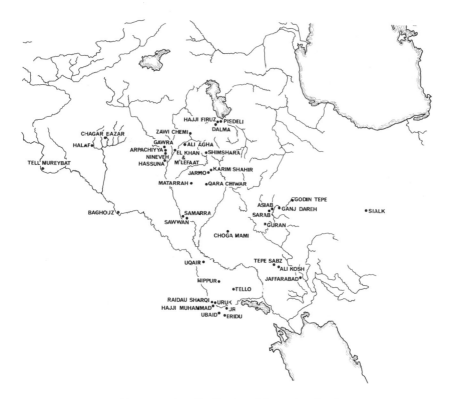

Figure 1.3. Greater Mesopotamia—distribution of sites referred to in text.

	Iranian Plateau	Lake Urmia Basin	Inner Zagros	High Zagros	Piedmont	North Mesopotamian Plain	Deh Luran & Khuzistan	Tigris-Euphrates Alluvium
Hunting & Collecting 9000 B.C.				Zarzi Cave Shanidar B$_2$ Zawi Chemi				
Intensive Collecting & Primitive Cultivation				Asiab	Karim Shahir M'Lefaat			
7000 B.C.				Ganj Dareh? Basal Guran	Gird Chai Qara Chiwar		Bus Mordeh	
Settled Villages & Developed Cultivation				Sarab	Jarmo Kani Sur Khora Namik Ali Agha		Ali Kosh	
5000 B.C.	Sialk I	Hajji Firuz	Godin VII	Upper Guran Shimshara	Matarrah Nineveh 1-28 El Khan	Hassuna Tell-es-Sawnan Samarra Baghouz	Mohammad Jaffar Sabz-Susiana a	Eridu (Ubaid 1)
Agricultural Colonization and Developing Regionalism		Dalma	Godin VI		Arpachiyah	Tell Halaf	Khazineh-Susiana b	Hajji Mohammad (Ubaid 2)
3500 B.C.	Sialk II	Pisdeli			Gawra XIII Gawra XII		Mehmeh-Susiana c	Ubaid 3
Urbanization			Godin V				Bayat-Susiana d	Ubaid 4 Uruk

Figure 1.4. Chart showing approximate chronological and environmental relationships of sites and phases of sites referred to in text. For more chronological details see Dyson (1965, 1968) and Porada (1965).

Earlier attempts to explain the eventual development of food production in this context have quite rightly emphasized the issue of domestication (Braidwood and Howe 1960; Childe 1936) and have tended to consider the development of permanent settlement as the *result* of the successful domestication of plants and animals. However, a considerable degree of sedentism *without* domestication can now be documented throughout Southwest Asia at sites such as Tell Mureybat and perhaps El Kowm in Syria, Manhatta in Palestine, Suberde in Anatolia, and possibly Ganj Dareh in the Iranian Zagros. Some of these sites (Tell Mureybat, for example) are classic "Neolithic" villages. If we reverse the traditional cause-and-effect relationship between domestication and permanent settlement patterns on the basis of these data, keeping in mind the character of the changing natural environment as we now understand it, and add to our considerations the demographic factor, it may be possible to bring the several variables involved in the origins of food production into a more intelligible mosaic.

General trends toward a wetter and warmer climate in Greater Mesopotamia after 12,000 B.C. were of great importance to man. Yet we hesitate to see these climate changes as a "trigger" mechanism for the development of food production. Rather we might consider their effect as having created an environment of "maximal permissiveness" given the then-existing technological and social levels of human environmental adaptation. Increased stands of wild cereal grains (wheat and barley) in certain suitable microenvironmental niches created and encouraged by the trend to a warmer and wetter climate (see van Zeist 1969: 45) would have permitted, indeed encouraged, a continued increasing emphasis by man on the gathering aspect of his hunter-gatherer pattern of subsistence and would have also permitted and encouraged a comparative degree of sedentism by man. That such a pattern of intensive exploitation of wild cereal resources is possible is attested by Harlan and Zohary's demonstration (1966) that stands of wild cereals can yield crops nearly as abundant as fields of domesticated cereals (and of even greater nutritive value). Probably some human groups in the area were, because of their previous orientations, better prepared than others to take advantage of this situation and also to make the change to a greater degree of sedentism. The important role of climate change in the equation is that it created an environment that made selective, preagricultural sedentism

possible, at times even on a rather grand scale. Man's role at this point
in the equation was that he, again selectively, supplied the level of technology necessary to exploit the changing environment intensively.

It is at this point that demographic factors may have begun to play an
important role in creating disequilibrium in the equation—a disequilibrium that led to further developments such as true food production.
Relatively few writers have dealt with this issue (but see Clark
1963; 1967: 130 and Sauer 1948: 76). With specific reference to Greater
Mesopotamia, Flannery has recently introduced the demographic issue
in a stimulating way (1969). But perhaps the most explicit statement on
the relationship between demographic change and the origins of food
production is by Binford (1968), who suggests that an increased dependence on aquatic resources in terminal and immediately post-Pleistocene
times led to increased sedentism and disturbance of the population density equilibrium, and that food production developed in this context (see
also Sauer 1948 for a similar suggestion). Binford proposes that the subsequent marked population growth and pressure would strain against
available food resources under two circumstances (deteriorating physical
environment, and changes in the demographic structure of a region as
one group impinges on the territory of another) and that this would lead
to a situation of stress during which plant and animal domestication
might develop. This is consistent with Birdsell's observation (1957) that
it is possible for human migrants into new territories to double in population with each generation even among preagricultural groups in unfavorable environments, until an equilibrium is reached. Our own hypothesis
is not far from Binford's in some respects, though we do not think his first
and second causes are necessarily exclusive and we hesitate to see aquatic
resources as an important factor in sedentism in Greater Mesopotamia.

We postulate considerable population growth as a direct result of the
development of preagricultural sedentism and the comparatively easy
exploitation of the "permissive" environment created by climatic change.
The causes for such population increases are, of course, both social and
biological and are central to the theme of this volume. For our purposes
here, however, we need mention only a few of the factors that may have
been involved as sedentism developed. More assured and perhaps more
nutritive food supplies, patterns of life involving fewer fatal accidents,

better health and less strenuous conditions for females before and immediately following parturition may all have contributed to the increase.
More important, the decreased emphasis on mobility would probably
have led to spacing children at shorter intervals as more sedentary conditions of life permitted a relaxation of controls on child carrying (see
Birdsell 1968). Again, we can postulate that increased sedentism and the
exploitation of large stands of wild cereal grasses that required reaping
during a few brief weeks would have made it adaptively useful to have
more harvest hands, on the principle that "many hands make light work,"
and that increased population would permit a more thorough exploitation of the environment. Sedentism in the context of Greater Mesopotamia at this time, therefore, would be a positive spur to population
increase. An analogue perhaps exists in aboriginal Wisconsin, where the
unusually high population density in parts of the region was due to the
utilization of wild rice (Kroeber 1939: 89), while Deevey (1960: 202)
suggests that "a shift from animal to plant food, even without agricultural labour and ingenuity, would practically guarantee a 10-fold increase, for a given area can usually produce about 10 times as much
plant as animal substance."

Eventually disequilibrium between population density and the carrying capacity of the environment at the existing technological level of
exploitation would result from continued population growth. Climate
changes as we now understand them for Greater Mesopotamia will not
explain this disequilibrium. Rather it is to man as an overexploiter of his
"maximal permissive" environment that we should turn for an explanation of why things got out of balance. Only certain microenvironments
were suitable for intensive, settled, preagricultural exploitation. As population increased within those environmental limits, population density
increased. As population density increased, the degree of overexploita-
tion of the environment increased. Yet through sedentism man had, in
the meantime, developed certain new social and economic patterns that
had become the cultural norms. We might expect a reluctance to deviate
from these norms in some cases at least. Under cumulative pressures resulting from the interaction of his social, economic, and environmental
circumstances, all influenced by increased population densities, he gradually began more and more to manipulate the plants and animals with

which he was now so familiar and which were so important to the maintenance of "normal" patterns of culture. It may have been under such
circumstances that the initial attempts at transferring cereals from their
original ecological niches to slightly different ones began—probably as
Flannery has suggested (1965: 1251), by nothing more drastic at first
than moving them from a hill slope to a valley floor. It is also in such
circumstances of population pressure and disequilibrium that variable
ecosystems (Flannery 1965) were able to enter into a creative and mutually advantageous process of production and redistribution (see also
Hole and Flannery 1967: 197 and, for the application of the ecosystem
approach to somewhat similar problems in the New World, Flannery
et al. 1967). Thus it would be in situations of increasing population density within the stage broadly characterized by early selected sedentary
exploitation of wild plant (and/or animal) resources that we would see
the roots of domestication and the development of food producing in
Greater Mesopotamia. Food production is sometimes a means for effectively diversifying the food resources of a particular habitat.

Since we are dealing with a process and not a fixed chronological state
of economic and cultural development, it is difficult to define this stage
archaeologically with precision. In general, we may say that the behavior
in this "Mesolithic" context corresponds roughly to Braidwood's "terminal level of food collection" (Braidwood 1967). The early phases of
this stage are perhaps seen in the Zarzian of the Zagros and the early
Natufian in Palestine; the later phases in the late Natufian and in such
sites as Tell Mureybat and Suberde.

2. Processes of change begun in stage one would naturally lead unevenly
and at varying tempos to levels of economic and cultural variation sufficiently distinct from anything like the Zarzian or the early Natufian to
warrant the heuristic definition of a new stage of development. With
continued population growth, at least in selective circumstances, we can
imagine that certain zones of Greater Mesopotamia in the early Holocene
became more crowded for those groups which had remained more strictly
hunters and gatherers as pressure built up from the groups that were
now intensively collecting plant resources and had begun tentative manipulation of those resources. Under these circumstances, somewhat
reminiscent of the situation in nineteenth century Wisconsin, where the
Sioux and Chippewa were forced into a zone hitherto occupied by only

one group (Hickerson 1965), the competition for land and resources would increase sharply. As a result, more groups of hunter-gatherers, or at least those that survived the probable conflicts, would be forced to adapt themselves to the new means of exploitation, with the emphasis varying according to the biotope concerned: cereals in some areas, goats and/or sheep in others, or perhaps the cereals and animals combined at times. Of course, as more groups adopted the new subsistence techniques, population density with respect to resources available for exploitation at a given level of technological development would increase, thus accelerating the trend toward the development of new technologies, which in this context meant a more sophisticated manipulation of the domesticates.

This stage, corresponding with Braidwood's "level of incipient cultivation and domestication," is notoriously difficult to identify archaeologically.[11] It is probably best represented in the Zagros by such sites as Karim Shahir, Gird Chai, and M'lefaat (Braidwood and Howe 1960) and Zawi Chemi (R. L. Solecki 1964) in Iraq, and in Iran by Asiab (Braidwood, Howe and Reed 1961), Ganj Dareh (Smith 1968; Young and Smith 1966), presumably the Bus Mordeh phase of Ali Kosh (Hole, Flannery and Neely 1969) and possibly basal Guran (Meldgaard, Mortensen, and Thrane 1964). Ethnographically the Vedda of Ceylon provide an analogue as groups who were primarily hunters and gatherers but who practiced shifting cultivation to a small extent (Watters 1960: 65). It is in this context of growing populations that we might expect the first serious attempts at soil cultivation and dry farming to take place. Chronologically we are dealing with a long period in this stage, from about 9000 to 7000 B.C., and unfortunately we are not able to order the several sites within the period. Undoubtedly some of these sites are contemporary (perhaps Asiab and Ganj Dareh), while some fall at the beginning or at the end of the period (Zawi Chemi and the Bus Mordeh phase of Ali Kosh, respectively).

With respect to environmental conditions at this time, it is important to note that these sites fall in different zones within Greater Mesopotamia. Karim Shahir and M'lefaat are in the Piedmont, Zawi Chemi is on the border between Piedmont and the High Zagros, Asiab (in the Kermanshah Valley of Iran) is in the High Zagros, Ganj Dareh lies at the border between the High and Inner Zagros, Ali Kosh is on the border between the southern High Zagros and the South Mesopotamian Alluvium, and

Guran is in the southern half of the High Zagros zone. It may be significant that so many of the relevant sites in this stage lie on the borders
between environmental zones, but perhaps even more significant is the
fact that primitive agricultural techniques had already been adapted to
a variety of ecological situations. Whatever the exact type of initial agriculture, it would certainly have been, in Geertz's phrase, a "canny
imitation of the natural landscape rather than at first any bold reworking
of it, integrated into and maintaining the general structure of the preexisting natural ecosystem" (Geertz 1963: 16). As for the broader environment within the Zagros, this is the period in which grass becomes
widespread, oak begins to appear in increased quantities, the pistachio
trees are even more common than today, and *Plantago* appears in the
pollen record.

Thus it seems doubtful that the vegetation, in the Zagros at least, was
sufficiently dense at this time to call for Boserup's first stage of land use,
that is, forest fallow. Indeed, we might at best visualize primarily grasslands interspersed with some bush and occasional clumps of trees (reserving
the possibility that the number of trees may have been somewhat greater
in the Piedmont than in the Zagros proper). This may have involved no
agricultural disadvantage since, as Nye and Greenland have pointed out
(1960: 124–125), in temperate lands "open" areas or grasslands are
usually more fertile than forests, whereas the opposite is true in tropical
areas. Thus, some of the cultivators in this period may have started with
the equivalent of Boserup's bush fallow or practiced forms of shifting
cultivation in grasslands.[12] In any case, the variety of ecological zones
already occupied by the primitive cultivators of this stage, combined
with the observed variations in the several archaeological assemblages,
suggests that by no means can one speak of a single system of cultivation
in practice throughout the Zagros at this time. Long-fallow cultivation of
cereals involving the use of simple digging sticks—probably already known
in Pleistocene times though none is preserved in the local archaeological
record—might be inferred from the perforated stone balls found at Karim
Shahir, Zawi Chemi, and M'lefaat, which could have been used as digging stick weights. The absence of any tool in the record that can be
directly related to tillage in the assemblages from Asiab, Ganj Dareh,
basal Guran, or Ali Kosh in the Bus Mordeh phase might be taken as an
argument from silence for the use of the digging stick and long-fallow

cultivation at those sites. It is, of course, also possible that in the case of Asiab, Ganj Dareh, and Guran in the High and Inner Zagros conscious tillage of any kind was not yet practiced and the inhabitants may have still relied entirely on intensive gathering, or, as Mortensen has suggested, they may have emphasized herding as a form of food production suited to their local environment (Meldgaard, Mortensen, and Thrane 1964: 120); thus, these sites might properly be considered under stage one, described earlier, despite their date. At the moment the evidence can be read either way, but the analysis of possible plant remains from Ganj Dareh may help in resolving the issue. The recent discovery of large and small pottery vessels before ca. 7000 B.C. at Ganj Dareh is suggestive of organized storage patterns, although we cannot yet be certain that domesticated plant foods were involved (Smith 1968, 1970). In any case, agriculture certainly was being practiced in Khuzistan at Ali Kosh later in this period.[13]

The presence of stone implements described as axes at Zawi Chemi, Karim Shahir, and M'lefaat (tools conspicuously absent in other zones) suggests that in the Piedmont there may have been scrub and small trees that needed to be cleared in the practice of long-fallow cultivation. On the other hand, fire may very well have been used to dispose of any brush or high grass cover, for the people, like most hunters, would almost certainly have been familiar with the uses of fire to clear off forested or grassland areas even in Pleistocene times (Stewart 1956). Indeed, one writer has suggested that the cultivation of grain began in western Iran when the wild ancestors of barley and wheat were accidentally blown into the burned-off areas of hunters and were found to grow abundantly (Steensberg 1957: 66). Clarke (1966: 363) describes an analogous situation involving grass burning and the use of dibbles in New Guinea. There is, however, some evidence already at this period in the record for a selective progression to ever shorter fallow periods. Chipped and ground stone hoes, the implements associated with increasingly heavy grass cover resulting from a shortening of fallow periods, are found at Zawi Chemi, Gird Chai, and Karim Shahir, while ground stone hoes are known from M'lefaat. If we assume that the negative evidence for digging sticks from Asiab and Ganj Dareh implies long-fallow cultivation in the High and Inner Zagros, we would conclude from the absence of any stone hoes at these sites that here the population pressure was not as severe as in the

Piedmont and that shorter fallow periods dependent on the use of the hoe had not developed.

Thus we might view the long period between about 9000 and 7000 B.C. as one in which long-fallow cultivation based on the digging stick, along with mud-flat cultivation where environmental conditions permitted, represented perhaps the earliest form of conscious tillage in the Zagros but was already beginning to give way in some areas to the use of the hoe and ever shorter periods of fallow under selective increases in population density. Long-fallow cultivation itself would have encouraged the spread of heavier grasses onto the cultivated plots as tillage brought about changes in soil compositions, thus increasing the urge to move to hoes and shorter fallow periods. Possibly the risk of soil erosion was another factor encouraging the shift to hoe cultivation for, as Nye and Greenland (1960: 134–135) have emphasized, in modern West Africa firing of grass-lands is a wasteful and inefficient system in the long run since the burning checks the growth of shrubs and trees and encourages soil erosion. Do-mesticated grazing animals (goats and sheep) by eating off the seedlings would presumably by now have speeded up the trends toward the elim-ination of those trees and bushes that existed, just as in Neolithic Europe (Clark 1952: 97), thus promoting further the spread of grasslands. In sum, it is tempting to suggest that man himself may have had a hand in the maintenance and spread of the grasslands that are so predominant a feature of the landscape at this time according to the pollen records (Wright 1968), if not in holding back the spread of oak into the area as well. It is also a possibility (admittedly slim) that the abrupt rise in *Plantago* in the pollen rain of the period may be a reflection of this early stage of cultivation, since that plant is often associated with agriculture.

3. Continued population growth with selective increases in population density in those areas most suitable for tillage would have led gradually to the adoption of short-fallow cultivation over much of the Zagros high-lands, and we suspect that in the early stages of Braidwood's "Level of Primary Village Farming" (roughly the seventh and first half of the sixth millennia), short-fallow cultivation became relatively ubiquitous (see note 9). Those groups which continued to practice long-fallow cultiva-tion would probably have been forced into agriculturally marginal areas, and one might expect that by the seventh millennium relatively few groups were still subsisting entirely on the basis of hunting and gathering,

though such activities would have continued to provide important supplements to the diet of agricultural communities (for example, Ali Kosh
in the Ali Kosh phase; Hole and Flannery 1967: 176). Unfortunately,
these assertions are rather difficult to document, for, given the accidents
of archaeological field work, this period is in many respects less well
known than the preceding developmental stage. On the present evidence
it is even sometimes difficult, if not impossible, to distinguish typologically
assemblages in this time range from materials dating to the second half
of the sixth millennium or even later (for example, the somewhat confused relationship between Hajji Firuz, Sarab, Jarmo, Guran, and the
Mohammad Jaffar phase of Ali Kosh (Young 1966; Mortensen 1964:
34–36; Hole and Flannery 1967: 181).

These difficulties aside, it nevertheless seems clear that there are certainly more sites in this time range and that some of those sites are considerably larger than sites in the previous period. (Only three, however—
Jarmo, Guran, and Ali Kosh—are even reasonably reported in the literature). In the Piedmont, we have Jarmo, Ali Agha, Kani Sur, Khor
Namik, and Kharaba Qara Chiwar (Braidwood and Howe 1960); in the
Kermanshah Valley within the High Zagros we have Sarab and three or
four sites with comparable assemblages known only from survey (Braidwood, Howe, and Reed 1961; personal communication from R. J. Braidwood; and Young, unpublished survey data); in the southern half of
the High Zagros is Guran (Meldgaard, Mortensen, and Thrane 1964),
where the sequence undoubtedly continues into at least the late sixth
millennium; in the area of the alluvial fans and eastern borderland of
the Southern Mesopotamian Alluvium (Buringh, 1953), where the southern High Zagros meets the lowlands, we have perhaps three sites known
from survey only with Jarmo-like materials (J. Oates 1968); and in Deh
Luran we have Ali Kosh in both the Ali Kosh and Mohammed Jaffar
phases, plus two other sites with Mohammed Jaffar materials known
only from survey (Hole and Flannery 1967). Thus there are some sixteen
or seventeen known sites in this time range, as opposed to eight or perhaps nine sites from the preceding period. The data clearly indicate a
considerable increase in population, and it is significant that, in the main,
this increased population is concentrated in the same geographical areas
where sites were found in the early Holocene. Thus we might assume
perhaps a twofold increase in population density in the area—a situation

that undoubtedly put considerable strain on the food resources available given the tillage practices of the preceding period. However, such an increase would have supplied the necessary labor for a general shift to shorter-fallow practices based on more intensive hoe cultivation.

Hoes are well documented at Jarmo, justifying the assumption that short-fallow methods of tillage continued in the Piedmont, where we saw them practiced in the preceding period apparently side by side with long-fallow techniques. Hoes are also found at Guran, suggesting that shorter-fallow cultivation may now have been practiced in certain areas of the High Zagros as well, where, on the basis of at least negative evidence, only long-fallow cultivation could be assumed in the earlier periods. That only two hoes occur at Ali Kosh in the Ali Kosh or Mohammed Jaffar phases, we assume, indicates a continuation of "mud-flat" cultivation and the use of the dibble as a suitable adaptation to the peculiarities of the local environment (Hole, Flannery, and Neely 1969: 199, Table 39). Hole and Flannery (1967: 177), however, suggest that practices involving animal grazing and some system of fallowing had, by the Mohammad Jaffar phase, considerably altered the local landscape and removed much of "the natural vegetational cover in the vicinity of the site." This suggests practices other than simple "mud-flat cultivation."

We know from the palynological record that grass continued to be the principal component of the landscape throughout this period, and grass, as we noted previously, is what one expects to be predominant in the environment during a period of short-fallow cultivation. How much the maintenance of high levels of grass in the environment was a simple function of natural forces and how much it may have been the result of more widespread short-fallow practices is hard to assess, but it is certainly tempting to see a relationship between the two. We suspect that, related to this issue of widespread grasslands, domesticated animals at this stage may have played an increasing role in subsistence patterns. The herding of animals certainly seems to have increased at Ali Kosh at least, the one site from which we have positive evidence published on this point (Hole and Flannery 1967: 177–178). Shorter-fallow cultivation requires the artificial renewal of soil fertility, and the grazing of animals on field stubble and the grasses that spring up between croppings is one of the time-honored methods of fertilizing the soil in the Near East. Indeed, this function of domesticated animals is so important that it is hard to postulate a widespread adoption of short-fallow cultivation without also assuming an increased emphasis on domestic animals. Thus there might also appear at this time an increased emphasis on pastoral nomadism and the development of a symbiotic relationship between the pastoralist and the sedentary agriculturalist—the standard method used today of maximizing the exploitation of the natural resources within the Zagros (Barth 1961). Pastoralism, though outside Boserup's frame of reference, can itself be seen as a form of intensive land use under the spur of population pressure (see Chapters 10 and 11, this volume).

4. Over the course of the next 2,000 years Greater Mesopotamia experienced a series of radical cultural and economic developments that laid the foundations for the urban civilization to follow on the Mesopotamian plains in the late fourth and third millennia. In terms of the traditional Mesopotamian sequence we are here dealing with the Hassuna, Halaf, and Ubaid period (ca. 6000–3500 B.C.); in Braidwood's terms with the second half of the "Era of Primary Village Farming" (Hassuna and Halaf) and the "Era of the Developed Village-Farming Community" (the Ubaid). It is difficult to discuss Greater Mesopotamia in this time range in terms of overall developmental trends, for one of the period's prime characteristics is the growth of considerable cultural and economic regionalism. Nevertheless, two general points of some importance stand out against this background of diversification.

First, for the moment considering only the later sixth millennium, we can document a massive population increase over the preceding period which covered perhaps twice the number of centuries. Our best documentation of this phenomenon comes from Deh Luran and Khuzistan, where Hole and Flannery suggest a doubling of the population density in Deh Luran between the Mohammed Jaffar phase at Ali Kosh and the Sabz phase at Tepe Sabz (Hole and Flannery 1967: 188); and Adams (1962: 112) reports some 34 sites in this period (roughly Susiana a) in the northern half of the Khuzistan plain (see Figure 1.4). Elsewhere in Iran we can document an equally remarkable population increase based on the number of sites excavated and discovered through survey. In central western Iran, particularly in the Inner Zagros, we have Godin VII (Young and Smith 1966) and numerous similar sites known from survey (Young 1966 and unpublished survey data). Materials in the same general time range are also known from the Kermanshah area of the High

Zagros (Young, unpublished survey data), and the highest levels of
Guran probably date back to this period. In the Central Plateau zone is
Sialk (Ghirshman 1938). In the Lake Urmia Basin we have Hajji Firuz
(Young 1962) and at least three related sites in the Solduz Valley. In the
Piedmont and on the Northern Mesopotamian Plain, the area to which
Hassuna culture proper is confined, there are at least 12 sites where
relevant materials have been excavated, and perhaps as many as 25 or 30
sites known from survey (Lloyd 1938; D. Oates 1968).[14]

Finally, on the Southern Mesopotamian Alluvium are Eridu, whose
earlier levels fall within this time range (Lloyd and Safar 1947), and
several related sites that are known from survey but have not as yet been
the subject of a published report. On the crudest sort of estimate, therefore (and the lack of published data precludes anything but a crude
estimate), we are dealing with perhaps 100 or 120 sites in this period—
about 60 in Iran, perhaps 40 or 50 in northern Mesopotamia, and 10 or
20 in southern Mesopotamia. Even if we give little weight to the fact
that many of these sites are considerably larger than sites in the preceding
period, when we compare our gross estimate of the number of sites known
with our suggestion that perhaps 16 or 17 sites were documented for the
seventh and early sixth millennia, then it becomes clear that we are
speaking of something on the order of an eightfold increase in population
in a comparatively short period of time.

From the facts just summarized a second important conclusion follows.
We observe that now all seven zones of Greater Mesopotamia defined
earlier are occupied. Heretofore the known sites have been confined to
the Piedmont, the High and Inner Zagros, the fringes of the Mesopotamian plain, and the Zagros foothills in the south. Now occupations are
documented on the Southern Mesopotamian Alluvium, the North Mesopotamian Plain, in the Lake Urmia Basin and even on the inhospitable
Iranian Plateau. Thus, aside from the interesting question of the cultural
relationships in the Zagros past and present (Mortensen 1964), there is
little doubt that much of the population growth in the sixth millennium
and the pressure created by that growth was absorbed through colonization and migration. Even so, however, the density of the population must
also have risen markedly, as the data from Deh Luran and the central
western Zagros alone testify, and it seems reasonable to assume that,

along with colonization, more intensive forms of agricultural exploitation involving still further shortening of the fallow period were a feature of the period.

As usual, the case is difficult to document simply because not enough of the relevant archaeological data have been reported except in the most cursory form, and in much of what has been more fully reported those aspects of the data relevant to the hypothesis under examination have not been stressed.

Turning first to Khuzistan and Deh Luran, where good data are available, one notes two developments in the Sabz phase at Tepe Sabz (5500 to 5000 B.C.), which are perhaps of considerable importance. First, polished stone celts, implements very possibly used as hoes, appear for the first time in the local sequence (Hole, Flannery, and Neely 1969: 199, table 3). This fact, combined with the limited evidence available for the development of primitive irrigation techniques (Hole and Flannery 1967: 184), suggests a move away from "mud-flat" cultivation confined to the edges of marshes. Boserup has observed that in general the development of irrigation tends to accompany a shift to shorter fallow periods and to require a considerable increase in the available labor force (Boserup 1965: 26, 39–41). We suspect that this is at least in part true even if the irrigation techniques used are of a fairly simple type. One might argue, therefore, that the well-documented growth in population density, the beginnings of simple irrigation, and the appearance of hoes in the archaeological assemblage for the first time in the Sabz phase are related events involving the appearance of more intensive forms of cultivation in Deh Luran. The exploitation of local patches of alluvium through some system of short-fallow cultivation might explain the facts.[15]

In both Deh Luran and northern Khuzistan the population appears to have continued to grow down to the middle of the fourth millennium. In Deh Luran 12 sites are reported for the Khazineh phase (5000 to 4500 B.C.), and some 102 sites from the roughly comparable Susiana b phase are known in Khuzistan. For the Mehmeh phase in Deh Luran (4500 to 4100 B.C.) a population density of five persons per square kilometer has been suggested (over twice the density in the Sabz phase), and Adams reports about 100 sites for the same time range, roughly Susiana a, in Khuzistan. Nine sites are reported from the Bayat phase in Deh

Luran (4100 to 3700 B.C.) and 116 sites in Khuzistan for the Susiana d
period (Hole and Flannery 1967). Over the whole of this time range dry
farming remained perhaps most important, but by the Bayat or Susiana d
period the distribution of sites across northern Khuzistan tends to suggest an increasing emphasis on irrigation through the exploitation of
the natural aggrading watercourses of the Karkheh and Diz rivers
(Adams 1962: 113). Hoes continue in use, though it is interesting to note
their apparent decline in importance in the Bayat phase (Hole and
Flannery 1967: 195), a point to which we shall return later. On the
whole, despite the certain increase in the density of population in these
periods, one can probably assume that the short-fallow methods of exploiting the alluvium suggested previously as a development of the Sabz
phase, combined with somewhat more intensive irrigation techniques and
colonization, were sufficient to absorb the pressure of increasing population in this area at least to the middle of the fourth millennium.

For the High and Inner Zagros no data are available on the types of
agricultural implements used in the period between 5500 and 3500 B.C.
On the Iranian Plateau proper, however, chipped stone hoes are documented at Sialk in Period I and II (Ghirshman 1938: Pl. LVI: 3) suggesting the application of relatively short fallow methods of cultivation.
In contrast to the situation at Sialk, extensive excavations at Hajji Firuz
in the Lake Urmia Basin zone have failed to reveal any hoes, a fact that
holds true for the following Dalma and Pisdeli periods as well. What this
fact may mean is difficult to say, but it is possible that the absence of
hoes in the Solduz Valley might imply the use of digging sticks either for
"mud-flat" cultivation along the banks of the freshwater lakes and marshes common in the area or indicate some form of long-fallow cultivation
suitable to a region apparently not exploited before the beginning of the
sixth millennium.

Turning to northern Mesopotamia in the Hassuna time range, we
note that either the data are incomplete or no hoes were found at Samarra, Arpachiyah, Chagar Bazar, Halaf, Baghouz, el-Khan, and Shem-
shara. Hoes were common, however, in the lowest level of Tell Hassuna
itself, occurred in insignificant numbers in Level II, and then disappeared
from the assemblage entirely (Lloyd and Safar 1945: 269). A single celt,
which may have been a hoe, was found at Nineveh in Level 2b(?)
(Perkins 1949: 9). One celt was found at Matarrah (Braidwood et al.

1952: 34). Two celts that might have been hoes were found at Ali Agha
(Braidwood and Howe 1960: 38), and hoes were apparently relatively
common at Tell es-Sawwan (El-Wailly and es-Soof 1965: 22).

In the following Halaf period all excavated sites in northern Mesopotamia yielded polished stone celts (Perkins 1949: 35), but they appear
to have been small and not likely to have been used as hoes. In the Ubaid
period, still in the north, celts were found only at Gawra, where they
occur in all levels from XIX to XII, at which point they become rare
(Tobler 1950: 202–203). With only one or two exceptions, however (for
example, Tobler 1950: Pl. XCV: b: 3), all these tools, like their Halafian
counterparts, are much too small to have been used as hoes for tillage.
In sum, therefore, the hoe appears to have been known and used early in
the Hassuna period in northern Mesopotamia, to have survived perhaps
through the Hassuna period only at one or two sites, and to be missing
from the Halaf and Ubaid periods almost entirely.

It is tempting to suggest, even though it strains the data, that as agricultural settlement spread into north Mesopotamia roughly within the
limits of possible dry farming, sometime during the sixth millennium,
fallow practices developed in earlier periods in the highland areas were
applied initially in the somewhat similar environmental conditions that
obtained on the North Mesopotamian Plain: that is, some form of short-
fallow cultivation based primarily on the use of the hoe. Gradual population increases, creating greater densities of population within the areas
available for agricultural exploitation through dry farming, however, led
fairly soon to the introduction of the plow in response to ever shortening
fallow periods that eventually in certain favored and limited circumstances may have crossed the threshold to annual cropping. Thus it was
that the hoe disappears as a major tool in the excavated assemblages.
One might argue that almost from the beginning man found the comparatively heavy grass cover over parts of northern Mesopotamia difficult
to handle without some kind of crude plow, and, since cattle were undoubtedly domesticated by the Hassuna period (Hole and Flannery
1967: 185; Perkins 1969), suitable traction power was available for plowing. It is, of course, not until the Uruk period that we have our first firm
evidence for the plow in Mesopotamia (Childe 1952: 129). This plow,
shown in the pictographic script of the period is, however, of a relatively
sophisticated type, and we might reasonably assume that a long period

of development lay behind the plows of the Uruk period. Braidwood (1967) postulates the plow by Ubaid times at least. Also perhaps of some significance, the environmental record tells us that beginning about 6000 B.C. and continuing until around 3500 B.C. grass begins to decline as a component of the landscape partly, of course, because in the highlands at least it was being shaded out by an increase in the number of oak trees but also, perhaps, because shorter fallow periods, based on the plow, including annual cropping, had been introduced, thus preventing the growth of grass on cultivated land.

Turning to the South Mesopotamian Alluvium, we find a slightly different situation. Here our archaeological data are particularly poor, for little excavation has been conducted with cultural history in mind other than in terms of architectural (temple) and ceramic sequences. Nevertheless, small polished stone celts similar to those known from the Halaf and Ubaid periods in the north have been found at Eridu, al-Ubaid, Hajji Mohammad, Tello, and Uqair (Perkins 1949: 85). None of these implements can be dated with much accuracy, but in any case they are not of a size or type to be hoes useful in tillage. On the other hand, and in contrast to the situation in the north, chipped stone hoes that are undoubtedly proper tillage implements were found at Eridu, al-Ubaid, Ur-Ubaid I, Raidau Sharqi, Tello, and Uqair (Perkins 1949: 85). The precise dating of these objects is also problematical, but they might easily represent a more or less continuous tool tradition lasting from the earliest documented agricultural settlement in southern Mesopotamia in the Ubaid 1 period (basal Eridu, ca. 5500 B.C.) through to later Ubaid times.

Colonization of the Southern Mesopotamian Alluvium appears to have progressed from south to north (Buringh 1953) and probably was a relatively slow process. Even by Ubaid times little advantage had been taken of the agricultural possibilities of areas in the neighborhood of Uruk (Adams, personal communication), and settlement was anything but dense on the Diyāla plain (Adams 1965: 34 and personal communication, indicating even less density of settlement than the published evidence would suggest because of the subsequent realization that the clay stickle, heretofore thought to be a hallmark of the Ubaid period, dates to Uruk times if not later as well). One might postulate that agricultural techniques such as we described earlier for Deh Luran and northern Khuzistan, involving hoe cultivation in patterns of relatively short fallow, were those which were first applied in the Southern Mesopotamian Alluvium. As long as land remained available for colonization by a gradual move northward along the braided Tigris and Euphrates rivers, or until such time as we can demonstrate that the occupation of alluvial fans within southern Mesopotamia itself was not a case of shifting occupation and hence a particular type of shifting cultivation, we may assume that little pressure would have developed to change established agricultural practices. Eventually, however, population pressures were felt in the south. Small rural stetlements began to increase in frequency in early Uruk times indicating population growth, and in late Uruk times a sharp increase in settlement by a full order of magnitude is recorded (Adams, personal communication).

Once the closed environment of the south began to fill to the limits of its capacity with given systems of fallow and their related forms of social organization, pressures would have been exerted toward a change in fallow system as well as a change in accompanying social organization. In selected areas a shift to shorter fallow periods and possibly some annual cropping would have occurred, the plow would have been introduced, perhaps borrowed from the north, where it may have been developed earlier, and the hoes, apparently long since discarded in the north, might begin to disappear from the archaeological assemblage.[16] It is not possible, of course, to date even roughly this shift to the plow and shorter periods of fallow, but it may have happened as early as the late Ubaid or, more probably, in the Uruk period. From the only area where we have good excavated data, we have already observed the declining emphasis on the hoe in the Bayat phase in Deh Luran, where possibly a similar shift to the plow was taking place. In any case, it is striking that hoes seem to disappear almost entirely from excavated archaeological assemblages in southern Mesopotamia in the Uruk and Jemdet Nasr periods (Perkins 1949: 147–149).[17]

In sum, therefore, one might suggest that the plow and the shortened-fallow system associated with it may have appeared rather earlier in the north than in the south. Once shorter-fallow systems did take hold on the Southern Mesopotamian Alluvium, however, it would perhaps be natural that the south should experience accelerated cultural and economic rates of development in contrast to the surrounding highlands and the North

Mesopotamian Plain. The shorter the fallow period, the greater the need for artificial means of soil renewal. The grazing of animals on fields may be sufficient to renew soil fertility under some fallow systems, but it is possible that once the inhabitants of northern Mesopotamia (and the highlands as well) were forced to develop yet shorter periods of fallow, such simple methods of soil replenishment would have been insufficient to stem a general long-range decline in the fertility of the soil. The annual deposition of riverine alluvium on fields is one way nature has of restoring soil fertility, and massive silt deposition in Mesopotamia is confined to the central and northern parts of southern Mesopotamia. Such natural deposition would, of course, be enhanced through any efforts man might make toward artificial irrigation. Thus the cumulative prosperity of the south, accelerating in the Uruk, in contrast to the relative backwardness of the north and the highlands in the same period, might well be in part because nature solved for the southerner one of the major problems that must be faced under systems of very short fallow— the issue of declining soil fertility.

As for the development of urbanism in southern Mesopotamia beginning in the Uruk period and continuing through the Early Dynastic period, increased population densities most probably played an important role. Irrigation itself, on an increasingly controlled scale, can be viewed as a form of agricultural intensification, which became all the more necessary because of the "balling" of population in large settlements, as documented by Adams for the Early Dynastic period (personal communication). Particularly noticeable in both the archaeological and written records is the development of organized conflict, including the fortification of occupation sites of greatly increased size. We suspect that such conflict might easily be a direct reflection of increasing population densities and competition for land, particularly unsalinized land. The development of highly complex social and political power structures with social stratification and occupational specializations might also be directly related to the need for organizing larger blocks of labor, now available because of population increase, partly in order to intensify further the agricultural productivity of the region. (See Netting, Chapter 9, this volume, for discussion of the development of centralized political power in conditions of population pressure and circumscribed resources; and Carneiro 1961 for his circumscription hypothesis, which, we believe, is applicable to lower Mesopotamia.) These agricultural developments in turn would themselves contribute to a further development of urbanism, perhaps on the patterns already discussed which seem to have been operable in Europe in the twelfth and thirteenth centuries A.D. The details of these developments and the ramifications of our hypothesis with respect to urbanism, however, lie beyond the enforced limits of the present discussion. Research by Adams and Wright concentrates on southern Mesopotamia in these crucial periods and promises much information that may prove useful in assessing the applicability of our model in these time ranges in Greater Mesopotamia.

Conclusion

Central to our hypothesis and our problem is the issue of quantitative demography, one of the aspects of archaeology most difficult to investigate. Yet we feel that it is only by exploring more fully this very issue that archaeologists will be able to reach more profound levels of understanding and explanation of their data. Adams has stated, "the lack of data on population density and land use underlines the purely speculative character of all of these heuristic hypotheses which regard cultural change as an adaptive response to direct environmental forces" (1960: 290–291). While regretting as much as does Adams the lack of information on population growth and density and land use, we believe that this is not a hopeless situation if tackled properly. In this hope we are much stimulated by Adams's own efforts to struggle with the same problem (Adams 1965). Perhaps one of the principal advantages of our model is that it does not rely to any exaggerated extent on responses to "direct environmental forces" but sees the cultural changes as products of forces within the social and cultural matrix as they interact with the environment.

In the sense that we believe the changes involved in the formation of the Neolithic resulted from a desire *not* to change the social patterns built up during the initial period of sedentism based on food collecting, we can agree with Kroeber (1939: 1) that "on the one hand culture can be understood primarily only in terms of cultural factors." But we would insist on the external elements as well—in our case, the modification of the environment by extracultural forces—which permitted this initial situation to arise; and this viewpoint is in agreement with Kroeber's subsequent statement that "on the other hand no culture is wholly intelligible without reference to the noncultural or so-called environmental factors with which it is in relation and which condition it" (1939: 205). We do not claim that an important environmental change is always required to trigger this process of maximizing adaptation. We have suggested it here because the palynological evidence seems to support it, but perhaps in other regions, particularly in nonpristine situations, the process may have been instigated by other means such as population pressure from outside or the reduction for some reason of a traditional resource zone. Thus in the Lower Illinois Valley Struever (1968) sees no evidence for environmental change as responsible for the shift to "intensive harvest collecting" and a population buildup.

Again, our hypothesis does not rely on the role of purely technological innovation as the prime mover in effecting the changes during the period in question. In this respect we differ from Childe, who, following Morgan (1877), seemed to see technological advances as the agencies promoting the changes at various stages of his "revolutions." See, for example, Childe's discussion (1936, Chap. 6) of the role of the plow in promoting greater food production and expanded population. The questions that Childe and most other prehistorians did not answer satisfactorily are: Why did such innovations come about and why were they accepted? One gathers that in Childe's reasoning they came about either because in some way the environment made it necessary or because they represented rational decisions in the light of the progressive developments that went before. We do not think the instrumentation was so simple, and we propose to interpose another agency—that of population as an independent variable —into Childe's scheme. In this sense we tend to agree with Adams in his rejection of another technological item (large-scale irrigation) as an effectively independent cause of cultural development, though we can hardly side with him in his description of population pressure as a "misleadingly self-generating extracultural factor" (1966: 15). In our view as expressed in the present paper, population pressure is very far from being an "extracultural" factor, depending as it does on so many events determined by social and cultural decisions.

Is our model really inconsistent with the models of symbiosis or ecosystem interdependency suggested by other writers, or to what degree can it be reconciled with other explanations? We do not think there is any fundamental contradiction. After all, we emphasize throughout that the developments in Greater Mesopotamia proceeded at different rates according to ecological zones, so that there would be after the early beginning a number of zones at different levels of agricultural (and presumably social and political) complexity. It seems to us that it is in this context of unevenness that exchanges would become significant and interdependency would develop. In other words, one might very well regard our model as pointing to the causes for the creation of the symbiosis, which must surely have been due to factors other than simply the uneven distribution of certain natural resources. Far from being in opposition to the symbiotic explanations, we think our model goes some way toward explaining how symbiotic situations can arise.

The model we have presented here, we must emphasize again, is intended only as a tentative effort; it is probably far too schematic and undoubtedly will require much modification and refinement. In this brief outline we have not discussed other factors in detail, such as trade, commerce, settlement patterns, metallurgy, the development of artisan skills. They are important, especially in the later phases of the sequence, but perhaps they should be considered as dependent rather than independent variables. There has also been no discussion of changes in kinship, social organization, political structure, or land tenure, although one of the basic tenets of our hypothesis is that such transformations must have accompanied the technological changes. We have chosen, for the sake of simplicity, to neglect the role of ideological factors in determining or influencing such things as community size and patterns, though we are aware they may have been present and important (for example, see the statements by Helm and Rogers, among others, in Damas, ed., 1969; also Wagley 1951). Discussion of categories of material culture other than agricultural tools has similarly been omitted, although the stylistic and other changes in stone industries, pottery, architecture, and several other categories constitute one of the main focuses of the archaeologist's activities. Some of these artifactual changes were most likely linked directly with the propelling forces we have chosen to emphasize here; others may well be secondary or peripheral modifications. At the moment we cannot sort them out efficiently.

Perhaps most important, we have not had the time to deal adequately with certain important aspects of the demographic problem itself. For example, we have not considered at any length the possible results of *lessened* population densities in some of the areas in question at certain periods in prehistory. Rather, we have been interested primarily in one phenomenon that *did* exist—the indubitable general increase in population and population density in Greater Mesopotamia between about 10,000 and 3000 B.C. Yet obviously the possibility of temporary reversals, when population levels dropped for one reason or another, must be kept in mind as well. Archaeologists might find this aspect of the interpretation useful in helping to understand anomalous phenomena that violate expectations (for example, hypothetical reversion from more intensive to less intensive agriculture in certain regions which might be reflected in changing settlement types or sizes and by different tools in some assemblages). An example of such a situation might be the contrast between conditions that apparently prevailed in western Luristan in the Late Bronze and Early Iron Ages (Meade 1968).

Still another specifically demographic issue deserving considerable attention is the obvious reciprocal relationship between population growth and economic productivity; that is, there is a feedback process involved here just as there was, for example, in the reciprocal relationship between the development of efficient automobiles and of paved highway systems during the twentieth century. One illustration of this mutual reinforcement might be seen in the relationship between food production and increased numbers of children. Childe (1951: 61–62) had already pointed out that in the shift from hunting-gathering to agriculture there would be a greater incentive to have more children who could contribute at an early age to the labor force. To carry the point further, there seems to be a tendency among modern groups moving from shifting cultivation to more intensive agriculture in Formosa to have more children (B. Higgins, personal communication), and this is due not simply to an increase in the supply of food available but to the need for more hands as agriculture cumulatively becomes more labor-intensive. Geertz (1963: 69–70) suggests a similar process was operative in the imposed estate system in the nineteenth century Java. That is, it is not a case of more food equals more children but also a desire for and need for more children to provide manpower—in other words, a positive rather than a negative feedback system. In this, as in other aspects of the situation, we are dealing with a highly complex set of interactions in each case which we still cannot unravel. As Dumond has suggested,

For heuristic purposes it is possible to consider some of these factors—such as population growth, political stability, subsistence means—as short-run independent variables, the alteration of which will cause concomitant variations in the other variables. Thus a certain measure of population growth may be said in a particular case to be determined by a certain technological advance, or a major depression may be said to be determined by a depopulation following a severe epidemic. But the same technological advance may be argued to have been necessitated by population growth, and the response of the United States birth rate to the depression of the 'thirties is common knowledge. It is apparent that there is no independent-dependent relationship of population and the other variables in a permanent sense [Dumond 1965:320–321].

Thus we see that it would be easy to exaggerate the effect of population change and density and to view it as the sole *deus ex machina* or prime mover responsible for all cultural and technological changes. Such an interpretation would be a distortion, and undoubtedly other aspects of prehistoric activities will be directly explicable by processes that our hypothesis does not cover. Nevertheless, we are prepared to argue that, while of course population growth and technological development are mutually reinforcing, population growth is more of an independent variable than technology since it can occur in the absence of technological innovation, but it is unlikely that the latter will take place in the absence of population pressure.

We share the viewpoints expressed by Dumond that "in one way or another, an expanding society must be a changing society" (Dumond 1965: 318) and that "the relatively rapid pace of cultural change which has been manifest since the agricultural revolution owes as much to the rapidly expanding population as the increasing people owe to their developing culture" (Dumond 1965: 321). Population growth certainly does serve as a spur toward improvement of subsistence and, indeed, commerce; these, by raising total income, encourage the growth of further population. In other words, these relationships are reciprocal (Dumond 1965: 311). We agree with Dumond also that "it would not be well to consider that population increase is the only spur to agricultural improvement," and very likely he is correct in suggesting that active markets and a money economy may possibly be important (1965: 312). Nevertheless, these last two elements, whatever their importance in the later periods, especially after the growth of urbanism, would hardly have been relevant in the initial or takeoff stage of the food-producing sequence when the momentum was accumulating for subsequent developments.

Adams (1966: 7) has suggested that every stage of cultural evolution must be accounted for by some new principle or "qualitatively new causal factor and process." It is the new principle inherent in food production that explains the events after about 10,000 B.C., in Southwest Asia, and we believe it is the demographic factor that largely explains the course that this particular evolutionary stage followed. Finally, of all the issues that our hypothesis does not explain, one of the most interesting is that it tells us nothing about why individual cultures, building on the base of the food-producing subsistence system, developed such different forms and styles. For example, it does not show why Egypt and Mesopotamia were so different. The answer to this kind of problem probably is to be sought in other types of approaches.

The most important question to ask in evaluating our argument in this paper is: What kind of fit do we have between the archaeological facts so far known and the hypothetical sequence of agricultural development we have outlined for Greater Mesopotamia? We are very much aware that there are many weak and missing links in our chain of evidence, but on the whole we feel there is enough of a fit to be encouraging. In the meantime, the hypothesis provides an explanation, however imperfect, that does not rely exclusively on any one of the classical methods of archaeological explanation—migration, stimulus diffusion, relative inventiveness, external cultural stimuli, vague and undefined "influences." It does not place undue emphasis on either pressures of the physical environment or on the sudden implantation of technological innovations, nor does it utilize concepts such as orthogenesis, teleology, or undemonstrable notions of inherent cultural progress. Instead, it places the archaeological data in a framework in which the proper role of each explanatory factor may be examined and the variability in archaeological evidence investigated.

A second important question is: How can we specify the kinds of research needed to verify or invalidate the hypothesis outlined here? Limitations of space preclude a full discussion of this aspect of the problem. We suggest, nevertheless, that progress in this direction can be made by

following two lines of research. One involves the means by which archaeologists can detect the kind or kinds of agricultural land use in operation
at a given settlement. In this paper we have relied almost entirely on the
agricultural implements used (dibbles, hoes, plows), but it is almost
superfluous to point out that this kind of evidence alone is insufficient
and may even be deceptive. One obvious but promising avenue of research is in the examination of stone hoe blades for evidence of the peculiar polish that forms after use on soils with thick sod cover as on the
North American prairies (Witthoft 1967). In Europe and in the New
World soil furrows indicating plowing and hoeing have sometimes been
found preserved under ceremonial mounds, but we are not optimistic
about recovering this kind of evidence in Greater Mesopotamia. Nevertheless, Fowler's studies of Mississippian sites in the United States show
that there are several methods for distinguishing hoe-cultivated from
plow-cultivated fields, including studies of soil profiles, aerial photo-
graphs, and distribution of implements (Fowler 1969). Higham's analyses
of animal bones from European sites suggest that it may be possible in
some cases to say when oxen were being raised for traction plows
(Higham 1969). We are reasonably optimistic that further research on
this problem will enable archaeologists to make much clearer identifica-
tions of land use than we have been able to do in this paper by the crude
means available to us.

Another line of research is in the reexamination of archaeological
materials already excavated in Greater Mesopotamia and other regions,
together with new excavations purposefully oriented toward the hypothesis outlined here. The materials from Anatolia, the Levant, and even
Egypt should provide an idea of the degree of seaworthiness of our hypothesis within the Near East itself and show how the regional environmental variability operated to change or modify the details of the model
we have presented for Greater Mesopotamia. We are hopeful, too, that
the hypothesis may be applicable to prehistoric and perhaps historic
events in other areas of the Old and New Worlds, particularly in those
regions with arid, semiarid, and temperate environments (see, for example, the interesting discussion on Mesoamerica in Sanders and Price
1968: 84–94). We believe, from a rapid examination of the archaeological
literature from Peru, Western Europe, and several parts of North America, that the hypothesis could be used most productively in those regions

as well. Only the archaeologists working in those regions can decide whether our hypothesis is viable and whether it refers to a cultural regularity that is relatively independent of particularisms of time and space. Wherever the proposed new investigations are carried out, they should be based on establishing the long-term adaptive patterns through excavation of sites that will reflect as far as possible the whole range of variability that existed in the restricted region under study.

One of the traditional weaknesses of ecological approaches is that there tends to be an overemphasis on stability or equilibrium. We do not see the processes operating in Greater Mesopotamia during the nearly 10,000 years in question in terms of an equilibrium model but rather of long-term instability and conflict of forces. It is clear that our model does not offer a picture of man making himself solely through rational decisions or through the accumulated wisdom of his cultural heritage alone. Instead, our reconstruction of the events during the period shows a kind of forced-draft process by which the lines of development of many peoples were rather narrowly limited. Although not entirely without choices (emigration, internal population control, and so on), under certain circumstances the course to be followed in subsequent development was fairly predictable. While undoubtedly there was considerable impoverishment on the human, noneconomic side in the trends toward shorter fallow periods and labor-intensive cultivation, nevertheless there was also a progression in social and political and cultural complexity, in technology, and probably in certain arts to balance the disadvantages. It is not necessary to adopt a Panglossian attitude to agree that, by and large, it may have been a fair enough exchange.

Acknowledgments

We thank Brian Spooner for his encouragement in the writing of this paper and for much practical help in ensuring its appearance in its present form. Among those who have offered helpful personal communications and unpublished data or have read and criticized several drafts of this paper we are especially grateful to the following: Robert McC. Adams, Ester Boserup, Jacques Bordaz, Francois Bordes, Robert J. Braidwood, Hans Bobek, Robert Carneiro, Benjamin Higgins, Nathan

Keyfitz, Fumiko Ikawa-Smith, Hallam L. Movius, Jr., Robert McC. Netting, John Pfeiffer, Stuart Struever, and Eric Waddell.

Notes

1. We cannot evaluate here the recent claims that food production began in Southeast Asia at an even earlier date.

2. Human population density is of course a relative matter and must be regarded, not in absolute terms, but in relation to the resources and area available. Birdsell (1968: 229) defines it as "a ratio expressing the relationship between people and space." Thus there can be high population density in areas of absolute low population, for example, on Pacific atolls (Sahlins 1958: 125). Similarly there can be high population density and low population growth. In this paper we have taken the position that it is population increase (or decrease) causing alterations in the population density, rather than population density per se, that serves as the catalytic agency in technological and social change.

3. Childe's attitude seems to have been somewhat more flexible in his later writings, however, when he did concede that the dramatic increase in the population might *accompany* changes in economic structure and social organization, if they did not cause it (Childe 1950: 3).

4. According to C. Clark, "population growth has taken place, and will continue, because of improvements in medical knowledge and practice. It brings economic hardship to communities living by traditional methods of agriculture; but it is the only force powerful enough to make such communities change their methods, and in the long run transforms them into much more advanced and productive societies" (C. Clark 1967, preface). Kingsley Davis (1968) has convincingly challenged the accuracy of Clark's arguments in support of population growth in the modern world. Davis points out that Clark's economic benefits are based on a situation in which all other things are equal: "the benefits will be gained if population growth influences no variables in the system other than the ones it is supposed to influence favorably" (p. 133), and Davis maintains that other variables *are* influenced. However, Davis's arguments are not meant to apply to the preindustrial era with which we are dealing here, and it is not necessary to agree with the latter-day application of Clark's extreme position in order to concur with his acceptance of Boserup's thesis. In addition, as Davis points out, at no time in the past were growth rates comparable to those found today.

5. But Boserup does point out (1965: 18) that her classification of types of land use may be supposed broadly to "describe the main stages of the actual evolution of primitive agriculture during prehistoric times and in the recent past." And on page 53 she does propose a hypothetical sequence of development from hunting and gathering to intensive agriculture.

6. It should be noted that Boserup's types 1 and 2 are lumped together by some writers and called long fallow or shifting cultivation. Shifting cultivation may be defined minimally as "any continuing agricultural system in which impermanent clearings are cropped for shorter periods in years than they are fallowed" (Conklin 1961: 27). Settlements may be either shifting, moving as new plots are cleared, or permanent and inhabited for long periods by cultivators who commute to distant fields. The settlements may at times be fairly large (Carneiro 1960, 1961; Dumond 1961).

7. Obviously we must proceed with caution in applying the rules extracted from any one scheme of agricultural activity to another in a different context. As several writers have pointed out (for example, Watters 1960: 62) in discussing shifting cultivation, the practices vary widely in their degree of adaptation to the environment. There are dangers in

applying too literally examples from Africa, Southeast Asia, or even temperate Europe to the Middle East, where early Holocene conditions were undoubtedly not identical. For example, Nye and Greenland (1960: 124–125) point out that in tropical regions forested areas are usually more fertile than savanna areas, whereas in temperate regions it is the opposite, and open land is more fertile. In this paper we have used examples from the tropics because the problem has been best studied there where the system continues to the present day.

8. One can observe today in parts of central, western Iran (for example, the Kangāvar valley) the beginnings of a shift from annual to multicropping under increasing population pressure. This is evidenced by the growing of truck garden produce on wheat lands between grain harvests. Though the bulk of this increased production is disposed of as a cash crop, the need for such production can be linked directly to recent population growth in the villages involved.

9. Boserup, whose experiences were confined largely to tropical areas, found the plow associated with short-fallow cultivation (Boserup 1965: 24). We, however, are more inclined to concentrate attention on the relationship between the frequency with which the land is cropped and the type of tool used than to insist rigidly that the tool used, the frequency with which the land is tilled, *and* the nature of the landscape must always constitute an interlocking triad of features. This would seem to be a more prudent approach as we attempt to apply Boserup's basic scheme to the peculiar environmental conditions of Greater Mesopotamia in prehistoric times, particularly when the exact character of that environment cannot yet be determined with great precision for any given moment in time. For this preliminary discussion, therefore, we suggest that the introduction of the plow be associated with the latest stages of short-fallow cultivation, when the land is tilled very frequently and the grass cover becomes particularly heavy, and with the introduction of annual cropping under fairly extreme population pressure. The earlier forms of short-fallow cultivation would still use primarily the hoe, while the digging stick would be typical of long-fallow(forest- and bush-fallow) cultivation in general.

10. Boserup's argument is that the plow is essentially a device for dealing with tough grasses and sod. While this is undoubtedly true, we do not suggest that this is its only function. It is also valuable for stirring up the deeper and more fertile elements in the soil, for preventing moisture loss (in warm, dry regions) and preventing excessive wetness in cooler, damper regions. In some cases it may have served to make longer and straighter furrows to aid in distributing irrigation water. In agriculture there are usually at least two reasons for doing everything, as White, Jr., has remarked (1962: 55).

11. We may adopt Murdock's definition of incipient cultivators as those food producers who, though they do not depend for subsistence primarily on agriculture and/or animal husbandry, nevertheless produce more food by these techniques than they obtain through any one of the three food-gathering techniques alone, that is, from hunting, fishing, or collecting (Murdock 1964: 401).

12. It should be remembered that short-fallow and long-fallow systems are not necessarily restricted to regions where slash-and-burn agriculture is practiced. Thus in Europe variations on the infield-outfield system permit some fields to be cultivated only period-ically while others may be cultivated more frequently or even continuously with the aid of heavy manuring (Slicher Van Bath 1963: 58). Also, it seems possible that long-fallow techniques could be applied to grass conditions if agriculture begins in an environ-ment where there are no forests or extensive stands of bush, that is, where no preceding fallow types were possible. This was probably the case in the Zagros in this period, and therefore a better expression might be "long-fallow grassland cultivation." See, however, a contrary opinion by Sauer (1956, 1962), who doubts that primitive agriculturalists could have begun in bush or grassland and insists that the earliest cultivation must have occurred in forested lands. Our ability to visualize the details of "long-fallow grassland

cultivation" is hampered by our inability to find any references to long-fallow systems in Southwest Asia in recent or early historic times. Conklin (1961) lists no cases in this part of the world, and apparently it has long ago been superseded by more intensive systems. A few writers have speculated that it formed the basis for the earliest agriculture in the area (Childe 1936: 73; Whyte 1961: 79; Van Liere and Contenson 1964), but no archaeological or other evidence is given to support this assertion. Nevertheless, we believe the assumption that it once existed is justifiable,

13. The situation at Ali Kosh in Khuzistan raises the issue of what might be called "mud-flat" cultivation. Hole and Flannery see positive evidence in the botanical remains from this site for the planting of cereal grains on marshy ground (Hole and Flannery 1967: 171). For this kind of tillage a digging stick would suffice, or perhaps no planting implement would be needed at all. This phenomenon of "mud-flat" cultivation is one that must have played an important role in early agricultural adaptations to the southern Mesopotamian alluvium. We shall return to this issue later.

14. For this discussion we consider Hassuna and Samarra sites together.

15. It is striking that at least in the Deh Luran Plain of Khuzistan there was an increasing tendency toward rearing sheep rather than goats. Of little importance in the Bus Mordeh and Ali Kosh phases, after the Sabz phase sheep seem to equal goats in quantity (Hole, Flannery, and Neely 1969, Fig. 134). These authors have pointed out that sheep have a more efficient planting mechanism, and the thick fleeces also contribute to heat resistance. There may be another factor involved also, however: overstocking can render pastureland "sheep sick," and the animals become increasingly prone to disease, but breaking up the soil for cultivation restores the grazing potentiality (Higham 1968: 74). It is interesting that in the Sabz phase, where the first good evidence of hoes appears, sheep approach the ratio of half the caprine total, which they maintain until the end of the sequence.

16. Annual cropping, as strictly defined by Boserup, does not occur in southern Mesopotamia even today and is relatively rare in northern Mesopotamia and the highlands. The standard system of three-field rotation in practice in Greater Mesopotamia today can, however, be seen as a specialized form of annual cropping adapted to conditions in a semiarid region. While soil fertility is the prime concern of the annual cropper in temperate or tropical areas, moisture is the key issue for the semiarid farmer. Thus in temperate or tropical climates the farmer practicing annual cropping plants special crops on officially "fallow" fields either because they add nutrients to the soil directly or because they can be profitably plowed under in preparation for the future planting of the "cash" crop, which is the farmer's prime interest. In a semiarid environment, however, the farmer knows that to plant any crop is to remove moisture from the soil. A minimal increase in soil fertility can be tolerated during fallow periods if in compensation the moisture content of the soil is increased either through irrigation without cropping or natural precipitation. Here again the animals play an important role, for they keep the weeds down on the fallow field and thus prevent the "accidental" growth that might also lead to a decline in moisture content. Thus the farmer of Greater Mesopotamia is not practicing short fallow with the system of three-field rotation; rather he is annual cropping in a way uniquely suited to the local climatic circumstances.

The introduction of the plow in southern Mesopotamia may be as much related to its usefulness in creating long furrows well adapted to irrigation needs as to any change in actual fallow system.

17. Adams (personal communication) reports that from survey data, however, hoes are well attested in periods after the Ubaid in southern Mesopotamia. Hoes would, of course, have remained a tool useful for garden plot weeding and the manipulation of irrigation ditches long after the introduction of the plow and shortened-fallow systems.

2

Demography and the "Urban Revolution" in Lowland Mesopotamia

Robert McC. Adams

This chapter describes the process of urbanization that took place in the first of the seven zones defined in the previous chapter and at the end of the period that Smith and Young chose as their universe of study. The author examines the Boserup model in the context of this area and finds that it does provide a useful perspective.

This summary statement provides a guide to the latest findings (which were already in press when this volume was being prepared) by the foremost specialist on this chapter of human history.

An evaluation of the role of population growth in the achievement of urban civilization in southern Mesopotamia is both complex and beset with many uncertainties. The Sumerian city-state assumed its classical form at an early stage in the evolution of writing, so that textual sources provide little assistance with the problem. Because of the minute scale of excavations heretofore in relation to the size and number of available sites, and also because of the concentration of those excavations on monumental buildings in the major centers, there is also little help to be found from that quarter.

The only currently available approach to the question, then, stems from archaeological surface reconnaissance. Again the difficulties are manifest. They include the hazards of assuming a constant ratio of population to site area, the problems of distinguishing sequent from contemporaneous occupations, and the lack of comparability of data from single- and multi-period sites. At another level, they also include differences in the onset, density, and duration of settlement in different sectors of what is often—quite erroneously—assumed to be an undifferentiated alluvial plain. Finally, there are uncertainties as to the proportion of evidence recoverable from the present land surface, further complicated by differing combinations of alluviation and aeolian deposition and erosion in different areas. It should be obvious that no conclusive confirmation that population increases were or were not a major independent variable can be threaded through obstacles and qualifications like these.

Nevertheless, with due regard for all such reservations, it must also be said that a pattern has begun to emerge rather uniformly in the findings of recent surveys in several parts of the plain. Moreover, for all of the presumed limitations of topographic surveys it has been found empirically in at least some regions that settlement patterns of the late fourth millennium can be reconstructed to a degree approaching completeness. This has been particularly the case in the empty steppelands north and east of two ancient cities, Uruk and Nippur (for locations and sites mentioned in this chapter, see Figures 1.2 and 1.3), owing to widespread later abandonment and to the local predominance of erosional over depositional processes.

Briefly to summarize these recent findings, during the Uruk period there appears to have been an increase in the sedentary population of at least certain portions of the Mesopotamian plain by a full order of magnitude. The preceding Ubaid period, probably lasting into the early centuries of the fourth millennium, was characterized by widely and uniformly dispersed villages and small towns. During the Uruk period, probably lasting several centuries, a few ceremonial centers seem to have increased substantially in size and may have attained modest urban proportions. Probably even more important from a demographic viewpoint was the formation of dense clusters of villages and towns, whose distribution suggests that numerous small enclaves of settlement and cultivation grew up very rapidly along the anastomosing channels of predominantly natural watercourses. There is no reason to doubt that a major population increase was involved in this development. It is quite uncertain at present, however, whether the increase was a natural, local process under exceptionally favorable conditions (perhaps the refinement and spread of effective irrigation techniques) or instead was the consequence of massive immigration.

In any case, the most extensive development of the urban institutions characteristic of Sumerian civilization came after this period of population growth, in the last centuries of the fourth millennium (at least according to traditional chronologies; additional radiocarbon determinations should preserve the sequence but may shift it several centuries

earlier in time). At least in a few centers like Uruk the process of growth
not only was explosively rapid but was accompanied by profound structural changes, with massive fortifications, palaces, and political hier-
archies shifting the emphasis away from temples and their associated
priesthoods. But the important point is that this urbanization involved
redistribution of the population rather than a further increase. It was
accomplished, in other words, only through widespread rural abandonment and the more or less forcible relocation of former villagers and
townsmen in wholly unprecedented urban agglomerations. (For an extended discussion, see Adams 1969 and forthcoming.)

Thus a case can be made that the onset of the so-called Urban Revolution in lowland Mesopotamia followed in the wake of, and hence
possibly was triggered by, a massive population increase. Applied to this
region, Boserup's argument on how the triggering might have taken
place presumably would be that the increase in population density had
a number of interlocking effects: (1) it precipitated a shift from long- to
short-fallow systems, stimulating an increase in the efficiency of both
agricultural and nonagricultural labor; (2) at the same time, it fostered
an increasingly intricate division of labor, whose extension into nonagricultural activities had profound consequences for Mesopotamian
terms of trade with neighboring regions; (3) it also powerfully encouraged
improvements in agricultural technique, perhaps including refinements
in irrigation practices and the transition from hoe to plow cultivation.
But while all of these specific changes can indeed be shown or inferred
(with greater or less plausibility), it is also fair to state that both their
importance at the time with which we are concerned and their relationship to the subsequent achievement of urbanism cannot yet be documented satisfactorily.

Hence it may be worthwhile to outline another possible chain of relationship between population increase and the Urban Revolution, although more as an addition than as an alternative to the factors Boserup
adduces. Rapid population growth would have fostered competition for
scarce resources such as irrigation water. At the intracommunity level
this would have powerfully augmented trends toward social stratification,
of which politically organized state superstructures were a natural outgrowth. Between communities it would have been conducive to an

increasing emphasis on military hostilities—the natural outgrowth of which, in turn, would have been large, walled city-states.

In short, Boserup's thesis generates new insights and forces us to examine new causal relationships. The question of its validity as a general explanatory framework may not be quickly or easily resolved, but for the Mesopotamian plain it is currently useful.

3

From Autonomous Villages to the State, a Numerical Estimation

Robert L. Carneiro

In earlier publications Carneiro has dealt in specific detail with several aspects of the relationship between agriculture, population, and cultural evolution (Carneiro 1958, 1960, 1961, 1967, 1970; Carneiro and Hilse 1966). Here he seeks a way of quantifying, and therefore treating more exactly and scientifically, the processes that lead to exploitation of the total resources of an area and to competition and conflict over those resources. Thus, he is very conscious of the problems of defining an area of study. He sees the state (for which he gives a definition) as developing from conflict over the resources of the area. In contradiction to the hypothesis behind Netting's essay (Chapter 9; see also Dumond, Chapter 12), he claims that people never willingly surrender political sovereignty. An attempt is made to show how the conflict might take different forms in different areas.

This approach implies a point that is often missed: in anthropology quantification serves the primary purpose of providing a mode of exact expression of hypothesized factors and relationships, not a correct numerical answer to any general theoretical question.

The aim of this chapter is to explore in quantitative terms a question that has so far been treated only qualitatively:[1] Why in certain areas of the world did autonomous Neolithic villages give way to successively larger political units in a process that culminated in the emergence of the state?

To agriculture and population density, which Smith and Young (Chapter 1) regard as key factors in the process, I would add two others:

environment and warfare. It was by the interplay of these four factors— environment, agriculture, population, and warfare—that conditions were created that led irresistibly to the rise of the state.

My views on the origin of the state, which I have presented more fully elsewhere (Carneiro 1961 and, especially, 1970) may be summarized as follows.

I begin with the premise (the implications of which have often been overlooked by anthropologists) that autonomous political units never willingly surrender their sovereignty. The forging of villages into chiefdoms and of chiefdoms into kingdoms, therefore, occurs only through coercion, especially by conquest warfare.

This is perhaps something of an overstatement. Confederacies may arise by autonomous tribes agreeing to cooperate either in meeting aggression or in carrying it out themselves. Such federations, which usually weaken or dissolve when the situation creating them has passed, sometimes manage to outlast the occasion and become permanent. However, although nominally voluntary in origin, confederacies are almost invariably born out of war, thus showing that, in one way or another, war still lies at the root of the state.

Yet warfare is much older and more widespread than the state. Certain additional conditions, then, were required for war to give rise to the state. What were these conditions?

In areas of environmentally circumscribed agricultural land, it was population pressure that gave the necessary impetus to state formation. Competition over land arose first in those areas of the world where arable land was sharply restricted by natural barriers such as mountains, deserts, and seas. These circumstances not only led to warfare over land here earlier than elsewhere but also had the effect of leaving defeated groups with no place to flee, thus making them subject to forceful incorporation into the expanding political unit of the victors. It was by this process of successive conquests and amalgamations that the evolution of the state took place.

One has only to look at areas like the Nile, Tigris-Euphrates, and Indus valleys in the Old World, and the valleys of Mexico and Peru in the New to find that the earliest states did in fact emerge in areas of circumscribed agricultural land. On the other hand, in northern Europe, central Africa, the Amazon basin, and the Eastern Woodlands of North America—areas where arable land was extensive and relatively un-bounded—states developed late or not at all.

In my opinion it is entirely possible to identify the various factors that played a role in this development and to specify them in such a way that we can assign a numerical value to each. Moreover, we can fit these variables into an equation that will permit us to calculate how long it would take to bring about the conditions of full occupancy of arable land that precipitated the first steps in state formation.

Naturally, in constructing such a formula, we must be ready to idealize and simplify. The answers yielded by our formula may be expressed down to the last year, but we still cannot consider them to be more than rough approximations. Nevertheless, an estimate based on a careful weighing of quantitative data is better than a sheer guess and certainly better than no estimate at all.

The formula I propose for carrying out this calculation is as follows:

$$t = \frac{\log \dfrac{W}{C(Y + R)/Y} - \log P}{\log (1 + r)}$$

The symbols in the equation represent the following variables:

W = the area (in acres) of the arable land contained within the cir-cumscribed region being studied.

C = the size (in acres) of the plot of land required to provide the aver-age person with the amount of food he normally obtains from agriculture over the course of a year. (This phrasing would ex-plicitly allow for the fact that part of a person's subsistence may come from hunting, fishing, or gathering carried out in areas not involved in cultivation.)

Y = the number of years a plot is cultivated before being fallowed.

R = the number of years a plot is fallowed before being recultivated.

P = the total population of the circumscribed area at the time the calculation begins.

r = the average annual rate of population increase in the circumscribed area, expressed as a decimal fraction.

t = the number of years required for the increase in population of the
circumscribed area to bring all of the arable land into the agricultural cycle (that is, either in cultivation or in fallow), thus
bringing the area to its carrying capacity.

To see how this formula works, let us examine it part by part, beginning with the part expressed as $C(Y + R)/Y$. This portion of the formula
gives the area of arable land required to support the average person over
the full agricultural cycle. It involves, first of all, multiplying C, the area
of land required to support him for one year, by $(Y + R)$, the total number of years in the cycle. However, since an old plot is recovering its
fertility at the same time that a new one is being cultivated, the longer a
plot is kept under cultivation, the sooner in the cycle an abandoned plot
will be ready for recultivation. And the sooner recultivation of a fallowed
plot can begin, the less the total area of land required to feed an individual over the full agricultural cycle. To obtain the size of this area,
then, we must divide $C(Y + R)$ by Y.

The reasoning here may seem a bit obscure, but by working out a concrete example we can make it easier to grasp.

Suppose that it takes 1 acre of land to feed the average person for 1
year, and that this acre can be farmed for 5 years and then must be
fallowed for 5 years. According to the formula, then, the area required
to support the person indefinitely is $1(5 + 5)/5$, or 2 acres. The first acre
of land would feed him for 5 years and then become exhausted. The
second acre would feed him for the next 5 years and then it too would be
exhausted. But by that time the first acre would have recovered its fertility and could once again be cultivated. Thus, employing only 2 acres
of land, planting one acre for 5 years, the other acre for the next 5
years, and so on alternately, the person could be supported indefinitely.

Let us look next at the variable W, which represents the total area of
arable land within the circumscribed region. Since C and W are both
measures of land area and must be expressed in the same units, and since
it is convenient to express C in acres, we shall express W in acres as well.
If our sources of information give W in square miles, we simply multiply

when warfare over land will begin, as *by what time it will surely have begun*! Fighting over land is likely to start when the population of an area begins to approach the carrying capacity of its habitat rather than when it actually reaches that point. But it is again difficult to say what the margin of time between these two events may be. Nevertheless, since it appears that the earliest fighting over land occurs somewhat earlier than our formula predicts, it may turn out that the value it yields for *t* will give a fair estimate of the time at which incipient state formation begins after all.

To show what numerical results might be obtained by applying this formula, let us work through a hypothetical example.

For our circumscribed region we take an island, circular in shape, and 60 miles in diameter. To find the area of the island we use the familiar formula for the area of a circle, $A = \pi r^2$. This yields an answer of 2,826 square miles, which, multiplied by 640, gives us 1,808,640 acres. Let us assume that of the total area of the island 60 percent is cultivable. Taking 60 percent of 1,808,640 leaves us with 1,085,184 acres as the area of *W*.

As *P*, the population of the island at the time our computation begins, we will take a figure of 1,000. Our formula does not presuppose any particular settlement pattern for the population being studied. Thus it is irrelevant for our calculations whether, for example, settlement is in nucleated villages, as in most of Amazonia, or in dispersed house clusters, as in much of the New Guinea highlands.

Next, we need to assign values to the three agricultural variables in the formula, *C*, *Y*, and *R*. Let us assume that an extensive form of shifting agriculture prevailed on the island and that it took 0.5 acre to support the average person for 1 year, that a plot was cultivated for 2 years before being fallowed, and that it was fallowed for 20 years before being re-cultivated. Thus, $C = 0.5$, $Y = 2$, and $R = 20$.

Finally, let us suppose that the population of the island was growing at an average annual rate of 0.4 percent.

Substituting these figures into the equation, we have

$$t = \frac{\log 1{,}085{,}184/[0.5(2 + 20)/2] - \log 1{,}000}{\log 1.004},$$

and, solving through, we obtain

$$t = \frac{\log 197,306 - \log 1,000}{\log 1.004},$$

$$t = \frac{5.29514 - 3}{0.00173},$$

$$t = 1,327.$$

That is to say, under the conditions specified it would take 1,327 years for all of the arable land on the island to be incorporated into the agricultural cycle.

Before proceeding further let us attempt to make a few refinements in the formula. In the preceding calculations we tacitly assumed that during the entire length of t the mode of cultivation remained unchanged, so that C, Y, and R retained the same values throughout. Yet this is certainly unrealistic. We know from many cases reported in the ethnographic literature that as population pressure on the land increases, cultivation is intensified.[2]

This intensification would show up in our formula by changes in the values of C, Y, and R. As substantial increases in population occurred, we would undoubtedly find that (1) the area of land required to support the average person per year would be reduced; (2) the number of years a plot was cultivated would be increased; and (3) the length of the fallow period would be decreased. The amount of land needed to support an individual is, naturally, reduced by increasing the productivity of the land. This is ordinarily accomplished in several ways: by interplanting, by complete removal of stumps and logs from a field so that more of its surface can be planted, by the use of compost or manure, by more thorough weeding, and by fencing to reduce predation. The use of some of these measures also makes it possible to keep a plot under cultivation longer, and to make the fallow period shorter.

Let us suppose that as the population of the island grew, C, Y, and R changed so that by the time all the arable land was incorporated into the agricultural cycle their values were as follows:

$C = 0.2$ acre (instead of 0.5)

$Y = 4$ years (instead of 2)

$R = 7$ years (instead of 20)

At exactly what rate C, Y, and R would change in response to increasing population is not easy to determine empirically nor to surmise theoretically. Here we will simply average the values of C, Y, and R at the beginning and at the end of the period. Eventually it should be possible to assess these changes more precisely, and to express them more elegantly, but for the present we shall be satisfied with this approximation.[3]

The new values for these three variables then become:

$C = 0.35$ acre

$Y = 3$ years

$R = 13.5$ years.

Substituting these more realistic figures into the equation, we find it would now take 1,638 years (instead of 1,327 years) to bring all of the arable land into use.

This new higher figure for t makes it clear that the intensification of agriculture, by enabling a person to subsist on less land, reduces the aggregate need for land, and thus postpones the onset of competition over land.

A further effect of intensified cultivation should be noted. This is the extension of cultivation, by means of drainage, terracing, irrigation, and so forth, to land previously considered uncultivable. This would be reflected in our formula by an increase over time in the value of W. If the proportion that W represented of the total area of the island thus increased from 60 percent to 70 percent, we would deal with it, again, by averaging the two figures and using 65 percent of the total area as the value of W. This new figure, which comes to 1,175,616 acres (instead of the previous 1,085,184), would raise t slightly to 1,658 years.

It goes without saying that varying the remaining factors in the equation would also affect the results. Thus, if the initial population were higher, or the rate of population increase greater, the value of t would be correspondingly reduced. For example, by putting the initial population of the island at 10,000 instead of 1,000, and by taking the annual growth rate to be 1 percent instead of 0.4 percent, but keeping the other factors as specified, t comes out to be only 432 years.

Our calculations so far have been based on the supposition that the population being studied was growing within an environmentally circumscribed area. Very commonly, though, human populations live in regions that are not circumscribed. Thus, it seems desirable to try to modify our formula so it can be applied as well to regions where arable land is extensive and unbounded.

Actually, it should be possible for states to arise by warfare and conquest even in areas of uncircumscribed land if population growth is sufficiently rapid or prolonged to produce the critical factor of overcrowding. And overcrowding could occur in areas of environmentally uncircumscribed land if the increase in population taking place at the center of such an area could not be siphoned off into the peripheries at a rate fast enough to keep the central area from filling up to its carrying capacity. This buildup in population would naturally be slower here than in an area of circumscribed land, but it could occur. And once it did, the consequences of it for political evolution would be much the same as in the cases considered above.

But how do we represent this type of situation in a formula? Ideally, we would need to show the steady increase in population at the center of the area and its partial dissipation into the peripheries at a rate that diminished gradually and evenly with distance. I know of no ethnographic instance, however, where this process has been measured in any way that would permit us to represent it accurately in a formula.

The centrifugal expansion of the Tiv, surely the classic case of this type of population spread, has been well described by Bohannan (1954). However, his study does not present the kind of quantitative data we would need to devise a precise mathematical model for this expansion. Furthermore, even if the necessary figures were available, I doubt very much that my knowledge of mathematics would be adequate to the task.

Still, rather than give up the idea entirely, I would like to propose a highly simplified model that simulates at least the essential features of the process involved.

Let us imagine an extensive area of arable land part of which is occupied by a population consisting of autonomous agricultural villages that are more or less evenly distributed throughout their habitat. No geographic barriers or neighboring peoples exist to prevent this population from extending beyond the boundaries of its territory as the need arises.

Within the territory of this population we can distinguish a nuclear and a peripheral area. Just how we are to draw the line between the two I leave unresolved; I simply assume it can be done. The areas differ in that the periphery can expand outward to accommodate an increase in population, while the nucleus, limited by the surrounding periphery, cannot. Thus the same natural rate of population increase over the entire territory will lead to a higher density of population in the nucleus than in the periphery. Even the fact that part of the population increase in the nucleus is able to emigrate to the periphery does not alter the matter qualitatively, although it does affect it quantitatively.[4]

Let us assume that we know the extent of this nuclear area, the size of its population, and the rate at which it is increasing. Moreover, we also know the percentage of the population increase in the nucleus that remains within it. Now if we know this percentage, it is a simple matter to calculate the time it will take for the nuclear area to fill up. Let us attempt to illustrate this.

We begin by stipulating that of the increment in population in the nuclear area, half stays within it, with the other half moving out. If r, the rate of population growth, is 0.4 percent, as before, and half of this increase remains in the nucleus, this is exactly equivalent to a rate of increase of 0.2 percent, all of which stays within the nucleus. Surprisingly enough, then, the only modification we need to make in the formula to have it apply to this case is to use $0.5r$ in place of r. With $r = 0.004$, then $0.5r = 0.002$. Using this figure in the equation, along with the previous values for the other variables, and solving for t, we get an answer of 3,316 years.

It will be noted that 3,316 is just twice 1,658, the figure obtained in our earlier computation. Thus, with the effective rate of population increase in an area cut in half, the time required to fill up the area is doubled. We can see then how lack of environmental circumscription could be expected to retard state formation.

Next let us look at a somewhat more realistic example than the one just considered. The key factor in determining what proportion of the population increase of a nuclear area remains within it and what proportion moves out is the ability of the peripheral area to absorb the former's surplus population. If the peripheral area is geographically unbounded, and if the territory that lies beyond it is unoccupied, as we posited before, then this capacity is at its maximum. This is so because as the peripheral area grows in population, either by its own natural rate of increase or by absorption of persons from the nucleus, it can readily expand its boundaries outward to relieve the pressure of this increase.

In most cases, though, the peripheries of a population are bounded by other populations. This boundary may yield somewhat to pressure, but it still will tend to curtail the expansion of the peripheral area. This restricted expandability of the periphery reduces its capacity to absorb population from the nucleus, and this in turn curtails the percentage of the population increment within the nucleus that can move out.

The greater expandability of the periphery relative to the nucleus, which our model takes to be a normal aspect of centrifugal expansion, seems to me to explain quite readily what Bohannan (1954: 2) considers "one of the most puzzling aspects of Tiv expansion," namely, "that . . . it is precisely in those areas in which land shortage is least severe that the rate of migration appears to be the most rapid."

Since any bounding of the peripheral area is thus eventually translated into some degree of restriction in the net rate of population increase in the nucleus, it turns out that our revised model applies to cases of partial bounding as well as to those without bounding.

To illustrate this let us take a case in which the bounding of the peripheral area is tight enough to prevent it from expanding very readily, and thus from absorbing much population from the nucleus. Let us say that $r = 0.004$ again, and that of this increase in population 70 percent remains within the nuclear area. Using $0.7r$ in the formula, and holding the other variables to their previous values, we arrive at an answer for t of 2,032 years.

Suppose now that we alter conditions so there is relatively little bounding on the peripheries, and only 30 percent of the population increment occurring within the nuclear area remains within it. The value of t now rises to 5,570 years.

The marked difference between 5,570 and 1,658, the figure we obtained earlier for an area of geographically circumscribed land, makes very clear indeed the great assist that environmental circumscription gives to political evolution. In sharply delimited areas population growth is unrelieved and can thus exert its effect fully and unremittingly, accelerating thereby the fusion of smaller political units into larger ones. It is no accident of history, then, that most of the areas of the world where states first arose were precisely those areas in which environmental circumscription was strongly evident.

In closing I want to emphasize again that the formula presented here, even with its refinements, constitutes only a schematic model. Factors other than those represented by the variables in the formula are undoubtedly involved in state formation. And some of these factors must be of such a nature as to defy incorporation into a formula. Thus, any calculation carried out by means of this formula will be subject to a large and still unspecifiable margin of error.

But I do not want to be too apologetic. I think the equation developed here does single out the principal factors that have paved the way for state formation. Moreover, it shows how these factors can be quantified, the direction in which each of them exerts its effect, and how they interact to bring societies to a new stage of political development. The formula, then, may assist archaeologists by calling their attention to these factors, by encouraging them to try to find numerical values for them, and by indicating how they may have played a role in cultural development in areas in which they are working.

And if archaeologists are able to carry out reliable computations with the formula, they will be in a position to test the theory underlying it. Should such tests show the theory to be essentially correct, then archaeologists will have at their disposal a proven instrument to help account theoretically for what they have found to be true empirically. But should discrepancies arise between the theory and the facts, these discrepancies should serve as a stimulus to archaeologists to modify the theory and the formula in order to make them accord more closely with the facts. And if they succeed in this, they will have the satisfaction of having added more precise and serviceable tools to the working inventory of archaeological interpretations.

Notes

1. According to Spencer (1890: 376–377) ". . . the general advance of Science . . . is best shown by the contrast between its qualitative stage, and its quantitative stage. At first the facts ascertained were, that between such and such phenomena some connexion existed—that the appearances of a and b always occurred together or in succession; but it was known neither what was the nature of the relation between a and b, nor how much of a accompanied so much of b. The development of Science has in part been the reduction of these vague connexions to distinct ones."

2. The best single work demonstrating this intensification that I know of is Jacques Barrau's *Subsistence Agriculture in Melanesia* (Barrau 1958). Although it is essentially a synchronic study, Barrau is able to show very convincingly the probable course of this evolution by comparing a number of societies at different stages of agricultural evolution. (See also Clarke 1966.)

3. As already noted, the numerical values of C, Y, and R at the time the land is fully incorporated into the agricultural cycle may still be far from their optimal values. The additional demands made on the land by continued increase in population beyond the time of political unification generally leads to further intensification of agriculture (see Carneiro 1958). This continued intensification comes about partly through improved technology but perhaps mostly by even harder work in order to meet the tax demands of the state.

4. The situation I am attempting to describe here is one which Napoleon A. Chagnon (1970: 251) has aptly termed "social circumscription." He has proposed this notion in discussing the Yanomamö of southern Venezuela, and I have drawn on his discussion and incorporated his concept into my own thinking about state formation (Carneiro 1970: 737).

4

A Regional Population in Egypt to circa 600 B.C.

David O'Connor

Any application of the Boserup model or investigation of its validity involves, at least implicitly, the theory, the methodology, and the problems of historical demography. The following essay represents an exercise in historical demography which is unusual and valuable on several counts. Ancient Egyptian data seldom appear outside a purely Egyptological context. O'Connor is dealing here with an extinct culture and population, and his data are derived purely from burials. Further, the burials he has cannot represent the total population of any period, but for reasons that he gives they probably do represent a certain proportion, and therefore do provide a basis for an assessment of relative population changes and the relation between these and the environment.

An inquiry into the relationship between population growth and agricultural innovation in ancient Egypt should, in theory, be rewarding. The country's geography made the relationship a particularly close one; Egypt was an agricultural country, confined to a fertile but narrow valley surrounded by arid desert and almost entirely dependent on the annual inundation of the Nile. Moreover, a rich textual, pictorial, and archaeological record has survived, covering almost continuously a very long period. Unfortunately the pattern of preservation and archaeological exploration typical of Egypt has left important gaps in this record as far as population history and agriculture are concerned, and these topics have received much less detailed study than other aspects of ancient Egypt. However, it is possible to indicate the main factors, including agricultural developments, which affected the size of the Egyptian population and to study the fluctuations, over a long period, in the size of the population of one particular region. These fluctuations, at least in some instances, are of more than local significance.

Since late prehistoric times (ca. 3500 B.C.), the aridity of the deserts has confined the Egyptian population to the Nile's alluvial plain, which today has a maximum width of 130 miles in the Delta and of only 15 miles south of ancient Memphis, near Cairo (Figure 4.1). Apart from about 8 inches of annual rainfall along the Mediterranean coast, Egypt was virtually rainless, and its agricultural well-being depended upon the annual Nile inundation, which saturated the alluvium and refertilized it with a fresh layer of silt. As a result of these conditions there has been a kind of "differential preservation" of source material (Butzer 1965: 30–37; 1966).

Archaeological evidence exists in apparent abundance from prehistoric times onward while written documents appear in ca. 3100 B.C.; however, this material comes principally from the temples and cemeteries of Middle and Upper Egypt. Sites of all kinds in the broader Delta are comparatively less well preserved and difficult to excavate so that this area is much less well documented than the others. Throughout Egypt the settlements were naturally located on the alluvial plain so as to have convenient access to the chief water supply and means of communication: the Nile and its canals. As a result, settlement remains have suffered severely from the effects of the inundation, a gradual rise in the level of the alluvium, and the activities of a densely concentrated population over the millennia. Only a few comparatively well preserved but functionally rather specialized settlements have so far been excavated, although there is still considerable scope for settlement archaeology in Egypt in spite of the difficulties.

Monumental stone temples and royal funerary structures have, of course, survived better and have received considerable attention. Most important for our present purposes, however, are the cemeteries of all classes of society which, south of Memphis, were habitually dug in the uncultivated and uninhabited strip of low desert separating the alluvial plain from the steep cliffs of the valley side or else were cut into these cliffs. The cemeteries are often well preserved, and considerable numbers have been excavated.

As far as written documents are concerned, it is unfortunate that the kinds of greatest use to the demographer and agricultural historian, such as censuses, tax assessments, regulations and correspondence concerning agriculture and irrigation, and similar documents, were kept in the public and private archives of the towns and villages. Written on comparatively fragile papyri and ostraca, these records were probably often preserved in abandoned or sacked buildings or in the local rubbish dump. They are of course particularly liable to decay, and while some important collections of both Hellenistic and earlier times have been recovered, their total number is still small and unrepresentative. Systematic settlement excavation would certainly reveal more such documents as well as the vegetable, animal, and artifactual remains needed to reconstruct in detail the diet and food producing technology of the Egyptians.

Temple and tomb walls, as well as papyri and artifacts deposited in the tombs, are often inscribed, but the texts are mainly religious in content, although they sometimes contain important historical and geographical information. Decorated tombs are found at most periods and often depict the chief crops, animals, and agricultural tools, and some of the agricultural methods of the Egyptians, while actual examples of foodstuffs and some tools are often deposited in the tombs themselves. For demographic purposes the cemeteries are most important, for it can be reasonably assumed that they reflect the population size and the spatial distribution along the valley of the communities buried in them. Children were, it is true, certainly buried elsewhere or disposed of by other means, for although the ancient child mortality must have been at least as high as the modern one of 70 percent (Brothwell, 1963: Fig. 29), child burials are comparatively rare in the known cemeteries. However, the extraordinary stress laid upon adequate burial and funeral provisioning by Egyptian religion strongly suggests that most adults would have been buried in the community cemetery. References to the disposal of bodies other than by burial are in fact very rare and occur only at periods of great social stress. Only a few important religious centers, such as that of the funerary god Osiris at Abydos (see Figure 4.1), apparently attracted a "burial population" quite out of proportion to the size of the actual living population in the immediate area.

Although destruction through plundering or the extension of the cultivation has to be taken into account, cemeteries do provide the best continuous demographic record for ancient Egypt. It is true that cemetery evidence is not highly rated by historical demographers (Hollingsworth 1969: 43, 289–294), but given the cultural situation and the peculiar conditions of preservation in southern Egypt, cemeteries are a better guide than the demographic study of settlement remains. Apart from the inherent difficulties of this latter evidence (ibid.: 278–289), there are too few well-documented pre-Hellenistic settlements for them to be a reliable demographic indicator over a long period of time.

Having noted the general limitations of the available evidence, we are faced with two questions.
1. Can any major fluctuations over a long period in the size of the Egyptian population be detected?
2. If such fluctuations can be shown, what are the probable or at least possible causes; and, in particular, did any major population increases stimulate agricultural innovations?

There are as yet no reliable data for tracing fluctuations in the absolute size of the Egyptian population over time in the pre-Hellenistic and Hellenistic periods. It seems fairly certain that on an average the ancient and medieval population was always numerically much smaller than that of modern Egypt, but even so there must have been in the ancient period, as there certainly was in the medieval, substantial and important changes in absolute population size at certain periods. From ca. 2002 B.C. we have a record of a single rural household of about 20 individuals who worked an area of probably 90 arouras (Baer 1963: 12). The aroura is the Greek name for an ancient Egyptian measurement, the st3t; 1.5 arouras is approximately 1 acre. This suggests a rural density of about 1 person per 4.5 arouras, but the household in question was unusually prosperous and intent on working as much land as possible without having to hire extra labor. The more usual density was probably higher, perhaps 3 arouras per individual. If one assumes, as Baer has done for a later period (ibid.: 43), that 6,000,000 arouras were under cultivation, one reaches a rural population of about 2,000,000 and a total one of, say, 3,000,000.

Dealing with much better evidence from the Ramesside period (1320 to 1085 B.C.), Baer thought that a rural density of 1 person per 2 arouras was likely and, assuming a total cultivated area of 6,000,000 arouras, postulated a rural population of 3,000,000 and a total one of 4,500,000 (ibid.: 42–44). The crucial and as yet unresolved problem in all such calculations is of course the amount of land actually cultivated at any given period. The cultivated area of pre-Hellenistic Egypt was certainly less than that of today, and significant but incalculable changes in its area occurred at various points during the past (Kaiser 1961: 48–52).

It is true that a temple inscription of Senwosret I (ca. 1971 to 1928 B.C.) is believed by some to have preserved a record of the total arable land of Middle and Upper Egypt at this period (Montet 1961: 9). Unfortunately, the calculated area comes out larger than the modern cultivated area, which is certainly incorrect; either the nature of the areal measurements given in the inscription have not been properly understood, or else the measurements are in fact purely linear and give no areal information (Schlott 1969: 144–146; Nims 1965: 200, n. 10).

Despite the inevitable assumptions, however, the absolute population figures for pre-Hellenistic Egypt quoted here compare convincingly with those suggested for later periods. The highest figures quoted are 7,000,000, given by Diodorus as the population for Hellenistic times, and 7,500,000 (excluding Alexandria) quoted by Josephus as Herod Agrippa's estimate of the Egyptian population in 66 A.D. Russell (1966: 69–70) has queried these figures as being too high, pointing out that Diodorus noted that the population in his day (60 B.C.) was only 3,000,000. However, it should be noted that an official record of Ptolemy V (203–181 B.C.) states that Egypt had 9,000,000 arouras under cultivation (Schlott 1969: 160), which, at a density of 1 person per 2 arouras, would mean a rural population of about 4,500,000. In the urbanized and industrialized society of Hellenistic Egypt it is conceivable that as many as 2,500,000 more people might have lived in the towns. As Diodorus's reference to 3,000,000 inhabitants indicates, however, one must assume that there were considerable fluctuations in the size of the Hellenistic population in response to economic and political changes (Rostovtzeff 1959: 1137–1138).

Russell's (1966) careful analysis of the sources on Egypt's medieval population led him to conclude that from a peak of about 4,400,000 in the first century A.D. it declined to 1,600,000 in the tenth, and after rising again to over 4,000,000, it fell to below 2,500,000 in the fifteenth. These fluctuations were related in part to plague and to damage to the fields by floods but also to economic factors. It has been calculated that during the Mameluke period the population had an average size of 4,500,000 while the earliest censuses of the nineteenth century revealed a population of between 2,500,000 and 3,000,000 (Baer 1962: n. 113). Even in 1882 the population was still under 7,000,000, and its astronomical rise to about 30,000,000 (1965) has occurred only in the last 80 years.

Certainly the estimates of Waleck-Czernecki, who postulated an Egyptian population of between 20,000,000 and 14,000,000 in the last half of the first millennium B.C. and populations as high as 30,000,000 and 20,000,000 in the medieval period (Hollingsworth 1969: 307–308, 311), seem unjustified.

Trigger has attempted an estimate of variations in the absolute size of the ancient Nubian populations immediately south of Egypt (Trigger 1965: 160). However, even if one does not take into account the admitted hypothetical nature of these calculations, the special character and history of Lower Nubia makes it unrepresentative of developments in Egypt itself.

If we cannot establish changes in the absolute size of the Egyptian population over time, we can, at least in one region, trace relative changes in population size. The region involved, the west bank of the Nile between the modern villages of Matmar and Etmanieh (see Figure 4.1), is the only one that has been sufficiently well explored archaeologically to yield reliable data. The results must be relative since one small area was omitted and subsequent denudation and plundering have been serious enough to ensure that the 6,070 individuals represented in the archaeological record of 3,700 years do not represent the total population for that period.

The cemeteries and those settlements that happened to be located on the low desert of the 35-kilometer stretch between Matmar and Etmanieh were thoroughly explored and excavated by Guy Brunton between 1922 and 1931 (Brunton 1927; 1930; 1937; 1948; Brunton and Caton-Thompson 1928). Earlier work had been confined largely to some of the decorated tombs in the area (Porter and Moss 1937: Vol. V, 7–16), and a subsequent survey attempted no further excavation (Butzer 1961: 58–59; Kaiser 1961: 22–24). As a result of his work Brunton was able to identify a series of consecutive archaeological assemblages, each represented by a certain number of graves, usually containing only one individual. To each assemblage of the historical period Brunton assigned dynastic dates; therefore, since the absolute chronology of the Egyptian dynasties is well established (Hayes, Rowton, and Stubbings 1962), the approximate length of each assemblage can be expressed in years. Brunton's dating can in most cases be accepted as accurate; he was an experienced and able Egyptologist, and his thoroughly published data

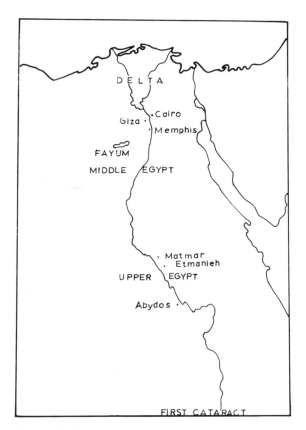

Figure 4.1. Egypt.

confirm most of his conclusions. Only the dates of one group of assemblages, which is particularly important for our present purposes, need some revision.

Most of the material Brunton discovered was already well paralleled elsewhere in Egypt, but the great mass of graves to which he assigned the dates Dynasties IV to XI (ca. 2613–1991 B.C.) was at that time the largest and best-recorded sample of that particular period. According to Brunton, the sample could be broken down into five assemblages, which were, however, difficult to date dynastically because of a paucity of inscribed material. Nevertheless, he did assign to each assemblage a date that he admitted to be very approximate, although he unfortunately chose to express those dates in precise dynastic terms (Brunton 1927). Subsequently, better-dated comparative material has been published, especially from the cemeteries near Giza, and as a result of a reanalysis of the material that I have done and that will be published elsewhere, the Dynasties IV to XI assemblages appear to break down as follows:
1. An early assemblage dating to the later Dynasty V and to Dynasty VI.
2. A chronologically intermediate assemblage that is certainly post–Dynasty VI.
3. A later assemblage that appears to be in large part contemporary with Dynasty XI.

Many graves with material that could be of either 2 or 3 have been divided equally between them in Table 4.1, although it is likely that the greater number belong to 2.

With these revisions in mind it is possible to compile the figures in the table. As a schematic expression of the demographic significance of these data, a rate of burial per year has been introduced; however, since our information on the absolute chronology of the prehistoric periods is so poor (Arkell and Ucko 1965), no effort has been made to express them in terms of years.

It is also of interest to plot, by means of the recorded cemeteries, the spatial distribution of the population at various periods (Figures 4.2–4.4), for these distribution maps reveal that changes in population size were sometimes accompanied by significant movements of the population within the region.

In brief, then, what is the population history of the Matmar-Etmanieh area revealed by these data? According to the table, the rate of burial

Table 4.1 Demographic Significance of Burial Data

Period	Number of Years	Number of Graves	Rate of burials per Year
Badarian	?	747	?
Nakada I–III (Amratian and Gerzean)	?	771	?
3100 B.C.			
Early Dynastic (Dyns. I–III)	490	220	0.4
Dynasties IV–early V	150	?	?
Later Dynasty V–VI (= earlier assemblage)	280	340	1.2
Intermediate Assemblage	60	733	12.2
Dynasty XI (= later assemblage)	110	388	3.5
Middle Kingdom (Dynasty XII)	205	116	0.6
Second Intermediate Period	210	428	2.1
1570 B.C.			
New Kingdom	600	135*	?
Dynasties XXII–XXV	300	562	1.9
650 B.C.			

* The principal New Kingdom cemetery was located but could not be excavated (Brunton 1937: 3–4).

per year increases from a very low figure in the Early Dynastic Period (ca. 3100 to 2613 B.C.) to an abrupt and extraordinary peak in the Intermediate Assemblage (ca. 2160 to 2100 B.C.); the rate then falls rapidly to a low figure in the Middle Kingdom and rises slightly in the Second Intermediate Period (ca. 1786 to 1570 B.C.). The New Kingdom rate is unknown, but that of the Dynasties XXII–XXV assemblage (ca. 950 to 650 B.C.) is close to that of the Second Intermediate Period. In interpreting these figures the peculiar nature of the evidence must be remembered; an increase in the number of burials made per year may indicate a numerically increasing population *or* a rise in the mortality rate and hence an actually decreasing population. Which of the two possibilities is likelier at any given point depends on the subsequent behavior of the graph that could be plotted from these data and on the known historical circumstances.

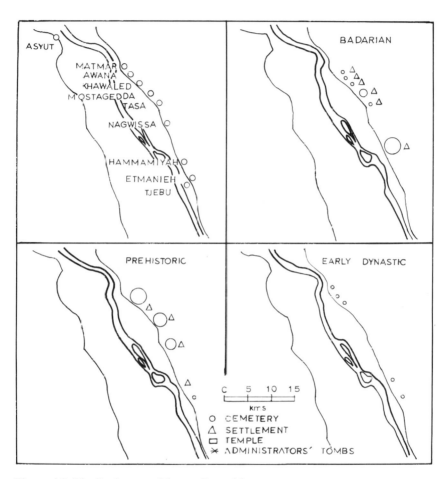

Figure 4.2. Distribution map, Matmar-Etmanieh, a.

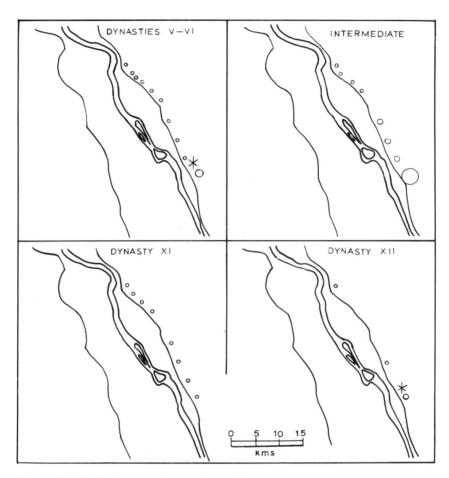

Figure 4.3. Distribution map, Matmar-Etmanieh, b.

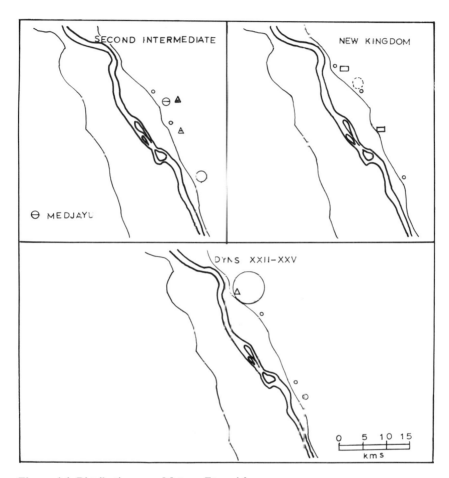

Figure 4.4. Distribution map, Matmar-Etmanieh, c.

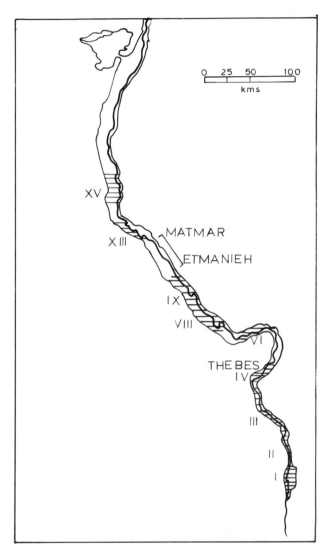

Figure 4.5. Areas (shaded) explicitly referred to as affected by famine between Dynasties VI and XI

The distribution maps show that the major population centers of the prehistoric population were north of Etmanieh, but that in the Early Dynastic Period the southern area between Hammamiyah and Etmanieh was the principal area of settlement. The importance of Etmanieh as a population focus is accentuated throughout late Dynasty V into the period of the Intermediate Assemblage, but its ancient population appears marginally smaller than that of other sites in Dynasty XI. Etmanieh appears to be the principal population center of the Middle Kingdom and Second Intermediate Period and remains important during the New Kingdom. However, the largest New Kingdom cemetery (unexcavated) lay considerably to the north at Khawaled, while in the latest period the population of the region was overwhelmingly concentrated at Matmar.

Are there reasonable explanations for these size fluctuations and spatial movements; and, if there are, are they of purely local origin, or do at least some have a national as well as local significance? Topographically the Matmar-Etmanieh stretch is typical of much of Middle Egypt; its alluvial plain today occupies about 100 square kilometers, although in antiquity its dimensions may have varied somewhat according to changes in the river's course. The northern and southern limits of the plain are formed by the steep limestone cliffs that come close to the river near Matmar and Etmanieh. Today and as far as we know in ancient times, Matmar-Etmanieh belonged to a general region of high agricultural yield and dense population (Wilson 1955: 217). The prehistoric landscape of a natural flood plain with woods running along the Nile levees was transformed during the fourth and early third millennia B.C. into fields devoted to the growing of wheat and barley, a variety of vegetables and fruit, and fodder crop for the cattle, sheep, goats, and asses, which were the principal animals of the Egyptians. The annual inundation was controlled and enhanced by a system of basin irrigation which appears to have existed by 3000 B.C. (Drioton and Vandier 1962: 148).

Apart from its agricultural richness the Matmar-Etmanieh area enjoyed no special advantages in historical times. It formed the east bank of the Xth Upper Egyptian nome (or province), the capital of which was Tjebu, near Etmanieh; a second capital may have developed on the west bank in the New Kindgom (Figure 4.2; and see Gardiner 1941: 44–45 fig. 2; 65–68; Gardiner 1947: 49–67; Montet 1961: 115–123). Economically the nome's importance was overshadowed by a concen-

tration of trade at Asyut to the north (Figure 4.2); Asyut dominated
the valley, particularly narrow at this point, and had easy access to the
routes in the eastern and western deserts. The Xth nome never contained
an administrative or religious center of national importance; it was not
especially significant for the control of the river, the principal means of
communication and transport, or for external defense; and it was never
an area of great public works such as the development of royal cemeteries.
However, its relatively uneventful history perhaps makes the Xth nome
more representative of general trends in population size and distribution
in Egypt than areas where there was an abnormal increase or decrease of
population for some specific purpose.

Turning to an examination of the data, we have already noted that
absolute dates cannot yet be reliably assigned to the prehistoric assemblages. However, the Badarian assemblage appears to have lasted for a
shorter period than the succeeding prehistoric phases, and it is therefore
striking that Badarian and later prehistoric graves occur in about the
same numbers between Matmar and Etmanieh. This suggests either a
numerically greater population in Badarian times or a considerably
higher Badarian mortality rate; both explanations are possible. The
Badarians were an intrusive group, originating in the then slightly better-
watered Red Sea hills, and the Matmar-Etmanieh area appears to have
been their principal entry point. Badarian remains are virtually confined
to this area, while their successors, the early Prehistoric (Nakada I or
Amratian) people are found as far south as the First Cataract and beyond, while Later Prehistoric sites (Nakada II or Gerzean) are distributed
between the Fayum and the Second Cataract (see Figure 4.1). There
may have been, therefore, an abnormally high population in the Matmar-
Etmanieh region while the Badarians adjusted to their new environment.

The process of adjustment may also have generated a higher mortality
rate, as the unusually high proportion of Badarian child burials suggests.
The Badarians were presumably nomadic in the Red Sea hills, and their
artifacts appear to reflect primarily hunting and gathering communities,
perhaps with a certain amount of pastoralism. Arrowheads, scrapers for
leather (?), and gazelle skin wrappings are fairly common; cattle, sheep,
goats (all domesticated?), birds, and fish were eaten; wheat and barley
(domesticated?) were harvested with inefficient saw-edged flint knives;
and linen was made from flax. In spite of the exploitation of the products

of the alluvium and although the valley was physically suitable for settlement, the fact that Badarian settlements clustered around the wadis on
the low desert suggests a reluctance to adopt a sedentary and agricultural
way of life. If, in fact, the Badarians were being compelled for climatic
reasons gradually to abandon a primarily nomadic life in the Red Sea
hills and yet were at first neither ideologically nor technologically prepared to exploit the resources of the valley efficiently, it may be that
during the transition period the problem of securing an adequate food
supply was not always successfully met.

Throughout the later prehistoric period there was clearly an increasing
reliance on agriculture: agricultural tools were common and more efficient, the production of linen became important, and by the end of the
period the Egyptian population was largely sedentary and agricultural.
Only early prehistoric settlements were to be found on the low desert,
since by late prehistoric times all settlement was on the alluvial plain
(see Figure 4.2).

The third millennium B.C. opened with the unification of the two
kingdoms in which the prehistoric people of Egypt had coalesced, an
event that generated or, at least, was accompanied by extraordinary
cultural advances. By 2700 B.C. Egypt was a literate civilization with
highly developed art and monumental architecture and was controlled
by a centralized bureaucracy dominated by a semidivine king. There are
indications from the poorly documented Early Dynastic Period that the
consolidation of secure royal authority was not achieved until Dynasty
III, and the apparently rather low population in the Matmar-Etmanieh
area at this time is perhaps due to a background of political and economic uncertainty. However, Egypt appears to have been well and efficiently governed throughout Dynasties IV, V, and much of VI, with
taxes in kind being regularly collected, the agricultural economy carefully regulated, and adequate provision made for supplying food to the
population in years of a low Nile inundation and hence poor harvest.

There is little archaeological evidence on the population of the Matmar-Etmanieh area in Dynasty IV and early Dynasty V, but throughout
the latter part of Dynasty V and Dynasty VI there seems to be a gradual
but distinct increase in the burial rate, which probably reflected a numerically increasing population. This presumably was due to efficient administration and security, for by the time of Dynasty IV royal estates

were being founded in the region (Jaquet-Gordon 1962: 130–131), and
reference is first made to the nome. By Dynasty V provincial administrators were being buried in rockcut tombs at Hammamiyah (Porter and
Moss 1937: Vol. V, 7–9) and the distribution of the population, with its
concentration near Etmanieh (Figure 4.3) shows that the administrative
center of the province was located here. The name of this capital, Tjebu,
is first preserved in records of Dynasties XI and XII, but its administrative importance was clearly established in the Old Kingdom.

The extraordinary increase in the burial rate after Dynasty VI can
hardly be due to a natural increase in the population, particularly as it
was followed by an abrupt and rapid decrease in Dynasty XI. There
seems little doubt that the data at this point record a great increase in
the mortality rate, generated by a complex set of factors. The latter part
of Dynasty VI and the succeeding period were characterized by an increasing fragmentation of political authority. The "nomes, once administrative districts of a strong central government, had returned to their
original status as small independent states. Each was governed by a dynasty of local princes . . . whose right to power had become hereditary and
who now dated events to the years of their own tenures of office, levied
and maintained their own armies, built and manned their own fleets of
ships" (Hayes 1964: 7). In these circumstances the overall control of the
national economy, irrigation, and flood control system inevitably suffered
at an especially unfortunate moment.

Butzer (1959: 109–111) has emphasized that it was just at this time
that the valley and the surrounding deserts were passing through a climatic crisis, with the slight desert rainfall disappearing entirely and the
level of the annual Nile inundation decreasing until it stabilized at about
2350 B.C. As a result recurrent famine struck Middle and Upper Egypt,
and it is from this general period that most of the known Egyptian references to famine come, direct and indirect. Of these approximately twenty-
two references, only one is dated to Dynasty VI, one to late Dynasty
XI, and one to early Dynasty XII; the rest appear to coincide in date
with the Intermediate Assemblage of Matmar-Etmanieh (Vandier 1936,
revised by reference to Hayes 1964 and Fischer 1968). Most, if not all, of
the area between the Ist and the XVth Upper Egyptian nomes, which
includes some of the most fertile land in Egypt, was affected (Figure 4.5).

The local governors sometimes had to close their frontiers against immigration, sending ships up and down the Nile to seek food, and there are at least two references, possibly but not necessarily exaggerated, to cannibalism (Vandier 1936).

The actual numerical decrease in the population of the Matmar-Etmanieh region must have been paralleled elsewhere in Egypt, and it seems likely that royal authority, gradually reconsolidated under Dynasty XI and firmly established during Dynasty XII, was faced with a difficult situation. Not only had the size of the population and hence of the agricultural labor force declined, but, if I have understood Butzer's arguments correctly, the height of the Nile inundation did not start to increase significantly again until New Kingdom times (Butzer 1959: 109–116). Undoubtedly, in the stable political and economic conditions of the Middle Kingdom, the population also started to increase again, as is indicated by the gradual rise to a distinctly higher rate of burial in the Second Intermediate Period at Matmar-Etmanieh. At the local level Tjebu appears to have lost its dominant position, according to the distribution map (Figure 4.3), during Dynasty XI, perhaps because the local administrative system, after surviving the earlier periods of distress, had finally collapsed. But the tombs of local governors appear once again in Dynasty XII (Petrie 1930; Steckeweh and Steindorff 1936), and Tjebu is again the major center of population (see Figure 4.3). A similar pattern undoubtedly occurred in other parts of Egypt.

Increasing population would of course have put a severe strain on the productivity of the cultivable land if this had in fact been reduced in area by a decrease in the level of the annual inundation. This would seem an ideal situation to stimulate agricultural innovation, since emigration for both psychological and physical reasons was not feasible. If we consider the climatic conditions of historic Egypt before Hellenistic times and if we assume that the available land was cropped at least once a year, we can conclude that any attempt to increase food production would require, possibly in combination:

a. More intensive agriculture or animal husbandry, involving cropping the land more than once annually and/or introducing improved or new plants and animals yielding more food.

b. Extending the area of land under cultivation.

Just such a combination is known for Ptolemaic Egypt, but it is not certain that it was a response to population pressure, although the population was undoubtedly high at the time. The usual explanations for the Ptolemaic innovations are that they were to satisfy the tastes of the Greek mercenaries who had settled in Egypt and more importantly to finance the Ptolemies' ambitious foreign policy by securing for Egypt "a favorable balance in international trade and thereby [securing] a good influx of gold and silver from abroad" (Rostovtzeff 1953: 353). The production of grains, oils, wines, and other commodities was therefore increased for trade purposes, although the Ptolemies were careful to maintain a good food supply for the Egyptian population, their chief source of labor (ibid.: 351ff.). Comparable innovations in intensifying agriculture or animal husbandry had not been detected in pre-Hellenistic Egypt, but the problem appears not to have been surveyed on a broad scale since 1923, so discoveries may yet be made (Hartmann 1923; Kees 1961: 74ff.).

Intensification of food production and the extension of cultivable area would involve the extension of or changes in the system of basin irrigation that was characteristic of Egypt until recent times. Because of the Nile's regime, basin irrigation in Egypt means that a good water supply is available for the fields only for three to four months of the year, but the introduction of large-scale perennial irrigation was beyond the abilities of pre-Hellenistic and Hellenistic Egypt. However, on a smaller scale the amount of water available for land not normally reached by the inundation and for use during the period of low Nile was substantially increased in Ptolemaic times by the introduction of an animal-driven water-wheel This was a much more efficient device for raising water than human labor and, from at least the New Kingdom onward, the "shaduf" of pre-Hellenistic Egypt. Lower Nubia, for example, appears to have been agriculturally rejuvenated by the introduction of the waterwheel (Trigger 1965: 123).

Canalization and drainage, however, were two means of land reclamation that were available to pre-Hellenistic Egypt, and both were used for this purpose. The principal areas open to reclamation were the Delta and the Fayum depression. The Delta is unfortunately poorly documented, but the major effort at reclamation here appears to belong to the later New Kingdom and especially to Dynasty XXVI (Kees 1961: 189).

This might be in response to population pressure (Matmar-Etmanieh evidence does not show a marked increase in population at this time, but this may be only of regional significance), or it might have been prompted by commercial motives similar to those of the Ptolemies (Gardiner 1961: 356–357).

In the Fayum, however, the history of land reclamation begins much earlier—soon after the First Intermediate Period—and it was perhaps as a response to population pressure that the rulers of Dynasty XII (Middle Kingdom) carried out a large reclamation project in the Fayum. Although the engineering capabilities involved have probably been exaggerated, archaeological and textual evidence indicates the addition of as much as 17,000 acres to the arable land of Egypt (Hayes 1964: 50). It is true that the laborers and, subsequently the maintenance of the cults and personnel of the great Dynasty XII royal monuments situated nearby would have required agricultural estates for their support, but the amount of land involved seems too great for this purpose alone.

Despite the division of Egypt between Asiatic rulers in the north and Egyptian kings in the south, during the Second Intermediate Period political fragmentation did not become as acute as it had been after Dynasty VI. Tjebu remained the population and probably administrative center of the east bank in the Xth nome, and its population had increased since the Middle Kingdom. This increase was not purely natural, for at this time several settlements and cemeteries of Medjayu, immigrants from the eastern desert with a distinctive and non-Egyptian material culture, appear in the region. The immigrants make up about 30 percent of the burials in the area at this time, and they are known to have settled in other parts of Egypt as well (Säve-Söderbergh 1941: 135–140; Bietak 1966: 61ff.).

Up to this point in time immigration had probably not had a significant effect on Egypt's population size, although there had been continuous small-scale infiltration through the frontiers. Throughout the New Kingdom and especially in its later phases, however, immigration—especially from Libya—becomes more perceptible and may have added considerably to the population.

Unfortunately, the relative size of the New Kingdom population of Matmar-Etmanieh is not indicated by the available data. However,

climatically the New Kingdom was quite favorable for agriculture (Butzer
1959: 109–116), and internal political and economic conditions appear
to have remained stable from the expulsion of the Asiatic kings in
ca. 1570 B.C. until the beginning of a new phase of disturbances near the end
of the second millennium B.C. It seems probable that the New Kingdom
population was in general quite large (Butzer: 1960: 7), and Matmar-
Etmanieh would certainly have reflected this. Curiously, although the
local "mayors," the New Kingdom equivalent of the earlier provincial
governors, appear to have resided at Tjebu and the cemetery of the town
reveals a considerable population, the major concentration of population
appears to have moved northward (see Figure 4.4).

The data do not indicate any increase or decrease during the periods
covered by Dynasties XXII to XXV, the last well-documented assemblage in the area. It is striking, however, that the bulk of the population
is now concentrated at Matmar (see Figure 4.4) and actually appears to
have lived within the shelter offered by the thick brick enclosure walls
of an earlier temple at this site (Brunton 1948: 60–65). This was probably
a direct result of contemporary political conditions and was probably
duplicated elsewhere in Egypt. Throughout Dynasties XXII to XXV,
Egypt was afflicted by a series of internal armed conflicts and finally by
an invasion from the Sudan. The records of the Sudanese conqueror
Piankhy (751–730 B.C.) show that the typical large town of Middle Egypt
had become heavily fortified and apparently served as a refuge for the
peasants of the surrounding countryside (Breasted 1906: Vol. IV, 816–
883). The inhabited temple enclosure at Matmar seems to be a variant
of this practice.

This attempt to trace fluctuations in the relative size and spatial distribution of a regional population in Egypt over a period of approximately
3,500 years has led to only very tentative conclusions. However, two
general points of interest have emerged and deserve recapitulation.

First, there is the problem of finding sufficient data to construct an
approximately accurate graph of fluctuations in the population size over
time for an entire country (or at least for a large area). For Egypt the
available evidence, which must be comparable to that from other parts
of the ancient world, is both textual and archaeological, and it is obvious
that this combination is more revealing than if there were only one type

of evidence available. The archaeological evidence is derived mainly from cemeteries, which—given the right conditions of culture and preservation—are potentially a most useful source, since they contain the remains of the majority of the ancient population. However, the relationship between the size of the burial population and the size of the living population at any given period is a complex one; the interpretation of this relationship can be aided by a detailed examination of the skeletal material (for age, sex, disease, malnutrition, and violence) and equally by a knowledge of the historical background. Although good archaeological data may be regionally limited, as in pre-Hellenistic Egypt, known historical facts may enable a wider significance to be given to those data.

The spatial distribution of the population at any period, even in a comparatively small region such as Matmar-Etmanieh, is a significant factor in examining population sizes, and data derived from a survey that does not include such information can be quite misleading. This is particularly evident for the Dynasties XXII to XXV population, which was overwhelmingly concentrated at Matmar, but it is true for other periods also. Finally, fluctuation in absolute population sizes seems to be impossible to obtain, but fluctuations in the relative size of a population over time can be established.

The second point worth emphasizing is the complexity of the factors affecting population size. Environmental changes had, at least once, a serious detrimental effect on the Egyptian population (in the later part of the third millennium B.C.), but this was coincidental with a marked fragmentation of political authority, and the cause and effect relationship between the two factors cannot yet be fully analyzed. In normal times a stabilizing influence on the population was the existence of an efficient, centralized administration under which the agricultural and irrigation systems were maintained on a nationwide basis, communications were good, and foodstuffs regularly stored for a variety of purposes, including the relief of famine. Immigration may also have been a significant factor in population growth at some periods. Plague and disease are not well documented for ancient Egypt, but they are known to have had demographic effects in medieval times, and their possible effect in antiquity should not be discounted.

Agricultural innovation, defined in terms of an extension of or addition to the cultivable land, is documented for ancient Egypt and probably occurred in the later third millennium B.C. as a response to population pressure created by a rather unusual situation. But it is important to remember that agricultural innovation could also be prompted by commercial and political motives, as it was in Ptolemaic and perhaps earlier times.

Population,	William T.
Agricultural	Sanders
History, and	
Societal	
Evolution in	
Mesoamerica	

As a test of Boserup's model as a whole, Sanders presents a series of population profiles from various geographical areas within Mesoamerica for the pre-Hispanic period (areas that vary strikingly in geographical characteristics), discusses the variations among them, and attempts to explain these variations in both ecological and nonecological terms. In the conclusion of his essay he discusses areas of both agreement and disagreement with the assumptions and details of Boserup's thesis.

In discussion Sanders agreed with Boserup's main points but pointed out that in her suggested correlation of agricultural tools with the frequency of cropping continuum she had ignored the possibilities of weeding with machetes. In Mesoamerica today, virtually no bush fallowers use the hoe. Instead, they slice the weeds down with machetes. Furthermore, grasses *can* be controlled with hoes, as ethnographic cases from highland Guatemala and West Africa demonstrate.

It is only recently in Mesoamerican studies that scholars have conducted intensive settlement pattern surveys (that is, surveys that attempt to include all kinds of communities within the sample, from isolated homesteads to cities) of relatively large local areas, and this is the only type of archaeological research that can provide reliable data on population history. There are, of course, enormous problems in translating archaeological sites into population estimates, but I feel that at least relative population profiles can be defined rather easily. By this I mean that, although it would be very difficult to say that in a given area there were 2,500 people and that the population had increased first to 5,000 and ultimately to 15,000 by 1519, one could state that the base population was probably no more than one-sixth of that in 1519. For our purposes here, this degree of accuracy is sufficient.

A major methodological problem is chronology. Most researchers deal in blocks of time involving hundreds of years. Conceivably in the history of an area, there could have been a period in which settlements were less sedentary and village sites were frequently shifted, followed by a period in which people lived in more stable communities. In this case a simple calculation of the total amount of habitation area or number of ruined houses of the various sites from each period would not give an accurate picture even of the relative population size for the two periods. If Boserup's arguments are sound, this would be precisely what one would expect in the history of land use of an area and would make a comparison of population sizes between the earliest and latest phases of occupation extremely difficult.

Another problem is the enormous variation in the quality of the data. In order to get a respectable sample in terms of total size and geographical spread, we have included studies that vary greatly in their quality and dependability. They are described here by levels of reliability.

Group 1 includes those studies where surveys were systematically conducted over fairly large areas, in which all sites were recorded, their occupational areas measured and dated by surface sampling. In all cases the author also presents his own population profile, often including absolute estimates. This level of reliability includes the Teotihuacán Valley study (Sanders 1965) the Texcoco-Ixtapalapa and Chalco studies by Parsons (1968, 1969, and 1970), the Belize Valley study by Willey et al. (1965), and the Nochixtlan Valley study by Spores (1969).

Group 2 includes those cases where surveys have been conducted or are currently in progress but in which published data are scanty and hence only a general impression of population history is available. This would include the Tehuacán Valley study by MacNeish (1964); the Tikal studies by W. Coe (1967), Haviland (1966, 1969), Bullard (1960); the Altar de Sacrificios study by Willey and Smith (1969); the Valley of Guatemala study by Sanders and Michels (1969); the Cotzal study in the northern highlands of Guatemala by Richard Adams (1965); the highland Chiapas study by Robert Adams (1961); the southwest

Tlaxcala-Cholula study by Tschol (1966); the north-central Tlaxcala study by Snow (1969); and the Central Valley of Chiapas study by Lowe and Mason (1965).

Group 3 includes those cases where general surveys have been conducted and where publications include summary statements that can be translated into rough population profiles. These areas include the studies by Grove in the state of Morelos (1968); cf the Pacific coastal plain and piedmont of Guatemala by Shook (1965), and Coe and Flannery (1967); the Valley of Oaxaca by Bernal (1965), Flannery et al. (1967, 1968); and various studies in northern Yucatán by Sanders (1960) and Andrews (1965).

In order to simplify the discussion for those who are not Mesoamerican specialists, I have converted all of the phase names used by the various authors to a master system for the Mesoamerican area as a whole. The chronological terms are as follows: Early Formative (2500–1500 B.C.); Middle Formative, Phase One (1500–1200 B.C.); Middle Formative, Phase Two (1200–900 B.C.); Middle Formative, Phase Three (900–600 B.C.); Late Formative, Phase One (600–300 B.C.); Late Formative, Phase Two (300–100 B.C.); Terminal Formative (100 B.C.–100 A.D.); Proto-Classic (100–300 A.D.); Early Classic (300–500 A.D.); Middle Classic (500–700 A.D.); Late Classic (700–950 A.D.); Early Post-Classic (950–1250 A.D.); Late Post-Classic (1250–1519 A.D.). The graphs are all plotted in terms of an absolute time scale, and population is given in terms of an arbitrary scale of intensity. Furthermore, it should be noted that, with respect to the scale of "population intensity," each graph and, in those cases where more than one area is plotted on a single graph, each profile is independent of all of the others. In each profile, therefore, the point of maximum population is always set at the maximum point in the population intensity scale (number 15) even though the different areas had strikingly different levels of population density during their respective peaks.

The Central Plateau

In the geographical heart of Mexico is a great tableland with an elevation averaging 2,200 meters above sea level and broken up by mountain ranges into a series of large basins (see Figure 5.1 for place

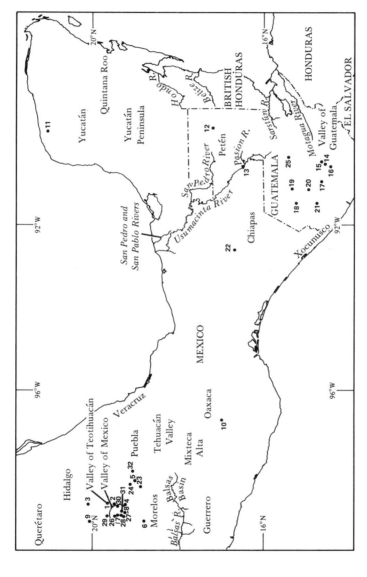

Figure 5.1. Archaeological map of Mesoamerica. Scale 1 : 9,100,000 or 145 miles per inch. 1. Teotihuacán   2. Texcoco   3. Tlaxcala
4. Chalco   5. Cholula   6. Xochicalco   7. Tenochtitlán   8. Xochimilco   9. Tula   10. Monte Albán   11. Tzibilchaltun   12. Tikal
13. Altar de Sacrificios   14. Kaminaljuyu   15. Chinautla   16. Amatitlán   17. Iximche   18. Zaculeu   19. Nebaj   20. Utatlan
21. Quetzaltenango   22. San Cristóbal   23. Atlixco   24. Huejotzingo   25. Cotzal   26. Azcapotzalco   27. Cuicuilco   28. Coyoacán
29. Quauhtitlan   30. Chimalhuacán   31. Ixtapalapa   32. Amalucan.

names). In 1519 the densest population in Mesoamerica was located
here. One of these basins is the Basin of Mexico, which was the locality
of the capital of the Aztec empire, the largest community in the history
of Mesoamerica. The plateau played a critical role in Mesoamerican
history during the entire Classic and Post-Classic periods, was the center
of at least one earlier pan-Mesoamerican empire centered at Teotihuacán. In Late Classic and Early Post-Classic times there were a
number of major polities centered at Cholula, Xochicalco, and Tula.
During the Early and Middle Formative period it seems to have played
a relatively minor role.

The region offers certain advantages and disadvantages to occupation by sedentary farmers with an agriculture crop complex centered
on maize. One of the many disadvantages is the elevation. In those
areas above 2,700 meters cultivation of maize is impossible because of
the prolonged winter frost season. Frosts between 2,000 and 2,700 meters
occur regularly from November until March—the dry season. In
normal years, the period from March to October is free of them, and
since this is the rainy season, the regime is favorable for summer maize
cropping. Unfortunately, however, frosts may occur as early as September and as late as April, and crop damage can occur. If the rains
are delayed until mid-June, a not-uncommon event, and frosts begin in
October and occasionally even as early as September, then crop damage
can be catastrophic.

Another problem is rainfall. In the valley floors where soils are most
fertile, annual rainfall varies from 500 mm in the drier northern portion
of the Basin of Mexico, Tlaxcala, and Puebla (in fact, averages as low
as 300 mm occur in the far northern edge of Hidalgo and Querétaro)
to 900 mm in the south, in the southern portion of the Basin of Mexico,
and at Cholula. Aside from the relatively low annual precipitation,
mid-season droughts are a common occurrence. The slopes receive
substantially more rainfall, reaching a maximum of 1,500 mm in a
few localities.

Compared to other highland areas of Mesoamerica, relatively flat
terrain, plains, and gently sloping piedmont are extensive, but since a
high percentage of land does consist of steep slopes, erosion is another
major problem. The region offers many advantages, however, that
offset these problems: the native vegetation is easily removed and

controlled; soils are fertile, easily worked with hand tools, and have excellent textures for dry farming methods of humidity conservation; plains are extensive; localized resources provide water for irrigation; and there are also fairly extensive areas of deep soil with high water tables.

Group 1 surveys have been conducted in four portions of the Basin of Mexico, the Valley of Teotihuacán (600 km^2), the Texcoco area (800 km^2), the Ixtapalapa Peninsula (180 km^2), and a series of small test strips in the District of Chalco in the southeastern part of the Basin (220 km^2). Altogether these areas make up approximately 25 percent of the total surface area of the Basin of Mexico. The completed surveys provide a good sample of the Basin of Mexico as a whole since they include a virtually continuous zone from north to south, from the drier portions of the Basin to the more humid south, and from east to west and extend from the lake shore plain, across the piedmont, and up the nearby mountain slopes. On the other hand, we lack data on the area west of Lake Texcoco, where the Aztec capital of Tenochtitlán and its numerous satellite settlements were located, so that data are deficient for this critical area.

Let us first examine the Valley of Teotihuacán profile (Figure 5.2). The following analysis is based on a survey that included approximately 800 occupations. The population estimate for 1519, the time of the Spanish Conquest, is based upon my detailed evaluations of sixteenth-century Spanish censuses. According to this study, the population in 1519 was approximately 130,000. My estimate for the Early Post-Classic period is based upon a comparison of the number of sites and the total surface areas of those sites with sites dating from the time of the Conquest, and then calculating the population on the basis of the resultant ratios. Since Early and Late Post-Classic sites occur in the same ecological setting in the valley and have similar characteristics, this method is undoubtedly a valid one.

The Early and Middle Classic population estimate is based on Millon's survey (1967, 1969) of the city of Teotihuacán, located within the valley, and with added data from our rural survey. Early and Middle Classic villages tend to be more densely nucleated than either Early or Late Post-Classic ones, and I have used the density figures from our test excavations at one of these village sites (TC 8) as a means

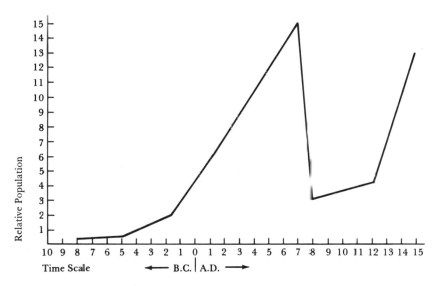

Figure 5.2. Teotihuacán Valley.

of estimating the populations of the others. The density figures from the village approximate very closely Millon's calculations of the density of population in the city itself.

For the Formative period, the estimates are less reliable. Many sites tend to be hamlets located in a different ecological setting from the Classic and Post-Classic settlements. The agricultural system was probably an extensive one, so that the probability of shifting settlements from one location to the other is great. Furthermore, the steep slopes were not as completely surveyed as the piedmont and valley floor, so that our survey is not quite as reliable in those areas. The possibility of undiscovered sites is great. Therefore our estimate of Formative period population is little more than a rough estimate.

The data indicate that there probably was not an agricultural population in the Teotihuacán Valley during the Early Formative and the Middle Formative, Phase One and Phase Two. The earliest evidence of occupation that we have dates from the Middle Formative, Phase Three. The profile shows a small population during this and the succeeding Late Formative, Phase One. In the Late Formative, Phase Two, there was a striking increase in population followed by a virtual population

explosion during the Terminal Formative phase (the earliest phase
of the evolution of the city of Teotihuacán). Our graphs show a rise in
population from perhaps 15,000 people by the end of the Late Formative
period to 60,000 by the end of the Terminal Formative (of which
perhaps 45,000 lived at the city of Teotihuacán). This population
further increased to a peak of 150,000 toward the end of the Middle
Classic phase (of which approximately 125,000 resided in the city).
In the final decades of the history of the city of Teotihuacán, there is
evidence of a complete nucleation of the rural population at Teotihuacán
and a total decline of the population of the valley and city, possibly to
about 100,000 people. Following the destruction of the city by invaders,
the total population of the valley plummeted to a nadir of perhaps
30,000 people in Late Classic times. This was followed by a steep rise
to a new peak by 1519.

   This demographic profile is closely paralleled by political and
economic history. The first ceremonial architecture and evidence of
ranked social structure do not appear until Late Formative, Phase Two.
During the Middle Classic period, the valley becomes the political
center of Mesoamerica; during the Late Classic and Early Post-Classic
periods, the valley was clearly marginal in every way to centers located
elsewhere, and it was a period of little building activity, small towns,
and villages. During the Late Post-Classic period, the valley was
tributary to, but part of, the core domain of Texcoco and registered an
increase in urbanism, including no less than six towns with populations
varying from 1,000 to 8,000 people each.

   The graph of the Texcoco area (an area immediately adjacent to the
Teotihuacán Valley to the south), which is based on unpublished surveys
by Parsons, shows some striking divergences from the Valley of Teotihuacán profile (Figure 5.3). Parsons's estimates of population all show
lower values than the ones we present here. This is so because his
survey did not include all of the area and we have established the
Aztec population on the basis of documentary sources, as we did in the
case of the Valley of Teotihuacán. We have thus recalculated his
estimates of the earlier period to higher levels, assuming that the un-
surveyed areas will show much the same settlement history. On the
basis of my studies of the area in 1519, the population must have been
very close to 150,000.

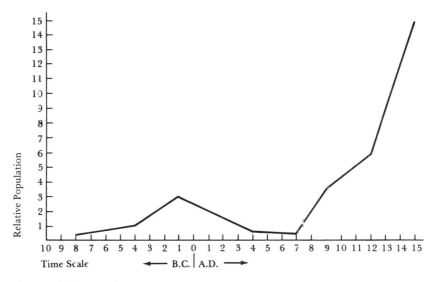

Figure 5.3. Texcoco Area.

Immediately apparent is the generally heavier Formative period occupation of the Texcoco area, and it is particularly concentrated in the piedmont zone. A peak is reached in Late Formative, Phase Two, but the inception of ceremonial architecture occurs in Phase One of the Late Formative, several centuries earlier than it does in the Teotihuacán Valley. By the Late Formative, Phase Two, we can define a series of small polities each consisting of a civic center and satellite settlements. In contrast to the Teotihuacán Valley, there is a striking depression of population during the Terminal Formative, Early Classic, and Middle Classic phases, and this period of depression is succeeded by a rise to a peak of 150,000 by 1519.

Of particular interest is the fact that the Terminal Formative decline corresponds very closely to the explosive increase in population in the Teotihuacán Valley, and the conclusion seems obvious that the two graphs show a process of migration to the emerging Teotihuacán city. If we combine the two into a single population graph as seen in Figure 5.4, then the result indicates two population peaks, one in the Middle Classic and another in 1519, separated by a substantial decline (but not as steep as the Teotihuacán Valley graph would indicate)

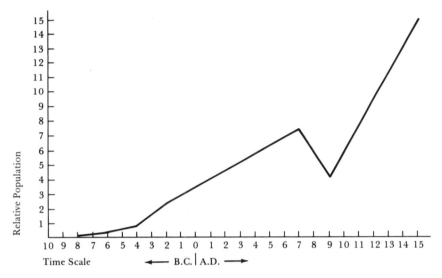

Figure 5.4. Teotihuacán Valley and Texcoco area combined.

during the Late Classic and Early Post-Classic periods. This Late
Classic–Early Post-Classic decline is probably the product of population
displacement related to new population centers emerging outside the
area.

I suspect that a graph representing the entire Basin of Mexico would
reveal a virtually continuous upward curve of population from the
Middle Formative period up to the time of the Spanish Conquest.
This suspicion is strongly reinforced by preliminary survey data from
the Ixtapalapa Peninsula and Chalco surveys. The reconstructed graph
(Figure 5.5) from this southeastern portion of the Basin of Mexico
reveals a Formative population that, in an overall sense, is denser than
in the two northern areas, begins earlier, and has a few substantial
villages dating from as early as Phase Two of the Middle Formative
period and with relatively large political centers emerging as early as
Phase One of the Late Formative period. The Late Classic–Early Post-
Classic population in this area was at least as dense and probably
denser than the Early and Middle Classic, thus at least partially
modifying the impression of a decline of population between the
Middle Classic and Late Post-Classic periods.

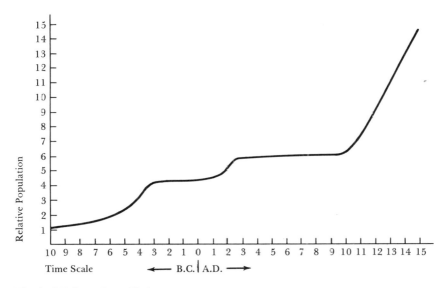

Figure 5.5. Ixtapalapa-Chalco area.

In Figure 5.6 we have combined the various graphs from the surveys, so that this graph is probably very close to the overall picture of the Basin of Mexico.

As the product of research conducted by Parsons (1968, 1970), Pedro Armillas (personal communication), Tolstoy and Paradis (1970), and myself (1969), an overall picture of agricultural and socioeconomic history of the Basin of Mexico can now be presented.

Insofar as it is known, the Texcoco area and the Teotihuacán Valley were not occupied by sedentary farmers prior to 900 B.C. Nearly all of the Middle Formative, Phase Three sites consist of hamlets or small, widely spaced villages on high ground, regardless of the particular area involved (usually above the 2,300-meter contour).

The settlement pattern data from both the Texcoco and Teotihuacán surveys suggest that, during this period of time, the system of farming was extensive and probably comparable to a variant of swidden agriculture still practiced today in the more humid regions of the Mexican highlands. There is little or no indication of more intensive practices of cultivation during these periods. All indications are that the social structure was tribal, in Service's (1965) terms. An exception to

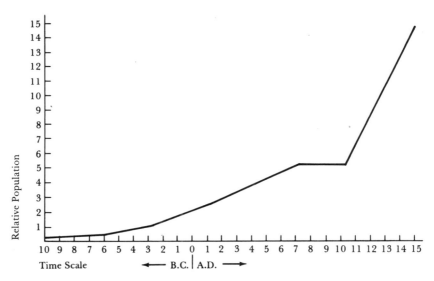

Figure 5.6. Basin of Mexico.

both the ecological and social rule is probably indicated by one site, a large village on the lower flank of the hill and adjoining plain at Chimalhuacán.

During Phase One of the Late Formative, a number of changes in settlement pattern do occur and are an indication of events to follow. Although the Teotihuacán Valley and Texcoco areas remained marginal, culturally and demographically, nevertheless substantial villages make their first appearance in both areas, two in the Teotihuacán Valley and three in the Texcoco area. In the Teotihuacán Valley both are located on the edge of the alluvial plain. It is probable that the appearance of these settlements is related to more intensive agricultural practices.

The southern portion of the Basin of Mexico was clearly more precocious in its population history, evolution of more intensive practices of cultivation, and evolution of more complex social systems than in the center and north. Generally, this is a more favorable region for cultivation that involves extensive practices of farming because of its generally higher rainfall, and from a historical point of view it can be expected that colonization would have occurred in this area prior to the drier north.

Occupation by cultivators apparently began in this portion of the Basin by Middle Formative, Phase Two, since Tolstoy has defined an earlier phase dating from about 1100 to 900 B.C. at one site (Ayotla). Parsons's surveys of the Chalco district did not reveal any additional sites, but they presumably do exist in that area. During Middle Formative, Phase Three, Parsons's Chalco survey has revealed at least one substantial village and during Late Formative, Phase One, ten communities with populations in excess of 1,000 inhabitants each are present, several of which have substantial civic ceremonial centers (and it should be emphasized that his survey included a much smaller area than either the Teotihuacán Valley or Texcoco surveys). Outside of his survey, in the southwestern corner of the Basin, was the huge site of Cuicuilco with its 20-meter-high pyramid-temple and a residential area conservatively estimated at 200–300 hectares.

Although much of the cultivation in the southern portion of the Basin during the Formative period was probably various types of long- and short-fallow swidden, there are indications of more intensive cultivation by Late Formative times.

Palerm (1961) has reported the inception of irrigation agriculture and a more intensive system of cultivation in the alluvial plain around Cuicuilco during the Late Formative, Phase One or Two.

During the Late Formative, Phase One, the overall population of the Basin increased, and we have a distinct gradient from south to north, with the densest population in the south. This growth is accompanied by the appearance of more intensive agricultural techniques in the area of densest population and the emergence of the first large political systems in the same area.

During the Late Formative, Phase Two, we have for the first time a major change in the ecological and political patterning of the Basin. There is a striking increase of population in the northern, drier zone coincident with definite evidence of irrigation, accompanied by the appearance of ceremonial architecture and large population centers. One of these is located within the area of the Early and Middle Classic city of Teotihuacán, covered a minimum area of 400 hectares, and had an estimated minimal population of 4,000 people. The settlement pattern data for the Teotihuacán Valley at this time indicate that the entire population of the valley, perhaps 15,000 people, was organized under the leadership of this nascent Teotihuacán city.

The Basin witnessed a series of dramatic and striking demographic, political, and economic changes during the Early and Middle Classic. Politically, it was a period marked first by the eclipse of Cuicuilco as a political center (in part the product of a volcanic eruption that wiped out the town and its ecological base, the irrigated alluvial plain) and second by the spectacular and dramatic rise of Teotihuacán as an urban center of 125,000 people.

The increase of population at Teotihuacán was the product of a variety of factors, as we have seen: the probable expansion of the irrigation system in the Teotihuacán Valley to a total extent of 5,800 hectares, the political unification of the Basin of Mexico and subsequent displacement of population from small centers to the city, and the expansion of the political and economic orbits of the city to include areas outside of the Basin proper.

The internal population movement from the small settlements to the city apparently did not affect the southeastern portion of the Basin since Parsons's survey has revealed great numbers of small villages and several towns, but the indications are that there was some reduction of population between Phase Two of the Late Formative and the Terminal Formative. The center of balance during the Early and Middle Classic had obviously shifted to the drier north for the first time. In all probability this shift is related to the expansion of canal irrigation in that area. The settlement pattern data suggest that most of the Basin was still cultivated by using extensive techniques and with only a core of intensively cultivated land in the immediate vicinity of the city. On the west shore of the lake was another large settlement near Azcapotzalco that was probably based on a similar but smaller core.

The demographic picture for the Late Classic and Early Post-Classic period is still somewhat obscure. First, a large portion of the Basin, perhaps all of it, was tributary to Tula, a center located immediately to the north of the Basin of Mexico. Second, the period witnessed a rapid and striking decline of the city of Teotihuacán. Unfortunately, since we lack settlement pattern data for the area around Tula, we have no idea about the repercussions of these political events on local population profiles there. Not surprisingly, the Teotihuacán Valley witnessed a drastic reduction of population from 150,000 to perhaps 30,000 over a period of a century. It is certain, however, that this was a strictly local process related to the decline of the city of Teotihuacán as an economic and political center. In fact, the loss of population was probably related to the sudden and rapid rise of population in the Texcoco area. In other words, this was not so much a decline of total population but a process of displacement and more even distribution. In the Teotihuacán Valley, the Late Classic population was concentrated in a few large villages and small towns around the edge of the alluvial plain. In the Texcoco area, there were apparently two heavy clusters, one on the southern edge of the area and the other on the north.

The Late Post-Classic period witnessed a dramatic rise in population over the entire Basin. We believe that the population may have been as much as three times the Middle Classic peak. This is clearly related to the further expansion of three types of intensive agriculture that all originated as far back as Early Classic or Terminal Formative times— swamp reclamation, canal irrigation, and terracing.

Perhaps the most significant of these new developments in agriculture was that subsumed under the heading swamp reclamation. Aside from the small area around the springs of San Juan Teotihuacán, perhaps not exceeding 1,000 hectares, this approach to land use was essentially a phenomenon of the Late Post-Classic or Aztec period. By swamp reclamation, I mean a system in which the major technique was one of excavation of systems of drainage ditches and the construction of dikes to reduce the water content of waterlogged soils. Most of the Texcocan lakeshore plain was apparently not utilized for agriculture until Aztec times, and by 1519 this area had become the major agricultural resource of the city of Texcoco, the largest population center in the eastern half of the Basin of Mexico.

In its most elaborate form, swamp reclamation involved the colonization of the fresh water lakes themselves in the southern portion of the Basin of Mexico and involved a system of cultivation in which dikes and ditches were constructed and artificial islands (*chinampas*) were built within the deeper portions of the lake itself. Surveys by Armillas (personal communication) indicate that approximately 10,000 hectares

of land were reclaimed in the two fresh water lakes of Chalco-
Xochimilco at the time of the Spanish Conquest. According to my
calculations, based on contemporary production figures, an area this
size could have provided an annual maize ration for 150,000–200,000
people, if all of the land was planted in maize. The system reached its
climactic development in the late sixteenth century when a portion of
the salty Lake Texcoco was diked off, provided with sluice gates and
fresh water by means of a system of aqueducts from the nearby hills,
and converted to *chinampa* agriculture, (Palerm, 1961). The total
population capacity of all types of swamp reclamation in the Basin of
Mexico cannot yet be established, but it must have been well in excess
of 250,000–300,000 people, a figure exceeding the entire Terminal
Formative population.

The second major development was terrace agriculture, and in 1519
virtually all of the cultivated slopes were covered with terrace systems.
This system of farming, combined with permanent or floodwater
irrigation, was developed in the Texcoco piedmont probably by
Terminal Formative times and appeared in the Teotihuacán Valley
by Early Classic times.

With respect to canal irrigation, the situation is less clear because of
a lack of surveys in several portions of the basin where large canal
irrigation systems existed in 1519 (Coyoacán and Quauhtitlán, for
example). We have data on the history of the systems only for the
Teotihuacán Valley.

As the product of the expansion of these various systems of intensive
agriculture, the population of the Basin reached its peak by 1519, with
an estimated 1,500,000 inhabitants. This was also a period of maximal
development of urban society. The Aztec capital of Tenochtitlán was
at least as large as Middle Classic Teotihuacán; Texcoco probably was
substantially larger than Middle Classic Azcapotzalco; and there were
at least eight or nine additional communities, each with population in
excess of 10,000 inhabitants, and forty towns with populations ranging
from 1,000 to 8,000 inhabitants each. Contemporaneous with this urban
development was a process of political expansion in which Tenochtitlán
emerged rapidly as the capital of an empire which at its peak involved a
population of at least 5,000,000 to 6,000,000 people.

Two additional surveys have been conducted in other portions of the

Central Plateau, outside the Basin of Mexico. These are in the states of
Tlaxcala and Puebla. Snow (1969) has summarized the settlement
picture for the upper portion of the drainage of the Rio Zahuapán in
north-central Tlaxcala, a region that fell within the Conquest period
Tlaxcalan state. Demographically and agriculturally, this was a marginal
region even during that period. It is a hilly region susceptible to severe
erosion, has an annual rainfall comparable to the drier portions of the
Basin of Mexico, and is lacking in major irrigation resources. Furthermore, the region is above 2,200 meters and is therefore within the frost
zone. Snow states that he recorded 59 sites, but he does not tabulate
his sites by phase, nor does he explicitly provide us with a comparative
population figure; so here we can present only subjective impressions.
Formative occupation in the area is both late (no earlier than the Middle
Formative, Phase Three) and light, with only one Formative site
with ceremonial architecture (dating from the Late Formative period).
Sites were small and located on the tops and upper slopes of sedimentary
hills, a location comparable to the Middle Formative and Late Formative, Phase One sites in the Teotihuacán Valley. During the Early and
Middle Classic period, there was a definite population expansion with
three substantial centers, including ceremonial architecture and numerous smaller sites. The total impression, however, is one of a strikingly
rural area not well integrated into the Teotihuacán political and
economic system (for example, Terminal Formative ceramics continued
to be used in the area, combined with trade wares from Teotihuacán).
The sites tend to be located on the lower flanks of the sedimentary hills
within a short distance of the edge of the alluvial plains, locations
comparable to contemporary villages today. Some of the lowest-lying
areas are frequently waterlogged with heavy textured soils and were
apparently not cultivated until the introduction of the plow in Post-
Conquest times. Snow provides no specific data on either the Late
Classic or the Post-Classic occupation but implies that the settlements
were located in comparable situations to those in the Early and Middle
Classic. There is also a definite impression that the maximum population was achieved at the end of the sequence.

Tschol's survey (1966) includes a much more significant region in
terms of the culture history of the plateau—the southwestern portion of
Tlaxcala and the Cholula plain in adjacent Puebla. Unfortunately, we

have only a preliminary statement of the results of his survey. As in the case of Snow's survey, the area is above 2,200 meters, but with substantially higher rainfall (750–900 mm), and also is in an area of very extensive, deep soil alluvial plains and gently sloping piedmont. Furthermore, it is ideally located in terms of water for large-scale canal irrigation since the plain is immediately below the snow fields of Popocatepetl and Iztaccihuatl. Within it are the site of Cholula, one of the largest centers in Mesoamerican history, and Tlaxcala, the capital of the Conquest period state. Tschol estimates his survey area to be 60 by 50 km and reports the locations of 165 sites. He estimates, on the basis of the test sample, that the area probably contains between 400 and 600 sites, a figure that can undoubtedly be increased substantially if major chronological phases at each locality are classified as sites, as was done in the Teotihuacán Valley survey. Among his sample of 165 sites he notes 30 with civic centers of modest to large size (5 to 40 mounds each). No quantitative data are provided, however, that would enable us to obtain an accurate picture of population history, but he does state that the Late Formative sites are numerous and include substantial civic centers. The site of Amalucan near Puebla is probably only slightly smaller than the contemporary site of Cuicuilco in the Basin of Mexico. There was a definite reduction of the number of sites in the Early and Middle Classic phases, a phenomenon that coincides with the growth of Cholula into a major population center. Although we have virtually no settlement pattern data, much of the volume of the great pyramid at Cholula has been found (on the basis of recent excavations by Messmacher and later Acosta—personal communication) to actually consist of a huge Teotihuacán-style Middle Classic civic center, indicating the presence of a substantial population center. The process of movement from small settlements to a large single center strikingly parallels the events previously described for the Teotihuacán Valley.

Cholula continues as the major population center in this area throughout the Late Classic and Post-Classic periods, but, as in the case of the Basin of Mexico, there were a number of other major centers (at least at the time of the Conquest) such as Tlaxcala, Huejotzingo, and Atlixco. On the basis of Tschol's survey and documentary data, the population undoubtedly peaked at the time of the Spanish Conquest, and the scattered, additional data indicate a curve of increase between the Early Classic and the Late Post-Classic periods similar to that which I have defined for the Basin of Mexico. My data from documentary sources would suggest that perhaps 500,000 people resided in Tschol's survey area in 1519.

With respect to the agricultural history of the area, there are scant data. The problems of cultivation in this region are very similar to those faced by cultivators in the Basin of Mexico. At the time of the Conquest, Cholula was located within one of the largest irrigated plains in Mesoamerica, but there are no specific data on the history of this irrigation system. There is evidence of terracing in close association with civic centers in some of Tschol's Late Formative sites. At Amalucan, Fowler (1968) reports evidence of a Late Formative irrigation canal. The Late Formative centers are in areas of alluvial plain with access to irrigation water, and the scattered data suggest that the emergence of large civic centers in Late Formative times does relate to the expansion of canal irrigation. The fact that Early and Middle Classic Cholula is located in the same place as Aztec Cholula and their apparent nucleation into a single major center by Early Classic times would also seem to indicate that the concept of a core-hinterland pattern as defined for Teotihuacán is easily adaptable to the situation at Cholula as well. The Aztec period here, as in the Basin of Mexico, was a period of population climax and full utilization of all ecological zones.

These ecological processes are undoubtedly linked with the political and economic development of the area. Cholula was probably politically dependent on Teotihuacán for at least a century or two, but the architectural evidence suggests that toward the end, there were striking divergences in style from the buildings at Teotihuacán, presumably representing a final period of political autonomy. During the Late Classic–Early Post-Classic period (the chronology of the site is somewhat confused), the huge Pyramid of Quetzalcoatl was constructed, the largest building ever erected by American Indians, and, as I have noted it was a major population center at the time of the Spanish Conquest. Cholula therefore played a dominant political role in Central Mexican history for a period of 1,500 years.

South of the Basin of Mexico and the Cholula-Tlaxcala plain is a region of gentle escarpment with elevations ranging from 800 to 2,000 m, the present state of Morelos and the southwestern portion of Puebla.

The region is drained by a number of tributaries of the Rio Balsas (Atoyac, Nejapa, and the Amacusac). Within the region are extensive plains and relatively abundant resources for canal irrigation. Rainfall is comparable to that reported in the higher valleys to the north and is equally seasonal. The region has the added advantage that it is frost-free. At the time of the Conquest it was densely settled—I calculate a population of between 750,000 and 1,000,000 in an area of 8,000 km^2, a density comparable to that in the Basin of Mexico.

No intensive surveys have been conducted in this region. It is included here because of its undoubted significance in the early phase of agricultural development of the Central Mexican area. Ecologically, it is similar to the Valley of Oaxaca and the Valley of Tehuacán, and is located within the zone of early plant domestication. Theoretically, the population density should reveal a definite precocity during the Early and Middle Formative periods, as compared to higher regions like the Basin of Mexico, both in terms of population and socioeconomic evolution.

Grove (1968) does state that Early and Middle Formative sites are numerous in the Morelos portion of the area and records at least six sites with substantial residential areas, some with ceremonial architecture, and all probably with special cemeteries for individuals of especially high rank. Some of these features probably date as early as the Middle Formative, Phase Two. At least one other additional center of this type is known for western Puebla (Las Bocas).

The sixteenth-century census strongly suggests a population maximum at the end of the sequence, but in the absence of data for the Late Formative and Classic periods, little more can be said about population profiles. The Late Classic–Early Post-Classic center of Xochicalco, in terms of size, sophistication of architecture, and size of the residential area, is far beyond anything known for the Formative period and would suggest a large population, but we have no surveys to confirm this estimate.

The Lowland Maya Area

The Lowland Maya area is one of the most interesting areas in Mesoamerica with respect to its culture history. It was the setting of one of

the most spectacular and impressive regional developments in all of
Mesoamerica. Environmentally, this is a tropical region with considerable variation in the amount of annual rainfall and the degree to
which its distribution is seasonal, but it has a basic unity in that the
plant cover is tropical forest in varying degrees of density, height, and
botanical composition and in that it is entirely below 500 m above
sea level. The total area involved is on the order of 200,000 km^2. The
contemporary population and, according to a number of Spanish
sources, the immediate Post-Conquest population as well were swidden
farmers. There is some indication, as we shall see, that more intensive
practices were characteristic of Maya agriculture in Late Classic times.

The major outline of Maya history and the occupation of this huge
region are fairly well known. Lexicolinguistics and palynological
evidence suggest an initial occupation of the southern portion of the
area (known as the Petén) by incipient cultivators by 2000 b.c. (Vogt
1964; Cowgill et al. 1966). Between 900 and 750 b.c. a series of new
population movements into the region resulted in a substantial increase
in population and the introduction of pottery for the first time. Between
this period and approximately 500 b.c., the vast forests of the Yucatán
Peninsula were gradually colonized by the Maya. In some areas, by
this later date, the population density had reached a point where the
construction of the Mesoamerican-type, civic-ceremonial center was
feasible.

Around the time of Christ, there is evidence of a new influx of population from outside—in small groups, probably non-Maya, and from
the eastern highlands of Guatemala and adjacent Salvador—who
introduced new ceramic types, the calendrical system, and certain
architectural characteristics. The specific combination of architecture,
sculpture, and epigraphic style that archaeologically characterizes the
Lowland Maya area became fully developed by 300 a.c. as the product
of these local processes of population growth combined with external
influences. Between 300 and 900 a.d. this huge lowland area was the
scene of one of the most spectacular Mesoamerican Classic civilizations
with at least a dozen gigantic ceremonial-civic centers, scores of smaller
but still imposing ones, hundreds of small ceremonial centers, tens of
thousands of hamlets, and a population that must have numbered in the
millions. The densest-settled area (and locale of the largest site of all—

Tikal) and the scene of the most intensive building projects was a heartland comprised of the northern portion of the Petén and the south central part of the Yucatán peninsula that embraces about 75,000 km^2 of land. Between 900 and 1200 A.D. this huge heartland was virtually abandoned for settlement and has continued to be abandoned until the present time. The Spaniards found a relatively dense population ringing this demographic vacuum on all sides in what is today the state of Yucatán, coastal Campeche, Quintana Roo, eastern Tabasco, western Honduras, and the foothills and plain immediately north of the Guatemala highlands.

This spectacular decline over such a large area has been a major problem of Mayan archaeology. Some writers have doubted that it did occur and have suggested that the Maya, through internal conflicts between peasants and their rulers, simply stopped building ceremonial centers but continued to live in the area in small agricultural settlements. Surveys comparable to the Basin of Mexico survey have not been conducted over a large enough area to establish definitely the validity of the argument of a major population loss, but there is a series of intensive surveys of small local areas which tends to justify the conclusion that, indeed, there was a massive decline. Unfortunately, some of these surveys, at Altar de Sacrificios, Tzibilchaltun, and Tikal, for example, have not been published in detail but only in summary fashion, so only rough evaluations of the data are possible here. The only fully reported survey is that of Willey et al. (1965) for the Belize Valley in British Honduras.

The Belize Valley is a river valley with a narrow ribbon of alluvial land (approximately 1 km wide) bordered by limestone hills. The researchers surveyed, at various levels of intensity, the alluvial plain for a total surface area of approximately 60 km^2. The drainage basin, in other words, the area up to the watershed on each side, covered approximately 600 km^2, and spot surveys were conducted in the neighboring hilly zone. In this area Maya settlement consists of a virtually continuous narrow strip of houses along the alluvium, with very few settlements in the neighboring hilly zone. For the climax of the population of the valley, the authors suggest an economic pattern in which the alluvial plain was used for commercial crops like cacao and maize, and other subsistence crops were grown in the nearby limestone hills using a

swidden system. On the basis of their local surveys, they estimate a
probable total population for the 600 km² of 24,000. On the basis of
the distribution of major ceremonial centers, they also estimate that
there were four polities in the area in Late Classic times with an average
population of 6,000 each. The graph presented in Figure 5.7 summarizes
the population curve estimated by the authors of this report (ibid. 1965).
The occupation by sedentary farmers begins in the Middle Formative,
Phase Three. Sites consisted of widely spaced hamlets. Ceremonial
centers are absent. The Late Formative Period witnessed a 25 to 35
percent increase of population and the appearance for the first time of
small temple platforms. The Terminal Formative and Proto-Classic
phases were times of rapid change: the population doubled; a complex
of new ceramic traits from highland Guatemala or Salvador appear in
the sequence; and for the first time there is evidence of ranking as a
principle in the social organization. Population seems to have remained
at roughly the Proto-Classic level throughout most of the Early and
Middle Classic phases and then to have gone through a final, minor
spurt of growth during the Late Classic. Following the Late Classic
period at approximately 900 to 1000 A.D., there is evidence of a major

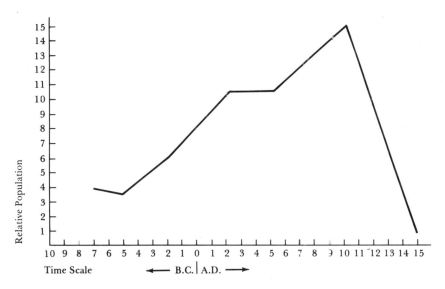

Figure 5.7. Belize Valley

population decline. Potsherds of the Early Post-Classic phase are found in minor concentrations on many of the house mounds, but there is no indication that any major construction took place either on the mounds or in ceremonial-civic centers. Probably the population had dropped down to a very low level, and a highly mobile population occupied and reoccupied the older Classic mounds at periodic intervals, using them as platforms for simple types of houses. By Late Post-Classic times there is no evidence of occupation in the Belize Valley. The profile then agrees with the impression of a total population decline of this heartland area.

At Tikal, a critical site since it is in the virtual center of the Maya heartland, detailed survey data are available only for the area of 16 km^2 around the civic center (see Figure 5.8). Aside from this, a series of tests have been conducted on strips in all four directions from the edges of the intensively surveyed area for an additional 12 km, providing somewhat wider coverage. Unfortunately, none of these data is published in detail. On the basis of the brief reports published to date and personal

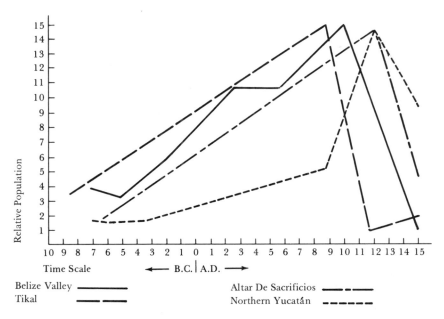

Figure 5.8. Lowland Maya Area.

communication with various individuals of the Tikal project staff, the following picture seems to emerge. During Phase Three of the Middle Formative and Phase One of the Late Formative periods, there is evidence of small hamlets of farmers in and around the site of Tikal. By Late Formative, Phase Two this population had increased substantially, and ceremonial building first appears at the site. The Terminal Formative and Proto-Classic phases witnessed a duplicate of the events that I have described for the Belize Valley: the arrival of a new elite group from highland Guatemala or Salvador, definite population growth, and a rapid development of the formal characteristics of Maya elite culture. By Early Classic times, a dense population was distributed over an area of approximately 165 km^2.

Major architectural effort characterized the history of Tikal at this time, and the scattered references in the literature suggest a substantial population increase in the Late Classic period. There is also evidence of concentration and resettlement of population within a compact area measuring 65 km^2. Haviland (1969) estimates the population of this core at 39,000. I would reduce this to 26,000, since I feel his average figure for the nuclear family is much too high (5.7). Given the conditions of growing population pressure characteristic of the final phase of the Classic period at Tikal, I would prefer averages somewhere around or slightly below 4.0—an average family size in areas of population pressure today in the Central Plateau. He estimated a density of 100 per km^2 in the remaining peripheral area (99 km^2), giving a population of 9,900. This I would reduce to 6,600, making a total of 32,600. The density of population in the total area would then average 200 per km^2. All of these calculations assumed that all Late Classic houses were simultaneously occupied, a dubious assumption.

The Late Classic period was a period of enormous building activities, and since the site in its present form was built during that period, the suggestion that there was a final population maximum achieved during this period is further strengthened. This is also supported by evidence from test surveys by Bullard (1960) in the northeastern Petén.

Again, as in the case of the Belize Valley, the surveys show a striking and dramatic drop in population toward the end of the Classic period. During the Post-Classic period there is evidence of minor ceremonial activities at the site, presumably then in ruins, that involved resetting stelae, but no building activities. The only population remaining in the general northern Petén area at the time of the Conquest was a small cluster around Lake Petén, approximately 30 km southwest of Tikal. One difference between the profile of decline at Tikal compared to the Belize Valley is that it seems to have occurred at least a century earlier at Tikal. On the basis of test pits in the house mounds around Tikal, Haviland (1969) suggests a 95 percent population drop between Tepeu 2 and 3 times or between 800 and 900 A.D.

Scattered evidence from other sites and other areas suggests that the very center of the Classic Maya area suffered an earlier population decline than those areas located in more peripheral positions. For example, at Altar de Sacrificios near the foothills of highland Guatemala, there is evidence of a substantial Early Post-Classic occupation, even involving some migration from Tabasco. This is followed by a very sudden and rapid decline in the Late Post-Classic period. On the peripheries of the Maya area, where the Spaniards report a substantial population, at the time of the Conquest, the evidence is for abandonment of the old Classic centers, but new centers were established and new building activities characterized the succeeding Post-Classic period. In this area there may have been some population decline a century or so prior to the Conquest, but if so it was in no way comparable to the decline that occurred in the Post-Classic period in the heartland. For example, I would estimate that at least 750,000 to 800,000 people still lived in the state of Yucatán, Quintana Roo and Campeche, at the time of the Spanish Conquest; between 300,000 and 400,000 people were still living in the eastern part of Tabasco; and perhaps an equal number in western Honduras. What we seem to have is an overall population depression in the Lowland Maya area, with its most intense manifestation in the center where the population was established earliest and where, during Late Classic times, it reached its densest concentrations. Around this heartland the effects of this overall depopulation decrease in a series of concentric rings.

With respect to the agriculture history of the Lowland Maya, we have very inadequate data from which to work. There are fundamental disagreements as to the nature of the basic crop complex and degree of intensity of cultivation. The usual model that has been applied by archaeologists to the Classic Maya is one derived from studies of con-

temporary Mayan agriculture in the state of Yucatán. This involves a
long-cycle swidden system with a ratio of cultivation to fallow of
approximately 1 to 4, with maize as the staple food. Yields of maize
per hectare are substantially higher in the wetter Petén and the regrowth of forest somewhat faster, so that the cycle in this area reduces
to about 1 to 3 around the occupied area of Lake Petén. In Tabasco on
unusually fertile and humid alluvial soils, double crops may be produced
with much higher yields (up to 3,000 kg per hectare if both crops are
included). The cycle can be reduced to 1 to 2 and still maintain these
high yields. If one allows for areas of uncultivated or marginal land, the
population permitted over this area probably ranges from 10 to 50 per
km^2. Some writers have argued that if root crops were utilized, these
estimates could be substantially raised. I would estimate (making
allowance for the lower-calorie yield of root crops versus grains per
weight) that these figures could be raised to perhaps 30 to 150 per km^2,
assuming the same pattern of cycling.

A major question is the possibility that the Maya may have reduced
the swidden cycle substantially and possibly even reached the point
where lands were continuously cropped. This would, of course, result
in a reduction of yield per hectare unless fertilization, irrigation, or
other means of maintaining high yields were available, and it is difficult
to see how these could have been available because of the lack of
animals and of water resources. If the soils can sustain continuous
cultivation in this area and still produce respectable crops, then even
though the yields per hectare would have declined, the total amount of
food could have been increased. Problems involved in this reconstruction
are twofold. First, one reason why the cycling system in vogue in the
area today is scheduled as it is, is to avoid the problems of the gradual
increase of density of certain troublesome weeds, particularly grasses.
The amount of labor in weeding increases enormously as fields are
successively cultivated. It is a serious question whether the Maya could
or would have attempted to resolve this problem with their Neolithic
technology. Second, in the absence of experimental work on the soils of
the area, we do not know whether high enough yields can be maintained in fields under continuous cropping to maintain a balanced and
stable family economy, and we have little information on the overall
deleterious effects on soil fertility involved in successive cropping. By a

combination of root crops plus some reduction of the cycle, if not continuous cropping, the population potential could be increased to perhaps double our previous figures. If the possibility of continuous cropping is considered, the density could possibly have been raised as high as 400 to 500 per km^2.

Another possible element in the Maya ecological system that complicates the picture is the possibility of a permanent subsistence tree crop. This would, of course, be the ideal solution to the Mayan subsistence crop problem, since the natural vegetation of the forest— trees—thrive on poorer soils than either annual grain or root crops, and land would then be kept in permanent cultivation. Until recently no one has suggested a possible tree crop. Many years ago Lundell (1937), in his study of plant geography of the northern Petén, noticed the close association of ramon trees with clusters of Maya house mounds. Puleston (personal communication) has recently presented a convincing argument that each Maya farmer, at least by Late Classic times, had a grove of ramon trees near his house and that the nuts were stored in underground chambers called *chultunes*, processed into flour, and ultimately into tortillas and other breadlike foods. He suggests this was the major food supply of the Late Classic Maya—at least of the lower class. The demographic potential of tree crops would be considerably higher than either grain or root crop cultivation using swidden systems since such land would be under continuous cultivation, and yields per hectare approximate those of the annual crops. In his model Puleston argues that ramon was the major calorie source, perhaps as important as maize is today (estimated by Steggarda 1941 as making up 80 percent of the diet of the Yucatán Maya). In his view much of the agricultural land around Tikal in Late Classic times was no longer in use, and the agricultural activities of the Maya of Tikal were concentrated within a small, compact area of virtually continuous ramon groves that coincided roughly with the Late Classic settlement area previously defined. Frankly, this interpretation, at least in the extreme manner in which it is presented, does not seem plausible. Tree crops are notoriously variable from year to year in the yield of their fruit. It is doubtful that the Maya would have placed full reliance on so variable a food resource. It seems more likely that there was at Tikal a multicrop, multisystem approach, with ramon orchards within the settled area combined with outlying root crops and maize fields cultivated by the swidden system.

Viewing the Maya ecological system diachronically yields the following outline. From the beginning of the agricultural exploitation of the area, the population probably had a large and variable crop complex as do the Maya today. During the Formative and probably as late as the Early Classic period, the population density was probably low enough so that a relatively long-cycle swidden system based on maize was the major system in vogue. Under the extreme population pressure of the Late Classic period, the Maya gradually shifted away from a long-cycle, maize-based swidden system to a short-cycle, root crop one, combined with permanent ramon orchards. The shift in settlement patterns between Early and Late Classic times is probably linked to these changes, and we can view the Tikal subsistence pattern as one of infield-outfield cropping, as Wolf (1966) uses the term, with the ramon grove as the infield crop. Evidence of palynology and studies of faunal remains strongly suggest that the lands were not cropped continuously, but that some version of a short-cycle swidden system was probably in use. There is evidence also of an increased reliance on seafoods (Lange 1969) brought through a regular trade system from the coast (a pattern made possible by the tightly organized political system in Late Classic times), which probably relates to the shift of food supply from grain to root crops and consequent decrease in protein vegetable foods. Ramon nuts could have provided an abundance of vegetable protein, but the evidence of stature reduction, nutritional deficiency, and general weakening of bone structure among the lower classes in the skeletal remains indicates that the Maya were having serious nutritional problems toward the end of the period and is further proof that ramon nuts were not the major source of food. The correlation of ramon groves with habitation sites is characteristic only of the northeastern Petén and consequently this solution to population growth was apparently not applied generally over the Maya heartland. Presumably, a combination of root crops and maize, based on short-cycle swidden cultivation, was in vogue in the balance of the area. By a combination of the various crops and systems of cultivation, the population density over much of the central portions of the Maya area probably did reach well over 100 per km^2, possibly reaching as high as 200 per km^2 in some pressure areas. The density was probably considerably lower in the peripheries where long-term swidden cycling based on maize was most probably the system of agriculture in use.

This brings us to the explanation of the peculiar demographic profile previously described. The loss of population in the core area is clearly not the same kind of process as the decline of population following the fall of Teotihuacán in the Teotihuacán Valley. The latter was essentially the product of changing local political fortunes, and of course we have the rapid recovery in Aztec times to roughly its former level. A variety of explanations have been offered for the Maya demise: internal troubles and wars, wars with foreign groups, earthquakes, changing climate (in some cases increasing rainfall is blamed, in others decreasing rainfall), problems with water supply, disease, and so forth. The first two (internal troubles and wars) are really symptoms and products of other processes rather than basic causes. There is no convincing evidence of earthquakes as the cause, nor are climatic changes justified by the palynological evidence. Water problems could hardly explain the decline in areas of abundant surface drainage, as in the Usumacinta River system, and there is no convincing evidence that disease was the factor other than the nutritional problems already noted.

The best explanation for the rapid abandonment of such a large area is still that of a critical change in relationship between the Maya and the environment. Two processes could explain the decline of population. One model is that increasing conversion to grassland by the reduction of swidden cycle (given the Neolithic level of Maya technology) stimulated migration to less densely settled areas; another model blames depletion of soil fertility under more intensive utilization. The whole must be seen in a context of the evidence of an increasingly more stratified sociopolitical structure, the increased size of the non-food-producing class, and the intense competition among the Maya polities over the key resource—land. As long as the upper classes were able to maintain control over the supporting population, the increasing demands placed on the peasant to produce surpluses and hence the increased burden of agricultural labor required to meet his own subsistence needs would not have resulted in migration. The Lowland Maya in the central area probably had moved to a very short cycle grass-fallowing system of the type discussed by Boserup. The ultimate result was probably intensive erosion and soil depletion, and even the tight control exercised by the upper class was unable to prevent a sustained and relatively rapid migration to the peripheries. The fact that the process started in the areas of densest settlement makes sense in this context.

Guatemalan Highlands—Pacific Coast

The Guatemalan Highlands and adjacent piedmont and Pacific-coastal plain is a topographically diverse region. The highlands occur as a series of three parallel east-west chains of mountains between which are a great number of small intermontane basins. The region differs from its Mexican counterpart in a number of respects. It is a generally humid area; much of the Guatemalan highlands has an annual rainfall exceeding 1,000 mm in stations located on the valley floor. The vegetation is primarily conifer and oak forest. In contrast to the Mexican highlands, few valleys are above the frost line; most of them, including the Valley of Guatemala, lie between 1,100 and 1,800 meters above sea level.

The northernmost massif is an ancient limestone formation. Between it and the central range are deep canyonlike valleys of the Rio Motagua system. The two other ranges are of volcanic origin with an older, more eroded middle range and a younger, steep-sided range fronting on the Pacific coast. Rainfall on the Pacific escarpment ranges up to as high as 5,000 mm on the middle slopes, drops to 3,000 mm on the piedmont, and generally averages from 1,200 to 2,000 mm on the coastal plain. Prior to alteration by cultivators, the Pacific coastal plain, piedmont, and lower escarpment were covered by a dense tropical forest. Today most of the coastal plain has been converted to artificial grassland for cattle grazing.

Since 1968 the author and Joseph Michels have been directing an intensive survey, combined with excavation, in one of these highland valleys, the Valley of Guatemala. The valley is really a terraced plateau with drainage flowing to both the Pacific and Atlantic sides. Elevations of the terraces vary from 1,800 m in the Canchon section of the valley and drop to 1,200 m near Lake Amatitlán. The City of Guatemala is on the 1,400-to 1,600-m terrace and is located within the most extensive alluvial plain in the valley. The plateau surface is generally deeply scarred by barrancas, and level land frequently consists of tonguelike pieces of land between barrancas. The valley is located between the two volcanic ranges, and the Guatemala City station records an average annual rainfall of approximately 1,200 mm. Even today many of the steep slopes are covered with conifer forests.

Our project involved excavation and surveys at the major site in the valley, Kaminaljuyu, and surveys of the surrounding area. The survey area is approximately 1,000 km². The analysis to follow is highly tentative since the project is not yet completed.

Shook (1952) conducted a survey and located seventy-three sites, including Kaminaljuyu. These sites are found well distributed over the survey area as a whole. He also provides mean dates and ranges of dates for each site, based on surface collections. All sites, however, with the exception of the Las Charcas phase, have civic-ceremonial centers; therefore the sample is biased in favor of the larger sites. Our survey has revealed at least twenty to thirty additional sites of this type.

Our major survey effort, however, has involved a systematic examination to locate the smaller rural communities. The valley has been divided into forty 25-km²-grid units. We intend to survey at least ten of them intensively as a sample. To date, only three units have been completed.

On the basis of the data at hand, Shook's survey, the test squares, plus our work at Kaminaljuyu itself, we would reconstruct the demographic and settlement pattern history of the valley as follows (see Figure 5.9). The earliest known agricultural occupation of the valley occurs during either the Middle Formative, Phase Three or the Late Formative, Phase One (the Las Charcas phase may be as late as the latter or as early as the former). All known sites of this phase consist of small rural settlements, and no definite ceremonial or civic architecture is associated with them. Shook's overall survey reveals fourteen sites, all outside the three test squares. At Kaminaljuyu, Las Charcas occupation has been defined in three or four localities. Intensive survey reveals a total of only five settlements in the 75-km² test area. The density of settlement was obviously quite low. Sites are found, however, all over the survey area. There is a slight tendency for them to cluster in the alluvial plain around Kaminaljuyu and on the El Canchon terrace.

For Late Formative times, the Shook survey indicates a definite and significant population increase. Approximately eleven sites with ceremonial-civic centers were located, not including Kaminaljuyu. These

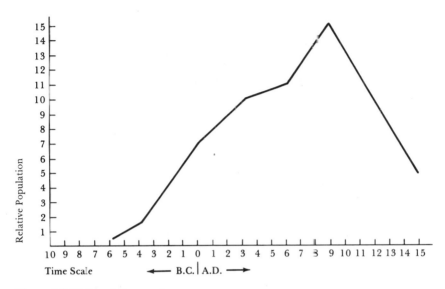

Figure 5.9. Valley of Guatemala.

ceremonial centers consisted of elongated, avenuelike plazas defined by high, steep-sided mounds and low earth platforms. Excavations at Kaminaljuyu have indicated that the higher mounds are burial mounds, and at the site we can define at least four of these ceremonial plaza complexes. The intensive survey to date is not definitive with respect to the impression of a substantial population growth, since only seven Late Formative hamlets versus five for the Middle Formative have been located. Most of the civic centers are located, as we noted, in two areas, and neither of these areas has yet been included in the intensive survey, so this discrepancy may be more apparent than real

During the Terminal Formative period, there is convincing evidence for a massive increase in population. The type of center now shifts to a relatively squarish plaza defined by temple pyramids and elite residential platforms—both constructed of earth—some including three or four mounds, others up to eleven. Each is the center of a small densely settled ward at Kaminaljuyu or a complete community in the sustaining area. At least a dozen such communities have been defined within the 5 km^2 that make up the site of Kaminaljuyu, along with a number of hamlets without ceremonial architecture. We estimate that the 5-km^2

area of Kaminaljuyu probably had a residential population of from 3,000 to 6,000 people at this time. Aside from this, at least seven small ceremonial centers are located outside Kaminaljuyu but within adjacent test squares; an additional seven are found scattered throughout the rest of the valley.

Interestingly, the Canchon Plateau, so important in the earlier phases, was abandoned for settlement at this time. In our three test squares, the number of hamlets rises to twenty-five, a striking and substantial increase.

The Early and Middle Classic period was a time of intensive contact and ultimately economic and political domination of the valley by Teotihuacán. At Kaminaljuyu itself, this is reflected by a shift of civic-center type to a single massive, acropolislike complex built in Teoti-huacán style. Along with this change there is convincing evidence of a gathering of the wardlike divisions of the Terminal Formative settlement into a single large settlement around the acropolis, possibly covering a total area of 100 to 150 hectares. In other words, it appears that the Kaminaljuyu community as a whole witnessed simply a rearrangement rather than any sizable increase in total population, and there is no evidence, as we shall see, that the sustaining rural population was moved to the center as was the case in the Valley of Teotihuacán. During the Early Classic period, small outlying centers were found in the surround-ing area, six located near Kaminaljuyu in the alluvial plain and eight others at greater distances. By Middle Classic times this number was reduced to three, and all were strung along a straight line between Kaminaljuyu and the route to the Pacific coastal plain, thus suggesting that they had some connection with a trade network. It looks as though virtually all ceremonial and civic construction during the Middle Classic period was concentrated at the acropolis at Kaminaljuyu.

Not only is there no evidence of a massing of the rural population at the Kaminaljuyu center, but there even seems to have been some growth in the total number of hamlets. In our test survey, we recorded twenty-nine Early Classic settlements and thirty-three Middle Classic ones.

The Late Classic period witnessed the rapid decline of Kaminaljuyu as a center with perhaps half a dozen small civic-ceremonial precincts widely dispersed through the site. Each consists of two adjacent plaza complexes, one functioning as a ball court, the other as a combination elite residence and temple. Small ceremonial centers of this type are found densely clustered in the general area of Kaminaljuyu, approximately thirty of them within a total area of only 100 km^2. Another cluster of eleven, including a huge site with thirty to forty structures, is found in the southwestern part of the valley near Lake Amatitlán, and three others are found on the Canchon Plateau, a grand total of about forty-four in all. The impression is one of a breakdown of centralized political control but with an increase in total civic-ceremonial construction and of population. The fact that forty-three hamlets were located in the three test squares supports the argument of a population increase.

The Post-Classic population and settlement pattern is characterized by some obvious and striking changes. First of all, Kaminaljuyu was abandoned as a population center, and a large new center emerged at Chinautla. This center consisted of at least forty public buildings arranged in several groups strung along the top of a narrow ridge with precipitous slopes on all sides. Shook's survey reported four other smaller centers in the southern part of the valley, all located on defensible positions. Surveys and excavations at Chinautla have revealed that the site is composed of a series of discrete civic centers, each made up of pyramids, temples, and elite residences and very comparable in their functional characteristics to the Terminal Formative and Late Classic civic centers. As in the latter cases, each is associated with a small, densely settled residential area. Because of the requirements for defense and the character of topography at Chinautla, these tend to merge together, forming a single settlement, but in any case the total concentration of population at Chinautla did not amount to more than a few thousand people. The ridge upon which the site is located is part of a large area on the north edge of the alluvial plain of Kaminaljuyu, which is composed of steep ravines and flat-top ridges. Preliminary surveys of this area indicate that each of the flat-topped ridges has a series of small, hamletlike settlements pertaining to this period. Apparently the requirements for defense involved a displacement of small settlements to the vicinity of the fortress-ceremonial center. The dependent sites were within easy reach of the center and only a few hours walk from the fertile, deep-soil plain around Kaminaljuyu. This skewed distribution of population increases the problems of estimating the total population of the valley during the Post-Classic period.

In spite of this problem, we feel that there is evidence of a definite and rather sharp total population decline of the valley at this time. Our three test strips, none of which is very close to Chinautla, reveal a total of sixteen hamlets.

In highland Guatemala today there is a striking variation in the degree of intensity of cultivation, certainly linked with population pressure and probably with variations in soil and vegetation charac-teristics as well. There are areas where long-cycle fallow systems are in vogue, others where short cycles are used, and a few areas where the land is cultivated every year, particularly around Quetzaltenango. In the latter area all of the hillsides around the valley are thoroughly worked over by iron hoes in a system of contour hoeing—a technique for controlling erosion on hillsides, similar to contour plowing. Pop-ulation density in the highlands today varies from a few people per square kilometer up to several hundred. A major problem is the appli-cability of this situation to the pre-Hispanic period. We suspect that much of the cultivation in highland Guatemala throughout all pre-Hispanic periods was of the long-cycle type. This impression is based upon established facts: the small size of the civic-ceremonial centers in all periods for the entire area and the demographic situation at the time of the Spanish Conquest. On the basis of Miles's (1957) study of the sixteenth-century population of the general region of the Valley of Guatemala and on projections back to the Conquest, which are based on my studies of the sixteenth-century demography, it is doubtful that the valley had a population exceeding 5,000 to 10,000 people at the time of the Spanish Conquest. This estimate is supported by our archae-ological survey data, preliminary as it is. This would suggest a maximum population (during the Late Classic period) of perhaps 15,000 to 30,000 people. If our three test strips (forty-four hamlets in an area of 75 km²) are typical of the valley as a whole, then these estimates are reasonable. For example, none of the hamlets could have had a population exceeding 100 people and probably averaged only 50 to 60 inhabitants. Even assuming all Late Classic hamlets were occupied simultaneously, we would have a density on the average of only 30 people per km², or 30,000 for the entire valley. This is a density well within the potential of long-cycle swidden agriculture. Our arguments are supported by pollen profiles from Amatitlán that not only confirm our population profile but indicate the use of swidden techniques throughout the history of occupation of the area. This conclusion is also supported by the fact that we have not located any archaeological examples of agricultural terracing anywhere in the area. The only exception is a Middle Classic site on the south slopes above Lake Amatitlán where the terraces seem to have been constructed, not for agricultural purposes, but as part of the residential area of the community.

The overall picture of population history for the Guatemalan highlands as a whole is unknown. Scattered data (see Borhegyi 1965 and Shook 1952) would indicate that a substantial Late and Terminal Formative population resided over most of the volcanic region. Whether the succeeding Classic period witnessed further growth is not known. It seems doubtful that the Post-Classic population as a whole suffered a decline comparable to our Valley of Guatemala graph since kingdoms or large chiefdoms are reported by the Spaniards, centered at Utatlan, Iximche, and Zaculeu.

The evidence from the northern limestone ranges, intermontane basins, and Petén foothills, however, does seem to show a divergent history from that of the volcanic basins to the south. Adams's Cotzal Valley survey (1965), plus earlier data by Smith and Kidder (1951) from around Nebaj, show a very marginal Formative occupation restricted to a few Late Formative rural settlements, and the population does not really build up to a respectable size (at which point moderately large sites with civic-ceremonial architecture also appear) until the Late Classic and Post-Classic.

General surveys of the Rio Negro portion of the area by Smith (1955), in which approximately sixty-six sites with civic-ceremonial precincts were located, agree with this picture, and his surveys would also indicate a major population buildup in Post-Classic times.

The major mountain chains of highland Guatemala extend westward into the Mexican state of Chiapas, and a survey conducted by Adams (1961) around San Cristóbal in the limestone valleys of that region shows a population profile that parallels to an extraordinary degree the corresponding profiles from Guatemala.

If we are correct in our assessment of the history of the Maya lowlands, the question may be raised "What about the effects of population growth and increasingly more intensive cultivation of other tropical forest areas of Mesoamerica?" Unfortunately, there are very few areas where we have even a rough picture of population history.

One of these is the Pacific coast and piedmont of Guatemala. Topographically this area consists of a wide, relatively flat coastal plain shifting to a narrow, gently sloping lower piedmont and ultimately to a steep escarpment. At the time of the Spanish conquest there is convincing evidence that the coastal plain was virtually uninhabited, the piedmont still had a respectable population, and the escarpment was densely settled.

Coe and Flannery (1967) divide the coastal plain into two segments, a coastal zone proper, extending 20 km inland, and an inland strip. In their publication they present a settlement frequency chart that can be roughly converted to a population profile. Unfortunately, the chart is based simply on a count of sites without making allowance for variations in site size. On the basis of subjective statements by the authors, we have reconstructed a population profile for a 130-km^2 test area as follows (see Figure 5.10). During the Middle Formative, Phases Two and Three, there was a concentration of settlement near the offshore lagoons, estuaries, and river mouths consisting of small villages or hamlets with a mixed riparian-agricultural economy. In the succeeding Middle Formative, Phase Three and Late Formative, Phase One, the sites become larger, and more of them occur well inland from the beach. They also report large earth mounds from this time period. The population was several times that of the earlier phase. Following this peak, Coe and Flannery report a decline in population—in the succeeding Late Formative, Phase Two, the Terminal Formative, and the Early Classic phases. In Late Classic times there was an explosive growth of population to a new and greater peak, far in excess of the Middle Formative, involving numerous sites with large numbers of earth mounds. This is followed by the virtual disappearance of population we noted for the Post-Classic period. Shook (1965), although he does not provide quantitative data, conducted numerous surveys along several river systems in the coastal plain. He did not make any distinction between the divisions of the plain suggested by Coe and Flannery. However, he does agree with them in that he sees two major peaks of population: an earlier one

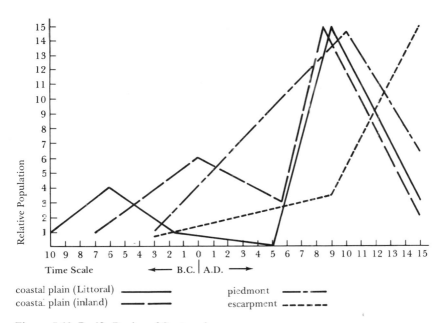

Figure 5.10. Pacific Region of Guatemala.

(which, however, probably reaches its peak in Late Formative, Phase Two and Terminal Formative times) that includes numerous sites with large mounds and a substantial population decline in the Early and Middle Classic periods, and a second, much higher peak during the Late Classic. Shook (1965) also agrees with Flannery and Coe that there was a massive population decline during the succeeding Post-Classic period.

Shook did not sort out the lower piedmont as a distinct province, but our impressions are that the Formative population was considerably less in density than on the coastal plain and that the history of the area shows a steady increase through the Late and Terminal Formative and the Early, Middle, and Late Classic periods; and that the Early Classic decline, which is apparent on the coastal plain, is not characteristic of the piedmont. The area seems still to have had a substantial settlement during the Post-Classic period but probably not comparable to the Late Classic maximum. At the time of the Conquest it was a center of commercial production of cacao and an extension of the province of Xoconusco in neighboring Chiapas.

The escarpment above the piedmont had a strikingly different population profile, with only small settlements during the Late Formative and with a steady rise in population through the various Classic periods, reaching a maximum population at the end. It is only during this final Post-Classic population maximum that substantial civic-ceremonial centers occur in this area, and they are not comparable to those in the piedmont and coastal plain.

With respect to agricultural history, we have little reliable information. Swidden agriculture based on maize and root crops as staples was undoubtedly the major system of cultivation through much of the history of this area, with the addition of commercial cacao grown on the piedmont. The population profiles are of considerable interest, both in terms of the cycling evidence and as compared to one another. The area was settled earlier than the Petén by sedentary farmers and apparently some centuries earlier than the neighboring highland valleys like the Valley of Guatemala. A relatively dense population was achieved strikingly earlier than in either the highland area or the Petén, as early as the Middle Formative. It is tempting to relate the two peaks of population represented in the coastal plain profile to a process of savanna incursion and forest recovery. The soils in the plain are unusually fertile compared to most tropical lowland areas, so that soil depletion was probably not a factor in the explanation of these cycles. As one goes through the various major periods of population history of the area, one gets the picture of an overall shift of population from the coastal plain to the piedmont and ultimately to the escarpment. Because of its much heavier rainfall, the piedmont would be an area where grass succession would be an extremely slow process and would occur only under conditions of extremely high population density. My impression of the coastal plain is that the conditions in this area, in terms of both soils and rainfall, probably are highly conducive to a relatively rapid shift from forest to savanna, and that the latter would emerge even under moderate population density conditions—this in sharp contrast to the situation in the Petén.

When compared to the graph from the Petén, the doubling cycle is of particular interest. We believe that it probably relates to the fact that the total population growth in the Pacific coastal plain was more rapid and earlier, thus providing room for a possible double peaking and retraction of population in response to grassland succession. In the case of the Petén, a substantial population did not occur until the Late Formative and Terminal Formative periods; thus, in effect, there was room for only one major climax. There are indications in the fact that the Lake Petén area was recolonized late in the Post-Classic period that the Petén area may have been getting set for a second major population growth when the Spanish conquest occurred.

In viewing the Guatemala-Chiapas Highlands and the Pacific Coastal plain as a whole, we seem to have a distinct gradient of population growth with the coastal plains as the most precocious area. The volcanic region shows a later, more sustained buildup, and the limestone region a strikingly retarded growth profile. There is also a strong possibility that some of the Post-Classic buildup in the latter area is related to the depopulation of the nearby Petén.

The Southern Mexican Highlands

The Tehuacán Valley in southeastern Puebla was one of the centers of early plant domestication in the New World. The valley is located between 1,500 and 1,600 m above sea level and has an annual rainfall that averages around 500 mm. MacNeish (1964) has presented a brief summary of the history of the occupation of the valley from the first utilization by a hunting and gathering population up to the time of the Spanish Conquest. He has also provided us with a series of relative population estimates for each of the major time periods represented in his study.

After a long period of incipient cultivation extending from 7200 to 3400 B.C., the local variety of maize became productive enough to permit sedentary residence (see Figure 5.11). Around 2300 B.C. ceramics appear in the region, and the Early Formative period begins (to follow the chronological system used here). MacNeish estimates a population of between 480 and 960 for the valley at this time, residing in a number of small villages. By the Middle Formative, Phase One, the villages had from 100 to 300 inhabitants. During the succeeding Middle Formative, Phase Two, community stratification appears for the first time, with

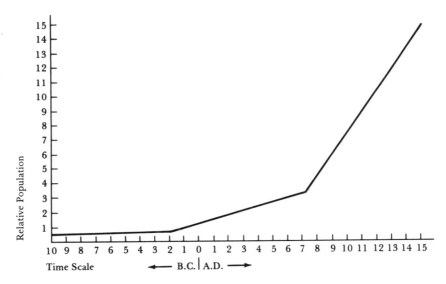

Figure 5.11. Valley of Tehuacán.

large villages serving as centers of small districts that include small villages as dependent settlements. Ceremonial-civic centers were constructed in the larger settlements. By the end of the Late Formative, Phase Two, the population had risen to approximately 1,000 to 3,000 people. During the equivalent of our Terminal Formative, Proto-Classic, Early and Middle Classic phases, these centers evolved into hilltop towns with large pyramids, ball courts, plazas, and elite residences. MacNeish estimates the population by the end of this long period at between 12,050 and 24,000 people. The maximum population was achieved at the end of the final period, which includes our Late Classic and Post-Classic, and the maximum population is estimated at 60,000 to 120,000 people.

The profile is somewhat peculiar in the steepness of this final population spurt. During the incipient agricultural period (Early Formative and Middle Formative, Phase One), the population apparently cultivated the naturally moist soils of alluvial terraces; by as early as the Middle Formative, Phase Two, small-scale irrigation appeared; and during the Classic and Post-Classic period, irrigation systems became considerably larger and more complex. The Tehuacán Valley, because it was both warmer and drier than the Central Plateau, probably never was an area of extensive cultivation, but intensive use of small, naturally humid lands apparently characterized even the earliest phase of its agricultural development.

The Valley of Oaxaca covers a total area of 3,375 km^2. Of this total, 700 km^2 is valley bottom or alluvium. A transverse profile of the valley reveals four major ecological zones: the contemporary floodplain of the river (a narrow, relatively minor zone); a higher floodplain that lies above it and is the major area of alluvium and key agricultural resource of the valley; the gently sloping piedmont; and the steep slopes of the surrounding mountains. The elevation of the valley floor is between 1,500 and 1,600 m and the annual rainfall varies between 500 and 800 mm in that same ecological zone. Known sites in one test zone of the valley during the Middle Formative, Phase Two include three widely spaced villages (one measuring 20 hectares), located either on the high alluvium or on the summits of low piedmont spurs immediately adjacent to them. During the succeeding Middle Formative, Phase Three, the sites doubled in number (one every three miles). They are located in the same ecological zone, but one such settlement covered approximately 40 hectares. The larger communities include stone terraced platforms, and variations in the quality of residences suggest significant ranking distinctions among the population.

The Late Formative, Phase Two saw major population expansion in the valley (see Figure 5.12). Bernal's (1965) survey of the valley revealed a total of 251 sites. Of these, he surface-sampled 164 and found 39 sites to have had occupation of this period, including the great center of Monte Albán itself. Many of these sites had substantial ceremonial architecture, and one, surveyed intensively by Flannery (1968), had a residential area of 80 hectares. During this phase there was also a substantial expansion of population up into the piedmont area, and both the piedmont and alluvial plain were under intensive cultivation. During the Terminal Formative and Proto-Classic periods, there were only 23 sites occupied within the valley, but all of these can be classified as relatively large population centers with massive ceremonial-civic precincts. This would seem to indicate a process of nucleation into fewer centers. Of them, seven were classified by Bernal (1965) as major centers, including Monte Albán itself. He also points out that Monte Albán was not strikingly larger or more monumental in its architecture than the other six—an indication that the valley was probably not politically unified at this time.

In the Early and Middle Classic periods, a period of Teotihuacán influence at Monte Albán, the number of sites rises to 30, all of substantial size. This was also a period of major expansion of the site of Monte Albán. It was probably at this time that the valley became a single political unit under the leadership of this center. In the Late Classic period, Bernal reports 18 large sites, one metropolis—Monte Albán—and over 90 medium-sized sites, all of which had substantial ceremonial architecture. At the end of the Late Classic period Monte Albán was abandoned as a major population and political center, and the succeeding Post-Classic period witnessed a series of new events. There is evidence of a final population growth (Bernal reports that virtually all of the 164 sites have Post-Classic occupation on them). The entire valley was used for cultivation, including even the steep mountain slopes, and apparently cultivated using a system of swidden cultivation. Bernal reports a number of centers, each as large or slightly larger than Monte Albán itself.

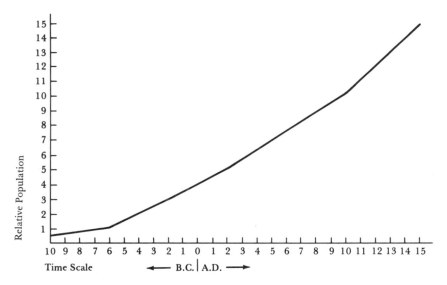

Figure 5.12. Valley of Oaxaca.

The Valley of Oaxaca from the Late Formative period on was a major cultural and demographic center in Mesoamerica. The influence of this area was felt over a huge region that includes most of what is today the state of Oaxaca, southern Puebla, and adjacent portions of Guerrero and Chiapas.

With respect to agricultural history, Flannery (1968) has demonstrated that the valley was one of the early centers of maize domestication with a record of incipient cultivation comparable in time depth and character to that recorded by MacNeish (1964) for the Tehuacán Valley. By 1200 B.C. the beginning of the Middle Formative, Phase Two, this development had proceeded far enough to permit the establishment of sedentary farming villages. There is convincing evidence that during this period the high alluvium was intensively cultivated by a system of irrigation that is still in use today and that is referred to by Flannery (1968) as pot irrigation. The water table over much of this zone is within three meters of the surface, and the villages are always located near those portions of the alluvium that have a high water table. Today farmers excavate shallow wells near their fields and irrigate by means of pottery vessels. There is convincing evidence that this technique was used as early as the Middle Formative, Phase Two. In the Valley of Oaxaca double cropping is also possible, since frosts do not occur during the winter season.

During the Late Formative, the piedmont was heavily exploited. We have definite evidence of small irrigation systems based on local springs and evidence for terracing of the sloping terrain. During the final phase of the history of the valley, there is evidence of ultimate colonization of even the steep slopes above the piedmont probably, as we have noted, utilizing a swidden system.

The Nochixtlán Valley is a small valley, situated in the Mixteca Alta in northwestern Oaxaca. The total area of the valley is approximately 400 km², including the adjacent slopes. The valley varies in elevation from 2,100 to 2,500 m above sea level and has an annual rainfall of approximately 427 mm. It is therefore comparable in climatic characteristics to the drier portions of the Central Mexican plateau.

Spores (1969) has conducted an intensive survey, comparable to those reported for the Basin of Mexico. The occupations are assigned to four pre-Conquest periods. These correlate roughly with the Late Formative,

Phase One; Late Formative, Phase Two, the Terminal Formative, and the Proto-Classic combined; the Classic period as a whole; and the general Post-Classic period.

He reports 8, 24, 36, and 78 substantial occupation sites for the four periods, in chronological order, and provides a population estimate for each period. On the basis of his data, I have constructed the population graph shown in Figure 5.13. The profile is very close to that for the Basin of Mexico and the Tlaxcala-Puebla regions, with a truly respectable population beginning only in the Late Formative, followed by a steady rise to a peak in 1519. If anything, the Nochixtlán graph shows a greater degree of marginality in the inception of well-established agricultural settlement, as compared to the Central Plateau area.

This population history closely correlates with agricultural and sociopolitical events. The Late Formative, Phase One sites are all small villages or hamlets located on low spurs or ridges extending out into the plain from the nearby hills. In this second period, which covers our Late Formative, Phase Two, the Terminal Formative, and the Proto-Classic phases, sites are concentrated in the same localities but are also found well up on the nearby mountain slopes—an indication of population

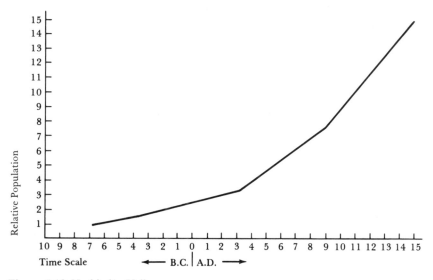

Figure 5.13. Nochixtlán Valley.

pressure and initial colonization of those areas. Sites also become larger in size, and some include civic-ceremonial complexes. One such site covers 100 hectares in area. In the Classic period there are no less than five major centers, each exceeding 100 hectares in settlement, and even small sites have ceremonial construction. The period witnessed considerable expansion of land use to the high mountain slopes, and there is evidence of intensive agriculture in the form of terracing at this time. The large population centers, however, were still located near the alluvial plain, either on hills within it or on high spurs overlooking it—presumably a pattern linked to intensive cultivation of the alluvium.

The final period witnessed a considerable expansion of hillside cultivation, and most of the terracing dates from this period. The largest communities and densest settlement, however, continue to occur near the alluvium. Of the 130 localities found in the survey, 111 have some occupation, and 78 show heavy occupations. One site has a reported settlement area of 3 km^2.

Conclusions

I will now evaluate some of Boserup's major theoretical arguments in terms of the data from Mesoamerican archaeology. The major postulate—that extensive systems of cultivation are generally more productive than intensive ones and that, given a choice, cultivators will select extensive systems of cultivation over intensive ones—is a perfectly sound one when applied to geographical areas characterized by high rainfall and an original forest vegetation. I will return to this qualification shortly. However, I would question the absolute manner in which some of the derived postulates are applied.

First, I would question the absolutely unidirectional cause-and-effect relationship between population growth and agricultural systems. If intensification of cultivation were the only aspect of change in agricultural systems, then the argument would be more defensible, although even here I must raise the semantic point that if population pressure leads to an intensification of cultivation, doesn't intensification relieve population pressure and then stimulate and permit population growth? If the process is viewed from this angle, then the relationships are really circular rather than lineal and represent the kind of feedback process that anthropologists generally feel characterizes much of cultural change. But even more importantly, agricultural evolution is not simply a matter of decreasing the periods of rest and increasing the period of cultivation. It is also marked by technological innovations as, for example, in the cases of canal irrigation, drainage systems, and terracing. These are specific approaches to the resolution of environmental problems, and their inception quite obviously permits and stimulates population growth. It is from this point of view, particularly, that I see the relationship as a feedback one and view both agricultural systems and population growth as dependent variables.

It is particularly in the area of the viability of agricultural systems and the role of environmental variation that I would disagree fundamentally with Boserup's hypothesis. I thoroughly agree that anthropologists have tended to grossly underestimate the flexibility of agricultural systems and have tended to think of such systems as relatively static ones, not susceptible to change. This is a major contribution of Boserup's hypothesis, particularly when applied to the tropical forest environment. It is this mistaken position that has made it so difficult for ecologically oriented anthropologists to understand the evolution of Lowland Maya civilization. The population history of the Lowland Maya area and increasing archaeological evidence on the history of Maya agriculture demonstrates the utility of Boserup's scheme.

It is, however, with the concept of an unlimited viability, implicit at least in some of her arguments, that I would quarrel. There are variations in soil fertility, and these variations quite clearly are significant in terms of variations in the history of agriculture. These variations explain, in part, differences in the precocity of population growth from area to area (a problem that Boserup's hypothesis does not explain). Furthermore, they place absolute limits on population growth and strongly affect the history of the specific areas.

The absolute position presented by Boserup is a reflection of the source of her data, primarily from southeast Asia, where there is a very special set of circumstances. First, the basic crop involved in this area is rice, a plant that can be grown in an artificial swamp, and, as Geertz (1963) has pointed out, it is not the soil that is the major source of nutrients for plant growth but rather the irrigation water in which the plant is growing. This reduces drastically the effects of variations in soil on population growth in that area. Second, in its later historical phases the area had domestic animals to provide both traction for plows and fertilizers for the maintenance of soil fertility.

In tropical Mesoamerica, in contrast, the basic crop was maize; draft animals and plows were absent; iron for efficient hoes was unknown; and the domestic animals available were too small in size to have provided adequate amounts of fertilizers for the maintenance of fields in areas of heavily leached or laterized soils. All of these factors would have placed absolute limits on the degree of intensity of cultivation and hence population growth. Furthermore, given the primitiveness of Mesoamerican tools, the labor-input–calorie-output ratio would be a significant factor stimulating migration or fission, even at relatively low levels of intensification of cultivation, since cultivators would not be able to cope easily and effectively with grasses or other difficult weeds, or would do so only under extreme political pressures. The extraordinary instability of population in the tropical lowlands indicated from our graphs is a striking demonstration of the limitations of the viability of agricultural systems with Neolithic technology and the absence of large domestic animals. What I am challenging here is the universal applica- tion of a principle derived from a very special regional situation. On the other hand, the agricultural history that we have outlined for the Lowland Maya in which the people shifted from maize to root crops to ramon and from long-cycle forest fallowing to bush fallowing and ultimately possibly to the grass-fallowing system is an excellent demonstration of Boserup's main thesis.

The Pacific coastal plain-piedmont-escarpment population profile from Guatemala is of particular interest here since there seems to be a gradual process of population movement inland by migration as a response to population pressure in the successively occupied ecological zones.

The basic principles can also be applied fairly well to the semiarid highlands of Mexico, both in the Central Plateau, the Balsas Basin, and the Oaxaca highlands with some qualifications. It is of particular interest that the pioneer occupation of the Basin of Mexico did, in fact, involve an early phase of extensive systems of cultivation followed by increasingly intensive ones. Furthermore, the pioneer occupation apparently involved a small population that selectively utilized the frost-free, more humid slopes, particularly in the southern part of the basin, for their initial occupation. As population pressure rose, instead of intensification of the use of such land, the population apparently spread out and occupied the smaller areas of similar ecological conditions in the drier central and northern portions of the basin, and it was not until these areas were occupied that more intensive systems of farming were adopted—a process that began in the more densely settled southern areas and gradually spread north, precisely as one would expect from Boserup's thesis.

In the cases of the Valleys of Oaxaca and Tehuacán, however, intensive utilization of the alluvium occurred virtually from the inception of sedentary agriculture in those areas. Since these valleys are all below the frost line, there was not the potential advantage in cultivating the wetter slopes (that is, where rainfall was higher), and, furthermore, the undependability of cultivation without irrigation of such lands apparently provided a major stimulus for a rapid evolution of irrigation and terracing. If there ever was a long period of extensive agriculture in the Valley of Oaxaca, it probably dates back to the incipient phase of agricultural development when the food supply was still based primarily on wild resources.

The semiarid or semihumid Mexican Highlands (with the qualifications just presented) do provide a good test case for Boserup's argument in the sense that this is an area of continuing population growth with all graphs peaking toward the end of the history of the occupation of the various areas, and this growth is very closely linked with increasingly more intensive patterns of land use involving new technological developments. However, it also demonstrates the great significance of geography in explaining the variations in agricultural history, since the population history of these areas differs strikingly from that in the tropical lowlands —differs in ways that are directly linked to variations in soil characteristics and density of the natural vegetation.

In viewing Mesoamerican culture history as a whole, the correlative relationships between the processes of population growth, intensification of agriculture, and increasingly complex social systems are clear-cut and unequivocably related.

The Early Formative Period (2500 to 1500 b.c.) was one of sparse

population (in fact, only certain areas were occupied by cultivators—
virtually all of them in the semiarid uplands), extensive systems of
cultivation, and simple band or tribal levels of social organization.
During the Middle Formative period (1500 to 600 B.C.), population
density rose strikingly in a few localized areas like the South Gulf coast
of Vera Cruz, the Chiapas-Guatemalan Pacific coastal plain, the Central
Valley of Chiapas, the Valley of Oaxaca, and portions of the Upper
Balsas Basin; agriculture became more intensive in some of the semiarid
highland regions with the inception of pot irrigation and possibly canal
irrigation; but, generally speaking, even in areas of relatively dense
population, the system remained one of forest or bush fallowing. It was
during the Middle Formative period that other regions of Mesoamerica
were colonized by sedentary farmers for the first time—for example, the
high mountain valleys in Central Mexico and Oaxaca, the Central and
North Gulf Coast plain, the Yucatán Peninsula, and the volcanic valleys
in highland Guatemala. In all of these cases the system of cultivation
was presumably various forms of extensive agriculture. It was also
during this phase that evidence of ranking as a factor in the social
organization emerges for the first time, particularly in the area of
densest population. The Late Formative period (600 to 100 B.C.) witnessed the appearance of complex social systems over most of the culture
area—a process that was correlated closely with rising population and
intensification of agriculture and that led to short-fallow systems in the
humid regions and to annual cropping combined with special techniques like canal irrigation, terracing, and swamp reclamation in some
of the more arid regions.

During the long period of time starting with the Terminal Formative
and extending up to the Conquest, Mesoamerican civilization went
through its final climactic growth, and the state level of political
organization became virtually universal, with large urban centers and
empires in the Central Plateau and other portions of the Mexican
highlands. This social evolution was clearly related to population growth
and increasingly wider distribution of more intensive systems of
agriculture.

These correlative processes are strikingly illustrated in every one of
our local histories, and I believe that it is here that the demographic
approach can make its most significant theoretical contribution.

Archaeologists have an unfortunate tendency to see the growth of civilization in a large area such as Mesoamerica as a process of essentially group-to-group diffusion. I do not challenge the fact that certain specific attributes of Mesoamerican civilization such as the 260-day calendar, feline rain god, and concept of a universe of thirteen upper layers and nine lower ones were diffused from single centers of origin. What is essential here is that the really significant development in the evolution of any civilization is the increase of societal size and internal heterogeneity, that is, the emergence of class and occupational divisions; and this is a process, not an invention to be diffused from place to place. As our local histories demonstrate, the most productive direction of research in understanding this development lies in the history of population growth and increasingly more intensive agriculture. In this sense each of our local histories represents an independent evolution of civilization. To a great degree, the variations in the precocity and retardation of development of complex social systems are the product of precocity or retardation in population growth. The latter is related to a complex set of processes, primarily ecological. In some areas, particularly those lying above the 2,000-meter contour, population growth was delayed until varieties of subtropical crops evolved that could be adapted to the frost cycle—as in the cases of the Central Plateau and the Nochixtlán Valley. In other cases, the characteristics of soil and/or vegetation limited population growth to a relatively low level that permitted states but not urban centers, as in the cases of highland Guatemala, and the Maya lowlands.

In Boserup's model, there is no room for a concept, rapidly developing in anthropological studies, of the special historical significance of particular ecological systems, and this again relates to her lack of interest in geographical variation. One of the more interesting aspects of Mesoamerican history is the close relationship between the appearance of large urban centers like Teotihuacán, Cholula, Tenochtitlán, and Monte Albán and hydraulic agriculture. The interrelationships between hydraulic agriculture and the emergence of these large urban centers and of the huge political systems that they governed can only be outlined very briefly here. Hydraulic agriculture provides first of all a new dimension of power—control of water as well as the control of land. The maintenance of an irrigation system also requires coordinated organization of labor in a way that other agricultural systems do not. Furthermore, irrigated land is universally private land because of the heavy investment of capital labor (that is, dikes, canals, and dams), and this stimulates class distinctions based on land ownership. Irrigated land also is permanently cropped land, and the demographic capacity of permanently cropped land of this type is considerably greater than any other system of farming. This permits a greater regional population density and the establishment of larger agrarian communities. Communities of this type with continued population growth and pressure may easily evolve into urban centers. A close juxtaposition of areas of hydraulic agriculture with their strikingly higher productive potential and nonhydraulic areas in the Mexican highlands furthermore is a powerful stimulus to competition. Thus it was no accident that the politically dominant communities became those with the control of hydraulic resources. Given the primitiveness of Mesoamerican technology and the absence of large draft animals, it was only certain environmental characteristics that permitted or stimulated the evolution of urban centers and macrostates—an example of the powerful influence that variations in the geographic environment have played in Mesoamerican culture history.

6

**Plow and
Population in
Temperate
Europe**

Bernard Wailes

**In this essay Wailes provides a beautifully detailed
and readable guide through the available data on technology, ecology, and historical demography in medieval Europe—a period that presents particular problems for the study of the development of agricultural
technology. Though he is unable to draw any positive
conclusions for the central theme, he does point out
some interesting possibilities for the relationship
of population growth and agricultural technology.
Indirectly he poses another related problem: Why
was the process of urbanization in Europe so slow?**

Introduction

Our knowledge of temperate Europe for the last two millennia is good,
compared to what we know of the agricultural technology and population of most of the rest of the world. I have started my consideration
with the pre-Roman Iron Age, since this is the earliest period for which
substantial advance in plow technology has been postulated, and since
the immediately succeeding Roman period provides the earliest documented population figures. I end with the later fourteenth century A.D.,
since by then population data are sufficient to provide only modest
variation in estimates, and plow technology is also well enough understood. Moreover, the relationship between agricultural economy and
population by this time was becoming increasingly affected by wider
economic problems (for example, the widespread commercial production
of wool) and so was less likely to be applicable, as any kind of model,
to simpler economic situations. Owing to the exigencies of the population
information, England figures most prominently, France is treated more
lightly, and the remainder of temperate Europe only as particular pieces
of evidence dictate.

Improvements in the plow are cited by many authors as being among the most important innovations leading to increased agricultural production (see Figure 6.1). One notable example is the proposition that the advent of the "true" plow (as opposed to the ard, defined in the glossary at the end of this chapter) made possible the cultivation of the heavy and potentially high-yielding clay soils, thus permitting a large-scale extension of agriculture. The implications for population increase are obvious, regardless of whether this follows or stimulates production. Lynn White (1969: 9–10) presents a particularly forceful version of this argument linking the "true" plow to population rise.

The model developed here is based explicitly on the proposition that the true plow was, in its way, a truly revolutionary implement with a ground-breaking and tilling capacity quite beyond that of earlier plows or ards. Unfortunately, there is no clear agreement on the nature of this

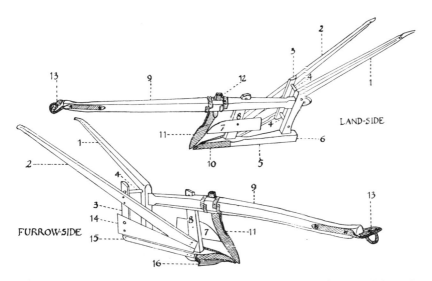

Figure 6.1. The parts of a plow (in the National Museum of Wales) of late eighteenth-century type. (Those shaded are iron, the rest are wood.) 1. Flow-tail (land handle) 2. Plow-stilt (right handle) 3. Drock 4. Rough staves (plow spindles) 5. Share-beam (chip, throck, sole, head) 6. Heel 7. Fen-board 8. Sheath (sheet) 9. Plow-beam 10. Plow-share (sock) 11. Coulter 12. Coulter-wedge 13. Hake (ear, copstol) 14. Moldboard (shelboard) 15. Ground-wrest (plow-rest, rice) 16. Wing of plow-share.
Reprinted with permission of the Royal Archaeological Institute, from F. G. Payne, "The plough in ancient Britain," *The Archaeological Journal CIV*, 1947, 82–111, Fig. 4.

new plow type, which is described variously as the true plow, heavy plow, or wheeled plow.

It is essential to consider these terms briefly in relation to the agricultural use of the implements they describe. A heavy plow, with no further qualification, means only something heavier than the light ard, the latter known as the only plow type in Europe prior to the Iron Age (see Wailes 1970). The imprecision of the term heavy plow can imply no more than that a more robust implement was required, presumably either for use on heavier soils, or for the cutting of deeper furrows, or both.

The wheeled plow seems to have no necessary functional significance. Payne points out that a swing plow may have as heavy a beam as a wheeled plow (Payne 1947: 96). Nor do wheels seem to have an advantage on heavy soils; indeed, the swing plow was evidently preferred to the wheel plow for working heavy, wet soils (ibid.: 97). The two arguments supposedly supporting the notion that a plow must have wheels are thus rebutted.

The significance of the moldboard plow is that it could turn a furrow, thus affording maximum aeration and drainage of the soil, factors of great importance when cultivating heavy and damp soils. It is not entirely clear, however, that the moldboard was essential for these functions, since the asymmetrical wear on ard shares (Steensberg 1936: 252; Payne 1947: 90) and asymmetrical furrows (Megaw et al. 1961: 207, 212) clearly indicate that ards were deliberately tilted, presumably to push soil preferentially to one side of the implement rather than the other. Whether this practice, in the hands of the skilled operator, could actually turn a furrow I have been unable to discover, but this might be possible. At all events, tilting an ard would tend to turn the cut sod on its side, even if not right over on its back, and would also deepen the furrow. Thus both of the main advantages of the moldboard would be at least partially achieved. Perhaps the moldboard refines this practice, making it both easier to execute and more effective, without being essential to it.

The term true plow is essentially meaningless; while presumably the plow was seen initially as different in some important respects from the ard and hence received a new name, we do not know what this critical difference was. Bratanić, in considering the linguistic evidence for the earliest plows and plow parts, writes "we still do not know the proper origin and the first meaning of the word plough" (Bratanić 1952: 56).

We are thus unable to insist that one innovation, or combination of innovations, truly defines the plow and distinguishes it from the ard. But from the crucial aspect of improvement in function three features seem most likely: the iron share, the iron coulter, and the moldboard. Both the iron share and the coulter would have greatly facilitated, or even made possible for the first time, the cultivation of relatively heavy soils. In addition, they would have made much easier the plowing of soil bound together with well-developed grass roots (for instance, a field left fallow for two or three years). The advantage of the moldboard has already been discussed. These three innovations, then, are all most advantageous in the cultivation of heavier soils and, separately or in combination, may well have been essential for this purpose. For ease of reference only I shall reserve the term plow for those implements with a moldboard. This distinction does not imply that the moldboard was necessarily the most important innovation.

At this stage it is necessary to discuss briefly the problem of soil classification, since it is evident that soil types are probably directly related to developments in plows and plowing. A detailed classification of soils is inappropriate in the present context. First, the complexity would obscure the basic issue of the broad trends that may be observable. Second, soil classifications are made normally in terms of development or formation, rather than in terms of variable suitability for varying agricultural purposes. Third, the long cultivation of much of temperate Europe has led to some change of its soils through cultural means (see, for example, Eyre 1963: 175–192), so that it may be difficult to determine just what type a soil belonged to when it was first cultivated, as opposed to what type it is now.

It seems preferable for present purposes to consider soils in the three very broad and general categories used by the British historical geographers: light, intermediate, and heavy. The light soils are mainly upland soils, thin and often (though not invariably) well drained; the intermediate soils are mainly the loams, heavier and richer than the light soils, but normally well drained and concentrated largely at intermediate altitudes; the heavy soils are largely low-lying clays, stiff, often poorly drained, usually difficult to work, but often potentially rich in agricultural terms. Fox (1959: 78–79) and Wooldridge and Linton (1933: 297–310) provide useful considerations of these broad soil types in relation to prehistoric and historic land utilization.

The Development of Plows and Plowing Techniques

Prehistoric Plowing

NEOLITHIC AND BRONZE AGE

Since I have discussed this topic elsewhere recently (Wailes 1970), I shall offer here only a brief review of the evidence, set out in terms of Boserup's proposed developmental sequence of increasingly intensified land use through progressively more frequent cropping and shorter fallow (Boserup 1965: 15–16). This sequence appears to suit the European evidence well.

Agriculture began in temperate Europe around 4500 B.C. (based on Carbon-14 age determinations, calculated on 5568 ± 30 half-life). It is generally agreed to have been an extensive method of forest-fallow cultivation. By the middle of the third millennium B.C. we have evidence for plowing with the ard, and by the middle of the second millennium, at the latest, a system or systems of settled agriculture had been developed. This settled agriculture is evidenced archaeologically by regularly demarcated field systems, lynchets, and manuring; botanically, it is demonstrated by evidence of sustained clearance of forest vegetation and an increase of open country flora, including indicators of cultivation (Godwin 1965: 20–22). In Boserup's scheme, either the stage of short-fallow cultivation or the stage of annual cropping had been reached in at least some areas of temperate Europe. It may be worth noting here that in temperate Europe herbs and grasses establish themselves rapidly on cleared ground and that the light ard used at this period could not have been well suited to breaking up a topsoil heavily consolidated by matted grass roots. I would suggest that, once the fallow period had been progressively reduced past the stage of bush fallow to a situation where renewed plowing would be on consolidated grassland, the difficulties of this process could well have spurred farming in one or both of two ways. First, the fallow might have been reduced to the briefest possible time in order to avoid more than the minimum development of grass roots: preferably, this would mean annual cropping and, inevitably, manuring. Second, the fallow might have been maintained as pasture for as long as possible in order to make the laborious breaking up of grassland topsoil as infrequent as possible. The concurrent practice of both systems on the same farm could have led to the development of the "infield-outfield" system, with the richer lands heavily manured and cultivated every year, or almost every year, and the poorer lands cultivated only at substantial intervals.

During this Neolithic/Bronze Age period of ard cultivation, the direct distributional evidence indicates that only the light soils were cultivated. However, I have argued that heavier soils were also being brought under permanent cultivation (Wailes 1970: 287), the intermediate soils being far more likely than the heavy soils. If this was the case, the appearance of widespread Iron Age farming of light soils would indicate, not the general initiation of settled farming, but the widespread extension of settled agriculture onto lighter and poorer soils. This might indicate population pressure on available cultivable land, or a change in conditions rendering the intermediate soils less advantageous, or both.

PRE-ROMAN IRON AGE

In the more northerly parts of temperate Europe, from which most of our evidence comes (that is, British Isles, Low Countries, northern Germany, south Baltic area), the introduction of iron technology coincides approximately with the climatic change from sub-Boreal to sub-Atlantic (which continues essentially to the present time) and is probably directly connected with the cultivation of rye and oats (Clark 1952: 109) for the first time, since both crops, in somewhat different ways, are hardier than wheat and barley. Evidence for the practice of drying grain also becomes common at this time (ibid.: 112) again probably directly connected with damper and cooler climatic conditions.

However, other evidences for change in food-producing methods at this time are less easily attributed to climatic change alone, since the manufacture of iron afforded the opportunity of technological advances that would have improved agriculture. Notably, the availability of iron made possible for the first time the metal plowshare; there are no recorded examples of bronze being used for this purpose, and indeed it would probably have been too brittle. With an iron plowshare, it is argued, the farmer could effectively till heavier soils. Thus iron technology may well have permitted for the first time, or certainly encouraged, the development of a heavier plowing implement suitable for more compact soils. In conjunction with the coulter, for which iron was certainly necessary, such a plow could also cope effectively with matted grass roots, cutting them both vertically and horizontally. We have already noted the additional advantage of the moldboard in cultivating heavier soils, but I incline now to the view that it was perhaps the iron coulter and share that were of greater importance in permitting the tilling of heavy soils (and probably the damper and heavier of the ~ intermediate soils also).

We turn now to the concrete evidence for plows and plowing during this period.

A. THE TOMMERBY PLOW (Steensberg 1936: 252–253). A curious feature of this plow, noted by Steensberg himself, is its close resemblance to recent Danish peasant moldboard plows. It is disappointing, but not altogether surprising, to record that a sample from this implement was recently subjected to radiocarbon age determination, giving a date of A.D. 1620 ± 100 (Tauber 1962: 30). Because of this, we must now conclude that this implement had indeed been thrown into a cutting in the peat and that the pollen spectrum (early sub-Atlantic) obtained for it was due to this accident.

B. CLASSICAL SOURCES. See the next section of this chapter.

C. PLOW PARTS SURVIVING IN ARCHAEOLOGICAL CONTEXTS. A number of iron shares and coulters of varying widths and sizes have been recovered from archaeological contexts (Payne 1947). None of these clearly demonstrates the presence of the moldboard plow. Heavy ards may have both broad shares and coulters—indeed, a broad share may well have necessitated a coulter. It seems plausible to suggest that such heavy ards were designed for heavier soils (though not necessarily the heaviest), particularly since, as Payne points out (1947: 90–92) some variety in these coulters, and particularly the shares, exists. This variety may well be deliberate and designed for differential uses, most probably on different soils.

D. PLOW FURROWS. Much evidence exists for cross-plowing in prehistoric Europe (Wailes 1970; Müller-Wille 1965: 108–114); this is argued plausibly to be the product of the ard, in most cases apparently a light ard. A few cases of one-way plowing are known, however, and are discussed briefly by Müller-Wille (ibid.). He considers them to be the product of the *Wendepflug* "swivel plow," "swing plow." Most of these could equally well be the product of a heavy ard (compare my arguments on the Gwithian early medieval plow marks, below). But one site, Feddersen Wierde, does appear to show evidence of true moldboard plowing—a properly turned-over sod. Haarnagel (1951, pl. 17, no. 2) illustrates this in cross section, and I find it difficult to propose any other method of plowing by which this result could be achieved, unless by skillful tilting of a heavy ard (see my comment in Introduction to this chapter). The date is late pre-Roman Iron Age. One would wish to examine the evidence in much greater detail, because cross-plowing with ards is still well attested (indeed, normal) at this period, as well as later (Müller-Wille 1965: 108–114). However, it seems possible to argue that during the pre-Roman Iron Age in the Netherlands–North German–Danish area no less than three distinct types of plow (moldboard plow, heavy ard with wide share, light ard) are represented by characteristic furrows, suggesting that different cultivation implements had been developed to suit different conditions.

Roman Plowing

CLASSICAL WRITTEN SOURCES

There are a few references, in the writings of classical authors concerned with rural economics and agricultural practice, that have been adduced to provide evidence for the introduction of the moldboard plow. These are summarized here.

A. PLINY THE ELDER (*Historia naturalis* 15.48) says that the Rhaeti had added wheels to their plows, the context indicating that this was evidently a novelty. This implement is called a *plaumatorum*, which is taken by many to mean plow in the sense of a heavy plow of some sort (presumably with wheels, if not moldboard). Gow (1914: 275) considers the passage somewhat obscure and concludes only that Pliny is discussing four different types of plow, of which the *plaumatorum* is one. Steensberg (1936: 265, n. 5) points out that the passage cannot be interpreted in a way that insists on the *plaumatorum* actually turning a furrow; he also interprets the passage to mean that the wheels were attached to the share, not the beam as is the case with the normal medieval (and later) European wheeled plow. Curwen (1938: 15) admits that *plaumatorum* is obscure and has several different readings but considers that it might be a corruption of a Teutonic word meaning "plow with wheels." However, examining the Teutonic languages (of a later date), Payne (1947: 94) points out that neither Old English nor Old Gothic has any word "plow"; OE used *sulh*, cognate with Latin *sulcus*—furrow, and the OE verb was *erian*—plow—cognate with Old Welsh *eredig*, both being variants of the *PIE *arə root. In early Irish (late 1st millennium A.D.) the only recorded word for plow is *arathar*, another clear *arə derivative, and Duignan argues that some form of heavy plow is the only type attested by the contemporaneous archaeological evidence (1944: 136). In other words, *arathar* was apparently the term used for implements with heavy iron coulters and shares. Furthermore, Bratanić (1952: 56–58) contends that linguistic evidence demonstrates that neither Teutonic nor Romance language groups contain the root word for plow, but that it must have come from further north.

B. VIRGIL (*Georgics* 1, lines 109–175). Nightingale (1953: 22) interprets *binae aures*, reasonably enough, as two ears and *duplici dorso* as indicating a keel-shaped underside to the share described; his contention is that Virgil refers to a one-way plow (see Glossary). Nightingale compares Virgil's plow to the well-known Romano-British bronze model plow from Sussex (illustrated in Payne 1947: 97); these would certainly help in preferential pushing of the soil to one side or the other of the implement, depending upon which way it was tilted, but they are not designed to turn a furrow efficiently, as is a moldboard. Indeed, Nightingale's interpretation of *duplici dorso*, as a keeled underside to the share beam to facilitate tilting in either direction, is consistent with an ard (however, developed with ground-wrests) rather than a moldboard plow, which, because of the moldboard, does not require tilting.

C. COLUMELLA (*De Re Rustica* 2. 2, par. 25) is similarly misinterpreted by Nightingale (1953: 22), who considers that the tilting of the plow implied in the passage indicates that it turned a furrow in the manner of a moldboard plow.

D. VARRO (*Res Rusticae* 1. 29, par. 2). PLINY (*Historia naturalis* 18. 180). The Orwins (1954: 31) say " . . . an important advance was made . . . by the addition of a moldboard on one side, or sometimes on either side.

... VARRO, and after him Pliny, mention ploughs thus equipped, were used, they say, to bury seed-corn." The Orwins clearly think that "ears" are necessarily moldboards. As I have just noted, this is not necessarily the case.

CLASSICAL ILLUSTRATIVE SOURCES

There are a number of Greek and Roman illustrations and models of plows. Gow (1914) is a convenient source for many, and Payne (1947: 99) mentions some models. With one possible exception all are clearly ards of one form or another. The Orwins, however, cite Gow (1914: 253) as authority for saying "the classical authors described the moldboard as an ear" (Orwin and Orwin 1954: 32). They refer to a relief on the pedestal of a statue of Demeter. First, Gow's illustration (1914: fig. 4) shows quite clearly a plow with two ears (Gow called them "earth boards"), which, no doubt, would assist in pushing the soil to one side or the other if tilted, or to both sides simultaneously if not tilted, but which are not moldboards in the effective sense of that term. Furthermore, Gow (1914: 253, n. 12) clearly indicates that this illustration (not his own) must be treated with considerable reserve: "this example is suspect," and "the drawing is probably not reliable for details."

ROMAN PERIOD PLOW PARTS

Payne (1957: 78) reports two asymmetrical iron plowshares from Roman period contexts in Britain. These, he maintains, were designed for use with a fixed moldboard plow since the share is clearly intended to guide the sod in one direction. In this connection, he recalls the asymmetrical coulters that occur in Britain from the later pre-Roman Iron Age onward: These, too, seem clearly for use with a plow that pushed or turned the sod preferentially to one side rather than the other. Despite Payne's authoritative deduction of a moldboard, it seems possible that an asymmetrical ard could be designed to assist such a practice and that the presence of a moldboard should not necessarily be inferred.

Plowing in the Earlier Medieval Period
(to the Eleventh Century A.D.)

PLOWS, PLOW PARTS, AND FIELDS

The breadth of this heading is justified by the paucity of evidence to be considered under it. Payne (1947: 103) states: "Let us look at the

evidence [for the Anglo-Saxon period]. We must pass by that of archaeology; there is none." Despite the rapid growth of medieval archaeology
in Britain since that time, the situation is very little better today. No
evidence can be put forward for the use of the wheel plow or the moldboard plow for the whole of this period. Nor have any field systems been
identified, with the exceptions to be noted and discussed here.

A. AT GWITHIAN, CORNWALL, SITE XX, cutting 1 showed one-way plow
marks at the base of a cultivated soil (Fowler and Thomas 1962: 67).
The small size of this cutting (3′ × 10′) prevented any determination
as to whether or not this was ridge and furrow plowing, but the broad,
slightly angled, plow marks (ibid.: pl. III) convinced the authors that
this was the result of plowing with a moldboard plow (ibid.: 77). The
dating of this plow soil, on the basis of numerous potsherds deposited in
the process of manuring, is put in the period ca. A.D. 550–850 (ibid.: 68).

B. GWITHIAN SITE XXI is a complete, small field cultivated by narrow
ridge and furrow (ibid.: 69–76). The dating, again by pottery, is put at
ca. ninth century A.D. to ca. A.D. 1100 (ibid.: 75). The method of
cultivation is considered to be by a fixed moldboard plow (ibid.: 72–73,
76) since "ridge and furrow depends primarily for its existence on the
use of a mold-board plow" (ibid.: 79). This assumption is based
particularly upon Nightingale (1953: 21–22, 26), who convincingly
argues that the use of a fixed moldboard plow will almost certainly
result in some form of strip cultivation being practiced.

However, this is not to say that ridge-and-furrow cultivation is
produced *only* by the use of the fixed moldboard plow. I suggest that the
skilled use of an ard, especially one with well-developed ears or ground
wrest, could also produce the ridge and furrow. On a light and sandy
soil such as that at Gwithian Sites XX and XXI, this process would
seem particularly easy. Of course, a moldboard plow would do the job
more effectively, but if a relatively light prehistoric ard could be tilted
to push soil differentially toward one side at the expense of the other
(Steensberg 1936: 252; Payne 1947: 90; Megaw, Thomas, and Wales
1961: 207, 212) and thus throw some form of ridge, it is surely possible
that such implements could be used to form the ridge and furrow.

C. HEN DOMEN, MONTGOMERYSHIRE. Barker (1969) has reported that the
first castle defenses, erected about A.D. 1070, covered ridge-and-furrow
cultivation.

Finally, we may notice that the three pieces of evidence for plow agriculture just cited are all from Celtic areas. They do not support the notion that it was the Saxons who were responsible for the introduction to Britain of the true, heavy, wheeled, or moldboard plow.

ILLUSTRATIONS

The frequently illustrated illuminations of a plowing scene from the Cottonian MSS., Tiberius B.V., and Julius Z.VI (as cited in Payne 1947: 103) are essentially the same. They supposedly date from late tenth and eleventh centuries A.D., respectively. The plow and team are depicted clearly enough: a four-ox team harnessed to a wheel plow with shifting moldboard (ibid.). Payne (ibid.: n. 70) cites Millar (1926: 20) to question the dating and provenance of these manuscripts; but even had they been of the dates proposed, they would still be Late Saxon and considerably later than the period of Saxon expansion into the claylands of Midland England. Thus they cannot be taken to represent the implement that the Saxons had available to them for their famous colonization of the clay zones. Furthermore, Payne (1947: 105–106) argues that this type of plow was unsuited to the first breaking of new ground, let alone heavy soil.

Other Late Saxon period plow illustrations show implements supposedly even less suited to the cultivation of heavy soils. All appear to be ards or at least are by no means clearly moldboard plows; some have coulters, some not (ibid.: 105–106). The plowing scene on the Utrecht Psalter (ca. A.D. 820–832), from which two of the aforementioned English plowing scenes were copied, shows an ard drawn by two oxen (Steensberg 1936: 262; Payne 1947: 106) rather than the four-, six-, or eight-ox teams that were supposedly the norm by this period.

DOCUMENTARY REFERENCES

A. The eighth century A.D. "plough riddle" of the Exeter Book (cited in Payne 1947: 106) does not mention a moldboard among the list of plow parts. The line "what I tear with my teeth falls to the side" might be taken to indicate a moldboard, but not necessarily, since an effectively tilted ard could so describe itself (ibid.). There are no other Saxon documentary sources to indicate knowledge of, much less use of, the moldboard plow.

B. White (1962: 51) points out that the English word "plough" appears to derive from the Old Norse *plogr*, and suggests that it was the

Scandinavian settlers in Britain who introduced the implement. However, the Norwegian Ohthere, who contributed information concerning his homeland for the late ninth century A.D. version of "Orosius" prepared by King Alfred, makes no mention of the *plogr*, but only the ard (Steensberg 1936: 261). Admittedly, Ohthere came from northern Norway, where the *plogr* perhaps was unknown, or not used owing to local conditions, but certainly we can derive no positive plow from this direction.

c. White (1962: 52–53) supports his linguistic argument by reference to the Scandinavian system of land division, attested from the eleventh century A.D. onward, in which the major unit was divided into eighths. This, he maintains, was clearly based upon the use of the "heavy eight-ox plough," since "the ordinary peasant holding seems to have been thought of as the *mark*, i.e., two one-eighth units . . . , i.e., the equivalent of a yoke of oxen." Since a similar type of land division was also known from Domesday, England, particularly in Danelaw, the main area of Scandinavian colonization, White argues that it had been introduced to Britain by Scandinavian settlers. However, an eightfold land division system does not necessarily reflect either an eight-ox plow-team nor a "fully-developed heavy plough" (presumably meaning a moldboard plow); moreover, the supposedly essential eight-ox plow team in fact appears to be only one variant of the more usual four-ox team (Payne 1947: 107–108).

d. For the continent White (1962: 50–51) argues that the *carruca* "wheeled plow" was used in southwest Germany in the eighth century A.D., and that it was widespread over northern Gaul by the early ninth century A.D. He implies that the *carruca* is derived from the *plovum* of seventh-century A.D. northern Italy. Even if the *plovum* really does indicate a moldboard plow (see Bratanić 1952: 56), the case is still far from demonstrated for the moldboard plow in early ninth-century A.D. northern Gaul, since the use of the different term, *carruca*, suggests at least that this implement differed in some important respect from the *plovum*. White derived this interpretation of the *carruca* as a moldboard plow from Bloch (White 1962: 46). However, Bloch (1931) does not anywhere insist that the *carruca* had a moldboard. Again, we seem to be left with evidence for different plow types but no entirely clear information as to the specific components of each type.

Later Medieval Evidence

The much greater quantity of surviving documents from the post-Conquest period makes it clear that during the remainder of the medieval period various plow types were in use. Steensberg (1936: 261–279) considers some of the better-known evidence, and, while I would disagree with him on the interpretation of some individual implements, his overall conclusion of moldboard plows being well attested from the twelfth century A.D. onward I find quite satisfactory. Payne (1947: 107) points out that the earliest unequivocal linguistic evidence for the moldboard in England is within the thirteenth century A.D.

Population

As a basic source I have used here Russell, 1958, since this is the most recent survey of the evidence for European populations from classical antiquity to the postmedieval period. I have condensed Russell's cited data and his arguments as much as possible, and the reader is referred to his publication (1958) for any further information. Needless to say, there are those who contest Russell's population estimates. Nevertheless Russell, having surveyed all the evidence over this long period and considered it systematically in one work, affords the only consistent appraisal of population in Europe over a period of nearly two millennia. If Russell's estimates are too low, they are fairly consistently too low, since he uses the same criteria to estimate population wherever possible, and his comparisons between one period and another are made on this basis. Not surprisingly, a substantial number of imponderables occur in the information on which medieval and Roman population estimates are based.

Roman

ROMAN GAUL

For Roman Gaul, the starting point is Caesar's population data, which Beloch (1899) uses to arrive at ca. 5.7 million for all Gaul. Russell, extrapolating from Caesar's figures for the Helvetii and their allies, arrives at ca. 4 million. Extrapolating from Caesar's figures for warriors of the Belgae, he estimates 8 million. Assuming urban population

density to be similar, he compares the walled area of fourteenth century
A.D. French towns to the walled area of the same towns in the Gallo-
Roman period, and on this basis reaches a population figure of around
5 million for Roman Gaul. Extrapolating from the Constantinian tax
assessment for Autun, he concludes that the total population of Gaul
was around 5.6 million. It is not surprising that all of these varied types
of estimate should produce such varied results, but these figures do seem
more realistic than the wilder guesses of other authors (anything up to
20 million for Roman Gaul). Nevertheless, an estimate ranging from
4 million to 8 million, even if more likely to range around the 5 million
to 6 million mark, is not a very satisfactory basis for further work,
especially in view of our ignorance of the details of population distribution and rural technology, that is, of the realities of land utilization in
relation to population during the period.

ROMAN BRITAIN

Roman Britain (which fortunately approximately coincides with the
area covered for the 1086 Domesday Survey) is even less adequately
assessed as to population. Using his hypothesis that the population of the
largest town is 1.5 percent that of the total population, Russell (basing
his estimate on Roman London) is disinclined to allow more than
300,000 for the population of the province (see Figure 6.2). However,
archaeologists with considerable knowledge of Roman Britain consider
this estimate too low. Collingwood (1929) suggests a population of
0.5 million. But Randall (1930) and Wheeler (1930) both consider this
estimate too small; Wheeler proposes a population of around 1.5 million.
Little (1936) concludes that the minimum population was probably
0.5 million and that the maximum probably did not exceed 1.0 million.
Again, the wide range of estimates is an unsatisfactory state of affairs.

Medieval

SAXON ENGLAND

The years following the demise of the Empire in the West are complicated, for our purposes of population estimates, by the problems of
plague, which seems to have begun around A.D. 543 and is assumed by
Russell to have been proportionate in its effects on the total population
of Europe to the Black Death of the fourteenth century A.D. Russell
suggests a population for England of around 0.5 million for A.D. 543,

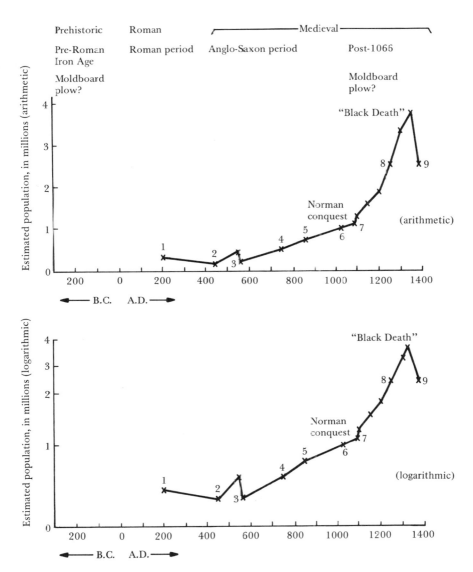

Figure 6.2. England: Iron age to fourteenth century A.D.—population and other items (population data taken from Russell 1953). 1. Extrapolated from town sizes.   2. Adventus Saxonum.   3. Sixth-century plague.   4. Tribal Hidage (Russell considers this eighth-century document a copy of a late sixth-century one).   5. "Peter's Pence." 6. Norman Conquest, A.D. 1066.   7. Domesday Survey, A.D. 1086.   8. Figures obtained by extrapolation from Extents, Inquisitions, etc.   9. Poll Tax, A.D. 1377.

immediately before the onset of the plague. This is based on his
population estimate for Roman Britain and allows for an influx of
Saxon immigrants. The seventh century Tribal Hidage affords Russell
the opportunity to estimate the mid-eighth-century population at around
0.5 million—a recovery to preplague level. In mid-ninth-century
Wessex, the "Peter's Pence," paid in support of the pope, suggests a
population for that area of 287,040, which is about 66 percent of
Russell's estimated Domesday population for the same area (432,958).
Extrapolating this to the country as a whole, 66 percent of Russell's
Domesday estimated population of 1.1 million gives an estimate of ca.
726,000 for mid-ninth-century England.

NINTH-CENTURY FRANCE

A. Using the levy figures on which was based the tribute paid to the
Normans and extrapolating them for the area of Roman Gaul, Russell
proposes a total population of about 5.04 million.

B. Polyptyque d'Irminon: the far more detailed figures afforded by this
early ninth-century survey would give a total population for the same
area of about 15 million, and Russell considers this far too high. The
reason for the apparent discrepancy lies in the population density
figures. For the very limited area covered by the Polyptyque d'Irminon
the population was ca. 26 per km^2, while for the very much larger area
covered by the Norman Tribute, the population density was much
lower, ca. 8.5 per km^2, or about one-third that indicated by the
Polyptyque d'Irminon. Presumably the area covered by the latter must
have been particularly densely inhabited by rural standards. Russell
suggests that many country areas at this time were still virtually uninhabited, being occupied by substantial populations only with the
extensive assarting (see Glossary) of the succeeding centuries.

DOMESDAY SURVEY OF ENGLAND (A.D. 1086)

A number of population estimates have been made from this source.
The essential difficulty of estimating population here is that Domesday
Survey is a survey of productive assets rather than of population per se.
Thus the basis for population figures is mainly the number of recorded
landowners, and estimates vary as to the number of additional persons
"per landowner" that should be allowed. This variation is considerable—
from 1.1 million to 2 million (Russell 1958: 11). For France at this
time Russell (1958: 105, Table 104) suggests a population of ca. 4

million—this is for France in 1326. For the area of Roman Gaul he proposes a population of ca. 7.3 million. This rough calculation is based upon the areal expansion of towns in France: additions to the Roman walls began in the eleventh century A.D. and continued during the twelfth and thirteenth centuries A.D. Russell concludes therefore that the twelfth-century A.D. population of the Roman Gaul area was about that of the Roman period, perhaps about 5 or 6 million.

FRANCE IN 1328

For the area that constituted France in A.D. 1328, Russell accepts the evidence of the Hearth Tax, and estimates a population total for that area of about 12.5 million. Here again, however, we must note a difficulty in assessing population from available records kept for other purposes. First, it is not certain that one hearth is the same as one household, since unusually detailed documentary evidence for a small area of the Spanish Pyrenees around A.D. 1400 gives the number of houses at 1,380 while the number of hearths is given as 1,405. The same source lists 1,494 heads of families. Second, there is argument as to the number of persons that should be computed for each hearth, house, or head of household. Third, it is not clear from the records how much of France was assessed in this way. Thus, even with such detailed data as the 1328 French Hearth Tax, there will remain some considerable margin for argument when it comes to computing total population. Extrapolation of the 1328 French population estimate (at ca. 12.5 million) back to England suggests to Russell a population for that country of ca. 3.5 million.

THE 1377 POLL TAX FOR ENGLAND

This tax (paid for all over age thirteen) is generally agreed to provide a fairly reliable population estimate of ca. 2 to 2.5 million. But we should note that, while the returns for 1377 incidated 1,355,555 payers, the 1381 tax, although admittedly assessed on somewhat different bases, indicated only 896,481 payers!

Summary of Population Estimates for the Roman and Medieval Periods

The foregoing synopsis of the major evidence for population in England and France from the Roman period to the fourteenth century is all too brief and simplified. As mentioned earlier, using Russell (1958) as the basic source has the one advantage of a degree of consistency. But it must always be remembered that, despite this degree of consistency, the variable nature of the raw data must make for variability in attempting assessment of population figures. As an approximation, however, we might accept tentatively the general nature of the "curve" displayed, while recognizing that it could be set higher or lower in terms of absolute population. If we can admit this, at least for temporary working purposes, it may be possible to suggest cautiously how other evidence, pertaining to land utilization and rural technology, might correlate with relative population figures. However, the hazards of deriving even relative population figures are such that I am most reluctant to do more than guess at possible correlations with other factors. As for absolute figures, their importance must not be underrated. For example, in relation to the extensiveness and/or intensity of land use in England in 1086, it makes a very considerable difference if the population is to be calculated at 1.1 million or 2.0 million, the second figure being almost double the first.

Prehistoric Population in Temperate Europe
In considering the evidence summarized briefly for Roman and medieval populations in temperate Europe, it seems impossible to make any very serious attempt to assess the prehistoric population of Europe, for which we have far less information. It is not only the lack of data on tax levies and so forth, but our woefully inadequate knowledge of what areas actually were occupied and in what manner. For medieval populations we have at least some information from place-name distribution, grants to assart, and the like with which to flesh out the bare archaeological evidence of actual physical settlements. But for the prehistoric period our distribution maps may be grossly distorted by the ravages of subsequent continued land use, and this distortion may well vary from area to area and period to period, depending upon the nature of the later land use.

Settlement Patterns

I have already hazarded the guess (in the introduction to this chapter) that by the pre-Roman Iron Age the population of temperate Europe was exerting some pressure on that land for which it possessed a suitable agricultural technology. Whether this pressure was exacerbated by the sub-Atlantic climatic deterioration or ameliorated by the introduction of iron technology is a matter for debate: clearly, though, these factors complicate the issue. Historically, it might be possible to see this suggested situation as a major cause for those westward population movements that brought Rome into conflict with the transalpine barbarians. One might go further to argue that the 400-odd years of Roman domination of Western Europe, keeping barbarian population expansion partly (though not wholly) in check, provided an incentive to those barbarians to intensify their food-production systems by continuing to improve their plows and extend the use of those improved plows. In addition, the founding of the terp and wurt sites (see Glossary) along the marshy North Sea littoral indicates that extension of occupation was also employed as a partial remedy. This was perhaps made possible by the improvement in plow types to the point where, under some duress, heavy and wet soils were taken under cultivation, at least in areas that afforded opportunity for insurance by diversification (for example, sea fishing, trading).

By the Belgic (latest pre-Roman Iron Age phase in southeast Britain) and Roman periods it is clear that there was settlement on intermediate soils, at least in some areas (Wooldridge and Linton 1933: 297; Wooldridge 1936: 114–115; Appelbaum 1958: 69; Fowler 1966: 54–55). As already indicated, I suspect that this was a pattern inherited from a period earlier than the pre-Roman Iron Age; it may have begun as early as the second millennium B.C.

While comparing Roman to early medieval settlement in England, one is led to suspect increasingly that the supposed dichotomy between Roman and early Saxon settlement is exaggerated, if not quite false. There is distributional evidence that the early Saxon settlers (whether foederati or invaders) did not colonize the heavy clay lands, after all (Wooldridge 1936: 114). It was probably not until a later phase of expansion that the Saxons tackled these heavy soils, which were until then perhaps virtually unoccupied. This is indicated by the proliferation of "-ley," "-den," and "-field" place-name suffixes, all of which indicate the assarting of wooded, and therefore probably lightly settled, areas (ibid.: 130–131). In gross distributional terms the largest area of heavy clay land lies in Midland England, to the west of the area of earlier Saxon settlement, so that Saxon expansion would naturally be in this direction and onto these lands. However, the avoidance of smaller areas of heavy soil was practiced in the areas of earliest Saxon settlement, in east and southeast England (ibid.: 114–115), making it clear that these were regarded as marginal, and that intermediate soils, especially loams, were preferred.

This contradicts the popular assumption that the Saxons preferred the potentially rich clay lands, but a probable answer lies in the adjective "potentially." Stamp (1969: 225 ff.) argues convincingly for long-term historical stability in the land use of England but points out that this is most true of the best and worst lands. Here he is working within the scheme of the British Land Utilization Survey (Stamp 1937–1947), which divided land into three major groups: good quality, medium-quality, and poor-quality land; these categories were determined, not by strict soil classification studies, but by observed agricultural use and potential (ibid.: 241–248). Stamp says of the medium-quality lands:

the maximum change is on land(s) of intermediate quality [that is, inter-mediate in economic potential rather than intermediate in grade of soil] which are abandoned in whole or part when agricultural prices are low, to be taken in hand again when prices rise. Particularly interesting are the good but heavy clay lands. . . . Not easy to manage, ploughable only when moisture conditions are just right and so workable only at certain seasons, they will yield the heaviest of all wheat crops when adequate labor is available.

This seems to provide a convincing reason for the apparent marginality of heavy clay lands in the prehistoric and early historic periods. The plow needed to cultivate such land had been developed, so it would seem, in the pre-Roman Iron Age—the heavy ard with iron coulter and share so necessary to cut, drain, and aerate such soils. Whether or not the moldboard was already added to this implement we do not know for certain, but perhaps this was more of a refinement than an essential component.

By the early ninth century A.D. the Polyptyque d'Irminon affords some evidence for reclaiming marshland (Russell 1958: 94), and Bloch (1931: 16) puts the major period of most extensive assarting as starting in the eleventh and twelth centuries and ceasing around A.D. 1300. By this time, he suggests (ibid.: 17) that the disappearance of considerable areas of forest was becoming critical, since forest was needed for a wide variety of purposes: grazing (especially swine), fuel, hunting, bark, wild fruit trees for grafting, and so forth.

The Domesday Survey of A.D. 1086 demonstrates clearly that much of the English clay lands had been taken up for agriculture by this time—in itself clear enough evidence for prior assarting. The survey gives little explicit evidence for assarting (ibid.: 180), because its organization did not include any formula for recording the process. However, there are references to assarting in Herefordshire and to *hospites* "probably colonists" along the Welsh Marches (ibid.). Furthermore, nine East Anglian villages, surveyed in both 1066 and 1086, show an average of a 58 percent decrease in swine pannage (clearly implying decreasing woodland) over this twenty-year period (ibid.: 183) which shows that assarting was being contemplated. Against this, we have to bear in mind the extensive areas set aside by William I as "Royal Forests," and the large areas, especially in the North, that were "laid waste" in the immediate aftermath of the Conquest.

We may note here that Gray (1915: 73) states that the two-field rotation system was used mainly on poorer soils, and the three-field system on richer soils; he points out (ibid.: 82) that, in 1086, the Midland clay areas—supposedly the richest soils available—were under two-field rotation for the main part, as opposed to predominantly three-field rotation elsewhere in England. This can be explained, as Gray himself hints, by noting some transition in the Midlands to three-field rotation in the thirteenth and early fourteenth centuries (ibid.: 192) and proposing that these Midland clay areas were still, in 1086, relatively thinly settled, colony areas, in which the less intensive two-field rotational system was still perfectly satisfactory—an explanation in accord with the relative marginality of heavy clay soils noted earlier. Subsequent documentation for the twelfth and thirteenth centuries affords considerable evidence for increasing pressure on the woodlands: increasing litigation over grazing lands, the rising prices of meadowlands, and explicit grants to assart (ibid.: 184–189). After the Black Death such information lessens dramatically.

Summary

Prehistoric Period

Although some potential population information is available (Piggott 1965: 47, 58, 68, n. 52), it seems premature to attempt seriously any population estimates, except to suggest strongly that, by the pre-Roman Iron Age, the population of temperate Europe was reaching a critical point in relation to its rural economy and technology. I suggest that substantial areas of intermediate soils had long been under cultivation by this time and that increasing population pressure is expressed in new and more varied forms of ard (and possibly the moldboard plow), and in the expansion of agriculture to (or, rather, *back* to?) lighter, poorer soils.

Roman Period

No evidence for any dramatic population increase exists for Roman-dominated areas. Outside this zone population pressure was at least maintained and probably increased. There is no clear evidence for improvement of agricultural technology, in either Roman or barbarian areas.

Early Medieval Period (up to ca. A.D. 800)

The substantial population flow westward may well account for much of the population increase in Western temperate Europe during this time. However, there is evidence that new land was being assarted before A.D. 800, indicating either continued migration from the east or expansion of the newly immigrant population.

About 800–1100 A.D.

There is increased evidence for assarting, land reclamation, and population increase but no evidence for increased efficiency in plow technology.

About 1100–1350 A.D.

Abundant evidence exists for assarting and population increase. Quite clearly a number of plow types were in common use, no doubt reflecting the requirements of different soils and perhaps different stages of assarting. However, we cannot say that this situation represents any clear improvement in available plow technology over the preceding periods.

Conclusion

The all-too-scanty evidence now available for our period, ca. 500 B.C. to ca. A.D. 1350, tends to indicate that the major varieties of plow were available before the Roman period if one accepts the furrow evidence from Feddersen Wierde. If this is so, one can discern no obvious improvement right through the whole period. In consequence, one must attribute the increased agricultural yield to expansion of the areas under cultivation, and perhaps also to intensification and improvement of such factors as manuring and crop rotation. If, on the other hand, one cannot accept the evidence for the moldboard plow in the pre-Roman Iron Age, I can see no clear evidence for its appearance prior to the twelfth century A.D. In this case, the apparent great increase of assarting around this time could be connected with the new implement, if indeed it was so revolutionary in its effect.

It is impossible, on this evidence, to determine whether population increase precedes increase of agricultural yield, or vice versa.

Glossary

Plows:

Ard
From *PIE root *ara, of which variants survive in many Indo-European languages. While we do not know just what the original word meant (see remarks by Cowgill at end of Wailes 1970), it has been taken to mean a "scratch plow," that is, an implement that scratches a furrow without turning the sod right over as a moldboard plow does. The scratch plow is quite satisfactory in the Mediterranean and on lighter soils in the temperate part of Europe. However, it is less well suited to the tilling of heavier and damper soils in temperate Europe, since these latter soils require good drainage and aeration. Hence, the arguments about the changes in plow type in relation to soil type.

Wheel plow (carruca, charrue)
Simply, a plow (of some sort) with a wheel, or wheels, supporting the beam of some heavier form of plow. A wheel plow is not necessarily a moldboard plow: it may be technically an ard with a wheel.

Moldboard plow
A plow with an attached moldboard, which "catches" the sod cut by the coulter and share, and turns it over so that the original top of the

sod is lying downward. This greatly assists aeration and drainage of the plowsoil.

Turnwrest plow, or one-way plow
This implement is a moldboard plow on which the moldboard may be attached to either side of the plow, enabling the plowman to turn the furrow either to left or right at will (a normal moldboard plow has the moldboard attached to the right side, thus turning the furrow that way only). The effect of the "one-way" plow is that a whole field can be plowed with all the furrows lying one way (hence the misleading term "one-way" plow).

Swing plow
A fixed moldboard plow without wheels.

Coulter
A large knifelike object set vertically just ahead of the share. It cuts the sod vertically, the share cuts it horizontally. On a plow with fixed moldboard the coulter is set just to the left of the share, so that the cut sod is turned to the right. On a "one-way" plow the coulter is adjustable, so that it can be set either to right or left of the share.

Fields, etc.:

Assarting
The "taking in" of land hitherto uncultivated, or not cultivated for a long time and thus covered with regenerated arboreal growth.

Celtic field (Danish "Oltidsagre")
Small, squarish field normally (but not necessarily) bounded by banks, walls, ditches, or other apparently intentional boundaries. So called because this type of field is still the normal field in the Celtic areas of the British Isles, and was not replaced by the "Open Fields."

Open field
Large field, often of irregular shape, containing a number of smaller holdings within it. These smaller units are not normally bounded permanently, and may be of various shapes and sizes—squarish or long and narrow. The open field system is often associated with strip cultivation, but the two are not synonymous.

Strip cultivation
Plowing in long, proportionately narrow, "strips." This is very often associated with "ridge and furrow."

Ridge and furrow (rig and furrow)
Caused by turning the sod inward toward a central line, which thus becomes a "ridge"; the line from which the sod is turned on each side becomes a shallow ditch—the "furrow." A field thus plowed appears to

have a corrugated surface, the ridges being of varying widths ("broad rig," "narrow rig") to suit different drainage conditions.

Lazy beds
Hand-cultivated (usually with spade) ridges that appear superficially similar to "ridge and furrow," except that the ridges are normally much shorter in lazy beds. Apparently an adaptation to conditions (especially very stony areas where surface is irregular) in which there is need for (a) concentration of thin soil into piles to promote crop growth, and (b) drainage.

Lynchets
Formed by downhill soil creep from top to bottom of a cultivated area on a slope: a "negative lynchet" forms at the uphill side, a "positive lynchet" at the downhill side. Well-developed lynchets are thus indicative of cultivation of the same area for a considerable period of time; of "settled agriculture," in other words. See Wailes 1970 for fuller discussion.

Other terms:

Terp, wurt
These are artificial mounds on which habitations were built. They are found along the coasts of Friesland and nothern Germany, and date from the Iron Age, Roman period, and migration period. They were evidently intended to afford relatively dry occupation areas in low-lying marshy coastal lands.

7

Some Aspects of Agriculture in Taita[1]

Alfred Harris

Harris, writing as a social anthropologist, finds Boserup's model generally stimulating but feels that it requires modification, noting that while population growth is *a* factor in agricultural change, it is not necessarily *the* factor. To support this view, he sketches briefly and selectively certain aspects of agriculture among the Wataita of Kenya. He concludes that although this is, in conventional terms, a "simple" agricultural system, it is nevertheless impossible to understand it fully without paying careful attention to variation and to social relationships connected with landholding, land use, and exchange. Experimentation, too, is built into the technology, and it induces change independently of demographic or other factors. His argument suggests that ultimately a multifactor model should be constructed and an attempt made to specify the conditions under which various factors assume greater or lesser importance in fostering agricultural change.

In the course of his argument the author draws attention to the range of simple technologies that make up both the system of adaptations of the logical universe of study (as he would define it) and the annual cycles of the individuals of the society. His data lead him to seek a redefinition of technology in tune with the reasoning of Adams (see Introduction, this volume), to include those aspects of social organization which allow the range of relationships necessary for the activities of cooperation and distribution which are integrally involved in the society's subsistence.

The Taita Agricultural System

The Wataita of Kenya occupy three discrete areas near the coast, approximately 140 miles north of Mombasa. I will consider only the largest of these areas, a rectangle roughly 14 or 15 miles square which includes two main blocks of hills (Dabida and Mbololo) and had in 1948 a population of approximately 40,000. With an area of about 200 square miles, the average density was thus close to 200 per square mile, though there is great variation in density of population if subareas are considered.[2]

Despite the small area, Taita displays a remarkable ecological diversity. The kinds of variation (and their degree) are recognized by Wataita and are either taken into account in agriculture or actively utilized. The lowest part of the plains next to Dabida lie at 2,400 feet, while the highest peak is 7,200 feet. Both plains and hills are marked by great variability and a real scarcity of level land. The topographic character of the area strongly affects the rainfall regime, modifying it so that there are not only altitudinal variations in the annual rainfall received but also some seasonal variations that arise because the hills screen differentially in the two rainy seasons. Rainfall is a good example of how extreme variation is: the range is from an average of 20 inches or less on the plains to an average of over 60 inches in the highest parts of Dabida. Correlatively, there are important differences in vegetation, though reconstruction of general patterns would be difficult since nearly the whole of Taita has been subjected to cultivation, and save for small relict patches there is little climax cover remaining. Soils, drainage, the occurrence of groundwater, and a variety of other less obvious elements (insolation, winds, and seasonal mists, for example) vary as well.

Not only do Wataita have detailed knowledge of practically all aspects of their environment, but this knowledge is actively used in the conduct of agriculture.

Everywhere in Taita three main sorts of cultivated land are recognized. These can be glossed as dry, moist (that is, perennially watered, as are swamps and seepage areas), and irrigated fields. A few areas used as pasture may never have been cultivated, but other areas, large and small, are known to have been used in different ways at different times. Fields may revert to pasture, and pasture may be taken over as dry fields. Areas once irrigated may become dry fields also. The areas I call moist are the most stable, though not immune to change. There are now three major ones, two of which are of substantial size. The third was said formerly to have been much larger, and a fourth (not in the area being considered) disappeared entirely as a result of a European mosquito control drainage project early in the century. The third area's reduction must have taken place at the same time. In addition to these major areas, all three of which are on the southern edge of Dabida, at the plains-hills margin, there are many far smaller moist areas within the hills.

In very broad terms, the various classes of land have a patterned distribution such that the largest proportions of pasture, browse, and dry fields are to be found on the plains and at lower altitudes. The largest areas of moist land are nearby, close to the plains. With increased altitude, particularly in the middle reaches of the hills, irrigation increases, while pasture and dry fields decrease.

There is a discernible zonation of land use, based upon but distinct from ecological zones, which can be seen as one moves from south to north and from lower to higher altitudes. There are, however, important differences between the southern and the northern hills. A line running northeast-southwest, connecting the major peaks in Dabida and that of Mbololo, divides the entire area under consideration into two, with the northern part having on the order of half of the total area but only about 20 percent of the population.

These two major areas have much in common, divergent though they are in important respects. By analogy with ecological usage, I term them the northern and the southern phases of a single agricultural system. The northern phase makes far more extensive use of dry plains fields. There are associated differences in settlement patterns. Northern phase agriculture tends strongly to be associated with large (sometimes very large) aggregated settlements. Residential densities may run to 4,000 per square mile, or higher. Southern phase agriculture tends strikingly to be associated with dispersed settlement. In these areas, residential aggregation does not begin to approach that found in northern phase areas and villages do not ordinarily exceed twenty households. Density of population more nearly reflects actual population distribution in the south, where small villages are scattered about. In the northern phase areas large and substantially uninhabited (though not unused) areas intervene between the aggregated villages.

These differences appear to depend on the proportions of dry fields, relative use of the plains, and the availability of water. In general, agricultural practice is the same in both areas with regard to the crops grown and the methods of cultivation. There are, however, important differences in the proportions of various crops.

Wataita stress the key importance of three kinds of crops—grains, legumes, and roots—in both their agricultural system and their diet. Maize, which had reached the area by 1848, is the most important of the grains and has almost entirely displaced millets and sorghums. Tiny quantities of rice are grown in a few areas. Of the legumes, beans are the most important and yams and cassava are the main root crops.

Though these crops predominate, the list of cultigens is large and, as new items are introduced and spread, constantly growing. Upward of twenty-five field crops were widespread in Taita, as well as several tree crops, including bananas, oranges, lemons, papaws, granadillas, and so on.

In addition to adoption of new crops, there is quite obviously a great deal of selective breeding about which, unfortunately, I know too little. For example, at least thirty varieties of beans were known, and these were said to be established strains suitable for particular combinations of soil, moisture, insolation, and wind conditions. As far as I could tell, other crops have fewer varieties, but the principle of deliberate selectivity is well established.

Some consideration of the cropping regime is necessary, though this is complex in practice. Thus only its major principles can be dealt with here.

The first kind of variation to be noted is that, as might be expected, the different categories of arable land are planted to rather different crops. This is critical in two respects. First, it is cumulative. Since the kinds of land are differentially distributed, and since they are not by any means of equal value for all crops, some areas outproduce others fairly regularly. Parts of the area given over to northern phase agriculture, for instance, produce very large quantities of beans. Second, any one household head will try to obtain the maximum workable mixture of different categories of land so that his household has to place minimal reliance on exchange or purchase for provision of foods not self-produced. The resultant of areal differences as countered by householders' efforts is to reduce interareal production differentials somewhat.

These efforts, however, are limited, for by no means do all households have available to them fully adequate amounts of the right kinds of land, appropriately situated. Various means are available for the adjustment of landholdings, in both short- and long-range terms, but these are best kept distinct from practices more immediately and obviously connected with the cropping system.

Of the latter, two may be mentioned as especially significant. The first is that the two rainy seasons have rather different characteristics, even within Taita, and cropping is adjusted to these differences. Second, clean planting of single crops is rare. Interplanting serves a number of different ends—water conservation, reduction of erosion, and protection of seedlings are among them—in addition to effectively increasing crop acreages and diversifying foods.

The cropping system, then, is conducted so as to reduce (but never entirely to eliminate) differences in production between comparable households as well as between different parts of Taita. In reasonably good years the expectation that some food will be available from the fields during every month of the year is fulfilled. This does not, of course, mean that every household has all of its needs met. Nor is field storage the only kind undertaken, though it is probably more important than in many similar systems.

Cultivation must be integrated with demands for grazing and brows-ing areas, for Wataita keep cattle, a few sheep, and goats. (They also keep chickens, dogs, and cats). In general, these demands are more difficult to meet within the hills than on the plains, and they are more easily handled in the north than in the south. Thus individuals in hill areas with more beasts than they can find grazing for locally (that is, readily accessible from their homes) must make provision for their care elsewhere, often in the hands of someone else for at least part of the time. Such arrangements, while common, are often difficult and time-consuming to arrange and maintain.

One striking characteristic of Taita agriculture is the relatively limited tool kit and the correlatively low investment in capital equip-ment. The key tools are bush knives (the panga, close kin to the machete), hoes of two types, and the digging stick. Various other tools (for example, knives and winnowing trays) are important, and so are the storage facilities and stabling needed by many farmers. In terms of crop production, however, the need for reasonably light and transportable tools is—almost everywhere in Taita—critical.

Who uses the tools—and when they are used—is more complex. It is necessary to note here that such tool-using activities as clearing bush, cultivating, weeding, baboon hunting and bird scaring, reaping or picking, carrying from the fields, preparing for storage and storing, herding, and so forth, are, in my view, only part of the work that is done to keep Taita agriculture going.

More narrowly, however, it is easy enough to establish that field-related work is undertaken by people of both sexes and of nearly all ages. Men do the heavy clearing and often break ground as well for their wives, the latter undertaking further preparation, planting, weeding, and harvesting. Men are in charge of herding, often assisted by young children, and a variety of other tasks, such as work on irrigation channels, are their province.

While the outlines are reasonably simple, the nuances are not. Many tasks are undertaken cooperatively, women being aided by daughters and daughters-in-law or men by sons and sons-in-law. What is particularly significant in this connection is that task allocation or cooperation varies a good deal in rigidity or flexibility. Some tasks, such as preparing a field for planting, can easily be given to particular types of hired labor (a young girls' cultivating club, for example). But others are more rigidly allocated: for instance, a woman's own husband *must* clear her fields of bush for her. On occasion her sons will perform the task.

A second kind of variation is to be met in crop assignment. While the main subsistence crops are grown by women, men grow a variety of other crops (largely nonessential) if they are grown at all. For these, of course, they must perform tasks normally undertaken by women.

It is incumbent upon a man to provide the fields cultivated by his wife or wives. Though some of these may be, and often are, patrimonial fields (use rights being passed from a man's mother to his wife), others are not. Few, if any, men in Taita hold for cultivation only inherited fields. Gaining others (by purchase, exchange, rental, borrowing, or, rarely, by opening new or unclaimed land) takes much time and effort, and I consider these activities to be a matter not only of politics, which they are, but of agricultural labor as well. The same is true, I feel, where negotiations and transactions over herds and their care are involved. Women enter into all these negotiations, most directly in land matters, which they frequently take into their own hands, informally (and illegally) exchanging fields or using land another woman chooses not to cultivate.

Discussion

Whether considered from the point of view of individual cultivators or in overall terms, agriculture in Taita is not "simple" in any reasonable sense. In more or less conventional terms, it might be characterized as predominantly a bush-fallow system, but this would not adequately account for the place of irrigation and moist fields and their produce. No one field type or cropping technique constitutes a distinct kind of agriculture in Taita; all are required. They are intimately connected not only in the practices of individuals but in the total system.

The same is true of areal differences. No part of Taita is wholly self-sufficient, even in good years. The interdependence of areas within Taita is even more apparent in years when poor rainfall accentuates differences in production. In general, the distribution of individuals' rights (to fields and to grazing areas) and the regular exchange of produce provide clear evidence of areal interdependence. Under especially adverse conditions, exchange increases and temporary population movements may occur.

What is especially important here is the ways in which Taita agricultural practices and the various kinds of land tenure are related to one another. Not only are adjustments possible; they are constantly being made in both, and though there is a tendency toward reduction of individual and areal differences, these nevertheless persist. Exchange is an important added element in the specification of connections between individuals and areas within Taita.

This view of Taita agriculture suggests that even though cropping practices are relatively uniform, an examination of them is not sufficient to specify the agricultural system. Any adequate specification would have to include all of the previously mentioned variations and the population involved. In practice this would include all of Taita since smaller units— of area or of population—would not embrace all of the variations and relationships.

The data on population growth and agricultural change in Taita do not provide strong evidence for or against Boserup's thesis that population growth is an independent variable in agricultural change. The data do, however, suggest that even if the case for this position appeared plausible, it would have to be examined with great care. Part of the difficulties stem from the generally held view that systems such as that in Taita are simple. Although this is true in relative terms, the system is nonetheless sufficiently complex (if adequately described) so that determining whether change was a response to population growth or, alternatively, a matter of the way in which the agricultural system works would be a challenging analytical task. I believe that Taita is similar to other so-called simple systems and that all pose the same difficulty.

Part of what is involved may be seen somewhat more clearly by considering briefly the question of technology and its status in agriculture. Boserup (1965: 56–57 and passim) tends to use "technology" to mean mainly tools and the techniques associated with their use. I believe this usage is unduly restrictive since it excludes many kinds of knowledge essential to agriculture, and it also excludes relationships crucial to its successful conduct. In Taita agriculture, even a full mastery of tools and techniques would not provide one with sufficient technical knowledge to survive very long.

A different view of technology would seem to be needed, and I have found that offered by Merrill (1968: 585; cf. Adams, Introduction, this volume) both helpful and productive. He points out that, among other things, " . . . a technology . . . is a flexible repertoire of skills, knowledge and methods for attaining desired ends and avoiding failures under varying circumstances."

This view serves to direct attention away from tools alone, or tools and techniques narrowly and rigidly conceived, and forces one to place them in a broader context. It leads me to a number of points about Taita agricultural technology, which are more concisely formulated in the following list:

1. Agricultural technology in Taita must be seen as being involved in a variety of social arrangements, without which the agricultural system could not operate. Even though many of these arrangements can be considered in terms of kinship or politics, this does not preclude their having a technological aspect as well. Such matters as gaining access to

land for cultivation or herding, or transferring it, are crucial parts of
agriculture.

2. There is, clearly, a relatively low investment in obvious capital goods.
Tools, seeds, supplies, and even the irrigation works require relatively
small investment. There is a very high investment, not readily calcu-
lable, in knowledge and in social arrangements. Continuity in these is
essential.

3. An important part of what is required to maintain Taita agriculture
in a viable state are ways of experimenting. The constant selective breeding and the testing of new crops provide one kind of evidence for this.
Certain shifts in task allocation provide another, for experimentation in
social arrangements that bear upon production can surely be viewed as
having a technological aspect.

4. There are significant rigidities as well, which must also be taken into
account. Social arrangements do not have unlimited flexibility, some
tasks cannot be reallocated, certain foods simply are not grown, and
so on.

This list of points could be extended, of course. They will serve to
illustrate the issues that seem to me critical in the context of Taita
agricultural technology. Too narrow a definition of technology would
blind one to some crucial aspects of how the agricultural system as a
whole works. At the same time, a broader definition makes it immediately apparent that there is a sense in which Taita technology, at the
least, *is* strongly autonomous. However, this does not necessitate its
being always progressive as well.

The kind of autonomy that must be stressed is implied by the freedoms
that exist in this agricultural system. These are freedoms—and techniques—that permit adaptation to both short-term and long-term
alterations of various factors. Wataita can and do make adjustments to
conditions arising in nature, to new possibilities of various sorts, to
changes in population distribution, and so on.

There may well be circumstances under which changes in population
can be linked firmly with changes in agriculture. However, the situation
in Taita provides clear evidence that there are various other possibilities
for the inception of agricultural change independent of population
increase. Borrowed cultigens, selective breeding, responses to population
movements (which do not result only from population pressure), and

changes in task allocation are a few of the more obvious elements that must be taken into account. They must first, however, be discovered, and this calls not only for careful observation but for theoretical formulations that will direct attention toward rather than away from them.

Even a cursory examination of the literature on other agricultural systems, in Africa[3] and elsewhere, provides hints that this point of view has some validity. These are generally systems of remarkable adaptability and flexibility, geared—as Merrill (1968: p. 585) suggests—to " ... attaining desired ends and avoiding failures under varying circumstances." In most parts of Africa, at least, failure is a nearly constant threat, and responsive technologies are of major importance in coping with it.

Notes

1. The field research on which this paper is based was supported by the (then) Colonial Social Science Research Council and was undertaken by my wife and me from July 1950 through August 1952. I am deeply indebted not only to the Council but to all those Wataita who patiently and generously helped us. The present sketch is to be expanded, I hope quite soon in a monographic treatment of Taita ecology, agriculture, and social structure. Christopher Day and Grace Harris read drafts of the paper, and their suggestions improved it greatly.
2. Detailed consideration of areas, populations, and densities of various sorts is beyond the scope of this paper, and these figures are approximations, albeit very close ones.
3. Excellent starting points for accounts of such African systems, providing references to fuller accounts, are Allan (1965), Biebuyck (1963), and McLoughlin (1970).

8

Farm Labor and the Evolution of Food Production

Bennet Bronson

This essay has a different orientation from much of the rest of the book. It finds its place here because it is concerned with agriculture: specifically, with questions of productivity and the evolution of technology in primitive agriculture in both the prehistoric and the ethnographic contexts. Bronson questions the historical validity of Boserup's model and therefore, also by implication, its general interpretative potential (though not necessarily the particular thesis of any of the other contributors to the volume). One of the basic differences between Bronson and Boserup is in the evaluation of data and statistics, in particular those in which investment—by either recent or distant, earlier generations—is a hidden factor. This brings us back once again to the question of the logical universe of study, though in this case it is not the spatial or geographical but the temporal universe that is in question.

The essay consists of two semiautonomous sections. The second section discusses the general problem of evolutionary models for agriculture. But before that a more specific issue has to be dealt with: the first section presents certain empirical and a priori grounds for questioning the contention that in typical cases output per unit of labor would decline when a given population in a given territory replaces extensive primitive agricultural methods with intensive ones (Boserup 1965: 41 and passim).

I. The Productivity of Primitive Labor

The validity of the Boserup model depends on the "law of least effort": since most farmers are concerned primarily with the minimization of effort and since each stage of agricultural change is less labor efficient than its predecessor, farmers in general prefer the most extensive system possible and intensify only when forced to do so by population pressure. This reasoning seems logical enough with regard to the early stages in the evolutionary sequence. Short-fallowed (and otherwise unimproved) land produces less food per cropped acre than long-fallowed land. It also requires less work, but this advantage tends to be offset by a lower yield, so that the farmer's net labor efficiency is decreased (moderately long fallows are clearly preferable to short ones). However, a difficulty arises when we move further up the sequence to annual cropping and multi-cropping. Swiddeners may usually prefer to use long fallows if they have a choice; but do multicroppers tend to aspire to be annual croppers, and annual croppers swiddeners?

It is clear in the first place that, if they do, their preference is probably not based on considerations of labor economy. Although the literature contains few quantitative data on the productivity of agricultural labor in other societies, such data as exist point to a conclusion somewhat at odds with our commonsense expectations. In point of fact, shifting cultivation is not always, and perhaps not usually, easier work than permanent field farming. These data are summarized in Table 8.1.

The conclusion comes out quite plainly. A great deal of shifting cultivation is monumentally inefficient. No extensive system for which data are available is as productive as the developed forms of wet rice growing and European dry farming. And although relatively inefficient intensive agriculturalists do exist, none of them seems to receive as little for their efforts as the great majority of extensive farmers. These data are plausible enough; however, they fall short of being completely convincing.

The difficulty is that they are cross-environmental and cross-cultural: a comparison of English wheat farmers and African cassava growers must disregard many differences in environment and economy. In order to control these variables, it seems best to find examples of groups who practice both intensive and extensive agriculture at the same time and in the same place.

The first case in point comes from the work of Stadelman (1940: Tables 11 and 12), from which one can calculate productivity statistics for four of the five stages of agricultural evolution. The figures pertain to maize farming in Huehuetenango, in highland Guatemala. The annually

Table 8.1 The Productivity of Agricultural Labor

Place	Group	Type of Farming	Crop	Productivity (bushels/ man-day) [a]	Source
Szechwan [b]	Chinese	Intensive irrigation [c]	Rice	1.41	Buck 1937: 225, 307 ff.
Yangtze Basin [b]	Chinese	Intensive irrigation [c]	Rice	0.99	Buck 1937: 225, 307 ff.
Northern Thailand	—	Intensive irrigation [c]	Rice	1.55	Moerman 1968: 172
Central Thailand	—	Intensive irrigation [c]	Rice	1.51	Janlekha 1955: 106
Japan	—	Intensive irrigation [c]	Rice	0.50	Beardsley, Hall and Ward 1959: 175, 178
Sarawak	Iban [d]	Extensive	Rice	0.40	Freeman 1955: 90, 93–98
Sarawak	Dayak	Extensive	Rice	0.32	Geddes 1954: 65–68
Gambia	—	Extensive	Rice	0.12 ⎫	Clark and
Upper Volta	—	Extensive	Rice	0.16 ⎬	Haswell 1969:
Nyasaland	—	Extensive	Rice	0.43 ⎭	90 [e]
Medieval England [f]	—	Intensive dry farming	Wheat	1.12	Slicher van Bath 1963: 173–176, 183–184, 302
Japan	—	Intensive dry farming	Barley	0.50	Smith 1956: 52–53
Guatemala [g]	Maya	Semi-intensive	Corn	0.31–1.07	Stadelman 1940: Tables 11 and 12
Yucatán [h]	Maya	Extensive	Corn	0.91	Steggerda 1941: 130
Quintana Roo [h]	Maya	Extensive	Corn	0.75	Villa Rojas 1945: 60, 62, 77
Guatemala	—	Extensive	Corn	0.87 ⎫	
Gambia	—	Extensive	Corn	0.16 ⎪	
Ghana	—	Extensive	Corn	0.19 ⎬	Clark and
Upper Volta	—	Extensive	Corn	0.28 ⎪	Haswell 1967 [e]
Nigeria	—	Extensive	Corn	0.29 ⎪	
Nyasaland	—	Extensive	Corn	0.21 ⎭	
New Guinea [i]	Kapauku	Semi-intensive	Sweet potatoes	0.61	Pospisil 1963
New Guinea [i]	Kapauku	Extensive	Sweet potatoes	0.36	

Place	Group	Type of Farming	Crop	Productivity (bushels/ man-day) [a]	Source
Upper Volta	—	Extensive	Cassava	0.48	
Nigeria	—	Extensive	Cassava	0.23	
Nyasaland	—	Extensive	Cassava	0.81	Clark and
Ghana	—	Extensive	Yams	0.32	Haswell 1967 [e]
Upper Volta	—	Extensive	Yams	0.11	
Nigeria	—	Extensive	Yams	0.54	

a. Productivity is calculated by dividing man-days per land unit by yield per land unit. A man-day is taken to be ten man-hours long. When yields are given in the sources by weight, they are converted to bushels according to the following ratios: 27.22:1 (wheat, sweet potatoes), 20.41:1 (rice), and 25.40:1 (corn). These are the weights in kilograms of the U.S. standard bushel.

b. Buck's sample is massive in size but may be slightly skewed in the direction of larger-than-average landholdings (Perkins 1969: 267–268). This should not affect the validity of his data on yields and labor input.

c. All five of these examples are classic Asiatic wet rice systems. The Chinese and Japanese are double-croppers, while the Thais take only one crop per year. The Thai systems are not as technically elaborate as the others; they involve little manuring or—in the Northern Thai example—large-scale engineering.

d. The Iban are famous in the literature as prototypical *mangeurs du bois*, long fallowers inhabiting a virgin forest area. Their poor showing on the productivity scale is significant. It should be remembered, however, that dry rice is not an efficient crop compared to corn, sweet potatoes, cassava, and yams.

e. Productivity here is expressed in "wheat equivalents," a nutritional unit derived by Clark and Haswell (1967) from a comparison between the caloric values of other crops and wheat, with the results weighted according to the other crops' relative protein content. Wheat equivalent figures are somewhat lower than actual production figures. The latter can be obtained by adding one-third (for corn) and one-fourth (for rice) to the wheat-equivalent figures, and by quadrupling them for root crops.

f. Since it seemed desirable to have some estimate for the productivity of European-style intensive dry farming, in the preindustrial period the figure of 1.12 bu/man-day was calculated from data in Slicher van Bath (1963: 183–184). They pertain to English agriculture in the thirteenth century:

Threshing	18	man-days/hectare
Harvesting	5.5	man-days/hectare
Plowing	3	man-days/hectare
(Haying and carting)	6	man-days/hectare
Other	3	man-days/hectare
	35.5	man-days/ha/yr.

Since he gives no figures for medieval haying and carting, these have been interpolated from eighteenth-century data (p. 302). Yields were very variable during the Middle Ages (pp. 175–176); 37 bu/ha is lower than the average. It is abysmally low both by modern standards and by the standards of many primitive agriculturalists—even the Iban get 60 bu/ha. But since the labor input is also extremely low (compare the Dayak at 250 man-days/ha, and the bush-fallowing Orokaiva of New Guinea [Crocombe and Hobgin 1963: 69] who expend 358 man-days on an average hectare), the net efficiency of the medieval English system is impressively high. The labor figures include estimates (haying and carting) for man-days of work incidental to feeding plow animals (see Smith and Young: Chap. 1, this Vol.) but do not make allowance for time spent actually caring for stock. However, even if this additional labor is counted, European-style intensive farming still looks more efficient than almost any extensive system.

g. The figures refer to production on refuse-fertilized infields. The corresponding out-fields are much less efficient.

h. Villa Rojas's figures have been converted as follows: 20 *mecates* = 1 hectare, and 1 kg of cob corn = 0.55 kg of shelled corn. The latter ratio is suggested by Cowgill (1961). Both the Yucatán and the Quintana Roo groups are unusually efficient for shifting cultivators. It is interesting to note that they attain this efficiency by using very large fields, often several hectares in extent, and by working the land rather lightly—a strategy similar to that used by the medieval English.

i. The "semi-intensive" fields are drained bottomland gardens; the "extensive" ones are bush-fallowed hillside swiddens. There are a few swiddens in the bottomlands as well; they are even more efficient than the semi-intensive fields. The data are presented in order to give some idea of the potential productivity of primitive intensive systems. It is quite respectable. For the sake of comparability, the figures have been converted into wheat equivalents. This is the only instance where data that are not from Clark and Haswell have been so treated. The rest are in the original, nonwheat equivalent form.

Table 8.2 Productivity of Maize Farming According to Evolutionary Stages (calculated in bushels per man-day)

	Forest (Long) Fallow	Bush Fallow	Grass (Short) Fallow	2nd-Year Fields	Annual Cropping
Santa Eulalia	0.33	0.34	0.16	0.34	—
San Mateo Ix.	0.36	0.38	0.21	0.34	0.31
Soloma	0.29	0.42	0.29	0.36	0.52
Concepción	0.41	0.42	0.34	0.54	1.07
Todos Santos	—	0.42	0.28	0.42	0.74
San Miguel A.	0.50	0.38	0.24	0.38	0.60

cropped fields listed are permanent infields, fertilized mainly by domestic refuse; the designations forest, bush, and grass fallow refer to the type of vegetational cover present before burning and correspond only approximately to the Boserup categories long, bush, and short fallowing. Nonetheless, the data are provocative. Long and bush fallowing seem to be equally productive, while short fallowing is inferior to the other two. But none of the shifting regimes are a match for annual cropping from the standpoint of labor efficiency (see Table 8.2).

The same conclusion is reached when we compare the productivities of bush-fallowed (dry) and annually cropped (wet) rice for Gambia (Clark and Haswell 1967: 92) and the Land Dayak of Sarawak (Geddes 1954: 65–68) in Table 8.3. The wet rice in question is grown by simple flood-farming methods; hence, this particular kind of annual cropping

Table 8.3 Productivity of Wet and Dry Rice (calculated in bushels per man-day)

Place	Wet Rice	Dry Rice
Gambia	0.22	0.05
Sarawak	(0.29 (0.39	(0.15 (0.31

Note: The Sarawak data derive from a sample of only four fields

cannot be compared with such truly intensive regimes as those of the Thais and the Chinese. However, the example is relevant to our subject. There can be no doubt that the less extensive regime is, on balance, the more labor efficient.

I have no actual information on the relative productivity of shifting versus permanent cultivation in societies that practice one of the two major intensive systems, Asian irrigated rice growing or European stock-grain mixed farming. Perhaps, however, some such estimate can be gained indirectly by considering cases where a choice between intensive and extensive techniques seems to have been made at some time in the past. This type of reasoning has occasionally been used to prove a thesis opposite from the one presented here. Some authorities believe that instances of technical regression show the superior efficiency of extensive agriculture. The literature contains a number of cases of this kind, of Italians and Germans beginning to swidden when transplanted to Brazil (Boserup 1965: 63), of the hit-and-run methods used by tobacco farmers in Virginia and the Carolinas during colonial times (Sauer 1956: 63), and of the persistence of outfield or lea farming among the peasants of Ireland and Germany. These data are used by Boserup and others to support the thesis that swiddening is easier than intensive farming, but the evidence for regression from intensive farming to swiddening is very thin. None of the above-mentioned examples actually proves the contention. The Brazilian colonists had been transplanted to a new environment where arguably their former intensive techniques did not work. The Virginian tobacco farmers were slaveholders; their choice of swiddening may have had little to do with a desire to economize on human effort. And the survival of shifting practices in Europe can be more plausibly explained by the marginality of the land and the impoverishment of its inhabitants than by economic preference. Much of this land—in Ireland and Scotland, for instance—

cannot be farmed permanently even now, especially by people too poor to own enough stock to maintain its fertility. In point of fact, European cultivators have historically been reluctant to avail themselves of the supposed advantages of swiddening except when moved to marginal or radically new environments. Western Europe did not revert to bush fallowing after the collapse of the Roman Empire in spite of the thinning out of population. And the nonplantation sector of the American economy during the land-rich colonial period was based on farming techniques just as intensive and labor demanding as those of the teeming mother countries.

In Asia also it has been claimed that swiddening is so much easier than the dominant permanent methods that the natives will abandon their rice paddies for shifting *jhums* or *ladangs* whenever they get the chance. Gourou (1956: 345), for instance, cites the immense difficulties experienced by French administrators in persuading the Montagnard Rhade of Vietnam to adopt wet rice farming in place of their ancestral swidden techniques and concludes that this is because "permanent rice fields, without manure, give a lesser output per day of work than *ladang*." But the qualification "without manure" suggests that this particular example is not decisive. The persuasive effort apparently did not extend to providing the Rhade with sufficient equipment (that is, animals for draft and manure) and training for them to have had a real choice between remaining swiddeners or becoming successful wet rice growers like the ethnic Vietnamese.

One suspects that inadequate planning and funding, together with shortsightedness among the administrators and caution (if not obstinate conservatism) among the administratees, often account for the failure of such agrarian improvement schemes. Many colonial and postcolonial governments have sought to sedentarize shifting cultivators (Boserup 1965: 66), feeling that annual croppers do less damage to exportable timber resources and are perhaps more easily found and taxed. When the schemes fail, the blame tends to be placed, not on administrative failings, but on native indolence. There can be no question that the law of least effort and the notion that swiddening is easy both owe much to this source, to the frustrations of administrators and the excuses of their subordinates, among whom are numbered many authorities on agricultural development and economic anthropology. Unless they are backed by hard quantified information, we would do well to take statements on the subject with a grain of salt.

Actual cases where established wet rice farmers have reverted to swiddening are very rare indeed, probably even rarer than instances of Europeans becoming shifting cultivators. Ho (1959: 145–148) cites one example: in early eighteenth-century China, a combination of extreme population pressure and the introduction of efficient new dry crops (corn and sweet potatoes) caused numbers of impoverished farmers to emigrate from the crowded Yangtze Valley into the uninhabited hilly regions nearby. They turned swiddener and seem to have thrived in the new environment, and by 1800 or so the hills were thickly populated. But then the trend seems to have reversed itself. Through the depopulations wrought by the Taiping Rebellion and its extraordinarily savage suppression, large tracts of rice-farming lowland became available. Immediately, many of the former emigrants reemerged from the hills and settled down again as multicropping intensive farmers. Quite clearly, shifting cultivation in this particular case was not an equally attractive alternative to irrigated rice growing.

This seems in fact to be almost a general rule in East and Southeast Asia. Most of the politically dominant plains-dwelling peoples grow wet rice and show no interest in changing over to shifting cultivation. Central Thailand, for instance, contains a great deal of wasteland that is politically secure, physically accessible, and flat enough to be cultivated with plows, but unsuitable for making rice paddies (mainly because of the porosity of the soils). At present this land is virtually uninhabited. The question is, why? If swiddening is easier and more profitable than growing wet rice, and if ease and profitability are worthwhile objectives from the standpoint of the local people, why did not some of them move into these wastelands long ago? The obvious answer is that it is not easier. Unlike the Yangtze Valley in the eighteenth century, the Menam Valley is still not overcrowded. Its inhabitants own their own land, are relatively prosperous, and judging from the statistics presented in Table 8.1, we can conclude that they do not have to work as hard for their food as do most swiddeners. The choice of intensive methods of rice growing must often be explained by simple economic rationality.

This may not always be true, however. Although in some places (for instance, in much of Central Thailand) irrigation requires relatively little effort (the paddies are filled by river flooding and monsoon rainfall), in other places sufficient water is hard to come by and may require a considerable investment of labor and capital. It is not clear, for instance, whether the Yangtze Valley Chinese would have been so eager to revert to wet rice farming if they had not been able to take over a going concern, with the major canals, dams, and weirs already dug. Perhaps, if wet rice is really as productively superior as it seems to be, even a large initial investment would be amortized within a few decades or so. But one suspects this would not always be realized. It would be useful to have another motive besides economic rationality to explain why wet rice growing is so popular.

Cultural preference is a strong possibility. Let us consider the Thais again. The inhabitants of Central Thailand may avoid swiddening for economic reasons, but actually almost *all* speakers of Thai languages avoid it and raise wet rice if they possibly can, whether in Thailand, Laos, Burma, or China (Lebar, Hickey, and Musgrave 1964; Leach 1965). Even in mountainous areas where irrigation is extremely labor consuming the Thais remain loyal to wet rice and leave the unirrigable uplands to non-Thai groups of swiddeners. It is possible, of course, that they do this because irrigation is more labor efficient than swiddening under all circumstances, but it seems more likely that an element of cultural preference enters in. Perhaps they irrigate because irrigation is part of their cultural identity, because wet rice farming seems a civilized, "Thai" way of earning a living.

For the moment, however, the theme of noneconomic inducements to intensification must be set aside. Our immediate concern is with agricultural devolution and the notion that most intensive farmers hanker after it.

The foregoing arguments have tried to show that the practitioners of the Asian and European types of permanent field farming should not and do not wish to be swiddeners, except in doubtfully significant instances of changed environments and government-inspired development programs. However, one might still contend that some of the more primitive intensive systems, as well as some versions of the advanced ones, are actually quite labor consuming and therefore not popular with the people who use them. This is not disputed here. Netting (1969) states that the Kofyar in Nigeria have recently begun to farm more extensively and that this has enabled them to increase their per-man-day output. And other formerly intensive groups—the Chagga of Tanzania (Allen 1965: 162–166) and the Gwembe Tonga of Zambia (Scudder 1962: 44–61)—are known to have recently expanded their territory to include land that they farm (probably out of necessity, because of water supply problems) by shifting techniques. Although it is rarely clear whether they are caused by overcrowding on the original land or by a desire to take advantage of the laborsaving possibilities of the new land, there is no question that intensive-extensive progressions have been a widespread, if minor, feature of recent agricultural history. It would be rash to deny that they are sometimes motivated by considerations of labor economy or that some of the original intensive systems did not involve very hard work indeed. But this cannot be generalized into a law. As far as the available evidence goes, there is no justification for regarding intensive regimes, whether primitive or advanced, as a priori more efficient than extensive regimes. If anything, the opposite is true.

The Law of Least Effort

Let us now discard the arguments of the preceding pages and assume axiomatically that labor efficiency and land-use intensity *are* inversely and regularly related, so that bush fallowing is more efficient than short fallowing, short fallowing more efficient than annual cropping, and so forth. The question then arises, can the Law of Least Effort be made to generate an evolutionary sequence of agricultural stages? There is reason to think it cannot.

The difficulty is that it depends too heavily on two rather doubtful assumptions about the way things work in rural societies. First, one must assume that the effort-minimizing tendency is very strong; in order to be the basis of a model of agronomic change, it has to be overwhelmingly the primary consideration for people choosing a subsistence system. And second, the concept "effort" must itself be cross-culturally meaningful; enough general agreement must exist on what constitutes effort for most peoples, long fallowers and multicroppers alike, to evaluate the labor requirements of different subsistence methods in the same fashion.

It would seem that an average farmer, faced with a choice between a more and a less extensive system of cultivation, might consider a number of factors other than effort minimization:

1. SECURITY FACTORS

Most farmers, whether primitive or modern, are more interested in minimizing risk than in minimizing work. If a farming system is better adapted to environmental conditions or is less vulnerable to natural and social catastrophes, it has a good chance of being chosen in preference to another system, no matter how labor efficient this second system might be.

2. ECONOMIC FACTORS

The choice of a subsistence regime is closely dependent on the nature of the regional economy. If markets or other systems of exchange exist, they may have specialized requirements. If the required produce can be cultivated only in annually cropped fields (like rubber, cocoa, fruits, and most varieties of rice), or if the location of the farm is such that transportation possibilities and land value dictate both crops and techniques (as in suburban market gardening, see Chisholm 1967: 76–110), then the cultivator may have no real choice. He may find himself willy-nilly an intensive farmer.

Moreover, scale factors also may affect the decisions of farmers. Intensive systems that involve high initial capital investment usually must have a break-even level of production that has to be sustained in order for the system to be feasible. Above this point per-unit costs are substantially lowered, but below it they are unaffected or even increased. Adopting some kinds of intensive regimes (for example, large-scale irrigation) might be a rational move for farmers in a market economy but foolish from the standpoint of a group that has no use for more corn or rice than it can eat. It has been suggested that scale factors may be operative even in such matters as whether draft animals can be profitably used (see Clark and Haswell 1967: 134).

3. POLITICAL FACTORS

Apart from the obvious forms of political pressure resulting from conquest and slaveholding and feudal institutions, even the most democratic states have means to encourage farmers to work harder than they might otherwise. And so, for that matter, do societies that are completely uncentralized and unstratified. The essence of political inducement to intensification is that the inducers do not propose to do the extra work themselves. But it may be that this principle of separating decision and execution can be applied to political transactions that occur in even the least statelike of societies. In a simple unranked community where men do the deciding and women the farming, already the casual links between the choice of a system and its execution begin to seem somewhat tenuous. Are the men not likely to be less conscious of the labor cost of a subsistence change when it involves their wives and children than when it involves themselves? The political power differential within a nuclear family may not be great enough to impose a sudden and labor-demanding basic alteration in subsistence. But as one goes up the line of organizational complexity—to the extended family or the lineage, perhaps—the separation of deciders and doers may sometimes increase quite rapidly. There must be a number of instances (perhaps the Sonjo, Gray 1963) where a labor-intensive system has been instituted by quasi-political force long before the societies in question have arrived at the stage of using slaves for agricultural work.

4. CULTURAL FACTORS

Some factors in subsistence decisions may be logically inexplicable but have considerable force. Food preferences and dislikes, especially when religiously reinforced, may have a decisive effect on a group's choice of agricultural system. Rice, for instance, is highly valued as a food over much of Asia. In the past many groups must have made the transition directly from bush fallowing to wet rice agriculture. If, as seems often to have been the case (Spencer 1966), the original bush-fallowed crops were the efficient yam or taro, then the changeover to intensive rice growing cannot be wholly explained as a rational response to population pressure.

Moreover, it is not uncommon to find peoples who have preferences for systems themselves rather than just for the kinds of food they produce. The possibility that some of the Thais may practice wet rice farming for reasons of cultural identity has already been mentioned. A still better example is that of nomadic pastoralism, which, in terms of caloric return per man-day expended, is a highly inefficient method of getting a living. Yet, as is well known, pastoralists tend to put a high value on their mode of subsistence and have on occasion violently resisted governmental efforts to settle them as cultivators. European plow farming is also a highly valued system among some groups. Western agronomists condemned tropical swiddening for many years before they were brought to the realization that, in those conditions, the systems of the natives were often superior to their own. One suspects that the agronomists' former vehemence had much the same irrational source as the nomads' attachment to herding. European plow farming was regarded as a badge of civilized identity and as evidence of the manifest superiority of their own culture.

It might be argued that all these considerations apply only to farmers in semideveloped economies and that true primitives will still be guided mainly by their desire to do very little work. But semideveloped in this case includes almost all peoples who are at the food-producing stage— as is shown later. On the other hand, locational factors and market requirements can be operative in very primitive economies. And in most economies all of these considerations are not only influential in sub- sistence decisions but quite capable of overriding the natural desire to minimize work.

Finally, there is the problem of what the idea of effort or work means cross-culturally. In most societies, effort is not measured by man-days or man-hours and is not closely correlated with physical expenditure of energy. Enjoyable tasks are easy even when time consuming and phys- ically taxing; unpleasant ones are hard no matter how little energy and time they demand. And because of these definitional problems, the least-effort concept is almost impossible to apply.

A group of farmers probably will not be able to evaluate labor efficiency objectively and, still more probably, will disregard such evaluations anyway. Several other attributes of a subsistence system will weigh more heavily in their judgment. And even if this hypothetical group is able to estimate labor costs and attaches an inordinate im- portance to them, there is still no guarantee that it will choose swidden- ing. The empirical data indicate that permanent field farming would often be the better choice.

The Rationale for Swiddening
A final problem remains to be discussed in this section. If efficiency and intensiveness are not inversely related and if even the Law of Least Effort is problematical, why is shifting cultivation used so widely among

primitive peoples? Obviously, primitives do not practice swiddening
because it is primitive or because Neolithic practices have tended to
survive longest among the more backward peoples. A behavior pattern
as widespread as extensive agriculture must have some functional
utility; it cannot be explained as a mere survival. Backwardness in
auxiliary branches of technology is also not an explanation. The soft-
ware aspects of primitive subsistence technologies are often highly
sophisticated. Some of these technologies (for example, those of the
Hanunoo of the Philippines and the central African Zande) compare
favorably with those employed by modern American farmers. And the
level of hardware technology a society possesses does not appear to be
closely correlated with the intensiveness of its agriculture, if one allows
for the recent diffusion of European plow farming. Many of the world's
intensive systems are today patterned after the European, which is
notably hardware dependent. But other earlier systems are not. Wet rice
cultivation, for instance, needs only two items of advanced hardware,
the plow and the ox or water buffalo, and both of these can apparently
be dispensed with. The wet-rice-growing Diola of Senegal (Dr. Olga
Linares, personal communication) use hand plows without draft
animals, as do several other African irrigators (including some of the
ancient Egyptians) and, according to legend, the poorer Chinese.
Several Southeast Asian groups use buffaloes without plows, their only
function being to trample the field into a properly muddy consistency.

The more primitive intensive systems are virtually hardware free.
The New Guineans and New Caledonians maintain relatively intensive
regimes in grasslands, armed only with digging sticks (Barrau 1958: 21
and Bartlett 1961: 57; see also Cowgill 1961: 277 for digging stick
savannah farming in Guatemala). Pre-Columbian irrigation and
chinampa cultivation in Mexico were carried on without either plows or
hoes. A majority of the more intensive African systems are plowless, and
it is by no means certain that taking their metal hoes and mattocks
from them would cause a critical loss of efficiency. It is possible, in fact,
that forest swiddeners may be more dependent on metal tools than many
intensive farmers. One can imagine that a Kofyar or Haya (Tanzania)
annual cropper could substitute wooden picks and crowbars for his iron
hoes more easily than could an Iban (Borneo) use a stone ax in place of
his steel machete.

Thus neither conservatism nor technological backwardness can account for the fact that so many primitives are swiddeners. A better explanation, it seems to me, depends on a principle introduced earlier: the primary concern of most farmers is security. In this respect, shifting cultivation has several major advantages.

First, it minimizes environmental risk. Newly cleared land may or may not give better yields than land that has already been cropped and refertilized, but it is more likely to *have* a yield in the first place. By shifting his fields each year, the swidden farmer insures himself as much as possible against the disasters that periodically wipe out the crops of permanent farmers. The soil structure in virgin land is better, thus seeds are more likely to germinate and growing plants are better able to resist a drought. Moreover, frequent field shifting and the intense burning that is possible when the fallow cover is high both serve to minimize damage from pests and soil-borne plant disease. The buildup of crop predators is cumulative as the same crop is sown on the same field each year. Rotation and intense burning are the only methods available to primitive farmers for preventing this buildup (and the only ones available to modern farmers in some circumstances—see Clark, Zaumeyer, and Presley 1957: 327, 337–338).

Second, it also minimizes some kinds of social risk. In the more militarily insecure primitive societies, it is clearly undesirable to tie up too much labor and capital in vulnerable assets. Dependence on animals for fertilization is a valid alternative to fallowing only when one can be reasonably confident that the stock will not be stolen. The feasibility of expensive land-improvement schemes (such as heavy manuring, irrigation, or the use of cultivated fallows) is also dependent on social stability. Members of a warlike or slowly migratory society like the Tiv (Nigeria) would be foolish to invest heavily in land that they could expect to lose to someone else within the space of a generation. Shifting systems have the great advantage of being relatively invulnerable to expropriation, since no more than a single year's work can be lost at any one time.

Third, there may be no possible, or rational, alternative. Some places with poor soils and broken terrain are virtually unfarmable except by swidden methods, even when modern equipment and expertise are available. This appears to be the case in parts of Zambia (Allan 1965: 72–73) and Ceylon (Farmer 1957: 48–49). Moreover, there are other places where shifting techniques are quite efficient and productive even when judged by recent Western standards. The carrying capacity of the Hanunoo system is said to be about 150 persons per square mile (Conklin 1957) and that of various West African bush-fallowing systems appears to be at least as high (see below). It seems likely that very few intensive systems could match the productivity of fallow fertilization in these particular environments. In some instances, therefore, swiddening may be practiced simply because it is superior in the same way that annual cropping is superior elsewhere—because it makes the most efficient possible use of the land.

These advantages seem sufficient to account for the prevalence of shifting agriculture. It should be pointed out, however, that swiddening is not a great deal more secure than some forms of permanent cultivation. Tree horticulture, flood farming, and various kinds of infield-outfield farming are very nearly its equals and, indeed, are widespread in the primitive world. In some environments, irrigation and infield-outfield farming may be even more secure. The superiority of extensive agriculture is not exclusive to it nor overwhelming in importance. The swiddener may decide that an intensive system is equally risk free. And even if it seems riskier, his natural caution can be overcome quite easily by many kinds of considerations, for example, the pull of the economy and the push of politics and demography.

II.   The Evolution of Agriculture

Agriculture has been divided into five main types—long fallowing, bush fallowing, short fallowing, annual cropping, and multicropping—which are also evolutionary stages (Boserup 1965: 15–16). It has been suggested that this model of gradual intensification may be applied in prehistory to explain the slow emergence of large populations and complex societies (see Chapter 1).

If it is considered purely as a synchronic taxonomy of cultivation systems, the five-stage sequence has a number of shortcomings. The single criterion of cropping frequency not only makes some systems (for example, tree farming) difficult to classify but also tends to give an overly simplistic picture of the enormous diversity of the world's farming methods. Thus more complex classifications have been suggested (for

example, Conklin 1957: 3, and Brookfield and Brown 1963: 160–167).
Moreover, there is not an especially close correlation between a system's
cropping frequency and the attribute that interests us most, its carrying
capacity. In fact, there are bush-fallowing systems that support dense
populations.

The main problem, however, is that as an evolutionary model it is
essentially unilinear. It has been a common assumption in anthropology
and cultural history that the development of agriculture is a substantially
regular and predictable process whereby an initial extensive type of
farming slowly, through the millennia, becomes intensified. A key
element in such models is the idea that swidden cultivation is intrin-
sically simpler and easier to invent than other farming systems. It seems to
be assumed that the first farmers practiced swiddening because swiddening can be discovered almost by accident: they simply learned to move
their farms whenever yields became intolerably low. And, by contrast,
the development of the more complex and difficult permanent farming
systems is thought to have been a laborious, long-drawn-out process.

This is a slightly extreme but not, I think, unfair picture of the model
that exists in the minds of many students of the subject. The Boserup
model of agricultural evolution is different. Although unilinear, it
represents agricultural change as caused entirely by outside agencies
such as political pressure and population growth. Boserup might well
agree that, if these factors were present at the outset of the Neolithic,
then intensive agriculture would have appeared immediately. This is the
contention advanced in the following pages. At the same time, it is
argued that unilinear models in general are inappropriate for use by
researchers in agricultural history and that a multilinear model might
better suit the available evidence.

The Putative Earliness of Permanent Farming

Swiddening is in essence no more than a technique for maintaining the
fertility of arable land. In many primitive farming systems cropping
frequencies are low because fallowing is the only method used for restoring nutrient reserves to depleted soil. However, if one wishes to
crop the same field continuously, there are several strategies one can
follow. (1) One can use fertilizer such as composted human and animal
excrement, green (plant) manure, domestic refuse, soil, or mud. (2) One

can use water that contains dissolved or suspended nutrients, either from canals and wells or from natural floods. (3) One can choose soils so rich as not to require fertilization. (4) Or one can adopt a regime that is ecologically balanced enough to mimic the fertility-conserving qualities of the natural vegetational cover of the region. All of these strategies are used by modern primitive farmers. Systems employing them can be found or imagined that are as easily invented, and thus perhaps as early, as long fallowing.

1. FERTILIZATION

Deliberate fertilization is unlikely to be as old as swiddening except under special circumstances because (1) without wheeled transport it is often excessively labor demanding, and (2) its beneficial effects are not always obvious—a dressing of manure or plant compost does not invariably result in a noticeably increased yield. However, accidental fertilization methods are a virtual certainty. Some early farmers undoubtedly discovered that discarded household refuse made the land permanently cultivable within a certain radius of the house. Some botanists (for example, Anderson 1967) have maintained that many of our modern crop plants were first domesticated in these permanent kitchen gardens. But the word "garden" may be misleading. The refuse-fertilized radius can be large enough to supply a significant proportion of a family's food, as among the Zande and some of the Mexicans (see the "calmil" system in Palerm, 1967), and can thus be called a true infield.

If early farmers were herdsmen as well, and if they were in the habit of folding their stock near the house at night, then a full-fledged infield-outfield system on the Celtic pattern (Evans 1956: 229) must sometimes have appeared without deliberation on the farmers' part. Infield-outfield farming with animal-fertilized infields is probably as early as the type that uses refuse-fertilized infields, at least in those places where stock breeding is coeval with crop farming. Both systems offer significant advantages over pure swiddening in terms of carrying capacity and, through diversification, of providing insurance against crop failure.

2. WATER

The fact that water is important to growing plants must have come to be generally recognized quite early in the Paleolithic. A preagricultural group might well have observed that wild food plants near streams remained green during the dry season and might have come to the conclusion that artificially extending the stream bed would produce more food. This seems actually to have happened among Steward's (1929) famous irrigating Paiute. It is probable that other, earlier groups also became irrigators before they became farmers. Irrigation is a simple concept to invent, and its application is not beyond the capabilities of dispersed and unorganized groups (see Millon 1962). As Bartlett (1961) has suggested, it is almost certainly as old as swidden farming.

3. PERMANENTLY CULTIVABLE SOILS

If one is willing to accept low enough yields, many fields can probably be continuously cropped for long periods of time. Without fertilizers this is an uneconomic procedure on ordinary soils. But some exceptional soils can remain productive indefinitely under heavy cropping, especially if they are protected from erosion. This goes counter to our commonsense expectation that output must be balanced eventually by input, but it is a fact nonetheless. Such soils are found in volcanic regions of Java and Africa (Allan 1965, passim) and in steppe regions of the Ukraine and the United States.

A second class of permanently cultivable soils are those which are annually flooded, their fertility being maintained by deposition of silt and dissolved nutrients. Where the soils are clayey and remain water-logged for some time after the flood, they are farmed by techniques like those used in true irrigation. In such cases ditching (for drainage) may be necessary, and the ideal crops will be those which, like rice, are specialized for swampy environments. However, where the soils are well drained, the appropriate cultivation techniques are no different from those used in ordinary dry farming. They may be simpler in some cases. Lambrick (quoted by Allchin and Allchin 1968: 260) reports that the inhabitants of the lower Indus Valley plant their main subsistence crop, sorghum, by broadcasting it on the completely untilled flood plain. The general aridity of the environment there, combined perhaps with the effects of alternate desiccation and flooding, must act to discourage the competition of weeds and pests and thus make tillage unnecessary.

A third class are soils in swamps, where fertility levels are kept in balance by the decomposition of organic matter and by water-carried nutrients. Swamp cultivation seems usually to involve extensive mounding and draining and the periodic dressing of these mounds with mud, as in *chinampa* farming. With the exception of sago, there are few swamp-adapted crops that can be grown without fairly involved methods of field preparation.

Any of these soils were cultivable by Neolithic methods. However, some types (swamps and clayey flood plains) may have required more expertise than a dispersed, subsistence-oriented population could be expected to develop. And others (soils with exceptionally high nutrient reserves) may have been difficult to use permanently because of crop pest buildup. But perhaps the well-drained flood soils are not so vulnerable to this problem; some of them can certainly be farmed by simple methods. Like irrigation and some kinds of infield-outfield, this type of permanent flood farming could occur very early.

4. ECOLOGICAL ADAPTATION

If one could design an agricultural regime that fitted closely enough into a natural ecosystem, or imitated one well enough, soil fertility would be maintained automatically. One's fields would no more require fertilization than would an uncultivated forest. This seems to be the strategy behind mixed horticulture, a type of farming in which many staple crops with differing niche preferences are grown in a single field. The crop mix in the more successful systems usually includes tree crops, as these are able to reach and recycle nutrients that are too deep for smaller plants.

Mixed horticulture is widespread in the modern world, often as an infield system (as in Java, Terra 1954, and in Guatemala, Anderson 1967) but also as a main field system (with shifting fields among the Hanunoo; with permanent fields among the Gishu of Uganda, Allan 1965: 166, and the Guaymi of Panama, Gordon 1969). It may be more common than some students of the subject have believed. At least one expert (Andrews 1935: 23, 27) seems to have mistaken a cultivated garden in southern Thailand for natural forest.

In fact, there is a very narrow dividing line between forest gathering and dispersed, but permanent, forest horticulture. All it takes for gathering to become farming in these complex environments is for the gatherers to begin to encourage and plant useful trees, vines, and shrubs and also, perhaps, occasionally to destroy the useless ones. And it is reasonable to

suppose that this has actually happened on occasion. As various ob-
servers have noted (for example, Lévi-Strauss 1963), nonagricultural
forest peoples tend to tamper extensively with their floristic environment.

In this way, the transformation of a natural ecosystem into a partly
artificial one could be accomplished without deliberation on the part of
the transformers. The result might be a forest where the proportion of
useful plants has been somewhat increased. But technically, at least
when some of the plants are grown, and not just protected, this is farming—a form of permanent cultivation in an extensive state but with the
potential of being considerably intensified. It is quite plausible that
dispersed forest horticulture could have been the earliest of all types of
farming.

The Productivity of Early Methods
Many of the agricultural systems that employ these hypothetically early
fertilization techniques are not only permanent but highly productive.
Javanese mixed horticulture, practiced on infields, is said by Terra
(1954) to produce half again as much food per acre as multicropped rice
paddies. Mexican and New Guinean *chinampas* support very high
densities—in Mexico, at least several hundred people to the square mile.
Pure tree cropping among the ancient Maya, Puleston (1968) estimates,
could have supported populations almost equally dense, as does permanent banana farming among the Haya of Tanzania (Allan 1965:
171–175). Some irrigation systems, of course, have very high carrying
capacities.

Infield-outfield systems probably have, on the average, a somewhat
lower carrying capacity. However, where animal manure is used on the
infield, population densities are known to attain high levels, as among the
Kofyar and in northern Ghana (Allan 1965: 241). If the infields are
cultivated with sufficient care, even the use of green manure and household refuse (as in the Zande and Mexican "calmil" systems) can support
populations of between 50 and 100 people per square mile. Estimates for
carrying capacity under flood-farming regimes are not available. The
flooded fields of the Land Dayaks and the Gambians are not impressively
high-yielding. But it is possible that the ancient inhabitants of the Nile
and Indus valleys may have done as much flood farming of the dry field

type as they did irrigating. If so, one might conclude that the carrying capacity of flood farming in some places is quite high.

It should perhaps be added that there are efficient systems that do not use any of these fertilizing techniques. Fallow fertilization—swiddening—in the right environments and with the right crops can have carrying capacities that approach 150 persons per square mile as in the Philippines (the Hanunoo), Indonesia (van Beukelaer, quoted by Pelzer 1945), and West Africa (the Ibo, Stamp 1938: 35 and Meek 1946: 146; the Yako, Forde 1937; some Northern Nigerians, Clayton 1963: 350). With fallow cycles shortened to the point where they can no longer be considered shifting agriculture, but without any significant use of other fertilizing methods, some of these systems have an even higher carrying capacity. Morgan (1955) estimates that Ibo farming can support 450 persons per square mile. Bender (1969) suggests that Yoruba farming may have a maximum capacity as high as 1,100 per square mile. Even without the intensive systems for whose early presence I have been arguing, Neolithic agriculture was not necessarily limited in the size of the populations it could have sustained.

Neolithic Tools and Crops

One possible flaw in all this reasoning from modern ethnographic analogy is the possibility that Neolithic farmers may have lacked some of the technological apparatus (tools and crops) that modern farmers possess and that they were therefore prevented from practicing truly intensive forms of agriculture. Very few of the primitive intensive systems are especially hardware dependent; they need neither plows nor metal tools. The examples of New Guinea and the pre-Columbian New World demonstrate with fair conclusiveness that a great variety of cultivation systems can be based on a technology of stone, shell, bone, and wood.

As for crops, there are admittedly some that may have required a considerable development time before they became reliable and of high enough yield to support a large population. However, this is not true for the majority of the world's staple food plants. Many of these may have been bred to an efficient level with relative speed and ease. The vegetatively propagated tree and root staples (yams, cassava, bananas, breadfruit, and so forth) are no problem. Since all members of a given domestic population are genetically identical, the fixing of desirable characteristics requires a minimum of time. One has only to select a suitable individual from a variable wild population and to plant cuttings from it, and within a single plant generation one has a stable and dependable cultigen. But with seed-grown plants, the situation may have been different. The individual gene-carrying units in such plants are smaller and more difficult to handle physically; moreover, inheritance is harder to control. Some characteristics in the self-pollinated grain crops (wheat, rice, barley, and so forth) may have evolved quite rapidly, especially such automatically selected traits as nonbrittle spikes on wheat and barley (Zohary 1969: 60). Other characteristics, like seed size and the number of seeds in a head, must have taken longer to develop, for with these the rate of change depended on deliberate genetic manipulation. The seeds had to be meticulously sorted, and the best ones from the best plants had to be kept for the next year's sowing. Even this may have been accomplished fairly quickly with crops that were both self-pollinated and also productive in their wild state (for example, wheat; see Harlan 1967).

However, the free-pollinating grain crops (maize and rye) that have been extensively altered from their wild prototypes must have posed a truly formidable problem for the primitive plant breeder. The stabilization of desirable characteristics in these crops was necessarily a hit-or-miss affair, depending as it did on a technique—the isolation of selected strains—which cannot have been understood or easily controlled by early farmers. This is doubtless the explanation for the archaeologically demonstrated time lag in the development of maize, a period of several thousand years between its original domestication and the time when it became sufficiently productive to have been a possible staple for a demographically efficient system of cultivation.

Except in maize- and rye-growing regions, therefore, the tools and crops requisite for a reasonably productive style of farming were available in Neolithic times. The vegetatively propagated staples may have been available very early in that period.

It is of theoretical importance to note that one of the implied premises in the argument of this section can be turned around. The development of efficient tools and crops may perhaps have done as much to inhibit as to encourage the appearance of intensive farming.

Long fallowing appears to be comparatively rare in dense grassland regions among plowless cultivators, even when they possess metal hoes. Many savannah regimes employ long cropping periods and low fallow-cropping ratios, often as low as 2:1 or 1:1 (see for example, Allan 1965 and Miracle 1967). Animal fertilizers and green manures both seem to be used more frequently by grassland farmers than by forest farmers. It may be that these things are done in order to avoid the necessity of clearing a whole new field each year. Removing heavy turf with hoes or digging sticks may be such hard work that it is preferable to use semi-intensive techniques and to keep already cleared fields in production for as long as possible. And in premachete times the same tendency may have been present among swiddeners in high forest areas. A farmer equipped only with a stone ax may have found it difficult to clear virgin land and, as a consequence, may have preferred to use short rotations in second-growth forest. Semi-intensive agriculture may have been more common during the Neolithic than afterward, when the introduction of efficient tools (plows, metal hoes, and axes) permitted a general exten-sification of farming techniques.[1]

The absence of productive crops would have had a similar effect, except that here the intensiveness would apply only to the frequency with which the land was cropped, and not to the number of people the land could support. If one grew an early variety of a crop plant which had only half the yield of a modern variety under the same conditions, one would be faced with the choice of clearing twice as much land, with Neolithic tools, or improving the soil to the point where it was twice as productive. It is not impossible that one would choose the latter course and become a relatively intensive cultivator.

To summarize the argument so far, there are several permanent and potentially productive intensive farming regimes that seem likely to be as early as long fallowing, for they are as easy to invent, as technically simple, as secure, and as independent of tool technology. Among these are irrigation, flood farming, manure- and refuse-fertilized infield-outfield, and mixed horticulture. Furthermore, two types of semi-intensive swiddening—in forests and grasslands—have claims to antedate long fallowing in certain environments. Several of the other systems that have been considered (*chinampa*, dry farming on permanently cultivable soils) and some that have not been considered (plow farming, large-scale irrigation, suburban market gardening) may be later, since they are either technically more complex or ecologically less secure.

By refining similar lines of reasoning, one perhaps could produce an idealized sequence for the appearance of each farming technique—in other words, a full-scale model of agricultural evolution, based on the assumption that some kind of inner dynamic is operating in the history of farming, causing given regimes to succeed each other in fairly regular patterns. But such a model does not seem likely to be valuable. Moreover, sufficient demographic—and even economic—incentive may have existed in very early times to give rise to agriculture of almost any degree of intensity.

The Economy and Demography of the Neolithic

Economic interdependence, involving specialized production of food-stuffs, is occasionally found to exist between very primitive groups, especially in regions containing varied microenvironments. This is the case with the Didinga and Acholi in East Africa (Herskovits 1952: 221–223) and the many crop-fish-exchanging tribes in Melanesia and coastal New Guinea. Similar trading patterns may well go back to the Neolithic. It is possible that these patterns may have encouraged some early farmers to increase production to above-subsistence levels and thus to adopt one of the scale-dependent intensive farming techniques.

Probably more important in Neolithic times were locational influences. Modern agricultural economies often show productive zoning that is primarily the effect of location rather than of environmental and technological variation; the ways in which land is farmed are determined by differences in land value and market access. However, differentials in locationally determined value are not necessarily confined to marketized societies.

One can easily imagine, for instance, that an ancient farming-fishing symbiosis like those of modern Melanesia could create a situation where land close to the coast is more desirable than land further away—the closer one lives, the more fish protein one is likely to get. Coastal farmland might therefore come to be differentially valued. Population densities could become quite high, but farmers still might be reluctant to move farther inland to areas where farmland is more plentiful. As a result agriculture in the coastal strip might be considerably intensified, the farmers' willingness to accept the attendant risks being proportional to the strength of their desire for fish.

There is, in fact, no reason why it should be only exchange-generating institutions that act to produce land value differentials. A group's desire to remain near any resource—a river for the sake of communications, a spring for drinking water, a good flint mine, a plot of hunting land to which the group has rights, a sacred place, a caravan route, a trading post, or perhaps a city—could cause the group to intensify rather than to move to a less crowded place. Variations in the intensity of land use can thus be caused by factors that have little to do with variations in the land's intrinsic quality. Nonecological, purely locational factors must have been an important determinant of subsistence methods at a very early date, probably long before plants were first domesticated.

Demographic pressure, the third of the previously mentioned causes of intensification, is also likely to be of great antiquity. It is true that Neolithic populations were generally small; however, the certainty with which one can apply this statement decreases as one's spatial frame of reference becomes smaller. The overall density of continental populations was certainly low. The density of regions was probably low. But as one focuses on successively smaller geographical units, the probability increases that some of them have experienced very sharp population fluctuations during their history. Moreover, some of the upward fluctuations must have been quite early. If it is granted that some Neolithic farming systems were capable of feeding them, then it follows that at least some local Neolithic populations were extremely dense.

To put this argument another way, human populations under favorable conditions are able to multiply very rapidly. Both Java and mainland Southeast Asia sextupled their populations during the century beginning in 1830, much of the increase occurring before the introduction of modern medicine. Most earlier and more primitive populations are believed to have been relatively stable. The reasons are somewhat controversial. Some students of the subject are inclined to blame mortality-increasing agencies such as war, famine, and disease. Others prefer fertility-decreasing agencies and feel that most premodern societies practiced effective methods of birth control. But whatever mixture of causes is chosen, there can be little doubt that this equilibrium model is not universally applicable. Some small areas, especially when isolated by geographical obstacles, must often have escaped from the effects of war and plague for periods of several hundred years, and the populations of some of these areas must have been as reckless about birth control as almost all modern peoples are. A number of these populations therefore became quite dense and were forced into intensive agriculture. Furthermore, this probably happened early. Given the ability of humans to multiply through sheer fertility and the possibility of in-migration of refugees to these isolated areas, the time lag between the first appearance of agriculture there and the forced adoption of even the most labor-demanding and insecure intensive techniques cannot have been much longer than a few centuries.

These hypothetical expectations are in a way confirmed by a widespread ethnographic phenomenon. The primitive world contains numerous instances of circumscribed, defensible environments that contain intensive farming populations of great density. Clark and Haswell (1967: 50) call them "societies under siege." These authors cite ten examples: Naudemba, Lamba, Cabrais (Togo), Toura (Ivory Coast), Lamba (Dahomey), Mitsogo (Gabon), Nuba (Sudan), Sidamo (Ethiopia), Agoro (Uganda), and Kamba (Kenya). Other well-known ones include the Kara (Lake Victoria); the Chagga, Gishu, and Sonjo (Tanzania), the Unga and perhaps Lozi (Zambia); many oasis dwellers in North Africa and Southwest Asia; the Batak, Minangkabau, and Nias Islanders (Sumatra); the Ifugao (Philippines); many New Guineans; many Pacific peoples; and, conceivably, the ancient inhabitants of the coastal valleys of Peru and the highland valleys of Mexico.

Many of these groups irrigate; all of them practice permanent farming systems that manifestly have high carrying capacities. None of the systems, except some of the Southeast Asian examples, much resembles either of the intensive regimes favored by the great modern civilizations. For this reason and because they are distributed so widely and discontinuously, it is likely that most of the systems were invented independently. They came into being as a response to population pressure within small subdivisions of often sparsely populated regions. The inhabitants of these places, without outside help and without advanced tools, managed to develop satisfactory intensive systems from a wide spectrum of preexisting agricultural technologies. Almost any group, no matter how primitive, seems able to do this. Even the natives of Mer in the Torres Straits were able to work out a system that feeds 200 persons from each square kilometer of land (Haddon 1908).

These examples alone go a long way toward establishing the hypothesis that the inception of intensive farming was not a milestone or a rare event in human history. Rather, it is commonplace and has occurred repeatedly in the histories of the most primitive and backward of agricultural societies. It must have taken place often during the Neolithic.

Conclusion

We may, therefore, conclude that intensive farming was not only quite possible during the early agricultural period but also that it probably did exist. A priori reasoning indicates that some permanent systems, because they are easily invented, are as old as or older than shifting ones. Ethnographic analogy suggests that these systems and others as well were probably used, and used intensively, at an extremely early date. Shortly after the dawn of the Neolithic, within a space of time that is probably too short for present-day archaeological methods to subdivide, a number of agricultural systems of varying intensity must have come into being. There are no particular grounds for believing that the first of these was long fallowing.

Therefore, the unilinear long fallowing–multicropping sequence is not likely to prove useful as a model that we could reasonably expect to see confirmed in the field by archaeologists. A multilinear model may correspond more closely to historical reality and seems, moreover, a more cautious and open-ended research hypothesis.

An agricultural fact cannot completely explain a social fact; one cannot say that because a group practices a certain type of agriculture, it is therefore at a certain stage of sociocultural evolution. No model, whether unilineal or multilineal, can explain why Neolithic extensive farmers (if they were extensive) had dispersed, disorganized populations (if, indeed, they did). Shifting cultivation is quite capable of supporting large enough populations for almost any degree of sociocultural development to be possible. Except in severely limited environments, the dispersion or concentration of human groups has social, economic, and medical causes; the role of agriculture in these evolutionary processes is quite neutral and dependent. If it becomes necessary to concentrate, most populations in most environments are capable of evolving intensive farming.

Notes

1. On the subject of tools, it should be noted here that there is not necessarily a correlation between the intensity of an agricultural system and the type of tool used. Boserup suggests that hoes tend to be associated with the more intensive swidden systems and that plows are usually used by annual and multicroppers. But many intensive systems do not use plows or even hoes. The majority of modern long-fallowing regimes are practiced by hoe farmers; some (for example, in Bronze Age Europe or in the United States during the frontier period) have involved the use of plows. If there is any correlation at all, it might be explained by the recent diffusion of plows along with Western concepts of intensive farming.

The idea that digging sticks, hoes, and plows have specific evolutionary implications can be traced back to Ratzel and Eduard Hahn (Kramer 1967). That plows and civilization went together was quite clear to European scholars of an earlier generation. Because a great deal of new ethnographic and historical information has appeared since then, the notion has been allowed to fall into disuse.

9 Sacred Power and Centralization: Aspects of Political Adaptation in Africa[1]

Robert McC. Netting

Netting's contribution is also based on agricultural societies, but from a culturally and ecologically different region. Rather than the development or intensification of technology as a response to increased competition for resources, he is interested in the appearance and function of certain nonkinship roles that allow central appeal for political, ritual, and social action from a broad base of kinship-based groups. In situations of growing population pressure sacral leadership may provide psychological reassurance, more broadly based dispute settlement, and enlarged possibilities for trade. In response to this paper it was suggested that in other enthnographic contexts—particularly in the Islamic area—sacred places or shrines perform a similar role. It is perhaps significant that these are most characteristically developed among pastoral nomads.

The intensification of food production is one possible strategy for meeting the problem of a decline in available per capita resources. According to Boserup (1965) changes in labor expenditures and receptivity to new productive techniques arise, not from subsistence success and abundance, but from the failure of traditional methods to provide for a growing population with limited means. To the extent that the cultural coping devices are effective in supporting more people for a longer time in a more restricted environment, a further set of organizational problems become apparent. With increasing dependence on certain unpredictable factors of the physical environment, competition for resources, and a need for efficient allocation of scarce goods, a premium is placed on the adaptation of existing social institutions. This chapter examines some of the ways in which sociopolitical relations may be broadened and re-oriented to solve problems of integration and cooperation created by the pressure of population on a circumscribed subsistence base.

Specifically, what are the failings or inadequacies of localized polities in situations where the ratio between population and exploitable resources is significantly changing? By localized polities, I refer to those societies where the largest continuously effective political units are autonomous villages or residentially defined lineage segments in which authority is divided, temporary in application, lacking sanctions, and arising from personal leadership characteristics. Controls over behavior are exercised through local institutions such as corporate kin groups, territorial communities, or cross-cutting sodalities (Cohen 1969: 660–661). More generally, such societies are called acephalous or stateless (Fortes and Evans-Pritchard 1940: 5). Localized polities appear to be very widely distributed in "middle-range" societies (Fortes 1953) based on settled agriculture, and variations of this form of organization may well have characterized sedentary farming communities before the advent of the state.

Given localized polities of this kind under circumstances of expanding population with circumscribed resources, certain serious dislocations could be expected to occur. I want to consider the nature of these problems and to examine the factors leading to one possible resolution of them, that of physically enlarging the polity and centralizing its leadership under religious aegis. The emphasis is on the process by which mutually supporting demographic and productive developments contribute systematically to sacral-political intensification. I will attempt to show that individual feelings of incapacity and fear in the face of threats to subsistence, increasingly irreconcilable disputes over productive property, and hindrances to the local and regional exchange of goods create needs that may be met by expanding the moral community and its shared consciousness of religious identity while according temporal power to a personification of magico-religious potency. The instrumental means for handling such difficulties are not born either solely or necessarily from these needs, nor are they revolutionary. Rather, where they do appear, they (like intensive agriculture in the technological field) merely emphasize, improve, and widen the scope of preexisting cultural tendencies and social mechanisms.

In attempting to limit the flights of fancy often implied by any such general, comparative, and evolutionary hypothesis, I will confine my discussion to a series of African societies with either localized or minimally centralized polities. Material on these groups derives largely from contemporary anthropological accounts of functioning social systems. My purpose will be twofold: to isolate certain features of sacred and secular leadership in acephalous societies that are capable of progressive enlargement, strengthening, and specialization to meet newly generated problems, and to examine the nature of contradictions built into localized polities experiencing population pressure. The cases to be considered are those of the Kofyar priest-chief, the Tiv big man who founds a market, the Ibo oracle agent and trader, the Jukun divine king, and the Alur rain-maker chief.

The Kofyar Priest-Chief

The general pattern of the rights, duties, role, and status of the priest-chief is numbingly familiar to anthropological students of society. He is the famous *primus inter pares*, the essentially powerless figure who does not make independent decisions but voices the sense of the meeting. He leads by example or by persuasion. As chief he may have a title and an office, but his authority is circumscribed; he *is* something, but he *does* very little. As Sahlins (1968: 21) remarks, "the Chieftain is usually spokesman of his group and master of its ceremonies, with otherwise little influence, few functions, and no privileges. One word from him and everyone does as he pleases." Those who are used to the order, hierarchy, and chain of command in states find such a situation quaintly primitive egalitarianism at best and at worst, an exasperating contradiction of efficient administration. The first assistant resident posted by the British to Kofyar country delivered himself in this way: "There can be no punishment without authority; without respect and reverence there can be no authority. Both qualities seem to be lacking in the peoples of the Kwolla District, and the result is seen in the powerlessness of the headmen and in the general conditions of disorder and anarchy prevailing hitherto" (Fitzpatrick 1910: 20). It is easy to pass from "tribes without rulers" to "tribes without rule," and thus to miss the order behind the apparent anarchy. In fact, a leader even when he lacks most kinds of executive and coercive authority *does* do something, and he *represents* a great deal more. The term priest-chief is an awkward English approximation of an elusive political and symbolic position with typically multiplex social relationships. The emphasis rightly belongs on the word priest, because " . . . chiefly figures bring little in the way of power to their priestly roles. Instead it seems more accurate to believe that such small power as they control is likely to stem from their ritual status" (Fried 1967: 141).

Even the group I know best, the Kofyar of the Jos Plateau in Nigeria, do not think of chiefship in any simple or unitary way.[2] They refer to and address their chiefs by two different terms. *Miskagam* means literally "the man of health," while the title *long* is also the word for wealth or property. Let me discuss these two concepts in turn. *Mis* is a singular masculine prefix and a noun meaning husband. *Kagam* refers to physical well-being, and the standard question asked of a sick person is *"Goe wu kagama?"* meaning "Are you well again?" "Are you healed?" *Miskagam* is also a term of respect used by people entering a group discussion or meeting. A man wanting a drink from people around a beer jar bends a knee, slaps his thigh, and says, *"Hong gun, daskagam,"* meaning "Greetings to you, chiefs." It may also be an omnibus term used relatively for the chief and his family, his lineage, his clan, or all the men of his village. It may distinguish among specialists, for example, chiefs as opposed to diviners.

The chief in his aspect of *miskagam* is responsible for the health and general welfare of his group through certain ritual prerogatives and mystic associations he possesses. These relate particularly to natural and social conditions that seriously affect the life of the whole community. The special religious powers of the priest-chief may come into play when there has been (1) major and widespread crop failure or barrenness of fruit trees, (2) severe drought, (3) sterility of domestic animals or women, (4) failure of game on communal hunts, (5) intravillage dissension and the threat of violence, or (6) intervillage feuding warfare.

The priestly role reflects an extension of the individualized services of the *wumulak*, the magico-religious practitioner who doctors illness and deals with infertility on the homestead and in the household, and the *wupa*, the diviner who searches out the cause of misfortune and hears confessions. Yet in the most frequent assemblies for religious purposes, the meetings for discussion and prayer of lineage, clan, or village, the chief does little. The procedure resembles that of a Quaker meeting, and there is no overt sign of leadership or division of responsibility. It requires a natural calamity of major proportions to elicit the priest-chief's ritual, and this may take place only a few times during his tenure in office (Netting 1968: 190–191). The ceremony is called *ya fu yil*, "catching the mouth of the earth," and the chief who has the right to perform it may be known as *miskagam yil*, man of the health of earth. The earth is often sacred in West Africa, and among the Kofyar it is identified, if not very clearly, with the high god Naan. Men swear that if they are witches causing crop failure, sterility, or bad hunting luck, "the earth will catch" them. The rite is a sacrifice, usually of a goat, but in one case of both a black cock and a black sheep. The chief cuts the throat while another man called *wuyil*, "he of earth," holds the animal's nose to prevent any noise. The blood poured on the earth is variously said to be for Naan or for beneficent spirits called *moewang* who are friends and creatures of God. God is called on to witness the sacrifice and repair the earth. The meat is divided by the chief, his lineage, his neighborhood, and the magico-religious practitioners present. When certain sacred spots in the bush have been violated by gathering wood there or having a case of snakebite in the bush, the same ceremony is held with representatives of the neighboring villages in attendance. The rite "makes the place cool," that is, eliminates magical dangers and the power of witches. The chief may also summon village males for unusual evening prayers at the beginning of the wet season or in the event of drought. He opens the meeting by simply stating the reasons for it.

Though such rituals are infrequent, the chief observes certain prohibitions at all times, and his homestead has a particularly sacred character. It is said that he should not meet face to face with priest-chiefs of certain other villages, and his homestead precincts may be forbidden to red cloth, flutes, drumming and dancing, or horses. Special rules may govern the use of his brewing hut. Some of these same taboos occur at the homesteads of lineage heads. Indeed, few of the chiefly ritual responsibilities are completely exclusive since lineage heads or rainmakers wield some of them on occasion, but, taken together, they tend to cluster around the chiefship. Thus traditionalists argue that a Christian or Moslem could not become chief because of the associated ritual observances.

The ritual duties and stature of the chief both direct and validate his role as mediator and peacemaker. Though the Kofyar have no formal courts, the moots that handle disputes between members of different lineages within the village are held at the chief's homestead, and he usually states the consensual decision. Such cases often concern rights to land or other property, but traditionally they did not include the marriage disputes, which are the major business of modern tribal courts (Netting 1969). The chief was expected to seek the restoration of good relations between disputants. When his actions contributed to ill feeling, it was said that he "spoiled the earth," a social rupture being viewed as equally destructive and contrary to nature as a disturbance in the physical environment (see the Tiv expression to "spoil the country," L. Bohannan 1958: 41).

A chief had no power of enforcement of judicial decisions save his refusal to conduct earth ceremonies. A chief I knew who felt he had been unreasonably deposed credited poor hunting and high infant mortality to the cessation of these rites. (A similar withdrawal in an important ritual context is threatened when parents, quarreling with adult offspring, say they will not attend future divinations for any illness of the offender.) The only sanction of the group when a moot decision has been ignored is to deny cooperative work assistance and social drinking companionship to the guilty party. If a controversy could not be resolved, the chief often referred it to a poison oracle or ordeal in a neighboring ethnic group area. The final arbiter was then a magically efficacious system for distinguishing truth and falsehood.

The chiefly role in intervillage disputes was one of attempted peacemaking. In cases of incipient warfare, chiefs of affected villages might meet to try to head it off. Neutral chiefs might be called to arbitrate incidents of theft or trespassing. Truces during fighting allowed enemy chiefs to meet at their boundaries and discuss the causes of hostilities. A feud could finally be settled by the chiefs meeting on the battlefield, reconciling their differences and making a joint sacrifice in a rite suggestive of the earth ceremony. Chiefs are never mentioned as being war leaders or organizing raids.

As a function of his religious responsibilities and his activities as mediator, a chief had some opportunities to accumulate wealth. In this context the title *long*, wealthy man, has relevance. There are few economic distinctions in Kofyar society. Rich men (and women) are usually self-made, but a chief has slightly better access to affluence than most. He acts as a redistributor at the simplest level of valued commodities like beer. The *mwos miskagam*, beer of the chief, is a jar set aside whenever there is brewing. It is the most frequent recognition of the chief's status, and he usually invites others to share it with him on the spot (Netting 1964). The size of the jar is critically evaluated for any sign of *lèse majesté*. The beer is regarded as the chief's due in his role of earth priest, and he may continue to receive it even if he is replaced administratively by an appointee of the government. In one village claims to receive this beer by an administrative chief provided a major bone of contention. In some Kofyar villages the chief receives an annual tribute of grain, an iron hoe, or salt. His farm might also be cultivated and his thatching grass cut by village communal labor. Judicial action resulted in some payments of fines, perhaps a goat, and some contribution to the chief for his trouble in hearing the case. Part of this might be given back to village members who participated in the moot. A successful litigant often gave a small gift to the chief. Traditionally there were no regular markets among hill Kofyar, but barter of commodities like beans and palm oil for salt and iron often took place in the chief's large homestead courtyard, the *pe tong koen*, "place of sitting for salt." These activities usually resulted in the chief having a larger homestead, more cattle, horses, and goats, more wives and resident sons, and more cloth and hoes than the average villager.

Real authority and high prestige could be built on this flimsy institutional foundation only by men of personal force, sagacity, and long life. A chief was selected by his lineage from among the brothers, sons, and near agnates of the deceased chief. Where there was a more formal rule in larger plains settlements, the group of eligible candidates comprised all those agnates with the same great-grandfather as the chief. The former chief may have informally selected a "wise child" to follow him.

Tugunmaap, a chief of the fifty or so homesteads in Bong village, and a man whose career spanned the concluding decades of the nineteenth and the first thirty years of the twentieth century, illustrates these themes. His birth was in the hazy, long-ago time when Bong was besieged behind its defensive stone wall. His age and experience lent force to his special ritual relation with the earth. The prestige of his wisdom was such that he was called in by all surrounding villages to settle internal disputes about farm boundaries. In arbitrating a quarrel over a theft between a Kofyar and a Sura Chokfem village, it is said he received gifts of goats from both plaintiff and defendant for "treading the dew," that is, making early-morning trips to summon witnesses and organize proceedings of the moot. The courtyard of his now-deserted homestead near the center of the village remains a *pe wuyon*, a most sacred spot where solemn village meetings and prayer sessions are still held. A skull house for leopards and dead enemies is maintained there, and theft in its precincts is magically revealed and punished. Tugunmaap coordinated his brothers' activities and amassed considerable wealth. He offered large animals for the funeral commemorations of men who died without heirs, thus laying claim to their homestead farms, which could not be purchased outright.

But these achievements were largely ephemeral. The case shows the stature that a man of impressive bearing, long life, and intelligence who was also born into a chiefly lineage could attain. But the respect that surrounded him, his personal authority, even his wealth could not be passed on intact. None of his successors could consolidate his gains; no stories are told of their skill as adjudicators, and no one secured inter-village unification. Those who followed Tugunmaap had short terms in office, further marred by vacillation in dealing with British colonial forces. In recent years when the new office of chief of the young men was introduced in Bong, borrowed from the immigrant Hausa, the chief refused to recognize the choice of the youth. He put forward instead a member of his own lineage, causing dissension between the two major clan groupings in the village. When the chief was dismissed by higher authorities for this quarrel (called "not bringing health") and for suspected peculation (an effort to redistribute tax money?), the other clan seceded politically, holding separate meetings, collecting tax money on their own, and refusing to join the communal hunt. Only the recent death of the ex-chief amid accusations of witchcraft plus the resumption of village hunting blessed with the killing of a bush cow allowed the partial return of amity between kin groups. Beneath any heightening of chiefly authority lie fissiparous tendencies held only temporarily in abeyance.

Though chieftaincy does not appear to occupy a central place in Kofyar conceptions of social organization, there seem to be general notions of what a chief should do and the relative importance of his functions. The legend is told that Kofyar himself, the ancestor from whom all villages trace descent, had two sons. One of these, Tuupyil (literally "lungs of earth") he placed to succeed him as chief, while his other son, Paya, was to assist. Tuupyil was a great magician, a wanderer, and a fighter. Since the day-to-day business of the chiefship made him restless, he left his brother to judge cases and went adventuring, founding towns on the plains and magically repelling the slave raiders who menaced them. Paya felt that since he was doing the work of the chief, he should be the chief in fact, though his brother had warned him that the land was not his to hold. A two-year drought reduced the country to famine, and only when Tuupyil deigned to return to his home village in the hills did the rains follow him. Paya admitted his fault, saying that Tuupyil was indeed the rightful chief. His point made, the wonder-working brother allowed Paya to remain as chief, and the chiefly lineage of Kofyar is to this day Moelapaya, "the sons of Paya." The Kofyar seem to be saying that magico-religious powers are the necessary foundations of chiefship, while arbitration and the preservation of social peace are its continuing justification.[3]

The Tiv Big Man

It is perhaps useful to compare leadership roles and functions in other Nigerian societies, not too far from the Kofyar, which also lacked centralization. Whereas the Kofyar have chiefs in autonomous village polities structured internally by unilineal kin groups, the Tiv are a classic segmentary lineage society with certain elders arising to personal preeminence. The Ibo, on the other hand, traditionally dispersed local authority among village councils, title associations, and age groups. Though the formal outlines of the system differ in each case, the nature of authority and the style of leadership appear to me remarkably similar.

In a series of important publications (Bohannan and Bohannan, 1953, 1968; P. Bohannan 1955, 1958; L. Bohannan 1958), the Bohannans emphasize the egalitarian nature of Tiv society, its lack of anything resembling an office, the inability of individuals to gain wealth by exploiting the labor of others, and the relative nature of leadership according to whether segments are united in opposition to a more distantly related group or split over the local interests of equivalent units at a lower level. But they also take pains to elaborate the mechanisms by which men do indeed attain influence and prestige.

Mystic qualities are so intertwined with political activity and social power that these categories themselves appear blunt tools for analysis. Magico-religious rituals are prerequisites to the achievement of political mobility; supernatural powers are the automatic attributes of success and influence. Leadership may be aided by the holding of *akombo* fetishes, inheritance of magical properties such as *swem*, and the experience of learning from an important man. But a man who has achieved influence without these advantages is also said to possess *tsav*, the beneficial control over people by the talented "born leader," that is also the fearsome power of the cannibal-witch causing all death (P. Bohannan 1958). Laura Bohannan has aptly captured the connotations of these ideas.

Valid leadership is in idiom correlated with the legitimate possession of *swem*, the emblem of truth and mystical protection against the evil of man and hence of witches. *Swem* prospers the land (*tar*) in all its meanings of farms, people, and government; crops grow well and abundantly; rain falls and sun shines at the proper season; man and beast are fruitful and multiply; kinsmen live at peace and in amity with one another; no blood is shed; none die . . . [L. Bohannan 1958: 59].

Talent, power, luck, wealth, strong character—all these are manifestations of the possession of *tsav* (a witchcraft substance). Relative influence and relative wealth thus can be, and are, phrased as ranking in degrees of *tsav*, and *tsav* is believed always to operate at the expense of others [ibid.: 54].

These mystic attributes directly inform and define the activities of leaders. The amazing amount of jural discussion and litigation that Tiv elders conduct in their moots carries as its principal sanction the threat of allowing those who refuse its decision to be bewitched. Such elders may be skilled in arbitrating disputes over debt and inheritance, wrangles over land, and troubles among kinfolk. "Treaties, peace-making, theft, homicide, childbirth, widow inheritance—almost any

field of social activity one can mention—eventually involved the performance of magical ritual which is in the hands of the elders" (Bohannan and Bohannan 1953: 33). Governmental activities in general, what
Tiv call "repairing the Tar," cannot be conceived apart from their
religious ideology and practice.

It is particularly interesting to note that this politico-religious complex, because of its operation in a context of segmentary lineages, gives
very little continuing jural authority or administrative control above
the most local level. In building up prestige, a man must seek affluence
at home and ultimately influence the economic activities of others by his
control of a market. Personal redistribution involves gaining financial
aid from agnates, other relatives, and age mates and using this to stage
feasts and farming parties, give gifts, and purchase titles having a certain
mystic prestige from the neighboring Jukun and Chamba tribes (Bohannan and Bohannan 1953: 35–36). Slaves could be bought to form a gang
of henchmen and extort protection payments from strangers (L. Bohannan 1958). Sacred tree drums and powerful fetishes might also be
purchased.

In order to flourish, a market in Tivland had formerly to be "in the
hands of a strong capable man of influence who could keep the peace,
ensure safe conduct to travellers, and protect those who came to trade"
(Bohannan and Bohannan 1968: 158). It was necessary, therefore, to
consecrate the market by the erection of an *akombo* fetish that could
punish breaches of the market peace with serious disease. The members
of the various tribes and lineages who attended the ritual establishment
of the fetish were thereby bound together in a peace pact. Such a market
is an appropriate place for intergroup negotiations even in time of war.
The rewards of market administration were considerable.

. . . a man in control of an important market is in a very strong position:
men used to pay him tribute for safe conduct; as market owner he is
approached on disputes occurring in the market and, if his opinion is
thought generally valuable, has legitimate standing as an arbitrator in
troubles between people of segments where his influence would otherwise
not extend; the market tribute is a source of wealth; a consecrated
market is a channel of diplomatic negotiations between contributing
segments at all times and between others at war on their own grounds
[L. Bohannan 1958: 63].

As the Bohannans (1968: 146) note, a market is "a political institution

of major importance because in a society that is dominated by the lineage principle it is a means of overriding that principle."

Among the Tiv the power of a true big man who combines forceful
personality, elder ritual status, prestige, and economic affluence is
certainly greater than any Kofyar chief, but his authority is even more
limited in duration and popular acceptance.[4] Tiv are always attempting
to balance their need for physical and mystical protection and their fear
that the protector will use his power against them. Thus anti-witchcraft
movements appear periodically to whittle down those who have crossed
that impossibly fine line separating the constitutional and beneficent
use of power from its selfish or illegitimate application. Elders are dis-
credited, *nouveaux riches* reduced, government chiefs frightened, all by
cults relying on medicines, sacrifices, magical emblems, and spirits
(P. Bohannan 1958). The market that projected the image of one man is,
after his death or eclipse, often run by committee with different individuals holding the fetish, managing the market, and settling disputes
there. In each case a rigidity in power relationships is broken. Just as
those who live by the sword are supposed to die by it, so the Tiv leader
who burgeons with magico-religious vapors is finally blown away by the
selfsame winds.

Ibo Oracle Agents-cum-Traders

A somewhat greater development on the same themes of leadership in
acephalous societies is discernible in the case of the Ibo of Eastern
Nigeria. The traditional ethnological interpretation of Ibo society (we
except here Onitsha and Western Ibo) has emphasized the existence of
over 200 independent political units called tribes, clans, village groups,
and so forth, with no political superstructure such as a confederacy or a
kingdom (for a recent review of Ibo political organization see Smock
1968). Recently it has been suggested that processes of "partial state
formation" were taking place during the period preceding colonial
domination (Stevenson 1968: 190). Though there had always been
various extralocal contacts of marriage, warfare, or commercial alliance,
shared cyclical ceremonies, consultation of diviners, and the use of
neutral elders to settle disputes, the growth of long-distance contacts
and political integration appear again to stress the importance of

arbitration and trade operating under the umbrella of magico-religious sanctions and guarantees.

This development was represented most clearly in the spread of agents of the Aro Chuku Ibo from their home villages near the Cross River and directly northwest of the trading ports around Calabar during the period 1650 to 1850. The Aro represented a powerful oracle, the Ibini Okpabe or Long Juju, in their own area, and acted in the dual role of solicitor-merchants. They overcame local parochialism and hostility by traveling under the protection of their oracle, who was reputed to kill anyone harming its agents. A full roster of legal services and magical solutions were offered to clients who came from far and wide in Iboland. Ottenberg (1958: 303) suggests why such aid should be eagerly sought:

Under the common Ibo system of group leadership, of councils of leaders —usually of elders—it was sometimes difficult for families, lineages, clans, communities, and other social groupings to reach definite decisions in certain cases. This was particularly noticeable in land disputes, in property and inheritance disagreements, and in settling persistent warfare. Sometimes the only recourse that could be agreed upon was to consult an outside agency, the Aro or another oracle. . . . Poor crops, continued illness, epidemics, lack of children, and other matters were brought to the oracle for explanations when they were not solved by local action. [See also Dike 1956: 38.]

The oracle prospered with fees and fines, and in some cases the party who lost the decision was liable to execution or sale into slavery. Colonies of Aro not only managed oracular consultations but carried on extensive trade in chickens, cloth, iron tools, palm products, and especially slaves. Mercenary armies were used for raiding. Slaves provided porterage for trade goods, and profits from trade could be invested in moneylending enterprises. Doubtless the Aro Chuku florescence owed a great deal to European slaving opportunities, but it is interesting that these commercial ventures should be so intimately linked with shared religious beliefs and a reliance on magical justice. There is little doubt that the oracle system contained serious disruptive patterns and that it was still far from a centralized hierarchical unit. Nevertheless, it did provide "a method of organizing a widespread group of persons with a common identification in contrast to the segmentary characteristic of most Ibo society" (Ottenberg 1958: 312).

Was the religious belief merely an idiom for conveying political and economic relationships—an ideological superstructure—or was it genetically crucial to these developments? A case of an individual Ibo creating a leadership position is instructive:

At Enu-gwu a travelling trader combined his business with the profession of "doctor," making a considerable success of the latter. Later he remained at home and his patients came to him. His villagers soon saw how successful he was as a medical man and asked to share in the business. He agreed on condition that he become "head" of the village, which was granted. The villagers began to solicit and to guide patients to him. With the help of a son-in-law, he moved his headquarters to a thick grove and began to take on important cases of the kind typical of oracles. He affected a mysterious and hidden voice, and elaborated the secrecy and the ritual until an oracle with supernatural powers and agents was, in effect, developed [Ottenberg 1958: 309].

Despite the Wizard-of-Oz flavor of the anecdote, the functional ties of supernatural, economic, and jural-political behavior are again striking.

Religious Arbitration and Economic Allocation Related to the Weaknesses of Localized Polities

Though a comparison of three societies may be too limited for generalization, I would suspect that a similar combination of ritually sanctioned arbitration and economic allocation might characterize leadership in a great many uncentralized societies, and that these aspects would be more regularly conjoined with each other than they would with military activities and the direction of war. Perhaps this complex has been obscured by the persistent focus of political theorists on coercive power and the whole machinery of legal enforcement and organized warfare that characterizes the modern state. There can be no doubt that military means and penal sanctions have, in threat and in fact, been able to bring centralizing tendencies to many societies. But cases such as that of Shaka, who created the Zulu nation as a conquest state, are possibly more dramatic than frequent. A similar de-emphasis of the role of war leaders in political evolution has been made on theoretical grounds by Fried (1957: 105), and the conquest theory of state formation in Africa has been questioned by Lewis (1966: 406).

Let me suggest that political development in many cases takes place internally and voluntarily rather than by imposition or wholesale borrowing from neighboring groups,[5] and that the main lines of development and channels for change are prefigured in existing institutions and patterns of behavior.

Why should a ritual role that may be seldom exercised, a special relation to divinity, and a set of beliefs relating the chief, big man, or agent to the health and well-being of the community occupy the crucial integrating position in the concept of leadership? Is magico-religious power the cornerstone of a new political edifice or merely the window dressing for what is essentially economic manipulation and power brokerage? I would claim that on the road to statehood, society must first seek the spiritual kingdom, that essentially religious modes of focusing power are often primary in overcoming the critical structural weaknesses of stateless societies.[6]

These weaknesses are by definition those of a society based on localized, highly autonomous units.[7] To integrate a number of such units or to allow an existing unit to expand without fission, ways must be found to keep the peace while enlarging personal contacts beyond the range of kin group and locality. Myths of common origins, segmentary lineages with single pyramidal genealogies, overlapping clans, interethnic religious congregations, and trading associations are all attempts in this direction. But central leadership is forever hampered by necessary identification with a specific kin group and a particular place.[8] Even when a larger group can be formed and coordinated to meet external pressure, it can seldom survive the return to normalcy where the interests of internal segments must necessarily clash. The overwhelming need is not to expand existing political mechanisms (they are in certain respects radically inelastic) but literally to transcend them. The new grouping must be united, not by kinship or territory alone, but by belief, by the infinite extensibility of common symbols, shared cosmology, and the overarching unity of fears and hopes made visible in ritual. A leader who can mobilize these sentiments, who can lend concrete form to an amorphous moral community, is thereby freed from complete identification with his village or section or age group or lineage. The cultural devices for actualizing such a status are as varied as human imagination—serving an earth god rather than a lineage shrine, receiving visions, establishing oracular contact with divinity, consecrating a market, providing real sanctuary for a murderer, introducing a foreign cult, and so on. Sometimes an alien, a subordinate, or a slave can do this better than a member in good standing of the community's elite. But it is this supersocial religious identification that confers the prestige, the extraphysical power, and most of all the sacred neutrality to settle disputes that clans or villages could not resolve. The jural community can thus be widened in area and rendered more pervasive in its operation.[9] The threat of violence, feud, and resulting migration is proportionally lessened.[10] In the same way, the contacts with strangers needed for expanded trade can be mediated, adjudicated, and ensured. The entire scope of what is right, who can be trusted, and where one can go with safety can thus be radically extended, not by force of arms (which may, in fact, be unavailable), but by a sort of covenant, a suprahuman contract among otherwise unrelated people. The sacrifices, the emblems, and the religious ideas need not be new, but they are activated on a new and more inclusive plane. Kofyar intervillage arbitration and peacemaking, the Tiv consecrated market, and the network of Aro Chuku oracle legal and commercial influence represent tentative steps in this direction.

If political positions have been monopolized by outsiders, or if an emergency threatens a locally structured group, a similar process, drastically accelerated, may result in a millenarian or revitalization movement.

Such communities, then, united by common interests but without any political forms through which to express and utilize this unity must perforce *create* suitable political forms. Any leader who wishes to unite these divided social groups must dissociate himself from narrow allegiance to any one of them. To unite them he must stand above them: he cannot afford to be identified with any one village or one clan. One of the most effective ways of doing this is to project his message on to the supernatural plane. He brings a message from God or the ancestors, and appeals to the people to join the movement on the basis of a common allegiance to a religion and an organization which stands above them all and unites them all [Worsley 1957: 27].[11]

Worsley also notes that such unity can be effected by quite secular devices, but perhaps similar ideological commitments characterize even the slower, more independent growth of centralized states.

Ecological Problems and Centralizing Tendencies

Even if we have characterized a valid set of preliminaries to centralization, are we any closer to knowing how the actual process takes place? We would not like to be guilty of the comparative shorthand that

implies a naive and mechanical kind of continuity between lineage
organization and the segmentary state. We cannot insist that any of the
societies considered were on the verge of political "takeoff" before colonial
penetration or that existing states passed through earlier stages similar
to the examples here. Indeed, centralization may be one of those protean
social processes like unilineal descent group formation that serve a
variety of functions and proceed from a multitude of causes, acting
together or separately.

But let us indulge ourselves just one moment in the unanthropological
luxury of speculation. What circumstances applied to a society with
priest-chief or lineage head or village council might render adaptive a
more continuous recognition of paramount status, an institutionalization
of powers formerly achieved by personal ability, an acceptance of
decisions as binding? It may be that certain internal and external
stimuli cause an increased demand for those services customarily performed by local leadership. My own work on agriculture, demography,
and social organization has suggested that a change in the man-land
ratio resulting from either growth in population density or shrinkage of
land resources may set in motion a chain of events resulting in more
intensive agriculture and individuated land tenure (Netting 1969b).
With higher land value, more clearly defined boundaries, and more
elaborate rules of ownership and inheritance come increased friction and
litigation. The largest Kofyar chiefships in which a species of para-
mountcy united a number of adjacent villages were found on the plains
where population density was highest and competition for arable land
keenest.[12] The Tiv system of having "no boundaries, only arguments"
would certainly become exacerbated to fighting or to one unending
moot if all opportunities to move into new land were removed. Neighbors who must cooperate find some of their vital interests seriously
opposed.[13] Land scarcity may indeed lead only to a vicious circle of
feuding warfare, expulsion, or enslavement, but more advantageous
solutions are at least imaginable. The leader who can mediate such
quarrels and preserve intergroup harmony under religious validation is
performing an obviously useful task that the various segments may do
ineffectively, if at all, when left to their own resources. The same problems might arise among diverse immigrant groups coming into significant

contact with each other in a new territory. Moreover, we may hypothesize that restrictions on arable land plus the threat of natural catastrophes to the farmer's limited subsistence would produce heightened
personal insecurity and anxiety. In these circumstances, a claim to
control the rains or promote fertility with annual ceremonies may take
on an impressiveness and power to convince proportional to the need
for control of the habitat. People want to believe that those conditions
most vital to their existence are in some way subject to their will, and
the ritual of increase performed by kings may embody this wish.

Such necessities of life as food may be wiped out in one area while
remaining plentiful elsewhere. Trade not only can supply districts of
scarcity but can also allow for movement of labor to areas where needed
and promote specialization. In this way, interlocking ecological niches
may be more effectively exploited.[14] An enlargement of effective commerce may have rapid adaptive effects, increasing population size and
stability. (The Aro markets and trade routes throughout Iboland are
thought to have promoted just such expansion [Stevenson 1968: 208]).
Even where land is not at a premium and food scarcity is infrequent, it
may be profitable to import or export certain goods, for example, salt,
iron, and cloth. Localized gift exchange and redistribution are rather
inefficient methods to secure substantial long-distance trade. Only with
protected routes and markets where the peace is enforced can commerce
thrive.[15] Again the benefits are generally obvious, and people have good
reason for believing in the fetishes or oracles that ensure commercial
tranquility. Growing desires for alien goods lend support to market
expansion and the politico-religious efforts of leaders to create and
preserve them (see Chapter 12, this volume).

A leader who can simultaneously reassure farmers worried about their
harvest, adjudicate their quarrels, and profitably redistribute or promote
the exchange of valued goods is obviously not the same as other men. He
occupies a central social position. A higher social status is both functionally necessary to his activities and an appropriate reward for his
services. To the extent such a role is institutionalized, a system of ranking, perhaps with conical clans, may be formalized, and incipient
stratification may appear (Fried 1967: 109–184; Sahlins 1968: 24).
Political chiefship may be dignified by titles and inherited through more
rigidly defined kinship links. Regular differences in access to resources,

control of services, and possession of valued goods may emerge. Privilege becomes both more overt and increasingly ascribed. Both the powers and the prerequisites of a highly ranked individual or group are justified by ritual status. Such people aresingled out fundamentally by their relationship to sacred things and suprahuman potency.

The Jukun Divine Kingship

Is there any evidence for such speculation? Do some or all of these factors figure in more centralized polities? The Jukun state, a classic divine kingship, was formerly situated on the Benue River between the Tiv and the Kofyar, and it has had at least indirect historical contact with both. Historically the Jukun king was regarded as the incarnation of deity. He conducted a daily liturgy and was secluded most of the time. He was not supposed to eat, sleep, or die as a mortal, and his body was charged with mystical dynamism. Meek (1931b) states that his "primary function [was] to secure for the people a successful harvest," and he controlled winds and rains. The king reigned over but did not govern a number of widely dispersed villages with small, localized, and possibly ambilineal descent groups (Young 1966). A group of titled administrative officials ran the state, prosecuted war, counseled the king, and carried out priestly functions.

The king's religious and symbolic role was so dominant that the kingship has been thought "more meaningful among Jukun when considered as ritual rather than political institution" (Young 1966). Whereas a priest-chief may promote the health of his society through ritual and jural means, the Jukun king was supremely responsible not only for good harvests and the regular natural phenomena on which they depended but also for the delicate harmony of interrelations between his people and the gods (Young 1966). Jukun subsistence farmers relied on their crops and credited both prosperity to the activities of the king and natural failure to the king's incapacity, arising from divine repudiation and requiring regicide. Though the king functioned jurally only as a supreme court of appeal, litigants had to swear with their hands on the royal mat, risking death if they lied. Religious symbolism, beginning with an elaborate investiture, had so transformed the king that he existed above kin group and sectional rivalries and represented the whole society rather than any one of its segments. Though land scarcity does not appear to have been a Jukun problem, the king did provide reassurance to individual farmers and the conceptual unity that the scattered Jukun would otherwise lack. If neighboring groups may be cited as an example, he also presented a standard around which non-Jukun could rally and thus secure admission to the Jukun political community.[16]

Meek's account is lamentably deficient in economic data, but there are some indications that Jukun unity was advantageous in terms of trade. Villages on the Benue and some of its tributaries must have made use of the natural communications artery, just as did the centralized Igala,[17] Onitsha Ibo, Nupe, and northern Yoruba[18] on the Niger. Meek (1931b: 29) suggests Jukun slave-trading contacts with Ibo middlemen such as the Aro. Perhaps even more important were the salt springs and pools throughout the area controlled by the Jukun. Salt was a prized commodity among inland peoples and conferred a "peculiar sanctity on any district" (ibid: 428). For the Jukun who ritually collected it, the salt may have exercised considerable influence in state formation. The king certainly received tribute in grain and beer from the capital and in specialty products from the outlying towns (ibid.: 345), but if the pattern followed that of his subject Goemai chiefs, he also organized, protected, and profited from most long-distance trade. Though the Jukun have a semilegendary reputation for conquest, the king seldom led armies or even went to war. The parallels throughout to the Shilluk (Sudan) case analyzed by Evans-Pritchard (1948) are obvious.

The Alur Segmentary State

Perhaps the most cogent discussion of centralization in process is Aidan Southall's characterization of the Alur "segmentary state" on the Uganda-Congo border. There local kin-based institutions were integrated with chiefly political authority and an administrative hierarchy incorporating chieflets and lineage heads (Southall 1953: 28). The Alur chief's aura of supernatural efficacy was based largely on his rainmaking activities, the performance of an esoteric ritual complex that inheres in the chiefly lineage: " . . . autonomous political activity never exists

among the Alur without the validation of rainmaking" (ibid.: 94).
In addition the chief's personal ancestor worship and service at ancient
shrines were believed important in the control of the weather and
seasons. These powers invoked fear and reverence for the chief's person
supposedly strong enough to stop fighting when he appeared.

In settling disputes, the Alur chief had the power to hear cases of
murder and levy fines and to respond to calls for assistance and protection. He could burn and plunder clans in his territory that failed to
keep the peace and thereby threatened free movement. In these jural
matters as well as in the realm of the supernatural, the chief had "general
and ultimate responsibility in the minds of his subjects for both their
material and moral well-being" (ibid.: 239). The greater chiefs maintained a large body of retainers and courtiers who tended their extensive
herds of cattle. Regular tribute was delivered as thanksgiving for the
chief's manipulation of rain and fertility, meat from game came to him
by right, labor service was given on the chief's farm, and fines plus
court costs were collected. Salt, ivory, dried fish, ironwork, and basketry
from different ecological zones also played an important part in the
redistributive network of which the chief was the node (ibid.: 81). The
chief received girls as payment of fines and gave them as wives to
favorites and the destitute. With grain and livestock he gave feasts.

Not only does the institution of chiefship appear to be adaptive, but
also its advantages were evidently recognized by societies lacking in
centralization. New subjects were attracted to the Alur chiefship, and
Alur expansion appears to have taken place by voluntary submission
and without the use of force (ibid.: 230). The acceptance by other ethnic
groups of Alur chiefs seems to have been motivated first by their rain
power and the self-confidence with which it was wielded, a particularly
potent magic in an area of highly variable rains and unpredictable
drought, against which the ordinary individual was defenseless. Second,
such segmentary lineage peoples as the Madi and the Lendu saw the
desirability of dispute settlement at a more inclusive level:

It thus appears that many groups entered the Alur system to escape from
factors operative within, not outside their societies. It is claimed by the
dominant groups, and admitted by the Lendu subject groups that the
latter resorted to Alur and Hema as arbitrators, and then as suppressors
of the feuds which they were themselves unable to terminate, and by recognizing the limited jurisdiction of Alur chiefs or chieflets over them,

they attained a political order less restricted in range and less constantly disturbed by violence than they had possessed in independence [ibid.: 234].

It is difficult to tell whether ecological pressures were acting on the existing populations, but a highlands density of 112 per square mile under a mixed regime of farming and herding suggests this possibility as does the presence of insoluble disputes. The benefits of chiefly redistribution and protected trade would also be increasingly obvious under such conditions.

Conclusions

Throughout this discussion, the mastery of socially inclusive religious rituals and the embodiment of sacred forces have been viewed as crucial attributes of emerging institutionalized leadership in localized polities. Rather than viewing sanctity as a functional alternative to political power vested in discrete authorities (Rappaport 1967: 236), it might be seen as the most compelling quality of a focal figure in establishing a sense of common identity and unified political action among a collection of autonomous groups. Certainly sacred conventions may decline in importance when a state with considerable technological and military development gains a monopoly of physical coercion. But the initial growth of centralization insofar as it responded to internal socioeconomic problems under conditions similar to that of "pristine state" formation (Fried 1967: 111) may well have seen a widening of the span of religious mutual understandings, a deepening of ritual involvement, and an increasing severity in the application of sacred sanctions. This does not mean that the symbolic content of traditional observances of the local religion must change. It refers instead to the recognition of a more extensive group within which a common belief in certain magico-religious powers is already present, allowing a more effective mediation of extralocal conflict and the peaceful pursuit of complementary economic activities. If religion is the enshrining and deification of society as Durkheim suggests, the social field may be most aptly expanded and rendered cohesive in the minds of men by symbolic rites and ritual representations.[19] In situations of ecological pressure the greater the potential benefits of psychological reassurance, centralized arbitration, and regular redistribution, the more rewarding will be any movement in this direction.

It would be unrealistic to credit the initial process of centralization solely to internal factors. A change in the man-land ratio is often the result of the loss of territory to militarily superior outside groups or the restriction of opportunities to handle population growth by budding or migration. Organization for aggressive warfare or defense obviously profits by central coordination, a recognized hierarchy of command, and measures to ensure discipline. The type of outside military threat and the defensive possibilities of the local environment may alter in subtle and complex ways the adaptive responses of a society.[20] The sacred leadership that I have examined may also exercise its charismatic qualities in mobilizing fighting men and focusing group hostilities against enemies. The Tiv big man of the market had his henchmen who used force on disturbers of the peace. Aro Chuku agents commanded hired troops. The relationship of war to centralizing political tendencies has been so often stressed, however, that it has come to be taken for granted. My point here is that other pressures relating to demography and subsistence may frequently occur even in the absence of severe warfare, and their resolution may often be sought in the voluntary re-orientation of localized polities through sacred leadership centrally administering rituals of increase, mediating intergroup disputes, and extending the sphere of peaceful exchange.

In summary, then, it is possible to say that the growing pressure of population on circumscribed resources may render adaptive not only agricultural intensification but also a rudimentary political centralization under sacral leadership. This provides traditionally sanctioned and increasingly institutionalized means for handling the interrelated problems of: (1) greater personal insecurity stemming from reliance on relatively fixed resources and unpredictable variations in the environment; (2) increased interpersonal and intergroup competition for circumscribed resources with a corresponding rise in the frequency and severity of disputes; (3) developing economic interdependence among specialized producers and ecological zones, putting a premium on the redistribution of goods, protected trade routes, and peaceful markets.[21] All of these problems reflect the difficulty of managing scarce resources for the mutual benefit of a population within which kinship relations and ties of local contiguity are no longer sufficient to the task. Where organized coercive mechanisms are weakly developed, these ends may be achieved most effectively by the concentration of magical potency in a leader, the expansion of his religious authority, and the crystallization of a more inclusive moral community.

Notes

1. This essay is dedicated to the memory of my father, Reverend Robert J. Netting. An earlier version was presented at African Studies Symposium of New York University. I am grateful for the perceptive comments of Igor Kopytoff, Tom Beidelman, Nicholas Hopkins, and Brian Spooner at various stages of manuscript preparation.

2. Field research on the Kofyar has been generously supported by a Ford Foreign Area Studies Fellowship, a Social Science Research Council grant, and supplementary funds from the Ethnocentrism Project under the direction of Robert Le Vine and Donald Campbell.

3. A similar pattern of role and status in matters religious, jural, and economic is found in other stateless societies of Nigeria. Meek (1931b: 437) notes that among the Yungur each district has a priest-chief of outstanding importance. Because of his ownership of the rain cult and his performance of the annual rites for corn, he was regarded with considerable religious awe. Signs of respect included removal of sandals and clapping of hands by any subjects passing his house. The ritual importance of the priest-chief was emphasized by his special burial and the use of his jawbone as part of rainmaking paraphernalia. His religious status allowed him to arrest theft subjects, impose blood wealth payments on the family of a murderer, support the results of the poisonous sass-wood ordeal for witchcraft, and arbitrate between two fighting villages in order to restore peace. His position also made him an economic focus. Priest-chiefs supposedly descended from wealthy immigrants who had purchased the rain cult. They received gifts of mats at initiation time, and novices worked on their farms. They retained a part of the fine levied in homicide cases.

4. Sahlins's (1963) useful discussion of the relation of Melanesian big men to Polynesian chiefs points out both the indispensability of big men for the creation of supralocal organization in tribes normally fragmented into small independent groups and the comparative instability of a political order built on acquired magical powers and the demonstration of personal superiority.

5. I would, therefore, directly question the inclusiveness of Carneiro's contention that "the forging of villages into chiefdoms and of chiefdoms into kingdoms . . . occurs only through coercion, especially by conquest warfare" (Chapter 3, this vol.) It may well be, however, that development of ritually sanctioned ranking as sketched in this paper both logically and temporally precedes a process of stratification relying more heavily on warfare and the subjection of certain social groups (see Chapter 12, this vol.).

6. Sahlins (1968: 98) has similarly pointed out that ritual or religious concepts come into play "at points of stress in the economic and social order where ordinary procedures and arrangements are insufficient to sustain the system. Supernaturalism can be expected in connection with economic uncertainty, whether occasioned by inadequate technical means or untoward natural events. It acts to blunt contradictions and conflicts of interest in one's social relations. It collaborates with politics at the latter's points of weakness, to buttress authority, consecrate peace, or mobilize war."

7. At an earlier stage of development, it is possible that high population density triggers

the formalization of localized agnatic descent groups (Keesing 1967: 15). Here the relatively open organization of local descent groups including cognates and acknowledging bilateral links seems less effective in handling competition for scarce land.

8. The authority of those acting as intermediaries in intergroup strife depends primarily upon their disengagement from the web of kin, caste, and territorial affiliations (Tuden 1966: 282). Ritual functionaries such as the Nuer leopard skin chief achieve a measure of impartiality by standing "outside and above the system of lineages" (Middleton and Tait 1958: 16).

9. The function of religion in rendering political action legitimate has been stressed by Swartz et al. (1966: 168–169), though the emphasis on separation and balancing of priestly and chiefly power differs from that of this essay.

10. "Conflict of interest is countered by various institutions that provide for the affirmation of joint as against sectional interests. This seems largely to depend upon non-empirical factors, which include a common set of religious values, a common God or body of ancestors to whom constituent units and their representatives feel responsibility for their actions, and a common mythology" (Middleton and Tait 1958: 26).

11. The distinction between an emerging chiefship and the formative stages of a religious movement may be unclear. Middleton and Tait (1958: 18) indicate that "some types of chiefship seen in religious terms and especially in the form of prophets or messianic leaders who acquire political power may well develop as a response to external stresses, some of which at least are due to pressure of population and ecological factors."

12. It is very difficult to demonstrate the buildup of population pressure from African examples. The density at which a change in agricultural systems becomes adaptive depends on local factors of soil fertility, rainfall, topography, etc. The paucity of demographic records and the problems of estimating population trends in the past are obvious. Until more adequate data are available on specific cases such as that of the Ibo, we cannot judge the precontact rate of population growth or the point at which this increase might stimulate economic alterations and sociopolitical readjustments.

13. The mere increase in proximity and frequency of encounter under circumstances of settled agriculture and high population density may lead to heightened interpersonal hostility. "The sheer number of Browninan contacts, hence of possible conflicts, increases" (Sahlins 1968: 8). Rappaport (1967: 116) discusses the geometric increase of the "irritative coefficient" in such circumstances. "Such irritations are produced by close living constantly do threaten to arouse anger so intense that it can be relieved only by mayhem or murder. The cultural solution is religious . . ." (Wallace 1966: 21).

14. This contrasts sharply with a society of self-sufficient, sovereign communities in which "each group, exploiting like environmental opportunities, underwrites by its ecological completeness, its political autonomy" (Sahlins 1968: 22).

15. "In order to trade, man must first lay down his spear. When that is done he can succeed in exchanging goods and persons not only between clan and clan but between tribe and tribe and nation and nation, and above all between individuals" (Mauss 1954: 80). See also Sanders and Price (1968: 93) on the integrative effects of traditional repetitive market encounters of people from different communities.

16. A somewhat similar phenomenon has been suggested to account for the presence of a Poro-type secret society among the linguistically diverse but culturally homogeneous peoples of the Central West Atlantic region in Africa (d'Azevedo 1962: 516, 527–528). Among neighboring rice-growing groups of relatively dense population such as the Mende, Gola, and Kpelle, Poro provided a "sacred and secret arm of political authority and intergroup diplomacy. . . ." It was also a mechanism allowing transition from kinship-based political units to territorial and federated chiefships with ranked lineages. In earlier times the Poro society seems to have regulated the distribution of the iron so necessary for agricultural tools and weapons.

17. An aspect of divinity is frequently its power to resolve conflicts. Boston (1962) records

the tradition that the first Ata of Idah was reared in the bush by a leopard, and eventually became accepted as ruler "through skill in arbitrating disputes." Another story that derives the Igala ruling family from Jukun presents the significant first step in statehood as the uniting of the original nine Igala clans.

18. The Yoruba kingship similarly has the major function of sacred mediation. The prosperity of a town is thought to depend on the proper attention of the king or oba to ritual. The oba "is the personification of his town: the Yoruba say that no town could exist without its oba, for the lineages would start fighting among themselves and so destroy the unity of the settlement" (Lloyd 1965b: 567). Interestingly, the oba had no control of the army or police activities.

19. See Durkheim (1912: 426) on the extension of this process, leading finally to the creation of great international gods.

20. Richard Dillon (n.d.) has admirably demonstrated these differences in his reanalysis of Harris's (1965) data on Mbembe political organization, showing how the basic idiom of a peace cult was developed by three tribes in different ways according to the unique problems each faced in external threats, land scarcity, communication, and the organization of trade.

21. A convergent approach to similar questions is evidenced in Wheatley's (1971: 302–305) recent consideration of the role of ceremonial centers in urban genesis. He emphasizes the role of religion in assuaging anxiety over food shortages resulting from population increase, in promoting a system of economic redistribution under divine authority, and in providing a greatly amplified ethical system integrating new values into a sacrally sanctioned moral order.

10

The Iranian Deserts[1]

Brian Spooner

This chapter marks a transition in the volume from agriculture to other subsistence bases. It is concerned particularly with the effects of environment—and the technologies used to exploit it—on the culture and identity of pastoral nomadic groups, mining colonies, and certain agricultural communities specializing in different ranges of crops. It deals with an arid region where these three occupational categories are closely linked and interdependent economically. It suggests that before agricultural technology reached a stage of development that would allow exploitation of such a marginal region, exploitation by other means (for example, pastoralism) was not possible either, and excess population from the lush peripheries was not able to overflow into the deserts.

The Alburz, Zagros, and Hindukush ranges in Iran and Afghanistan enclose an immense area (about 500,000 square miles) of desert and semidesert plains.[2] Though they can by no means all be strictly defined as desert, for convenience I refer to these plains throughout as "the deserts." Unlike most similar areas in the world, they lie at the very center of a culture area. For at least two and a half millennia the same culture has extended far to the east and west of them, and for most of this period there have been major cultural centers of one and the same culture on all sides of them. The deserts as a whole constitute a natural barrier to communications only to the extent that the traveler cannot live off the land. He will perish if he runs out of supplies on the way, but he is otherwise unlikely to die of exposure to the natural conditions of the environment. However, the very nature of the deserts causes him to move faster than he would over a similar distance through settled country. Therefore, two cities a thousand miles apart on either side of the deserts will be closer in time than two cities similarly spaced on the same side—though people may be less ready to travel between them. The emptiness of the deserts enhances mobility and favors the hit-and-run methods of raiders. It is not surprising, therefore, that traditionally the deserts have been the natural element of raiders, as the Persian Gulf was of pirates (see Toynbee 1934: 39ff.). The deserts link the territories on either side of them while at the same time they separate them. And this paradox is the key to an understanding of their role in the history of the area. They have never contained a major regional center, but a glance at the place names sprinkled through them even on the inadequate maps available suggests a degree of human activity that requires investigation, and my own field surveys substantiate this.

The desert center of the Iranian culture area therefore is not a vacuum. The purpose of this essay is to discuss on the basis of data presently available the demographic processes operative both within the deserts and between them and the major cultural and political centers outside and around them. These processes must be discussed against the background of the natural environment and the ability of the various elements of the population to exploit it—that is, the various technologies. We are concerned with small oasis settlements with optimum populations determined by the level of technological achievement, and we are able to elicit information concerning settlement, communications, political, military, and social movements, and levels of technology and investment over a time span of up to and even exceeding a thousand years.[3] There is no evidence of change in agricultural technology during this period. In my interpretation the available data suggest that pressure of population on resources tends to lead to intensification of labor and investment up to a certain point (which is a function of both environment and culture), beyond which it is diverted into marginal pursuits in marginal areas. The culture and ecology of the marginal areas can be properly understood only in the context of the total cultural and social universe and, in particular, the relationships with the (primary) agricultural settlements on the periphery of the deserts.

The Physical Environment

The accompanying map (Fig. 10.1) is designed not only to show the extent and location of the deserts but to illustrate some of the topographical factors that are important to the discussion. It so happens that practically all the area below the 1,000 m contour is desert or near desert, and everything above the 1,500 m contour is mountainous or narrow plateau corridors between ranges. The space between the two contours coincides very closely with the fertile and comparatively well-watered country of the alluvial fans, which slope down from the mountains to the depressed desert center of the plateau, rather like the rim of a saucer. A number of cities, many of them of considerable antiquity, lie within this space. Many of these cities have at one time or another been the major political and cultural centers of the Iranian world, and the written history of the Iranian plateau has been primarily the history of these cities. The major capital of the Iranian world—when it has not been on the plateau—has moved between points as far west as the Tigris (Ctesiphon and Baghdad) and as far east as Samarqand. During the very few brief periods of cultural eclipse it has moved even farther afield.

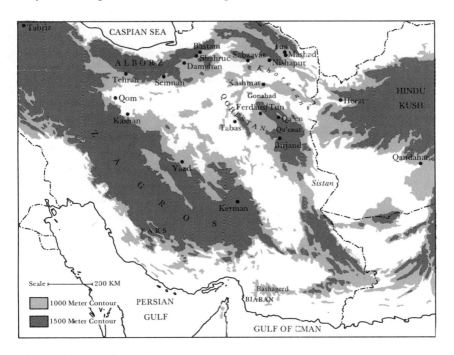

Figure 10.1. The Iranian Plateau.

Situated roughly centrally between these extremes, the deserts are doubly circumscribed—socially and naturally—by the relatively dense population and lushness of the fertile belt around them and by the mountainous barrier beyond.

Within Iran the deserts fall naturally into two main parts: the northern, which contains great expanses of saline mud flats (*kavir*); and the southern, which is characterized chiefly by rolling gray gravel plains. The latter receives less drainage from the surrounding mountains and contains fewer springs. It has been characterized as one of the most forbidding deserts of the world. The *kavirs* are generally treacherous. The water table is very close to the surface. Precipitation in the surrounding mountains finally drains into these sumps, and they become literally impassable bogs (cf. Hedin 1910). However, caravans did make crossings over traditionally well-defined routes (see Fig. 10.2). Along the southern and southeastern borders of most of these *kavirs* there are considerable accumulations of sand, which is a general characteristic of the larger expanses of plain on the plateau. But, generally speaking, sand is not a feature of the Persian deserts—as it is, for instance, of the Empty Quarter of Arabia—and both its advantages and disadvantages are absent over most of the area.[4]

The major sources of water in the deserts are cisterns built for travelers at intervals along the major routes, which catch and conserve runoff. In addition there are frequent potable springs,[5] and in a few places, where there is cultivable soil, *qanats*[6] are viable. There is one town, Tabas, which traditionally relied on a perennial river (see Stoecklin et al. 1965: 7). Pasturage tends to be confined to wadis and runoff channels. Although wells are found, they are rare.

The arterial routes, which traditionally crossed the deserts, linked the east and west, and (less significantly) the north and south of the Iranian world. In periods when the greater political situation allowed, the plateau constituted a crossroads on the scale indicated in Figure 10.3. This was a crossroads not only of commerce, individual travel, and communication but also of mass movements of armies and peoples. The present distribution of cultural and linguistic groupings on the plateau derives historically from this condition.

But the deserts are not only a system of throughways. They are also a cul-de-sac. They contain many groups of people that went in one side

Figure 10.2. Traditional routes of communication within the deserts.

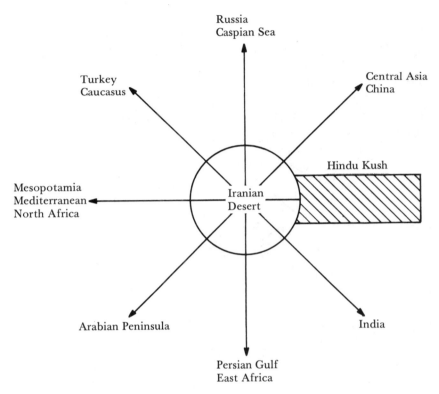

Figure 10.3.   Schematic representation of traditional long-distance communications relevant to the area of the Iranian desert.

but never came out the other. It is the combination and complementarity of these two factors that form the background of the discussion in this essay. I am interested in the relationship between population and resources in the cul-de-sac, but this relationship is not comprehensible without an appreciation of the existence and role of the throughways.

Occupation, Technology, and Identity

The great attraction of the deserts as a field of study is that social units within them are relatively small and well spaced, so that, superficially at least, it is relatively easy to isolate social processes in space. The social identity of individuals derives from their membership in a particular

social group. In the deserts social groups and occupational groups tend
to be coterminous. The identity of the individual is generated by the
relationship with the natural environment that is involved in the occupation of his social group. However, the composition of the groups changes
continuously. This continual redistribution of population between social
and occupational groups is caused by demographic processes: unequal
fluctuation in the population of various groups causes pressure of population on the available resources in one place and a relative vacuum in
another. Individuals have to change groups. Often this requires a change
in occupation that results in a change in ideology and identity. Therefore,
in order to arrive at a better understanding of the demographic situation,
it is necessary to investigate the ecologies and technologies of the various
groups.

A minimal survey is sufficient to show that—in the traditional, or
predevelopment, situation—activity can be summarized under three
main headings. These are subsistence, communications, and security.
Communications are on two planes, linking (a) the cities on either side—
the principal channels of trade, pilgrimage, and administration—and
(b) the various scenes of activity within the deserts. Subsistence comes
from agriculture, pastoralism, or mining; and security is both locally
organized by the subsistence communities and delegated by the peripheral political centers for the security of their own back doors and of
the caravan routes. It is the caravan trade generated by the peripheral
cities which gives rise to the raiding and thus necessitates the security
arrangements. Further, the caravan trade constitutes an auxiliary
resource that may be exploited for subsistence within the deserts.

The sites and distribution of each of these three categories of activity
are predictable to a high degree. Traffic follows the shortest route from
city to city with due allowance for natural obstacles (such as *kavir*, sand,
and mountains), the natural corridors between them (natural passes,
torrent beds, and wadis), water sources, oases, and, occasionally, also
shrines. Caravanserais are not so common within the confines of the
deserts as they are on the great routes that go around the north and west
of them (see Siroux 1959, map), though they are found on stretches of
the Kerman-Meshed and Yazd-Meshed routes. The foundation of a
caravansarai requires reliable water supply and security, both of which
are scarce. It is in the absence of these facilities that chains of cisterns

are constructed, generally at one-parasang intervals, which catch and conserve the runoff from the occasional precipitation. These are built and maintained largely by private investment.[7] Owing to the vagaries of the precipitation pattern, even when they are kept in good repair, not all of them will contain water at any given time. But the traveler will usually find water in one somewhere along his route. They were built on minor as well as major routes, and kept water fresh for surprisingly long periods (for details of construction see Siroux 1959).

Sites of potential agricultural activity are predictable where accumulations of cultivable soil coincide with a supply of water that the local population, with the level of technology at their command, can exploit for irrigation. Pastoralism is predictable in a similar way. However, while it is possible to delineate areas where pasturage (of rather poor quality) is generally available—and unlike the Arabian situation these areas are fixed by the topography—nevertheless, the pasturage they afford appears not to be sufficient to support independent groups of pastoral nomads. This does not mean that pastoral nomadism or pastoralism is therefore nonexistent. Rather, the pastoralist must also have access to other resources in order to subsist. Where there is an oasis settlement fairly close by, the pastoralist turns out to be an agriculturalist who uses pastoralism as an auxiliary resource. This situation is general in the northern two-thirds of the deserts. Where areas of pasturage are not close to settlements—a situation typical of the more arid southern part of the deserts—nomads rely on pastoralism as one of a number of resources, often the main one, but their nomadism must include the exploitation of other resources in order to attain a level of subsistence.

Further discussion of social process in the deserts requires some understanding of the different technologies involved in the exploitation of the resources of the descrts. I do not wish to give the impression that I consider any of these technologies physically restrictive, in the sense that they necessarily require long apprenticeship or inhibit change of occupation. However, technology is an important factor in a man's identity. Men are born into social groups, and in the traditional situation birth tends to determine what a man's occupation will be. There are processes whereby he may change his group membership and his occupation, but when these changes do occur, other factors are often also involved. The differences between a miner and a peasant and a nomad are not simply differences of occupation and technology: they are differences of Weltanschauung or ideology and identity. And most significantly in this context, they entail very definite differences in attitude toward the environment.

The nomad, insofar as he is pastoral and nomadic and does not also cultivate, relates to a total and unimproved environment. He may be compared to a hunter-gatherer. He hunts and gathers for his animals as well as himself. He does nothing to improve or modify the physical environment that is his habitat, except (in some areas) to dig occasional wells.

The agriculturalist, on the other hand, must improve his environment. He must irrigate. Irrigation on the plateau is by *qanat*, spring, or river. *Qanats* are constructed where there is cultivable soil. Where waterflow is available from spring or river, fields of cultivable soil must be *constructed*. This is done by means of terracing and *bands* (drystone walls and earthworks enclosing soil). The agriculturalist concentrates on his small improved enclave within the total environment and on his title and his investment within that. Though he may also hunt and gather outside it, and will almost certainly travel outside it at least occasionally for purposes of trade, pilgrimage, and now also business with the larger administrative centers, his main relationship with the world outside is conditioned by his interest in the defense and security of his small improved enclave.

The miner is different again. Ideologically he is best characterized as a member of a desert proletariat. Although he generally retains at least some residual title to membership in an agricultural village community, he relates primarily to a vast area in which the fixed points are mine workings at various stages of exploitation. There is a general camaraderie among all miners that is based on a common experience (despite differences in mineral mined), on the mobility from old to new workings inherent in the occupation, and in the common dialectal elements that develop.[8]

Therefore, the sites, the ideologies, and the technologies of the different types of human activity are both highly predictable and generally fixed and permanent in the traditional situation, with considerable histories, though there may be continual movement of individuals between them.

We must pause here to consider some aspects of the technologies in greater detail, in order to appreciate the potentiality of the environment in general and the fixity of the communities within it. These are factors that regulate the size of social and subsistence groupings independently of demographic fluctuations and therefore stimulate mobility of individuals.

The relationship between technology and social organization requires much more attention in anthropology. Much of the basic technological information we require for any analysis is not available in the literature. Ethnographers have concentrated too much on the relationships within the social structure and the cultural system, and the ecological approach is only just beginning to bring out the importance of the technology of adaptation, as distinct from the mechanics of adaptation, just as it is only recently that the size of the group has been seen to be an essential datum.

Although it is possible to make general statements about the ecology and the organization of nomadic populations, there is wide variation in the details of their ecological adaptation (see Spooner 1972b). Briefly, there are almost as many different types of nomadism as nomadic groups, whereas, at least from the ecological point of view, the cultural ecology of peasants is basically similar. Peasants (that is, sedentary agriculturalists—I use the term for convenience, since all tend to be involved in some way in both agriculture and pastoralism) all improve their environment in basically similar ways. They make an investment in a piece of land that enables them to grow the crops on which they lay the greatest emphasis in their subsistence pattern and in so doing tend to make it similar to other such improved pieces of land. Nomads do not improve their environment and thus do not homogenize it. Therefore, nomadic groups vary widely in the environment they exploit, as they do in the main animal of exploitation, in the patterns of movement entailed, and in the main end product of their pastoralism (for example, cheese, ghee, meat). They also vary significantly in level of affluence and in the degree to which they can in fact specialize in the exploitation of one species of animal. It would seem that only the most affluent nomads are purely pastoral nomads, and a more generally valid stock epithet for nomads would be "multi-resource" (Salzman 1969). Furthermore, nomadic societies are made up of primary social groupings formed for the purpose of efficient herding of the animals. A combination of factors of individual ownership of the animals and the optimum size and composition of herd leads to a high degree of instability in the composition of the human herding group. Nomadic societies in the Iranian area display only two common features: this basic instability in their primary social grouping and a strong, uncompromising ideology. The latter idealizes the unimproved environment and its efficient exploitation and proclaims both the nobility and freedom of nomadism as a way of life and the despicableness and bondage of peasanthood. I have suggested elsewhere (Spooner 1972a) that the strong nomadic ideology may be seen as compensating (vis-à-vis the peasants) for the inherent instability of the nomads' primary social grouping.

The agriculturalist owns his agricultural resources as an individual. He owns or has rights to one or more parcels of land and a number of time units of water to irrigate it. The water may come from a *qanat*, a spring, or runoff (controlled by dikes). In the case of the *qanat* he will be involved in a corporate investment interest, but in all three cases he will be involved in some measure of cooperation with his neighbors—at least those who own the immediately adjacent parcels of land—in order to maintain the efficiency of the irrigation and repair irrigation channels and *bands*. The water flow continually erodes and changes the configuration of these and so gives rise both to one of the major causes of disputes in this type of community and to the need for some corporate structure for the settlement of these disputes. However, such corporate structure is generally minimal in this area, and the identity of the village is a function of the unity of the land area cultivated rather than the social or political structure. A man is a member of the village community by virtue of the fact that he owns and works part of that land.[9]

There are a number of jural terms for different types or degrees of rights to land in Persia (before Land Reform): for example *malek, ra'yat, iqta', tuyul, suyurghal,* and *mubasher*. Some have been constant; others have varied and been used in particular historical periods only. Together they constitute the model of the Great Tradition. However, they represent a series of social and political relationships involving rights in cultivation and might be represented more usefully (for anthropology) by a model of four levels from (1) actual cultivator, through (2) local noncultivator, (3) absentee noncultivator, to (4) government. Where all four levels are represented the actual cultivator (1) will typically be a sharecropper; the absentee noncultivator (3) will take the major share of the produce via his local representative, the local noncultivator (2), but will be expected by the government (4) to pay taxes on it. Where the local noncultivator and the absentee noncultivator are missing, the actual cultivator will be a smallholder, etc. The sharecropper may in some circumstances be the original owner of the land, whose title was usurped when one or another type of tax farmer was set up between him and the government (for example, under the *iqta'* system, see Lambton 1954 and 1967). Further discussion of the political and social organization of the village would require analysis of the pattern of intermarriage that integrates the community and of the oligarchical superstructure that links the villages of each region (cf. Spooner 1965b and Parsons 1964: 161–162).

Although peasants may be considered ecologically homogeneous when compared to nomads, nevertheless from the point of view of group composition, identity, and native models they are quite heterogeneous. There is at least one case in the literature of the Middle East of a village community where the people all describe themselves as "sons of the village" (Peters 1963). But many village communities (including Peters's) are strongly divided by considerations of class, religion, or other larger classification. In some cases it is difficult to see why and in what way such divisions form one community—why they identify themselves by one name. The proposition that it is simply the distribution of land rights that integrates the divisions is at least worth investigation, but it begs historical questions. The proposition that the identity of a community is in the land that it collectively owns is not new and has been exaggerated. A full analysis would have to seek the evolution of the pattern of land rights, on the one hand, and the evolution of the social groupings, on the other, in any historical material, which may or may not be available.

But given that people identify themselves first as members of their community, what does this mean? Identity is of course relative in that it distinguishes one grouping of people from the rest, and is therefore more clear-cut in the deserts, but the criteria of the distinction may be social or environmental. Village nomenclature is not homogeneous. There are cases where one residential cluster equals two villages. In my experience such cases result from the coresidence of two groups who cultivate separate land or depend on different sources of irrigation water. In any case no general rules can be drawn up which do not require investigation of the name of the village itself. For instance, is it primarily the appellation of the whole community itself; was it originally the name of one group to whom other groups later attached themselves; or was it the name of a natural feature or landmark by means of which groups living in geographical juxtaposition identify themselves? In other words, is it a purely social or historical, or a geographical, or ecological identification?

The village of Nayband provides an interesting example. It is situated at the foot of a 9,000-foot mountain of the same name in the deserts of eastern central Persia and is very isolated; its history spans at least a thousand years. In the village nearly eighty families huddle together in tall houses of several stories on a crag overlooking their dry riverbed cultivation—historically for reasons of defense against marauding Baluch. A score more families live at other points around the mountain (within a range of forty miles) in groupings of from one to ten families. They identify themselves first as being of the community of Nayband but also have distinguishing names for their particular settlements. They all own land in Nayband village as well as where they are settled. The name Nayband, therefore, in present usage, denotes (1) the main village, (2) the mountain, (3) a community of all the settlements around the mountain. It is now also applied to the lead mine workings some forty miles to the east, which are closer to Nayband than to any other settlement but in a different geographical region. In this case, therefore, the name seems to be elastic and capable of covering any settled activity within an undefined radius of the dominating natural feature.

In all agricultural communities in the deserts and in Persian Baluchistan, membership in the community involves rights to cultivate and irrigate land and/or rights to a share in the produce of that land. The relationship between the social grouping and the environment in which it has made an investment proceeds on the two parallel planes of the individual and the community. Further details of these relationships depend on the choice of crop, which in turn determines the technology of cultivation and the ecological relationships. In the oasis villages I have in mind, the range of crops grown includes rice, wheat, sorghum, dates, and alfalfa. In order to satisfy subsistence requirements each of these crops entails a different relationship with the land a different level of investment in terms of engineering or labor, and a different ratio of land to cultivator. Of course, these five crops do not exhaust the total range of crops grown in the area, but they are the most significant in the present context. Rice is the least common. There are villages where all five are grown, primarily in the southern half of Persian Baluchistan. However, for the sake of simplicity and in order to make a point, I shall treat them separately as though any given community was conditioned by the cultivation of only one of the five. Alfalfa is the exception, in that it is of course grown for animal, not human, consumption. The alfalfa grower is therefore a sedentary agricultural *pastoralist* and is interested in agriculture simply as a means of augmenting the feed of his flocks. In effect, within the occupational category of pastoralism he has made the ecological choice to become settled rather than nomadic and is therefore now ideologically a peasant though his primary means of subsistence is pastoralism. The village of Nayband, already mentioned, is a case of this type of adaptation. The people of Nayband grow many other crops besides alfalfa. However, since they were continually subject to raids, and since rainfall is both scant and irregular though necessary for a good grain crop because of the mineral content of the spring water, the production of any crop fit for *human* consumption from wheat, sorghum, or dates was always chancy. Consequently, the tendency was to consider each of them, and especially the dates, as extra feed for the flocks and count them a bonus if good for human consumption. In this situation the ratio of population to resources is obviously very different from that of the ordinary agricultural village, since in fact the agricultural resources are only auxiliary in the economy, even though primary in the ideology.

Nayband is not the exception that it might at first appear. Many other communities, whose subsistence is based primarily on other crops, are ecologically not so different. Variation between rice, wheat, sorghum, and dates is to some extent—but not totally—determined by environmental factors. Rice requires a reliable water supply sufficient to keep it submerged throughout the growing season. Wheat requires a more reliable water supply than the sorghums. The various millets and sorghums have a high tolerance of drought, and the date crop is vulnerable only to severe drought, rain, cloud cover during the ripening season, or severe frost in winter. Sorghum and dates, which have high tolerance of marginal conditions, are typically dual purpose. When these crops fail for human consumption, they nevertheless provide feed for the flocks. Rice and wheat are highly valued and are the ideal foods in the cultural system. Millets and sorghums are generally considered at best poor-quality substitutes for wheat. Dates are a delicacy when fresh, and in their preserved form they constitute an important staple but are not considered fit food for guests. (These relative cultural values probably derive solely from the Great Tradition of the cities.) It is not surprising, therefore, that wheat is grown at least in small quantities almost everywhere, except where all the land is given over to rice (for although the growing season is different, land used for rice is useless for most other crops). Even rice is grown in many places where, simply on the basis of the water supply, it would not be expected. For, however meager the water supply, it can be entirely devoted to a little rice during the summer months. There is evidence that much more rice was grown as a supplementary summer crop in the past before the introduction of cotton as a cash crop at the beginning of this century.

The most significant difference between these major crops in the context of this paper lies in the relationship between the individual and his land according to which crop is primary in the agricultural cycle. For the crops vary significantly both in yield per hectare (in quantity and in food value) and in the man-hour labor input required to obtain that yield. The extreme case is that of the date palm, which will produce up to 400 lb of fruit per year per tree, with a normal productive life of upward of 75 years. Apart from the organization of irrigation (where necessary), the labor involved is almost negligible. A good tree must be cultivated from a sucker. It will start producing in its fifth year or thereabouts. It must be artificially pollinated in the spring. When the fruit turns color a month before ripening in the summer, care must be taken that it does not fall before it ripens. Finally it must be picked, and the lower fronds should be cut back. One man can easily tend fifty trees and still work only three weeks in the year.

However, though dates may be an important staple, no community lives on dates alone. Date growing is commonly linked with pastoralism. Since most good dates are also grown by peasants because of the irrigation requirements, date cultivation forms one of the most important bridges between nomad and peasant.

Only affluent communities in relatively lush, nondesert environments can afford to specialize in occupation and depend more or less exclusively on one resource, whether pastoral or agricultural. In the deserts every community or social grouping, whether nomad or peasant, is obliged to depend on more than one resource. Each resource that is exploited entails a different technology and a different cycle and constitutes a different niche. In the case of any particular community the cycle and technology entailed in the exploitation of each resource are dovetailed together to form an overall system. Each system will demand either nomadism or permanent settlement, and it is from this distinction that the ideology of the group derives. And the ideology is a determining factor in the external relations of the group. The failure of one resource could change the total system.[10]

To summarize briefly at this stage, there are five major products: milk products, dates, wheat, sorghum, and rice. Their production entails a variation in the relationship between society and environment that can be seen as a continuum from a very extensive relationship to a very intensive one. Dates in particular require a low level of investment in the environment and a very low man-hour input of labor in return for a high output. Date cultivation takes up far less of a community's time than does rice cultivation, and it is likely to coincide with lower population density. Similarly, it allows more time and mobility for the exploitation of other resources. At the other end of the scale, rice cultivation requires a relatively high level of investment in the environment to ensure efficient irrigation and a high man-hour input of labor per unit of produce and per unit of land. Rice cultivation, therefore, allows less diversification of resources and requires higher concentration of population. However, it should be noted that rice cultivation and date cultivation are often combined.

Demographic Implications

I am dealing with two modes of society, with nomads and peasants, that are distinguished less by ecological adaptation, or technological specialization, than by the ideological polarization that is generated by their different relationships with the environment. In the Iranian cultural area nomads generally have close relationships with peasants, in some cases so close that both are included in one tribal structure; but more typically an ethnic distinction is made between the two. In this situation I believe it can be shown that agricultural activity and the size, and therefore the density, of population occupied in it have probably remained close to the capacity possible for the level of investment at any particular time or place—after one allows for certain social factors in the ownership of the land and the restriction of the peasants' freedom to buy, sell, or move. However, the level of investment has varied in response to certain exogenous factors.

Under these conditions nomadism took up the slack in the population. The nomad (in this cultural area) is a cultural satellite of agricultural settlements, markets, and cities, because he needs grain—more than he can grow himself, even if he does cultivate some. There is no independent nomadic cultural tradition. At times of political success the nomad apes the political institutions of the cities. Nomads do sometimes have a tradition of epic poetry, but even where this is composed within the nomadic society, it is in the "courts" of high-status chiefs. Not even pastoralism is a monopoly of nomads. In fact, the most significant cultural criterion for a general definition of the term "nomad" is ideological: a man is a nomad because he says he is. The primary function of this ideology would seem to be that it distinguishes its followers from the inhabitants of villages and cities and gives them an identity that they do not otherwise have.

Ideologies belong to groups, not to individuals. There are several different types of evidence to suggest continual movement on the part of individuals from the nomadic to the peasant life and vice versa (cf. Barth 1960).

If the ideological change is possible, then the technological change from peasant to nomad (or vice versa) need present no difficulty either, since it is likely anyway to be only a change in emphasis. However, it is worth noting here that the movement from peasant to nomad is a move in the direction of technological simplicity.

I am suggesting that on every plane—cultural, ecological, demographic, and historical—nomadism (in this culture area) is secondary to settled agriculture. This would mean that pastoralism must similarly be secondary to agriculture, and I would suggest the following ecological support for the historical validity of this argument. On the Iranian plateau flocks have to be watered in the same way as agricultural crops—in fact, much more often and regularly. Since flocks have to move to find pasture, they are dependent on supplies of surface water, which are very few and far between. The engineering that produces so much of the available water on the Iranian plateau is the work of settled agriculturalists, but—albeit with some exceptions—pastoralism is as dependent upon it as is agriculture. Peasants increase both the number and reliability of available water sources. Therefore, the spread of settled agriculture must have been a prerequisite for the spread of pastoralism into many areas.[11]

I found these arguments about the relationship between nomad and peasant in the desert environment epitomized in the situation I studied in the summer of 1969 at Nayband. The village was in existence at the beginning of the Islamic period, when it is described by the early travelers as "possessing a *rubat* or guard-house, with a score of houses round it, water being plentiful, enough indeed to work a small mill. Palms grew here, and many springs irrigated the fields . . . " (Le Strange 1930: 324). Since the occasional European traveler began to visit it in the nineteenth century, it is described as sustaining a similar population to that of the present day:

A picturesque village of about 400 inhabitants . . . It is perched upon a crag. Many of the houses have watch-towers, the position having been chosen entirely with a view to defence against the Baluchis. It has a small stream of good water, but the amount of ground fit for cultivation is very small indeed. Small quantities of wheat and barley are grown; but the principal product is dates. The chief resource of the people is selling provisions to the caravans, which pass through, pilgrims from Kerman going via Tun to Mashhad, and caravans of merchandise going from Yazd and Kerman to Birjand and Herat. The people of Naiband act as guides to these caravans across the desert. Supplies here are only procurable in very small quantities. . . . occasionally the date crop fails, as it did in 1881, when 2,000 date-palms were killed, and others damaged by a heavy fall of snow. Bands of Baluchis wander by Naiband occasionally, and plunder the country towards Tabas, or elsewhere [*Gazetteer of Persia*, n.d., ca. 1900]

The cultivable land around the village is built up into terraces along the sides of the wadis on each side of the rock. There is no sign that more land was cultivated at any time in the past than now. It is difficult to see how any more land could be brought under cultivation. The land is not nearly sufficient to support the population through agriculture. All members of the village community own land and rights to water for irrigation. Though my data are incomplete, it would seem that agriculture occupies the greater part of the time of those who practice it. But many rent out their plots to neighbors and spend their time on flocks. The mountain is surrounded by desert, and the only pasture is on the high slopes and vales within the mountain. It is a sixty-mile walk around the mountain. The village of Nayband commands all but one of the water sources in the area. The other is situated on a hillside a few miles south in the desert. A thousand years ago it was described as an "outlying spring, surrounded by palms, where there was a domed tank, of evil fame as a noted hiding-place for robbers" (Le Strange 1930: 324), and the description still holds good, except for the dome. Therefore, even though the flocks have to keep moving, they cannot move very far away from the village, and migration is not feasible. Furthermore, the available pasture is unreliable and, in most years, insufficient. Some of the land in the village is therefore given over to alfalfa to supplement the feed of the flocks. Because of the traditional insecurity of the deserts, the people were not willing to make the minor investment necessary for the cultivation of good eating dates, and the extensive palm groves produce fruit that is good for human consumption only when made into syrup. Most of the crop is used to supplement the feed of the flocks. The resulting situation is a community of pastoralists, who for reasons of ecology and simple geography build houses in one defensible place and cultivate in order to support their pastoralism. Ecologically they are nomads in all but the essential ecological adaptation—migration. However, according to the criterion suggested before, they are not nomads because they do not call themselves nomads. Furthermore, their ideology, particularly their attitude toward the environment, is characteristic of peasants, not nomads. It would seem that the very fact of being settled and therefore centered on an improved environment, which is therefore contrasted with everything beyond it, which is desert, is enough to explain the difference. But the interesting point here is that they exploit to the full the agricultural potentiality of the area they control before making up their subsistence from other resources. The primary other resource, which is in fact economically the most important, is pastoralism. In the past the caravan trade was another important resource, but this is now diverted by the redirection of routes brought about by the advent of the motor age. Finally, migrant laboring, especially in mines, has always played a part.

While knowledge of the technology and ecology of subsistence is basic to an understanding of the distribution of population in the deserts, the overall political situation, depending on exogenous factors, is also relevant. On any particular technological level it is the level of agricultural investment which determines the optimum population in agricultural settlements. Thus it should at least be noted that such investment shows a marked tendency to rise and fall with variations in political stability, which may or may not be related to internal or external population pressures.

The deserts have never contained any town of historical significance. Probably, with the exception of Tabas, and perhaps also Khabis, no single settlement has ever exceeded about 3,000 in population, and few have reached that figure. Since the cities on the periphery of the deserts were bound for their own security to guard their back doors, every named region of the deserts is traditionally appended to one or another of the peripheral cities. In some cases where there is not very much difference in the distance between the area and two or more peripheral cities—for instance, in the case of Khur-o-Biyabanak—it has been appended to one or another of them at different times, according to the relative distinction and political power of each. However, the deserts have never been entirely without internal political centers. And when the adjacent peripheral cities have been weak, the internal centers have come into their own. The nineteenth century in particular was an interesting period for the study of these internal centers. Birjand, Qa'en, Tabas, and Gonabad provide the most significant examples, though unfortunately our information is far from adequate even for these. The typical political pattern in the deserts consists of powerful families in control of forts in the centers of major agricultural regions. The family displays dynastic attributes. For example, it will give its women in marriage only to families that it considers to have a similar status. From the fort a varying hinterland is controlled, according to the capacity of the dynastic family, the alliances it can make, and the surrounding political conditions. Often the family is of tribal origin (see Spooner

1969a: 147–149). In general, there is a definite tendency for the political situation in the deserts to balance that on its peripheries. The desert, therefore, is never a vacuum either politically or demographically.

There are also religious factors contributing to the cultural ecology of the deserts. For example, religious minorities are drawn into the deserts because they are refuge areas. The most obvious case is that of the Bahais in the Boshruya area of Khorasan. The case of the Bahai shop-keepers in the Saravan area of Persian Baluchistan differs, since trade in Baluch society was traditionally conducted by non-Baluch.

Further, religion is significant in the siting of shrines. I have suggested a typology of shrines elsewhere (Spooner 1963: 90) on the basis of origin. From the ecological point of view, there would seem to be two main factors in the distribution of shrines, which in turn influence geographical patterns of human activity in the deserts. Shrines develop either from authentic graves or from what the ancients called the *naturalis deus uniuscuiusque loci*. The former type occurs typically either at settlement sites or on major routes. Great men whose tombs might develop into shrines are unlikely to die elsewhere. Other, "natural" shrines occur at natural features that for some reason attract particular attention in the culture. That is, it is the ecological relationship between the natural environment and the local culture that suggests the site of the shrine. A typical example would be a shady spring in an arid environment or a flat platform atop a rock or mountain in an unusually broken terrain. The appearance and degree of "success" of the shrine then has a feedback effect on the pattern of settlement and communications.

In this enormous area of such low overall population density,[12] it is impossible not to be drawn into the investigation of the apparently easy and ideal distribution of optimum or near optimum population among the resources that their technology allows them to exploit. Technology is obviously the fulcrum, for any change in technology will change the carrying capacity of the environment. But the agricultural technology is not very advanced. *Qanats* were a major technological leap forward, which must have vastly increased the area of cultivable land on the plateau. Unfortunately it is impossible to learn from direct evidence when they were introduced, though it is generally thought to have been well into the first millennium B.C. and possibly connected with the rise of Iranian political power. But *qanats* are more characteristic of the peripheries of the deserts than the agricultural settlements within them. In either case there has been no other technological innovation since then that would affect either the intensity or the distribution of agriculture until the introduction of cash-cropping, which again is not a factor in the small desert oases.

If the carrying capacity of the environment did not change throughout this period, by what processes was the population regulated? Apart from the movement back and forth from nomadism to peasanthood, there would obviously have been pressure from outside the area, which caused new groups to use the deserts as a refuge area. Also there was certainly migration out of the area, in the form of migrant labor, which was both temporary and permanent. Finally abortion appears to have been widely practiced in at least one village (Nayband), where genealogical data allow an average of only two children per family up until, but not including, the present generation.

The data we have suggest the following model in the context of Boserup's hypothesis. When a peasant becomes a nomad, insofar as he forsakes agriculture for pastoralism, he slides down the technological scale. He leaves behind a certain amount of capital investment and makes none in his new situation. He also moves from a situation of dense population to dispersed as well as mobile population. Moreover, he changes from an intensive use of the environment to an extensive use of it. Finally, he moves from a relatively rich (in terms of exploitable resources) to a relatively marginal environment. He leaves his community and makes these changes because of a reduction in resources relative to population—due, usually, to natural catastrophe or hostile activity. Either case is equivalent to population pressure on resources. Therefore, population pressure is forcing people into marginal environments, where in less dense groupings they make a more extensive use of the environment with a lower man-hour input per unit of produce but at a lower technological level. The nature of their new relationship with their environment—a far larger geographical area—requires that they make a much greater investment in the knowledge of that environment, which is in fact what occupies them when (to the outside observer) they often appear idle.

Presumably, in Europe, where the plow and and swidden coexisted (see Boserup 1965: 57), swidden was primary and the plow was used only where the pressure of population required the increased investment. On the Iranian plateau, however, if the present argument is valid, agriculture—the more intensive land use—is primary, and pressure of population forces people in the opposite direction. Presumably, original movement into the deserts resulted from the same forces, for why should any group move into the deserts if the richer land around them was available?

It would seem, therefore, that oasis settlement must be at least partly due to pressure of population outside the area, and nomadism to pressure of population in agriculture settlements, though the presence of arterial routes and frequent traffic must obviously be relevant to both types of activity. At the other end of the process excess population from the deserts moves into migrant labor and supplies not only the mines but the city proletariats.

Notes

1. This paper constitutes the preliminary progress report of a long-term program for the study of the desert areas of the Iranian plateau. The data, generalizations, and arguments presented here derive from extensive survey work and over a decade of familiarity with the desert areas. Intensive ethnographic inquiry, however, was begun only with a four-month season last summer (1969), during which I concentrated my efforts on the village of Nayband in southwestern Khorasan. Much of the argument has developed from working hypotheses that I formed on the basis of earlier work in Persian Baluchistan from 1963 to 1967 (see Spooner 1969a). In many ways Persian Baluchistan may be considered both an appendage and a microcosm of the desert areas of the central plateau.
2. Sistan, however, is excluded from this discussion. Though located near the center of the plateau, such a considerable area of intensive agriculture, irrigated by a Nile-like river, is too complex to be treated in this context except from the point of view of its external relations and communications.
3. The quantity and quality of the evidence decreases drastically the further back in time we look, and the main sources are present-day observation, ethnographic inquiry, and oral history. However, there is a great deal of literary evidence in the form of scattered chance data in Western travel accounts (back to the sixteenth century), medieval histories and geographies, and reports of the early Muslim travelers. Furthermore, there is the evidence of archaeological deposits and the linguistic evidence of the toponymy. The exploitation of each of these sources has just begun, but enough has been done to demonstrate the potential (cf. Spooner 1965a, 1969b, 1970, 1971a; Wertime 1964, 1967).
4. The advantage of sand is that, when precipitation does occur, it supports pasturage. The most important disadvantage is that it greatly slows or prevents communication.
5. Many springs are thermal. Many more are saline, sulfurous, or otherwise nonpotable.
6. Qanats are tunnels that bring water from the water table onto fields by gravity flow. For technological details consult English 1968.

7. This may be in the form of *waqf*, religiously institutionalized good works for the benefit of the community, see *Encyclopaedia of Islam*.

8. The common elements of dialect may to some extent be due simply to the preponderance of men from one place—Anarak—in positions of relative responsibility in mining enterprises throughout the deserts.

9. There are, however, also cultural considerations. When an outsider acquires rights to land in a village, he is not necessarily accepted straightaway as a member of the community, even if he works the land himself (cf. the case of Deh Salm in Spooner 1971b).

10. More general details of agricultural technology may be found in English 1966: 117–124.

11. It should be noted that I am dealing in this chapter primarily with an area where agricultural, peasant values are dominant. In an earlier article (Spooner 1969a) I showed how in Baluchistan nomads appeared to have taken over a peasant society, leaving a situation where nomadic values were dominant, although the nomadism was still secondary.

12. Unfortunately there are no figures, except for individual settlements, and these are unreliable.

11

Demographic Aspects of Tibetan Nomadic Pastoralism[1]

Robert B. Ekvall

Ekvall provides us with a rare case of population decline. As in Chapter 10, the area under discussion is one in which various agricultural and pastoral subsistence technologies are practiced, and individuals and groups can and do move from the practice of one technology to the practice of another. However, the most interesting feature of Ekvall's data in the context of this volume is that agriculturalists seek to become nomads, not because of pressure of population on resources, but because they are able to make the investment in animals that will allow them to become nomads—that is, from choice, not necessity. Ekvall thus provides valuable support for the obverse of Boserup's thesis: although the decline of population over centuries has left a surfeit of agricultural resources in the agricultural areas of Tibet, nevertheless population is continually siphoned off into nomadism—a less land-intensive technology—in the "high-altitude zone."

That this nomadic zone of the country has not thus become overpopulated is traced to biological (among other) factors, which are further discussed by Katz in Chapter 16.

Population

The Tibetan nomadic pastoralists are known to themselves and all other Tibetans by the all-inclusive term *aBrog Pa* ("high-pasturage ones."). Whatever, and however varied, may be the ingredients of their ethnic amalgam, they exhibit great cultural homogeneity, though they are widely scattered. They also are unequivocally Tibetan in important aspects of culture—language, religion, and sense of a common history. Yet they are markedly different from other Tibetans and, because of their habitat, subsistence technique, and the behavior patterns stemming from that environment and way of life, form a self-consciously distinct sub-society. As a "people of the black tents," they share many of the culture traits and something of the mystique of the nomadic tent dwellers from northern Africa to Central Asia. Because of a life-style affinity with Turkic and Mongolian nomadic pastoralists, which fostered contact, and—in the northeast of Tibet—because of geographical proximity to those populations, the Tibetan nomadic pastoralists probably also have a somewhat greater admixture of Turkic and Mongolian genes than do other segments of the Tibetan population. Indeed, there are some nomadic communities that, though apparently completely Tibetanized, are still called "Turk ones" or "Mongol ones," and take pride in the fact.

The relative size of the nomadic-pastoral subsociety, as compared with the sedentary-agricultural subsociety is the subject of ad hoc opinion that varies greatly. Majority opinion concedes, and some Western Tibet-ologists argue, with some heat, that the nomadic pastoralists are fewer in number than the sedentary agriculturists, and what fragmentary tax, or census, reports are available support this thesis. Parenthetically, such records are notoriously understated—no one wants to be listed on a tax record if he can help it, and the nomads have a situation advantage in such evasion. A number of Tibetans, however, insist that the "high-pasturage ones" do in fact outnumber the "deep-valley ones," "country ones," "soil-field ones," "village ones," or however else the cultivators may be designated. For example, the high Tibetan official who recently wrote a political history of Tibet flatly stated that the nomads are the more numerous (Shakapba 1967: 6).

This concept of relative size—actual or ascribed—takes on special significance because the only observable shift in population, which is mostly by individuals and small family groups, is from the sedentary to the nomadic. This trend is well substantiated by the origin and the direc-tion of culture change, as well as actual geographical movement, of so-called seminomads. These are, in all reported cases, from the sedentary agricultural to the nomadic pastoral in habitat and life-style.

Ecological Niche

The *aBrog* ("high pasturage") is the ecological niche occupied by the Tibetan nomadic pastoralists. Its location, extent, resources, and climate —each in its own way and degree—operate as population determinants and affect both material and nonmaterial aspects of culture. The niche consists of that portion of the Tibetan plateau which is suitable for grazing and lies between the highest limits of agriculture and the highest limits of vegetation. In terms of altitude this may vary from approximately 9,000–12,000 feet at 38° N to approximately 15,000–17,000 feet at 28° N. A large proportion of this zone forms a belt around the very high central part of the plateau, but it is not all contiguous, and there are many islands of high pasturage surrounded by lower land suitable for agriculture and at least partially cultivated. Considerable portions of this altitude zone are not part of the true high pasturage because of conditions such as extremely steep, eroded slopes, alkaline swamps and marshes of the internal drainage basin, rodent-denuded patches, and soil so rocky that nothing can grow. Only to a minor degree is aridity a determinant. Unlike the arid zones, which have generated the nomadic pastoralists of Africa and Asia, the *aBrog* is an altitude-determined zone, and the high-pasturage ones of the Tibetan plateau are altitude-zone nomadic pastoralists. This differentiation is of considerable significance, for it largely eliminates the possibility of exploitative competition for land between cultivators and herdsmen.

In the arid zone water may be captured by diversion, conserved by damming and karsh-well irrigation, or brought to the surface by wells of various depths. By such means pasturage may be taken away from the pastoralists, but, beyond some minor gains to be achieved by newly developed cold-resistant crops, little can be done to take land that is too high for cultivation away from altitude-zone pastoralists.

So delimited and conditioned, the actual extent of the high pasturage is very great; and much of it is not fully exploited. Considerable variation in the quality of the grazing, factors of accessibility, and security problems that follow any too wide dispersion, account for much of this inadequate utilization. What is basic, however, is that there is not sufficient pressure from factors such as wealth-accumulation incentive, uninterrupted annual increase of livestock, and population growth to fill any but the very best pastures. This leaves many spaces in the high-pasturage zone empty of human activity.

The resources of the *aBrog*, as related to the needs of animal husbandry are varied and frequently abundant. Along some valley watercourses and on slopes with a northern exposure, coarse grasses, other vegetation, and low-growing shrubbery furnish good forage for cattle. The fine soft grass that grows on slopes with a southern exposure is excellent for horses and sheep. On many of the high plains, thick and tall-growing grasses furnish good grazing in summer and, when ungrazed, persist as standing winter-killed hay for winter forage. Even at the upper limits of the *aBrog* —near the snowline or close to bare scree slopes—alpine thistle, dwarf shrubs, and a fine flat-lying grass known as "yak grass"—licked, not cropped, by the yak—have their value. The total of all this abundance constitutes *rTSa KHa* ("grass part"), which is the value factor of land in the pastoralist's universe of values.

Parenthetically, soil per se not only is neutral in terms of value but has negative connotations: for example, anthrax is "soil poison"; disturbance of the soil may arouse the wrath of the "soil lords," with the attendant possibility of disaster; and leprosy can be a "soil curse." Part of the pastoralist's feeling of superiority over the cultivator springs from the consciousness that he does not dig and disturb the soil to any great extent. The less "wounding of the soil" there is, the better.

In addition to suitable grazing for livestock, some of the vegetation of the *aBrog* constitutes minor resources to be exploited by gathering: for example, the collecting of wild-onion tops, wild leeks, and coriander seed; the extraction, from just under the surface, of the minute tubers of the potentilla; and the gathering of mushrooms and medicinal herbs. The latter activities are accompanied by some misgiving, for the soil is disturbed—though only to a small degree—in extracting the tubers or digging out herbs; and the mushrooms, because of value, color, and strangeness of growth, are regarded as "soil gold" that should not be plundered.

In a few areas real gold is placer mined to meet special tax require-ments. However, this is done generally, not by the pastoralists them-selves, but by itinerant miners who are regarded with aversion. The high-pasturage ones—with much less misgiving—also play a part in exploiting the salt and borax resources of the internal-drainage area of the central plateau.

Although hunting is inhibited by Buddhist scruples, combined with a more indigenous fear of poaching the preserves of autcchthonous mountain gods, the *aBrog* does have a considerable quantity of game. The herbivores—wild yak, wild sheep, antelope, and gazelle—supply appreciable amounts of meat and hides, and other game—such as stag for hartshorn, muskdeer for musk, and wolf, fox, snow leopard, and otter for furs—are subsidiary resources of considerable value.

The climate of this ecological niche is the product of continental land mass, altitude, and meridional position with relation to the sun. It is characterized by extremes of temperature and of alternate aridity and precipitation. The extremes of temperature are more diurnal than seasonal in character. Temperature changes within twenty-four hours of as much as 100° F have been reported, and although this is somewhat unusual, changes of up to 60° F are fairly common. The average diurnal range for both summer and winter is 40° F or more. Extremes of change are especially marked in clear weather (clouds at night tend to hold warmth in the atmosphere), and on a clear day steep-angle sunshine, through the thin air of high altitude, has a very special burning intensity of great ultraviolet content. The winters are largely dry, with little precipitation, but wide areas are drowned in torrential summer rains, and heavy snows occur in both late spring and early fall. Storms—rain, hail, snow, and relentless wind, which in winter may carry clouds of dust and sand mixed with pebbles—characterize the weather of the *aBrog*; but when sunshine comes, it is strong and promotes germination and growth of vegetation.

Resources: Power and Production

The basic production resource of cultivators is land that has been worked into fields. These fields may be ill-defined and temporary, as in swidden farming, or permanent and are worked with degrees of intensity, varying from long fallow to multicropping. Such resources are defined by the Tibetans as "soil fields." The basic production resource of the pastoralists, by contrast, is not land alone but a combination of the natural vegetation cover of the unworked land and the livestock that feed on it. Thus,

for the pastoralists, in a very real sense, livestock are the equivalent of
fields in the production cycle, as suggested in the title of my recent book,
Fields on the Hoof (Ekvall 1968). These "fields" are cultivated by pastoral
care and protection; and are reaped primarily in the taking of milk,
meat, blood, hides, wool, and dung. Selection of stock for sale is also a
form of reaping, but at the same time it is a subtraction from the fields,
total. There occurs, moreover, a continuing addition to that total in the
annual natural biological increase of the livestock. Livestock fields are
somewhat volatile in both size and value. At any point in time size is
dependent on such variables as: the annual natural increase; the number
of animals reaped as meat; the number sold or bartered; and attrition
by aging, disease, accidents, and weather-caused fatalities. Value, on the
other hand, fluctuates according to the quality and condition of the
stock itself and according to trade values, responsive to the law of supply
and demand.

The livestock that make up this production resource are yak, common-
cow cattle, a hybrid cross between these two known as *mDZo*, sheep,
goats, and horses. Though the numerical ratio between these animals
varies greatly throughout the *aBrog*, yak are the most important and are
indeed the essential livestock resource that makes Tibetan nomadic pastoralism possible. As uniquely high-altitude animals—in their wild state
indigenous to the Tibetan plateau and presently found nowhere else—
their importance and function in altitude-zone pastoralism are analogous
to the importance of camels in arid-zone pastoralism. Yak supply the
principal needs of the high-pasturage ones in: material for the black
tents; milk, blood, and meat for food; dung for fuel; and all the leather
for the innumerable artifacts necessary to a moving, pack-and-saddle
existence. They also supply the essential biological base for the breeding
of the extremely valuable *mDZo*. So important are the bovines that, to
distinguish them from the rest of the livestock, they are called simply "the
wealth." Sheep, a special breed called "high-pasturage sheep," that are
big and long-legged with many traits that indicate closeness to wild
sheep, far exceed the bovines in number, though the numerical ratio
between the two varies greatly in different localities. They are only
slightly less important in value, for they supply skins for clothing, wool
for felt and woolen cloth, meat, milk, and fuel; and wool is the commodity of prime bulk and value for export trade. Goats, like the common

cow cattle, are a small minority, being considered low-country—or farmer's—animals and not suited to conditions in the *aBrog*. Horses are not a production resource to the extent they are among the true horse nomads (for example, Kazakh and Mongol) as the Tibetans neither eat horsemeat nor milk the mares. However, the yield of natural increase does make the high-pasturage ones exporters as well as users of horses, and the prices the latter bring are a source of wealth.

Subsidiary forms of exploitation such as the furnishing of transportation and guide services for trade caravans, hunting, and raiding are not directly related to pastoral production; but the opportunities for such ventures and the capability to engage in them stem from or are associated with the behavior patterns and life-style of the nomadic pastoralists and substantially contribute to subsistence and the accumulation of wealth.

All of the domestic animals thus listed are also power resources. It is animal (yak, sheep, horse) power that is the essential element in operational pastoralism and that makes nomadism possible. It moves the livestock themselves out to daily ranging and grazing; it moves them again, together with the pastoralists—their dwellings, and all their possessions— from campsite to campsite in the seasonal utilization of pasturage and in the basic reality of nomadism. It is also horse and/or yak power that gives efficiency to the mechanics of herding and extends the capability of the herdsman, so that when mounted, especially on horseback, the guardian of the herds can control many more head of livestock than any man on foot can handle—particularly at altitudes where even walking is taxing and running is out of the question. This same animal power also moves—either on the hoof or by packing—the products of animal husbandry to favorable markets, thus completing the final stage in the production cycle; and the transportation capability that this power provides is a marketable commodity, which brings in wealth when hired out. Horse power raises this mobility to a particularly high level, increasing the herdsman's control of the herds he guides and guards, giving to his hunting additional range and effectiveness, and adding the entire behavior pattern of offensive raiding and defensive counteraction to the life-style of the high-pasturage ones.

The production resources and the power resources to exploit them are never pushed to their limits. Pasturage is rarely, if ever, exploited to its maximum potential. Indeed, some communities do not follow quite the same pattern of movement every year, and thus each year some pasturage is left completely untouched. This is not purposely leaving pasturage fallow for a year to help the soil recover. Grass grows as well after initial light cropping and simultaneous fertilization by livestock droppings as when it is left untouched throughout an entire season. What is crucial is the condition of the grass, and not the strength or the exhaustion of the soil.

Nor in general do the livestock fields ever reach their maxima in proportion to the available grazing. Bad weather, disease, and predators—animal and human—may take such toll as to diminish the herds at times, yet the general trend is for the livestock to multiply until they would reach such maxima unless otherwise limited. What does limit their increase is lack of manpower required for the degree of pastoral care needed. There exists a limit to the number of bovines and ovines that can be adequately taken care of by one herdsman. (In the case of horses this limit is much lower.) When the owner of herd or flock sees it approaching that limit, he must either cut down growth by putting the surplus into the channels of trade, where there is always a seller's market, or he must secure additional manpower. There appears to be, however, a chronic shortage of manpower within the communities of the high-pasturage ones, and so, instead of expanding the fields beyond limits that may be comfortably taken care of, the trend is to convert the potentially surplus livestock fields into other forms of wealth.

Because of this situation and within Asian and Tibetan contexts, the nomadic pastoralist subsociety is an affluent, though by no means a sybaritic, society. There can be no quantum jump to the luxuries of modern living. The extremely wealthy live on a scale that essentially is little better in comfort or the amenities than that of those not so wealthy. Wealth tends to be spent on: ostentation—for example, the best horses or rifle in the community, or the most amber and coral worn by wife or daughter; status—lavish hospitality and gift giving; and religious observance—great offerings to lamas and monastic establishments. This observance effects a transference of wealth from the realm of the here and now—mundane phenomenal living—to the realm of the supernatural and the hereafter. Thus the nomadic pastoralists are self-consciously affluent in both realms.

This does not mean that everyone is wealthy or that there are no poor;

but the relatively wealthy are many, and the poor can always supplement
their own production resources by selling their labor in a very good
labor market within their own communities. They live too in the expectation—or hope—that with good seasons their own livestock fields may
increase birth by birth. This general and relative affluence is evidenced
in the fact that the two segments or subcultures of Tibetan society that
concern themselves with the manipulation of wealth and its increments,
the trading community and the religious community, both focus their
primary attention on the high-pasturage ones. They are the ones who
control the wealth of the land, which is to be both gained and converted
into lucrative exports, religious celebrations, and monuments.

Demography

According to the Boserup model, such conditions might appear to point
toward population increase, if not indeed explosion; yet the population
of the high pasturage shows no sign of any such increase. Instead of
growth to take up the slack and move toward greater exploitation of the
available production and power resources of the ecological niche and of
the accumulated cultural gains and techniques, the population is at best
standing still. If indeed it is stationary, that equilibrium is due to a perceptible seepage of manpower from the cultivator communities and from
among the drifters that constitute a considerable segment of the Tibetan
population as a whole, and not because of adequate biological replenishment to compensate for the death rate. The birth rate is very low.

This demographic recession requires analysis in two contexts: (a) that
of population change among the Tibetan people as a whole and (b) that
of population change among the high-pasturage ones, which is distinct
from, and contrasts with, the population change among the rest of the
Tibetan people. Of the possible causes for these changes some are common to both a and b; some, though common to both, are intensified in
the case of the high-pasturage ones; and others seem to affect only the
latter.

Generally recognized indications (see Shakapba 1967: 6) are that the
population of Tibet is and has been a decreasing one since the time of
its peak, which was between 600 and 800 A.D. The nascent and expanding Tibetan empire of that period occupied oasis cities in Central Asia,

made contact with the Persian empire in the Pamirs, conquered non-Tibetan peoples in the west and south, levied tribute on Bengal, Nepal, Gilgit and Hunza, conquered—or displaced—Hunnic populations in the region of the Koko Nor, and contended on near equal terms with China of the T'ang dynasty for control of large areas in what is now north-western, western, and southwestern China. These are not the exploits of a shrinking population. From accounts of the armies fielded and Tibetan colonies established in newly occupied border areas at that time, it would seem that there must have been a population base of at least twice the size of the Tibetan population of the present time.

Currently, in many areas of Tibet, as evidence of a former agricultural production much greater than at present, there are many permanently abandoned fields. Leaders of quasi-independent principalities and chiefdoms have told me that people are more important than land, and they appear more interested in attracting the allegiance of populations than in taking over territories. The relative emptiness of the land and the challenge of unused fields—or soil fit for fields—are themes that appear repeatedly in discussions of Tibet and its people by the land-hungry Chinese. Throughout the country there is no sign of population pushing against resources. Instead there is evident population hunger, for in all communities transients and drifters are welcome and find employment and subsistence with relative ease.

During the earlier period of maximum population it is by no means certain that the birthrate was particularly high, because all Tibetans live at altitudes that are suspected of adversely affecting the birthrate through appreciable shortening of pregnancies with injurious effects to the neonatal. Even the agriculturalists live at altitudes of from 7,000 to 15,000 feet, and at the higher levels of that range male fertility is also adversely affected (see Katz, Chapter 16). Thus population growth may have been relatively slow, though reaching a maximum at some point later than the beginning of the ninth century, from which it has speedily decreased.

There is no evidence of ecological changes to account for this decline. Certainly the altitude did not increase significantly, nor, from all we know, were there any great temperature changes. From that time to the present the Tibetans have cultivated the same crops and have tended and used the same domesticated animals in numerical ratios that have furnished an adequate and well-balanced diet, rich in proteins. It is true that unknown ecological changes *may* have contributed to the shrinkage, but there are no known indications of such changes.

If not in the ecology, then were there any cultural changes—verifiable or hypothetical—that could have taken place since that peak period of population growth, which might account for very considerable population losses? There is a probability that one significant change in public health took place since that time. That high incidence of venereal disease adversely affects population growth is to be expected, and from all known data such disease is now widespread among the Tibetans. If, as seems likely, the spread of syphilis throughout the Old World is post-Columbian, then syphilis—at least—was brought to the Tibetans since the heyday of the Tibetan empire. I do not know whether any such fixing of time limits can be made for the introduction, or indigenous genesis, of gonorrhea. There may be a hint as to origins in the fact that one of the terms for syphilis is "Chinese sore." On the other hand, the term for gonorrhea suggests that it is due to the effects of geing cold. Parenthetically, treatment of hundreds of cases in one area of Tibet suggests that syphilis is more common among the sedentary house-dwelling agriculturalists, and gonorrhea is more common among the nomadic tent-dwelling pastoralists, which may have some bearing on a possible birth-rate differential in favor of the former.

One very great and important cultural change did, however, take place exactly within the period of peak population—600–800 A.D. Buddhism, after meeting with intermittent and—at times—very strong opposition for at least two centuries, finally became established as the dominant and, eventually, the state religion, which in turn remade the Tibetan polity into a religious state with ecclesiastical rulers exercising ultimate control.

Buddhism replaced an earlier religious system known as the Bon religion. The exact outlines and content of this system—before it was ever subjected to the overwhelming influence and pressure of Buddhism—are overlaid with Buddhist terminology, if not indeed ideology, and are blurred by disuse and the lapse of time. It appears, nevertheless, to have stressed the following: reverence toward the Sky—or Blue Sky—with worship of the sun, moon, and stars; an extensive pantheon of local deities—mountain gods and spirits of lakes, forests, cliffs, and so on; and a *cult of ancestor worship* in which the ancient ones were identified with mountain gods and kept in remembrance by tombs and monuments. The priests of the system were shamans; specializing in healing, exorcism, the ordering of funerals, the foretelling of the future, the demonstration of magical powers, and the claim of relationship to, and control over, spirit beings. Ritual was characterized by bloody sacrifices—sometimes on a large scale—that included human beings. All in all, it was much like the religion of the Mongols at the time when, under Genghis Khan, they began their conquest—or devastation—of half the world.

In replacing this indigenous religion, Buddhism did adopt—the Tibetan word is "subdue"—many of the local gods, but it forbade the sacrifices and disregarded the Blue Sky as being nothing more than blue sky and the heavenly bodies as little more than adjuncts of horoscope manipulation. It also substituted tantric experimentation for the shaman's magic and lost the ancestors completely in cycles of innumerable rebirths throughout the entire range of sentient beings—from the human to the insect and microscopic. Buddhism also brought to the Tibetans the ideal and practice of social and biological withdrawal, denigrating—if not actually forbidding—the procreative function and, by introducing monasticism, segregating the choice one-third of the males from the breeding pool. Thus there was created a great female-over-male imbalance in the breeding population.

Family and living ancestors and descendants too are thereby lessened in importance. The living ancestors, soon to lose their identity in the lottery of Karmic rebirths, are not a part of a long line that extends changeless into the far past and claims worship and remembrance in tombs and monuments. The living descendants too, though useful for facilitating the withdrawal of their parents from mundane concerns, do not have that crucial importance which belongs to those who will honor and worship their ancestors, for those parents will soon become generalized *being* instead of retaining identity as specific *beings*. They themselves feel no compulsion to have descendants to honor and worship them, for they too will soon lose identity in the changing cycles of rebirth. In such a frame of reference marriage becomes more incidental and a matter of economic convenience; and burial, though attended with ritual to send the soul on its way toward rebirth, is more a matter of simple corpse disposal, involving neither tomb nor monument of remembrance. The family too—whether monogamous, polygynous, or polyandrous—is more fragile and more subject to breakup. In such a universe of values there is no overriding imperative to have progeny.

The fact that this cultural change, as hypothetically summarized in the foregoing, did adversely affect population growth becomes a very reasonable premise when demographic comparisons are made with the Chinese, who are near neighbors. The latter have no ethic of social or biological withdrawal and no large celibate segment of the breeding population. They worship the sky but go their earthly ways, very much preoccupied with mundane concerns until death, and when that takes place, the funeral is celebrated with enormous formality: sons mourn fathers visibly—in behavior and attire—for years. Above all other worship is the worship of the ancestors who, rank on rank and generation after generation, are individual *beings* in the spirit world, demanding individual attention. It is indeed a kind of immortalism, but to be without male progeny is to end that immortal succession and become an untended, wandering derelict in the spirit world.

The desire to have sons is more than desire. It is a compulsion for both men and women. For the man it guarantees that the line of innumerable ancestors in the past linked to unending descendants in the future will not be broken and that when his turn comes, he too will be worshiped. For the woman it is the ultimate blessing as expressed by the ideograph for woman, which combined with the one for son signifies the basic— individual and ethnic—good. Thus the Chinese, who also have venereal disease and whose diet at times is meager, breed and breed; and there is no stopping population growth.

I once traveled through a frontier valley where Chinese live on one bank of the river and Tibetans on the other bank. Particularly good bottomland fields belong to one community or the other in an alternate pattern according to how the course of the river meanders from one side of the valley to the other. The crops were the same, the livestock were the same, and the ecological niche offered the same opportunity; yet, as noted at each stopping, by every criterion the Tibetan population appeared to be a shrinking one and the Chinese population a burgeoning one.

As the Tibetan population, in its entirety, has decreased in size, the high-pasturage ones have shared in that general shrinkage. Postulated

causes for the inhibition of population growth, such as the ethic of social
and procreative withdrawal and the effects of venereal disease, apply with
equal probability and degree to the high-pasturage ones as to those other
Tibetans. The nomadic pastoralists, however, have an even smaller population growth than other Tibetans. There is an absolute dearth of children. This appears to be due to an extremely low birthrate rather than to
any abnormally high infant mortality, for the few children that are born
are given relatively good care. Although weaned somewhat early by
general Asian standards, there is an abundance of yak and sheep milk
for substitutional feeding. Children who cut their teeth on chunks of
meat, gristle, and lumps of very hard cheese and are fed curds and yogurt
have no problem of protein deficiency.

This absolute scarcity of children in a nomadic pastoral community is
most marked. One of the few comments on Tibetan demography that the
Chinese Communists have made, since their take-over of the country in
1959, is to the effect that there are very few children among the tent-
dwelling herdsmen of the plateau. On my part, for a considerable period
I had a close and continuing association with a Tibetan tribe that was
half sedentary-agricultural and half nomadic-pastoral, and lived in both
villages and encampments. The number of children in the encampments
was perhaps less than one-half the number of children in villages of analogous size. Being considered a man of medicine—of a sort—I heard many
of the confidences that in our culture are heard only by doctors or psy-
chiatrists. Among the high-pasturage ones—never among the "valley
ones"—I frequently was asked by both men and women—individually
and in couples—for medicine or any advice that would make it possible
to have children. By contrast, only once in all that time was I ever asked
about birth control, and the request was made with no particular urgency.
The seemingly healthy and contented woman quite casually added to her
husband's plea the explanation that, having five children in ten years—
all still living—did complicate moving and following the herds. If an
unmarried woman does have a child, her marriage chances are correspondingly enhanced, and the chance—if it ever presents itself—to adopt
a child is accepted as an auspicious opportunity. As a result population
hunger among the tent people is very strong and reaches out in many
ways for manpower additions to the community—and with some success,
as is attested by case histories and names of individuals and families that

tell of other origins and of making the transition to pastoralism and nomadism.

The search for answers as to why the nomadic pastoralists are relative demographic failures—in spite of all their affluence, their great need for manpower to exploit available but unused resources, and their relative health and high-protein diet—must focus on significant differences in their ecology and their way of life in comparison with other Tibetans. Two items of major interest suggest answers. One is related to a special characteristic of their ecological niche, and one stems from activity and habits, connected with technique and available power resources, necessary to both pastoralism and nomadism.

Though all Tibetans are high-altitude people, the high-pasturage ones are a yet higher-altitude population, the difference being that between a 7,000- to 15,000-foot range and a 10,000- to 17,000-foot and over range. Many of the high-pasturage ones seldom if ever go much below the 16,000-foot level. This high-altitude factor as a possible, and even highly probable, cause of lowered birthrates can affect both women and men. If relatively low altitudes—6,000 to 10,000 feet—as in Colorado, can adversely affect the birthrate by shortening pregnancies, it may be assumed that the much higher altitudes of 10,000 to 17,000 feet have a disproportionately greater adverse affect on pregnancies, for such altitudes go beyond the 12,000-foot critical threshold of physiological reaction in the process of acclimatization. How, and to what extent, such oxygen-thin altitudes affect male fertility, by inhibiting the formation of sperm, have been studied in some depth, among the inhabitants of the Andes by Carlos M. Monge (1968: 176–185). Complete loss of sperm marks initial reaction to residence at 17,000 feet. This is followed—after a period, the duration of which varies with the individual—by degrees of recovery which again vary with the individual's success in generally adjusting to high-altitude conditions. Some do very well, some barely make it, and some fail in this adjustment. Recovery of fertility thus varies, but, in any case, there remains a residual disability that affects both the individual and the breeding pool of the population. This pretty well establishes one cause for a low birthrate among the high-pasturage ones.

As suggested earlier in this chapter, yak and horse power improved techniques of pasturing and facilitated and extended the range of nomadizing. This made riding an important part of the routines and habits

of both men and women. The many-faceted influence of riding as a factor
in the formation of a societal ethos and as a character determinant has
been touched on elsewhere (Ekvall 1968: 90, 91). Within the topical
parameters of this paper the problem is the relationship of riding—constant, hard, and rough, and at all times of the day and month—to the
birthrate. There are no discriminatory taboos on the basis of sex. Both
men and women ride—either using the saddle or bareback, according to
need—and some ride extremely well.

There are no data—only a strong suspicion—that such riding, through
its immediate effects on women of childbearing age, has an adverse effect
on the birthrate. Women have to ride, cutting out or rounding up stock,
at maximum speed over rough terrain without regard to what period of
each woman's menstrual cycle it is. It would seem inevitable that this
must lead to a considerable number of early miscarriages. In advanced
pregnancies some care undoubtedly is taken, but even in such instances,
if the community is shifting camp, the expectant mother still has to ride,
possibly for a long day, thus further shortening a pregnancy already
shortened by altitude.

How the effects of prolonged and hard riding, as a way of life, may
affect the procreative function in men is, on the other hand, somewhat
more than a mere suspicion. One aspect of such riding which may affect
male fertility is the clothing worn and the manner of riding, or seat, of
the rider. The high-pasturage ones wear sheepskin clothing with the
fleece inside. Riding a high-treed saddle with extremely short stirrups in
what is a pronounced "crouch seat," the rider has as many as three
layers of heavily fleeced sheepskin—winter fleece is as much as seven
inches long—wrapped closely around and under the loins so that the
genitalia are nested in fleece and, without question, have the highest
temperature of any part of the body. It was Dr. Anton Carlson of Chicago, who pointed out to me that such localized high temperature is
particularly deleterious to sperm and its formation and can well be a
cause of periodic male sterility.

A more important, or at least somewhat more credibly substantiated,
threat to the birthrate lies in the possibility that hard and continuous
riding contributes to male sexual impotency. There are references that
point as far back as the mounted Scythians, which suggest this possibility;
as do some accounts of the part played by brutally hard and punishing

riding among the Plains Indians in setting aside, or fitting, transvestites for their role as men-become-women. Nor should the generally known rumor in the French cavalry about horsemen tending to become impotent—cited even in Stendhal's writings—be lightly dismissed, for I heard much about male impotence among the Tibetan nomadic pastoralists. On many occasions men came to me to ask for medicine, treatment, or advice to cure impotency. Frequently their wives would come with them, and the problem in all its details would be discussed with utmost candor. Of particular significance is the fact that those who came were mostly the young and those most continuously active—the ones doing the greatest amount of riding. Of course, it could be that older, less-active men had given up their sexual role.

Note

1. The material presented here is largely a description of a culture and an economy as they were prior to the Communist Chinese take-over of Tibet in 1959. Propaganda notwithstanding, not very much is known about what has taken place since then, but what may be gleaned from Chinese sources (via the publications of the Union Research Institute, Kowloon) strengthens the thrust and argument of this chapter.

The Chinese were much impressed with the resources—inadequately exploited—of the ecology of the high pasturage, and with the value of the animal husbandry products produced by the nomadic pastoralists. They have imposed less coercive restriction on the high-pasturage ones than on any other segment of the population and appear concerned mainly with leaving the herdsmen undisturbed, provided only that the latter continue to produce. They bemoan the fact that production is less than it should be, and they have some things to say about increasing the birthrate by elimination of venereal disease. With great pride, they report increases in livestock and in the production of wool, meat, hides, butter, and animal fats; and they are obviously experimenting with projects and devices calculated to reduce nomadizing while maintaining full-scale pastoralism. Furthermore, though they are farmers no one has seriously suggested "opening new soil" and setting up farms anywhere in the high pasturage. That right still belongs to the Tibetans—the high-pasturage ones.

12   Population Growth and Political Centralization   Don E. Dumond

Dumond has constructed a model to explain the political implications of population growth. His essay is therefore to some extent parallel with those of Carneiro and Netting (Chapters 3 and 9), but his conclusions differ from theirs. His disagreement with Carneiro concerns the latter's contention that "autonomous political units never willingly surrender their sovereignty" (Chapter 3). Like Carneiro, he is concerned with the internal political dynamics of a group, while Netting is concerned more with the relationship between groups—particularly, between groups with a certain type of social organization.

In Chapter 13 Dumond tests the first part of his model against data from Eskimo Alaska. This part of the model is concerned primarily with the relationship between population growth and subsistence and might be characterized as a middle way between Malthus and Boserup.

In an approach parallel to that of Boserup (1965) but much less developed than hers, I argued earlier (Dumond 1961, 1965b) that population growth has consistently been operative in causing the adoption of intensive agricultural practices and that population growth alone may be expected to result in an increase in the degree of social centralization. But I concluded both that population growth should not be considered an independent variable, for population growth and the expansion of subsistence techniques are interrelated, and that the growth of relatively high-density population, while a necessary precondition of civilization and the state, is not alone sufficient cause for that development.

In this essay I present a model of the place of population growth in the evolution of political centralization in preindustrial society. Although I do not exclude all consideration of derivative or secondary incidence of civilization and centralized society, my focus is especially upon the pristine development of centralization (see Fried 1967: 231ff.). In the first section I treat the decisions involved in allowing the population to grow and in expanding subsistence, in the second the factors involved in the centralization of political control.

Population Growth and the Intensification of Subsistence Techniques

A recent statement about human demographic relationships of the early post-Pleistocene (Binford 1968: 328) builds upon the proposition that "equilibrium systems regulate population density below the carrying capacity of the environment"; hence disequilibrium occurs only during (1) a change in the physical environment that alters subsistence resources and (2) a change in demographic relationships within a region so as to bring about the impingement of one group—of themselves in equilibrium —on the territory of another, whose equilibrium is thus disrupted.

Yet I prefer to argue that virtually *all* animal populations, humans included, have a pronounced tendency to overpopulate. One view, which is perhaps now out of date, holds that given this condition, nonhuman animal populations achieve equilibrium only through the operation of factors outside the population—environmental factors like climate, predation, and food supply—that serve to select for successful characteristics within the population by inflicting death on the many less successful members. In this view, "equilibrium" is not a function of mechanisms within the population but rather is imposed upon the population by external conditions.

A second, seemingly more modern, view argues that few animal populations actually have been known to reproduce to the point that they exceed subsistence resources and experience mass starvation (but some have, as any wildlife management expert knows). This view holds that internal factors within animal populations *do* serve to restrict the size of the population; hence, the tendency toward equilibrium is indeed a feature of the breeding population itself. But even here, the apparent correction factor is not usually operative through a decrease in births— that is, in control of actual reproduction—but by the production of deficient offspring who are doomed to death from the outset or by the impulsion toward suicidal activity such as that for which lemmings are famous (see Stott 1962 for a recent review). That is, even here equilibrium is not achieved so much by limiting reproduction as by encouraging externally inflicted death in individuals already living.

In a very real sense, then, to any breeding population bent by definition upon reproducing itself, equilibrium is in a sense "unnatural," in that it is achieved through externally inflicted, "unforeseen" deaths. The anthropomorphic phrasing here is intended to highlight the coloring that is given to the maintenance of population-resource equilibrium among humans by two especially human characteristics—the power of foresight and the tendency to inject affection into close interpersonal relationships. The first of these allows advance warning of the possibility of at least some externally inflicted deaths. The second makes these deaths painful, not to those killed, but to those who survive. "Unwanted" deaths are deplored.

A simplified formulation of the decisions humans burden themselves with in order to minimize these unwanted deaths follows.

The Choice Model

Unwanted deaths—those that would be classed here as "external" controls on population—may be partially avoided by acts of three sorts:
1. *Limitation of population increase* either at or before birth.
2. *Migration of surplus members* outside the territorial sphere of the society.
3. *Expansion of subsistence techniques and resources* including hiving, migratory movements of so short a distance that communication is maintained and the parent society is not disrupted.

These choices are diagrammed in Figure 12.1. They are not intended to represent mutually exclusive choices, nor are they implied to be necessarily fully rationalized.

Given the degree of fecundity inherent in human populations, it must be expected that nearly all human societies have resorted to one or more of these measures throughout much of their existence (see Birdsell 1968: 236–237, but see also Durand, Chapter 17, this volume). To specify which of them would be chosen in any particular situation, however, is another matter. In general, I expect the decisions involve a balance among three components—the satisfaction of material wants, the satisfaction of affective relationships (including purely symbolic ones, as with gods), and the expenditure of least effort.

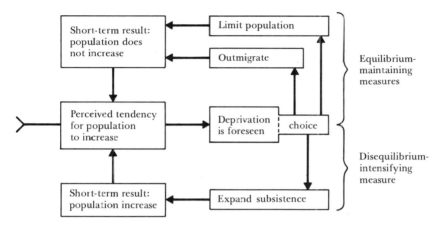

Figure 12.1.   The minimization of unwanted deaths.

This balance is not achieved by "maximizing" returns in any of these spheres. Rather, it is achieved by the minimization of relative deprivation. Relative deprivation is used approximately as it was presented by Aberle (1966: 323–329), who extends the concept to all spheres in which things or acts are valued—to matters of possessions, status, behavior, and worth—and defines it as a "negative discrepancy between legitimate expectation and actuality, or between legitimate expectation and anticipated actuality, or both" (Aberle 1966: 323). It is *relative* in that it is individually determined according to cultural standards and individual experience. Thus, although in any specific circumstance, given knowledge of cultural and individual facts, one could reasonably predict the decision to be made, one cannot in blanket fashion predict the decision for all societies or all individuals.

Although the diagram in Figure 12.1 has a beginning (for the convenience of the reader), it is without an end. This emphasizes that the choice involved is unending.

Results of the Choice
Equilibrium is achieved by most human populations through the exercise of constant foresight and the equally constant expenditure of human effort. The loops of the diagram indicate the constant nature of the

choice; decisions are ever renewed, and the potential for increase is always there.

However, in avoiding deprivation in the area of the three components mentioned earlier, certain populations have certainly achieved equilibrium with subsistence resources over long periods of time, without manifesting evidence of a constant fight to expand subsistence resources. Wagley (1951) has argued that certain expectations regarding population size itself may have been effective in this regard. More recently, Birdsell (1968) has pointed out that the need for a certain amount of mobility is in itself a factor strong enough to cause the Australian mother, in order that she may fulfill her responsibilities, to restrict herself to a maximum of about one infant every three years. He concludes that similar factors have entered into judgments to limit population through the Pleistocene as well as more recently (see Lee, Chapter 14, this volume).

Thus it is that in many populations the choice available in order to effect equilibrium with subsistence requirements has not in a practical sense included the third alternative (expansion of subsistence techniques and resources). Rather the decision is limited in a material sense by the subsistence organization of the society and in an affective sense by what (in sociological jargon) one might call the constraints of role taking. It is these populations that may be said to be characterized by an "equilibrium system" operating to adjust their numbers to their subsistence resources. But the important point is that this equilibrium system is commonly maintained only by the exercise of constant effort on the part of the individuals involved, is promoted only by certain specific (although here largely unspecified) aspects of social organization, and is potentially subject to instant rupture.

Given the nature of human reproduction and of the human infant, it seems reasonable to hypothesize that the single most compelling set of reasons for spacing live offspring is presented by a state of constant geographic mobility (see Lee, Chapter 14, this volume). Hence one would expect that the combined choice to permit more offspring to survive and to expand subsistence resources is strongly associated with sedentary living.

Obviously, the three choices in Figure 12.1 are not of equal portent for a society's future. The choice of the limitation of increase and the choice of long-distance migration both result in negative feedback or deviation-counteracting measures, bringing the population size toward equilibrium.[1]

But choice of the third alternative—the expansion of subsistence—initiates a positive feedback measure, resulting in a self-intensifying spiral as population increase and subsistence expansion reinforce one another, constituting what Maruyama (1963) has called a "deviation-amplifying" process. It seems clear that the adoption of the decision leading to this spiral portends other cultural adjustments.

In accordance with an expectation that this last choice will be made when a population is sedentary rather than mobile, one would expect that with the advent of sedentary living the population-subsistence spiral would begin to be reflected in historical and prehistoric record. This expectation seems fulfilled when the increasingly settled life of the Mesolithic is followed immediately by the development of large societies based on agriculture. However, the factors discussed are not considered to be effective only within those populations that take up agriculture.

One additional comment should be injected. By saying that population growth and subsistence are interrelated, I did not mean simply that a larger population requires a larger food supply. What I mean (although the question is finally an empirical one) is that a restriction placed upon either variable will result in a serious inhibition or a complete prevention of increase in the other, at least under conditions common to preindustrial society. A limit on the expansion of subsistence, for whatever reason, means a curtailment of growth in population; a limit on population growth, for whatever cause, entails a lack of expansion of subsistence means. The first of these is commonplace enough. The implications of the second for those of us concerned with the history of technology—particularly archaeologists—should also be obvious. Furthermore, because the interrelationship of population size and subsistence itself is the result of constant human effort, it follows that conditions of increase in population and a concurrent expansion of subsistence are under relatively conscious human surveillance and control and are subject to change at any time. Thus population growth is not an extracultural force that drives culture along an evolutionary path; it is rather a cultural fact in itself. That is, it is purposely induced, or at least consciously tolerated.

This is not to deny the existence of societies such as that described by Ekvall (Chapter 11, this volume) in which desired population growth is limited by certain extracultural, or at least involuntary, means. Nor is it to deny the operation of these and other factors pointed to by Katz

(Chapter 16, this volume); surely pure biological factors acting through fertility and mortality do affect population balance. Rather, it is to argue that in the long run human culture—a body of techniques that anthropologists seem to agree has conveyed a substantial advantage for survival, one oriented toward the preservation of the lives of its bearers and the lives of the descendants of its bearers—has been enough of a success that unforeseen deaths commonly *have* been diminished, enough so that in most societies at most times a level of fertility substantially above that actually achieved has been possible. In a previous study (Dumond 1965b) I was not able to document occasions in which the usual Malthusian checks (famine, warfare, and so on) had served to permanently restrict population increase. Furthermore, in situations in which a population has been seriously depleted through war or plague but in which the basic productive resources have not been rendered unobtainable or in which the productive organization has not been completely destroyed, population regrowth has been extremely rapid, matching the growth observed among people who enter a new, uninhabited environment (Birdsell 1957). These cases are most easily explained if the crucial factor of population control in most times and places has been human volition, acting instrumentally through individual, personal, private decisions, the observable modal expression of which we are apt to term *cultural*. For present purposes I therefore assume that most human populations have tended to increase, and that this increase has commonly been held in bounds by purposeful acts of the people themselves.

In the following chapter, the model presented thus far is examined against the prehistory of Alaskan Eskimo hunters. The next section of this chapter takes up the implication of a continued population-subsistence spiral for those societies in which it is allowed to occur.

Population, Subsistence, and Political Centralization

The Choice Model

The choice to expand subsistence leads immediately to further choices among means to accomplish this aim. The process is diagrammed here (Figure 12.2) as two orders of choices. The first of these is whether to use resources presently available or free, or whether to capture additional resources from someone else. If the first alternative of this pair is chosen, the immediate second-order choice involves a decision among:

1. *Increase in labor input per capita.* This includes labor applied directly to subsistence activities (more frequent weeding, more frequent planting, and so on) or labor applied in the construction of non-energy-producing capital goods (improved hunting, gathering, or farming implements, boats to improve fishing and shore collecting, irrigation canals, and so on).

2. *Increase in land used.* Included here are both land farmed and land collected (for instance, a fishing people may increase the number of places along rivers at which it fishes).

3. *Increase of additional power sources.* This includes draft animals (later, tractors). It also includes the adoption of the horse for hunting bison or herding sheep, or the development of sails. This choice implies the existence of capital goods of a certain kind, here conceptually separated from those that make use of only human power.

4. *Reorganization of production.* Examples of this are the organization of work teams for more efficient production (the organization of boat crews for taking whales, the organization of communal bison hunts, the organization of cooperative farm labor). These reorganizations often involve new ownership arrangements; the boat owner who manages the whaling crew is one example. Some of them may result in altered residence patterns, with implications for family form and kinship terminology. Extreme reorganization may be so far-reaching as to involve changes in land tenure among agricultural peoples, although this factor will be discussed separately.

To return to the first-order choice, the decision to rely upon warfare and conquest to expand subsistence leads to a similar set of second-order decisions:

1. *Increase in (captured) labor input.* This may be applied as in the case of previously available labor.

2. *Increase in (captured) land use.* This implies that people were not captured with additional land.

3. *Use of additional (captured) power sources.*

4. *Collection of tribute.* This does not imply the sort of social reorganization involved in choice 1, immediately above, but represents a form of indirect (but income-producing) rule.

Again, the choices are not conceived to be mutually exclusive. Indeed, because the population-subsistence loop of Figure 12.1 would have to be

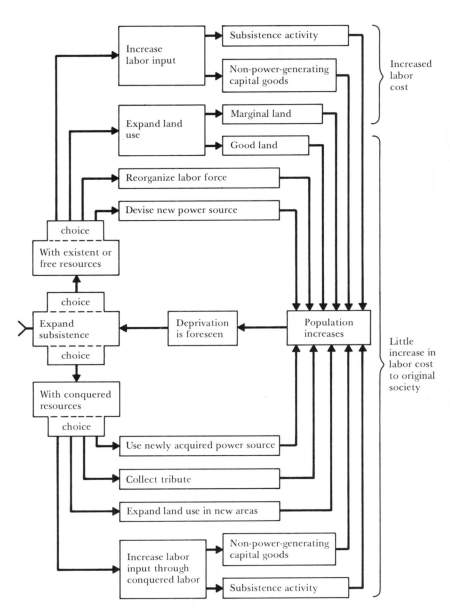

Figure 12.2.   The expansion of subsistence.

maintained over a period of time in order to be effective in inducing substantial social changes, one would expect that different choices would be made at different times. Hence it is reasonable to expect that if there is free and relatively adequate land available, the use of this additional land would be the measure chosen—a measure that constitutes filling the ecological niche. Beyond this, the choice is less predictable without specific knowledge of specific situations. In general one would expect that few societies would adhere to the labor intensification choice indefinitely. Although it appears that some societies—like, apparently, that of Java (Geertz 1963) and perhaps others in Southeast Asia and in Africa—have tended to do so, in many cases the picture is clouded by the varied effects of colonial rule. Nevertheless, whatever the decision, it is expected to be one that will minimize deprivation in the areas of material wants, affective relationships, and effort expended, and it need not be fully rationalized.

Clearly, the choices made would not be expected to have equal implications for the development of political centralization. But before proceeding to the results of the choices as they are diagrammed in Figure 12.2, some of the requisites for the development of politically centralized societies will be discussed.

The Course of Political Centralization

I follow Fried (1967: 52, 229) in his definitions of egalitarian society ("as many positions of valued status as there are individuals capable of filling them"), of rank society ("fewer positions of valued status than persons capable of filling them"), of stratified society ("adult members . . . enjoy differential rights of access to basic resources," and this situation serves to maintain in relative opulence an upper social class), and of the state ("power of the society is organized on a basis superior to kinship"). The achievement of two of these stages—that of simple (unstratified) rank society and that of stratified society—will be discussed here. For the purposes of this essay I shall follow Fried and accept that the state is the inevitable result of the successful achievement of a stratified society (Fried 1967: 185–186) and thus need not be considered separately.

THE ACHIEVEMENT OF RANK SOCIETY

CONTROL OF TERRITORY. Although not all basic resources are *land* in the agrarian sense, I can think of none that does not involve a geographical location, that is, *territory*. I conceive territoriality to be related both to the existence of specific geographical areas that provide dependable and productive resources and to population pressure on those resources. For example, with groups of Central Eskimos, the location of the most crucial subsistence resource, winter sealing places, is unpredictable from year to year because of local ice conditions. Since the size of population is restricted to one likely to survive the few critical times of year, more predictably productive resources—such as the streams with small runs of anadromous fish yielding food during the relatively rich summer—experience comparatively little pressure and are not "owned." That is, *place* as a resource is either untrustworthy, or when it is moderately trustworthy, it yields at a time when additional resources are relatively unnecessary. Territoriality, the sense of trespass, is weak or nonexistent. On the Northwest Coast, on the other hand, the large and predictable runs of salmon and other anadromous fish are vital subsistence resources. Fishing places are both owned and inherited by corporate groups.

Thus, increased pressure through increased population density makes for increasingly more specific (and rigid) rights to productive land. I interpret this to be the position of both Boserup (1965: 79) and Gluckman (1965: 65ff.). When the population density–subsistence resource relationship is equivalent to that of most horticultural societies, "ownership" is vested in a localized, kin-oriented group; each member has a general right to land (or territory) for his use, although his right may not extend to any specific piece of land, and if it does, the right normally does not include that of disposition by sale or other permanent transfer; the kinship unit has reversionary rights.

KINSHIP. With control of productive resources vested in a corporate, kin-based group and the automatic provision for inheritance of rights in the resources by upcoming members, the descent aspect of kinship is emphasized, and it is to be expected that kin groups based on considerable genealogical depth will appear. This seems implicit in Service's (1962) argument that kinship is a basic organizing principle both in his tribal and chiefdom levels of social organization, and in Fried's (1967: 120–128) discussion of rank society. Whether the tendency of these units is to regularly approach, as Gluckman appears to suggest, a depth of eleven to twelve generations approximately half of which are real (the rest fictive or at least compressed), I am not certain. If so, one might be able to specify a population size commonly organized by this principle.

POSITIONS OF RANK. With a kin-organized territorial unit of substantial size owning subsistence resources and to some extent controlling their allocation to members, some individual positions with executive functions are bound to emerge. These may be filled by individuals selected by genealogical position in a ramified kin group such as ramage (Sahlins 1958, after Firth 1936), conical clan (Kirchhoff 1955), or perhaps *obok* (Bacon 1958), or by election from the group or a certain segment of it.

I am asserting that formal leadership is always found when there is a regular and recognized problem of the allocation of basic resources within a kin-based society (at least in those cases in which the society is not so dislocated by strife as to remove the allocation problem entirely). This feature of the emergence of formal leadership related to the problem of managing the access of a large number of people to resources in less than infinite supply is seen even in such nomadic groups as the Indians of the American plains, among whom aspects of rank society were consistently the most marked during the time of year of maximum coalescence for the communal buffalo hunt.[2] An old-fashioned anthropological explanation of this would rely on the concept of limited possibilities, while more recent sociological thought would make use of the model of responses to a task environment that imposes problems surmountable only through interpersonal cooperation and organization (as in Collins and Guetzkow 1964: 72ff.). At any rate, someone specifically designated to do so administers or at least mediates the distribution of resources. The allocation of scarce resources is not the *only* kind of problem, however, that may be met by the development of formal leadership. Other problems may also be confronted in this way. Hence, some societies in which basic resources are relatively plentiful may have formalized rank, but no society in which basic productive resources must be carefully allocated is without formalized rank.

WEALTH AND REDISTRIBUTION. Although the discussion so far has related especially to the distribution of productive resources like land, the same principle should hold for consumables in a kin-based society, as goods are shared family-style by a system of redistribution in which the same high executive takes a key role (see Sahlins 1960). Furthermore, as communities become larger, the reciprocal gift-giving so often found in egalitarian society quite reasonably tends to be increasingly formalized, especially regarding gift-giving between communities that consider themselves to be related. So, for instance, the intercommunity exchange of the Messenger Feast found among most Alaskan Eskimos receives a special emphasis in the larger whaling communities, where it is organized around the work groups of the ceremonial house and gifts are channeled through the whaling captain (Oswalt 1967: 226, with references). (Still more extensively organized, kin-based, nonegalitarian communities may be expected to develop at least equally formalized systems of balanced reciprocity with neighboring and related communities.) The intra-community correlate of this, of course, is again redistribution: property is contributed to the senior representative of the community to be given to representatives of other communities in balanced-reciprocal fashion; return gifts are received by the same man and are distributed to his previous donors (see Sahlins 1965; also Gluckman 1965: 89–92). Thus, as an automatic outgrowth of increased density and the concomitant pressure on heritable strategic resources, redistribution appears as a common feature of rank society and chiefdoms (cf. Fried 1967: 116–118; Service 1962: 145ff.).

Obviously, a man of prestige in the role of community representative and redistributor is in a strategic position in the allocation of material wealth, a position that cannot help but redound to his importance and his richness. At the same time, peculation is not reinforced, because the economic system of the localized kin group in which all members—including the redistributor—have approximately equal rights to productive resources, makes for a roughly equivalent distribution of wealth and a concomitant shortage of purely luxury items. Rather than spend extra goods in riotous living, therefore, there is little for the redistributor to do but reinvest it in social support by giving it away (Gluckman 1965: 168) in an additional fillip of redistribution that serves to emphasize the inability of even the highest-ranking man to achieve a distinctly different style of life. This situation holds even when prestige differences are strong: in the potlatching societies of the Northwest Coast, with a plethora of titles and degrees of rank inherited or earned or both, there was almost no difference either in subsistence activity or in style of life between "nobles" and commoners. Thus there is rank but no social class in the sense of a social subgroup horizontally divided from the rest of society, both with a distinctive life-style and a tendency to associate with one another more than with members of other classes. This lack of class is an aspect of rank society.

SEGMENTATION. I have described a society composed of self-sufficient territorial segments organized around a principle of kinship in which there is no marked individual difference in terms of affluence. This is the description of a society with at least a measure of the segmentary qualities so clearly specified by Evans-Pritchard (1940) for the Nuer—a society with a tendency to meet external threats by coalescing within the largest lineage-based unit threatened and with an equally marked tendency to fragment again into lineage units when the threat is removed. Rank society in general manifests this property, although societies with more highly developed systems of rank than the Nuer may segment somewhat less readily and fluidly. Some rank societies also have superordinate but nominal rulers—"kings." And in some cases the symbolic value of these positions of rank is apparently strong enough to effect a measure of uni-fication. Hence the Shilluk "kingdom" in which the king is described as reigning but not ruling (Evans-Pritchard 1962) appears in definitional fact to be a group of related chiefdoms, or related rank societies in the terms of this discussion. Yet the Shilluk reportedly total more than 100,000 people and appear capable of at least occasional unified action. At this point I should add that whereas the existence of titles probably accompanies all ranking, the presence of titles of overwhelming symbolic value depends upon variables in addition to those that determine the existence of ranking. But whether the kingly titles exist or not, whether unified action exists or not, men of rank in simple rank societies have no autocratic control over productive resources and have no superordinate means of power at their disposal.

SUBSISTENCE. Most simple rank societies have been based upon agricul-ture, but some have been societies of herdsmen, and others societies of hunters, fishers, and collectors—such as the Indians of the Northwest Coast and probably early prehistoric littoral-adapted peoples of Peru, Mesoamerica, and elsewhere.

SUMMARY. I consider the principal attributes of simple rank society to be the following:

1. Localized, self-sufficient, kin-oriented social units control productive resources.

2. The rights to subsistence resources are distributed approximately equally among members.

3. There are relatively few formal positions of high status, which are held by individuals who are normally active in the allocation of basic resources but who manifest no marked difference in their style of living.

4. Commonly a redistribution system serves to add to the prestige of high-status individuals.

The transition from egalitarian to rank society can be explained by the interaction of factors constant to all egalitarian societies, plus at least one of the following two variables:

1. Increase in population size and density, with a corresponding pressure on basic productive resources.

2. Other persistent problems created by interaction with the external environment that are perceived as soluble by means of formalized leadership; continuing armed aggression may be one of these, but the variety of potential problems seems great enough to make unfeasible any attempt to list them here.

In fact, these two variables are one—a class of problems brought on by interaction with the external environment—but are separated here for the purposes of this essay.

THE ACHIEVEMENT OF STRATIFIED SOCIETY AND THE STATE

RIGHTS IN LAND. Stratified society as defined is attained either with the widespread realization of private ownership (including rights of permanent transfer) in land or other productive resources or with the recognition of rights of certain individuals to "tax" land or other productive resources, with these owners or tax recipients comprising a relatively small proportion of the society. Most society members are thus definitionally *peasants* paying something that may be construed as *rents* (Wolf 1966) to someone who may be construed to be a landlord.

It was argued in the previous section that pressure on basic resources tends to tighten concepts of tenure, so that in place of free use of plentiful land, the rights of use are ultimately vested in a corporate group that itself has rights of reversion when usable land is not employed. If this is true, it seems reasonable to think that continued pressure will further increase both the demand for land and the temptation to control it privately (see Boserup 1965: 86–87). The temptation should be especially great when land is irrigated. Irrigation can be seen as a population-density-related, labor-produced capital improvement that adds to the value of the land. Its importance is that it sharply defines an area of high land value. It is important in its influence on matters of land tenure, but not because of the managerial requirements of the irrigation system itself, which may be expected to be minor in cases of societies with only budding stratification.

The temptation to control land privately might be felt by both users and distributors of land. It thus seems logically possible that users could by clever manipulations become large landholders, and a class of these landholders could arise to form a stratified society. But pertinent examples of this are from areas under foreign domination, in which cash cropping and cash economies were imposed largely by colonial powers. That is, these are areas in which a ready-made higher level of living (that of the dominators) already exists, and in which the use of cash conveys advantages and motivations not present in subsistence economies.[3] It seems likely, then, that this means is a characteristic only of societies achieving stratification under the direct influence of other stratified societies.

A more promising mechanism for increased personal control of land is the extension of rights by the distributing official himself. It seems likely that the group as a whole is always potentially vulnerable to having its land appropriated through conscious design on the part of the high-ranking official. This would be most easily accomplished, not by wresting it from those using it, but by waiting until it becomes vacant and distributing it on bases other than those customary. In this way a chief could enlist the support of a group of subordinates who hold the land in true feudal fiefdom.

Yet the position of the men of rank is not without constraints. In addition to those informal checks provided by kinship, a society in which citizens hold approximately equal rights to land is probably a society in which they also constitute the army and the armory, in which case dumb loyalty to the men of rank may not be one of their qualities. Looked at in this way, the change in access to resources that forms the definition of stratified society appears to constitute a major reorganization—indeed, a revolution.

EMERGENCE OF CLASS DISTINCTION. One factor of importance in the achievement of such a revolution lies partly in the size of the total society. And there is a mechanism to explain the existence of short-term federations of unusually large size in the tendency of the segmentary society to cleave together when it is threatened externally. More broadly, this occurs when it perceives a "task" (Collins and Guetzkow 1964, Chap. 4), that is, a challenge or problem proceeding from the external environment, of which warfare is only one possible example.

Given, then, an increasingly large though unstable society made up of a number of segments, each with its few men accorded high status, it in time becomes possible for high-status individuals to count themselves numerous enough to form a separate social group. How many would this require? It is tempting here to refer to Birdsell's report (Birdsell 1968: 232–233) that dialectal tribes in Australia approach a statistical population of 500, a constant figure that tends to be preserved by fragmentation when a tribe becomes too large or by integration with neighbors when a tribe becomes too small. I do not mean to imply that the number 500 will be the number of the elite who come to perceive themselves as a separate social group, but rather I am suggesting that there is *some* numerical threshold that the elite must pass before they are inclined to place identification with each other above identification with their own localized kin units.[4]

At the same time, the sheer increase in societal scale necessary to reach this threshold would also tend to increase the availability of luxury items, which could serve as visible signs of class distinctiveness. If warfare also existed on the periphery—a condition providing a likely occasion for the original large federation of segmentary units and requiring a regularized leadership—it would both provide experience in the management of a centrally organized force and tend to increase the allocation of power to that leadership in the manner common in crisis situations (see Hamblin 1958).

The total situation outlined so far can be summarized as an elite increasingly interested in allocating vacant lands in directions of their own choosing, increasingly tending to identify with each other rather than with local kinsmen, increasingly wanting to acquire luxury items too expensive for their less wealthy kin, and increasingly finding skill in the management of forces of men (even though these men still have primary loyalties to their localized territorial base). All of these tendencies point toward the possibility of a basic horizontal cleavage in society, of class differentiation, and of the economic and social separation of elite from commoners. This is not to say that these factors are sufficient to *compel* such a cleavage, however.

THE NATURE OF THE LANDLORD. In part, the revolutionary appearance of stratified society may be the result of overstating the "landlord" aspect of the society. It seems clear that taxes imposed by a central authority may consist simply of the appropriation by (or from) the local chief of goods that would otherwise be redistributed by him, or of the assumption by him of rights not previously considered important. An excellent example is found among the twentieth-century remnants of the more or less independent Maya chiefdoms of Quintana Roo. There, during the chewing gum boom of 1917 to 1929 the accepted chiefs taxed foreign—that is, non-Maya—chicle collectors for personal gain, the income of one chief reaching one year the reputed sum of 40,000 pesos. Yet this was in a society so strongly imbued with the concept of common ownership of the land that when later (in the 1930s) the last quasi-independent remnants were induced to apply to the Mexican government for a formal grant of *ejido* lands, they consented to do so only on condition that the grant be made in common to the entire polity—people of nine villages—rather than to individual settlements (Villa Rojas 1945: 31, 67).

A view of the landlord as one with rights to tax that do *not* extend to rights of disposal of the magnitude of those implied by the term "private property" is in accord with the discussion of the landlord by Boserup (1965: 82ff.). So, for instance, in the description of the Inca government presented by Murra (1958) the labor tax imposed by the central government is identical to that traditionally self-imposed upon *ayllu* members. A very similar situation apparently existed in pre-Spanish Yucatán (Roys 1943). In neither case does there appear the implication that the government was supreme "owner." And the fact that this degree of landlordship seems to have been historically much more widespread than that carrying the right of total disposal suggests that the origin of stratified society has existed primarily in the extension of the privileges of the man of rank, rather than in consolidation of small holdings by an active producer. English society, after all, was stratified long before the commons were enclosed.

CONQUEST. Warfare, of course, may not have the result of imposing one group upon another at all. If land is the principal aim, the few people who are conquered with the land may be absorbed into social units approximately coordinate with, rather than subordinate to, those of the conquerors—as with the Dinka conquered by the Nuer in southern Sudan. Indeed, Fried (1967: 214–215) has argued that only conquerors from stratified societies impose social stratification. Yet examples like that of Ruanda suggest that this is not the case. Here Tutsi herdsmen imposed themselves as a superordinate "caste" over farming Hutu to produce a society that seems to me stratified in Fried's sense (Gluckman 1965: 186–190); and it is hard to think of the Tutsi herders as previously stratified. A similar, more completely developed statement has been presented by Spooner (1969a), drawing on evidence from Persia.

It seems that warfare may indeed be a means to social stratification. INSTABILITY AND STATEHOOD. Clearly, any newly formed stratified society would have sources of instability deeply embedded within it. Chief among these would be the still strong territorial loyalties of people and of leaders, made dangerous by the ability of common men to convert themselves into armies with territorially based organization. At this point, one would expect a budding upper class to make use of some means to divert at least some of the armed force from its traditional local loyalty and control. Examples of such attempts are seen in the armies of Ruanda and Buganda, described by Gluckman (1965: 180, 187). One would presume that attempts like these would be particularly effective when a sophisticated weaponry, not available to ordinary men, could be employed—firearms at a later day, cavalry at an earlier one. Success of such policies implies the arrival of the political state, with its non-kin-oriented monopoly of force.

The segmentary weakness would be eliminated for good and all, according to Gluckman (1965: 196), only under conditions of economic diversity with a corresponding decrease in the economic self-sufficiency of local units. Lloyd (1965a: 101) has observed, however, that in spite of this apparent defect segmentary polities may persist—indeed, some obviously have persisted—over long periods. In Africa this instability was apparently never eliminated; at least, all African kingdoms have been characterized as to some extent "segmentary" (for example, Vansina

1962), even though some would certainly be classed as states. On the other hand, and although sheer geographical isolation may be a strong factor, even into the present century Japan has been composed of localized units that were largely self-sufficient, with market systems and trade little developed on a common level, with a historically demonstrated tendency to cleave into territorial units dominated by unruly lords, yet with at least a symbolic unity that persisted for two millennia. This last consideration prevents me from introducing the factor of economic diversity into the rudimentary model being developed here (cf. Flannery and Coe 1968; Sanders and Price 1968: 188–191). I am inclined to think that economic interdependence and the market system must have an effect upon interregional unity, but I cannot regard them as crucial.

SUBSISTENCE. Unlike simple rank society, stratified society appears to have been based consistently upon agricultural production. It is possible that a very few exceptions to this may have existed from time to time among nomadic herdsmen, but in most cases when herdsmen came to constitute a ruling elite, the subjects were predominantly farmers.

SUMMARY. I consider the principal attributes of stratified society to be the following:

(1) An elite exercises superior rights to basic productive resources.

(2) A separate social class is formed by the elite, a class that is marked by a distinctive difference in life-style from that of commoners and by a tendency for elite members to associate with each other more than with individuals from other segments of the society.

The transition from rank to stratified society can be explained in two different ways. The first is by the interaction of factors constant to all rank societies, plus the following two variables:

(1) The achievement of a size permitting the separation of an elite class.

(2) A decision on the part of local leaders to seek their mutual interests with other such leaders, at the expense of their local kinsmen.

The second way is by the interaction of factors constant to all rank societies, plus the variable of conquest, with the imposition of the victors over the vanquished.

The principal attribute of the state is a monopoly of the legal use of physical force by the elite. For the present purposes I follow Fried (1967) in considering the transition from stratified society to the state to be automatic, based upon the necessity of a successful elite to maintain its position.

Expanding Subsistence: Results of the Choice

THE TRANSITION FROM EGALITARIAN TO RANK SOCIETY

As I have indicated, I believe that the presence of the important attributes of rank society may be explained by the interaction of factors constant in egalitarian society with the variable factor of increase in population size and density and the concurrent intensification of subsistence and pressure on resources. This view is supported by the apparent absence of high-density societies without attributes of rank society. On the other hand, I do not find pressure on productive resources to be the only situation giving rise to ranking, an inference that is supported by the existence of societies with apparently plentiful productive resources, yet with attributes of rank society.[5] Inasmuch as this essay is concerned with the relationship between population growth and features of social and political centralization, these other causal situations will not be explored here.

Of those choices in Figure 12.2, only that involving the increased use of free, good land—which does not imply subsistence pressure on available basic resources—may be expected *not* to result eventually in the achievement of rank society. All other choices imply an increased intrasocietal competition for resources and could be expected to lead to rank society.

This is not to say that all choices diagrammed in Figure 12.2 would encourage the development of rank society with equal speed. Those that imply some increased formalization of hierarchical organization would a priori be expected to promote such a development. Examples of such choices are the reorganization of work forces with clear status positions; the use of new power sources, either local or conquered, *if* it tended to foster new sets of obligations; other choices involving conquest *if* they tended to enlarge the society and increase pressure on resources (whether intended or not), yet not involving direct stratification. In addition, the choice of warfare for any aim—land, tribute, etc.—could favor the achievement of rank society by heightening the internal solidarity of the

society as attention was directed to the external task, and hence leading
to an increased formalization of stragetic (high-status) positions.

THE TRANSITION FROM RANK TO STRATIFIED SOCIETY

As I have said, I believe the presence of the important attributes of stratified society are explained in two different ways: The first is by the interaction of factors constant to all rank societies, plus the achievement of a
certain critical size and the decision on the part of local leaders to seek
their interests with other such leaders, rather than with their localized
kin groups. The second way is by the interaction of factors constant to all
rank societies, plus the imposition of one people over another by conquest.
I conclude that population growth and its attendant subsistence expansion are not alone enough to be considered causal. This conclusion is
supported by the existence of some high-density societies, with pronounced intrasocietal competition for basic resources, even with a tendency toward private land ownership by producers, yet without the
attributes of stratified society.[6]

Thus there seems to be no compelling evidence that population density
and the attendant intensification of subsistence techniques and pressure
on subsistence resources are *of themselves* sufficient to explain decisions to
embark on conquest or decisions on the part of an elite to cleave together
rather than to maintain ties with localized groups. To explain these decisions, additional information is required.

Of the choices listed in Figure 12.2, only that of the conquest of additional labor could be expected to result directly in stratification. Other
choices, even those involving warfare, could not be expected to lead to
stratification without the operation of the additional variable involving
a decision by high status persons.

The choice involved in this particular decision is diagrammed in
Figure 12.3. The alternatives are:

(1) Continuation of redistribution and resource allocation as traditionally
practiced, with retention of ties to the local group.

(2) Appropriation of lands and resources, the grant of lands to favored
people to create a network of personal allegiances, consumption of resources in the achievement of a style of luxury living, and the identification with other high-status persons.

The first alternative constitutes an equilibrium-maintaining mechanism.

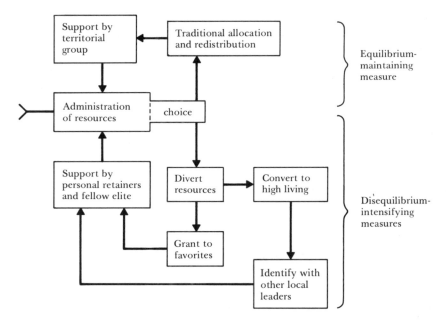

Figure 12.3.   The allocation of resources.

The second represents another deviation-intensifying device, portending social change. The decision between them may be analyzed in any particular case by reference to the values mentioned previously—material wants, affective wants, and energy expenditure—with the expectation that the attempt, whether rationalized or not, will be to best minimize deprivation for the individual concerned. Some elements thought to be necessary to the decision, such as the size of the society and its productivity, were mentioned; but it must be emphasized that this decision cannot be predicted in any particular case without substantial additional information.

Conclusion

In this paper I have attempted to present the following propositions:
1. The relaxation of population control and the resulting population growth with its attendant expansion of subsistence activity may be expected to occur with conditions of sedentary living.

2. Population growth and subsistence expansion are interrelated variables. Although it may at times be heuristically valuable to separate them, it is inaccurate to consider either an independent variable. The operation of external checks on either one of them will sharply inhibit the other.

3. The combined population growth–subsistence expansion variable is sufficient, if allowed to continue to operate, to cause the development of rank society; other necessary factors appear to be constant. (It is not, however, the only cause of that development.)

4. The population growth–subsistence expansion variable is not of itself sufficient to explain the development of stratified society, although its continued intensification represents a necessary condition for that development. A second variable is required; this may be either a decision to engage in warfare with the acquisition of a labor force as its aim, or a decision on the part of leaders to give their primary loyalties to other leaders, rather than to localized, corporate, kin-oriented groups. In either case this second variable is sufficiently independent of the population–subsistence factor to be considered separately.

Notes

1. Spooner's essay (Chapter 10, this volume) appears to me to illustrate a situation in which one or the other (or likely both) of these choices has been made for some time.
2. In another context, Netting argues in a similar vein (Chapter 9, this volume). Another example of the same process can be found in Ottenberg's description of the development of loan associations within more traditional associations of the Afikpo Ibo. In that case money, of course, is the important resource: "there is a strong sense of the loan group as a corporate organization holding property in common for the welfare and advancement of all, and that it is the job of the leaders to guide the group, but without personal gains, *other than in status*, for themselves" (Ottenberg 1968: 246–247, emphasis added).
3. Under colonial rule in Africa, individual farmers have on occasion been able to yield to this temptation successfully, contrary to customary procedure, either by calculated abuse of systems by which lands were traditionally pledged for temporary periods or by excessive payment to the traditional distributor of the land (Meek 1949: chap. 22 and p. 150).
4. Was it only accident that Mrs. Astor's famous ballroom held as many as *four hundred*?
5. The Maya splinter chiefdoms formed in Quintana Roo after the War of the Castes of the mid-nineteenth century are again a pertinent example. Descendants of the most militant of these people were described by Villa R. (1945). Except possibly for the decade of the chicle boom mentioned previously, these were an almost ideal example of rank society; defensive warfare against the government of Yucatán was the situation confronted by the groups (see Dumond 1970). But it is possible that the formation of rank society as the result of factors other than that of population increase with pressure on productive resources is commonly a "secondary" rather than a "pristine" phenomenon.

6. Thus having conceived population size as a necessary (but not sufficient) condition for the formation of stratified society and the state, it is not surprising that Sanders (Chapter 5, this volume) sees civilization in Mesoamerica accompanying relatively dense population, or that Adams (Chapter 2, this volume) finds that urbanization in Sumer followed on a time of explosive population increase. But the foregoing does not imply acceptance of the position expressed by Carneiro (Chapter 3, this volume, see also Carneiro 1970). That position is founded on the questionable premise that "autonomous political units never willingly surrender their sovereignity" (a logical extension of which must be that no human being willingly affiliates with another, since any affiliation involves a loss of autonomy) and proceeds to a second premise equally doubtful, that is, that population pressure always causes warfare, which in turn always causes the development of political states. Yet both of these premises are necessary supports for his presentation of a formula by which it is possible only to calculate the length of time necessary for a certain agricultural population, growing at a certain rate and using a certain fallow system, to fill up land of a certain size.

It is enlightening to compare, for instance, the societies and polities of the Yoruba and their neighbors the Ibo. The habitat, subsistence techniques, population densities, and history of warfare seem broadly comparable for these peoples. Yet at least some of the Yoruba (as described by Lloyd 1954) appear to have achieved a stratified society, while the Ibo did not, although it is clear they fit within the rank society category. Stevenson's (1968: chap. 9) contention that the Ibo were once part of a non-Ibo state and that they comprise a kind of secret state because of a control of trade exercised through the Aro oracle system, I find to be beside the point. I do not consider the Ibo stratified, as the term is used here, and clearly the indigenous—that is, properly Ibo—tendency has not been toward centralized polity and the monopoly of force. The Ibo situation seems to be repeated elsewhere. I take the Chimbu of New Guinea to form an example in a rather pristine—that is, only recently colonized—circumstance (see Brookfield and Brown 1963). In many areas the situation is confused by lengthy colonial rule and its attendant population growth, as has been pointed out by others (for example, Sanders and Price 1968:83). Nevertheless, I find it impossible to feel that the existence of societies like that of the Ifugao, with high population density and negligible internal political organization, can be squared with a conception of population density and growth as sufficient cause for the development of stratification and political centralization.

13

Prehistoric Population Growth and Subsistence Change in Eskimo Alaska

Don E. Dumond

Chapters 13 through 15 are concerned with hunters and gatherers—examples of peoples who did not develop agriculture or any other "intensifying" technology, whether or not the conditions of their physical habitat would have allowed them to do so. This chapter traces through three major cultural horizons the archaeological evidence for technological change and population growth among Alaskan Eskimos. Dumond uses this material to test the first part of the model he presented in the previous chapter.

In this essay I examine the relevance to the prehistory of a group of hunters—specifically those of the portion of Alaska and the eastern tip of Siberia now inhabited by Eskimos—of the first two propositions set forth in Chapter 12. These are:

1. The relaxation of population control and the resulting population growth with its attendant expansion of subsistence activity may be expected to occur with conditions of sedentary living.

2. Population growth and subsistence expansion are interrelated variables.

The area under consideration includes the coast and a strip of adjacent territory, largely tundra covered, from Kodiak Island and Prince William Sound in south-central Alaska, north across the base of the Alaska Peninsula (east of 159° W), and on northward around Alaska, including the tip of the Chukchi Peninsula in Siberia. I make occasional reference also to the Eskimo areas of Canada and Greenland. Specific Alaskan locations mentioned are shown in Figure 13.1.

I first summarize the archaeology and prehistory of the area in outline form, beginning with the time which most specialists take to be that of the initial settlement by ancestral Eskimos. I then turn to specific hypotheses derived from the two propositions from Chapter 12.

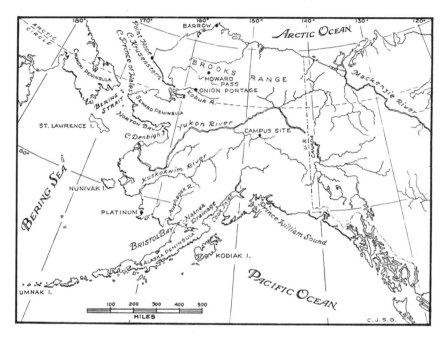

Figure 13.1.   Major Alaskan locations mentioned in the text (map drawn by Carol Steichen Dumond).

Eskimo Prehistory

I discuss the archaeology and its interpretation by means of three major horizons, referred to as "Arctic Small Tool," "Norton," and "Thule." These are represented over most of coastal Alaska, and the first and third are also represented in Arctic Canada and Greenland. For the sake of economy, voluminous references to primary data are omitted in those cases in which they may be found either in the recent general summary by Bandi (1969) or in a recent discussion of southwestern Alaska (Dumond 1969a). I have previously employed an approach similar in its ordering to that used here, though not directed toward population questions (Dumond 1965a).

Arctic Small Tool Horizon
This includes the Denbigh Flint complex in its various manifestations (as at Cape Denbigh, Cape Krusenstern, and Onion Portage) and all

other Alaskan assemblages commonly assigned to the Arctic Small Tool tradition. It does not include those assemblages from Anangula (off the coast of Umnak Island) and from the Campus site, both of which were assigned by Bandi (1969: 47–53) to his "Epi-Gravettian" phase.

DISTRIBUTION. From the Bering Sea side of the Alaska Peninsula, north along a strip adjacent to the coast. Representatives of the horizon are found neither on the North Pacific proper nor in Siberia. Beyond Alaska, materials of the horizon extend across northern Canada to Greenland.

DATING. No earlier (and perhaps somewhat later) than 3000 B.C. in the Bering Strait region; the horizon appears on the Alaska Peninsula after about 1900 B.C.; it is known in Canada and Greenland by 2000 B.C. (and perhaps somewhat earlier). In Alaska it ends no later than 1000 B.C. in any area with dating evidence, and perhaps by 2000 B.C. in some places.[1] In eastern Canada and Greenland representatives of the horizon develop into Dorset culture, the beginning of which is set in the first millennium B.C. and the end of which is marked by the arrival of Thule culture in Canada.

CLIMATE. The end of the hypsithermal, comparatively warm but cooling.

INVENTORY. Variety in stone tools is relatively restricted. Included are: end blades and side blades, often bipointed; burins, especially those struck on small bifaces; and microblades. Other artifacts probably present from the beginning include small adze blades with polished bits; a variety of scrapers; burinlike implements in which the struck burin facet is replaced by a polished face; and some knifelike bifaces of slightly larger size. There are no oil lamps. In the eastern Arctic, some small toggling harpoon heads of organic material are attributed to this period, and some lamps may have appeared by its end (for example, Nash 1969). Dogs are also reported from one site in Canada. Stone implements of the horizon are notable for their small and portable character, a feature that may be significant of aspects of the living habits of the time and certainly is welcome to airplane-chartering archaeologists. In their careful attention to minute technological detail and their adherence to miniature scale, these people have been said (albeit facetiously) to be *anal* in modal personality.[2]

PATTERNS OF SETTLEMENT. Chiefly temporary campsites, both on the coast and in the interior portion of their range. Inland these sites frequently occur along rivers. Constructed houses, presumed to have been

intended for winter occupation, are known only from three areas, all of
them in the interior: Howard Pass between the Noatak and Colville
drainages in the Brooks Range; Onion Portage on the Kobuk River; the
upper Naknek drainage on the Alaska Peninsula, where houses are
square, excavated into the contemporary surface, warmed by a central
fire, and entered by a sloping entry. In Canada some Pre-Dorset houses
are reported from coastal locations near Melville Pensinsula and near
Churchill, and temporary camps are known from both the coast and the
interior; in the succeeding Dorset period, occupation appears to be almost confined to the coast.

SUBSISTENCE. Balanced hunting and fishing, with emphasis upon caribou
and anadromous fish where available. Seasonal hunting of sea mammals
from temporary camps during periods of open water. In Canada there
was apparently more emphasis upon coastal hunting, but musk ox and
caribou were prime resources in the eastern Arctic. I know of no direct
evidence that winter sealing was practiced, but the predominantly coastal
locations of Dorset occupation suggest it must have been known in
Canada at least by that period.

CONTINUITY. Everywhere it is known, the first occurrences of remains of
this horizon are taken to constitute a break in continuity. In coastal
Alaska people of this stamp seem to have replaced a people oriented
primarily toward the boreal forest, who penetrated to the coast in a few
locations. In the Naknek drainage of the Alaska Peninsula, people of the
Small Tool horizon lived for nearly a millennium only some sixty miles
from slate-grinding, oil-burning, boat-paddling, sea-mammal-hunting
contemporaries of the north Pacific, with whom they had virtually no
contact at all. In the eastern Arctic, people of the Small Tool horizon
constituted the first human inhabitants of much of the area.

The details of the period following the end of the Small Tool occupation in Alaska are not well known. In southwestern Alaska there is a
hiatus in the established sequence that ends only with the beginning of
the Norton horizon. In the north the Brooks Range was apparently de-
populated, and at Cape Krusenstern there ensued several hundred years
with little or no occupation (Giddings 1967: 275). It is as though the
entire subsistence base of the Small Tool horizon had been suddenly
removed. Interestingly, the first millennium B.C. is a time of a major drop
in average temperature in the Arctic. It has been suggested that this

drop inspired the strong adaptation to coastal resources observable in later peoples (Dikov 1965). During this same cold period a transition was made in the east from Pre-Dorset to Dorset, and in northern Alaska, after the break in occupation already mentioned, the Choris occupation began. This occupation reflects somewhat the stone technology of the Small Tool horizon but seems also to reflect stone technology known from the boreal interior. Because of its ambiguous cultural position and its limited geographical extent, I do not include the Choris manifestation here. Continuity between the Arctic Small Tool and Norton horizons rests on typological evidence such as use of identical small polished adzes, identical bipointed projectile blades, identical polished burinlike implements, and—at least in the south—identical houses.

Norton Horizon

This includes Norton culture in its various manifestations (Cape Denbigh, Cape Prince of Wales, and Cape Krusenstern), phases of the Brooks River period of the Naknek drainage, early material from the Platinum vicinity, early material from Nunivak Island (M. Nowak, personal communication), Near Ipiutak, recently discovered material from Barrow (Stanford 1969), and material from extreme northwest Canada.

DISTRIBUTION. Coastal Alaska from the Alaska Peninsula almost to the Mackenzie River of Canada. No evidence is known for Siberia. Shortly after the beginning of the Christian era some elements of the horizon appear on the Pacific coast of the Alaska Peninsula, but these influences apparently did not carry farther into the North Pacific.

DATING. Known to begin around the middle of the first millennium B.C. on Norton Bay, appearing at Cape Krusenstern after the formation of the Choris-related beaches. Present by 200 B.C. in the upper Naknek drainage. It is thus presumed to have been spread throughout the area of its distribution before the beginning of the Christian era. North of Bering Strait the horizon ends by the early centuries A.D., with the appearance of Ipiutak. South of Bering Strait it does not end until the close of the first millennium A.D. In that area a steady evolution of cultures of the Norton horizon is observable for more than a thousand years.

CLIMATE. Warming after the cold period of the mid-first-millennium B.C.

INVENTORY. Pottery in the earlier portion of the horizon is chiefly fiber-tempered, with surface stamping in the form of checks or parallel lines.

Also present are: small oil lamps of stone; polished slate, some of the earlier material being both crude and rare; a variety of chipped projectile blades, including some similar to the bipointed projectile blades of the Small Tool horizon; small adze blades with polished bits, indistinguishable from implements of the earlier horizon. Organic artifacts include toggling harpoon heads. At Point Hope, at least, whaling harpoon heads are known.

PATTERNS OF SETTLEMENT. Almost entirely coastal, at least during the early portions of the horizon. Constructed houses—square, excavated into contemporary ground surface, with a central fire and sloping entrance—are known from the Platinum region, Seward Peninsula, Cape Denbigh, Point Hope, and are almost certainly present on Nunivak Island (M. Nowak, personal communication) and along the tidal portion of the Naknek River. Temporary campsites appear elsewhere on the coast and inland in the Naknek drainage. Collections I have examined suggest that some form of occupation from early in this horizon is also present in at least three other drainage systems around Bristol Bay. After the beginning of the Christian era, some constructed habitations of later phases within this horizon appear inland in the Naknek drainage. During this time in the north, most of the Brooks Range so favored by Small Tool people continued unoccupied; people of the Norton horizon are not demonstrably present at Onion Portage.

SUBSISTENCE. Coastal resources were favored. Whaling harpoon heads suggest the development of techniques for taking large sea mammals in open water, presumably through the use of the umiak and organized whaling crews. The use of interior resources in the south (the only place settlements are known to be in the interior) appeared to be slight in the beginning of the horizon, increasing steadily thereafter.

CONTINUITY. Culture of this horizon appears to include elements derived from Asia (pottery); from the north Pacific (polished slate and oil lamps); from the preceding Small Tool horizon (polished adzes, bipointed projectile blades, polished burinlike implements, house form). Inasmuch as Norton-like pottery is known from the Choris remains north of Bering Strait, it is tempting to see Norton culture developing in the south in all its characteristics—including techniques for hunting in open water but excluding the use of pottery—with people moving northward toward the Choris area by the middle of the first millennium B.C. At any rate, once

distributed, the Norton techniques underwent elaboration at Bering
Strait, where they resulted in the earliest manifestation of the Thule
horizon—represented by the Okvik–Old Bering Sea assemblages on St.
Lawrence Island and the adjacent Asian coast—shortly after the beginning of the Christian era (Dumond 1965a; 1969b; Larsen 1968). North of
Bering Strait, the Norton people were replaced by Ipiutak (similar in
many aspects of material culture and possibly in subsistence orientation,
yet without pottery, stone lamps, or polished slate). The relationship
between them is poorly understood. South of Bering Strait the early culture of the Norton horizon underwent a gradual evolutionary modification, uninfluenced either by Ipiutak or by the florescence at Bering Strait.
Meanwhile in the eastern Arctic the Small-Tool-derived Dorset culture
continued its relatively independent existence. Whether the Dorset use of
oil lamps was derived from Norton is unknown. Nevertheless, both
Norton and Dorset represent an intensification of the use of sea resources
and an apparent trend toward sedentary living.

Thule Horizon
In this I include all those manifestations of the midden-building, polished-
slate-using, lamp-burning, kayak- and umiak-paddling Eskimos of later
times. This subsumes all known Eskimo cultures of St. Lawrence Island
and the Asian coast (that is, from Okvik-Old Bering Sea onward), Birnirk, Nukleet, Eastern and Western Thule, and everything else in the
entire Eskimo area between about A.D. 1000 and the time of contact.
DISTRIBUTION. From Kodiak Island northward. Since this horizon includes
the movement of Thule people from Alaska to Greenland, the final distribution is coastwise from Kodiak Island to Greenland, including the tip
of Siberia.
DATING. Beginning shortly after the beginning of the Christian era at
Bering Strait; by shortly after the middle of the first millennium A.D.
north of Bering Strait (Birnirk of north Alaska and Asia); by shortly
before the end of the first millennium A.D. south of Bering Strait (Nukleet).
Among the ground-slate-using, sea-mammal-hunting people of Kodiak
Island and the Pacific, no shift in subsistence emphasis appears (Clark
1966). Rather, the beginning of the period is recognized by the intro-
duction of northern traits (especially of pottery) to Kodiak Island and
Cook Inlet around A.D. 1000. It may be inferred that this contact explains

the present distribution of Eskimo language (Dumond 1965a; 1969a). The horizon ends everywhere with the beginning of the period of European domination.

CLIMATE. A period of markedly higher temperature from around A.D. 900 to 1100 (perhaps as much as 2.3° C warmer than at present in much of Alaska), with deterioration thereafter.

INVENTORY. Thick, gravel-tempered pottery; predominant use of polished slate; oil lamps, often of pottery, with large lamps furnishing both light and heat in northern areas, including Canada and Greenland. Whaling implements appear in locations geographically favorable for the interception of migrating whales, where they were used by organized whale boat (umiak) crews. Sea mammal darts increase in variety, a manifestation of a general tendency toward specialization of equipment, much of it furniture for hunting kayaks. Such equipment includes projectiles, wound plugs, mouthpieces for inflating the skin of dead sea mammals, various hooks, toggles, and so on, to be used in towing sea mammals after a kill in open water. Sleds and dog harness were plentiful by late Thule times. Compared with the anal character attributed to the Small Tool people, these people must have been decidedly oral: trash heaps are large, debris is abundant, artifact collections are bulky and burdensome. Little wonder that large middens accumulated at village sites.

PATTERNS OF SETTLEMENT. The variety is considerable.[3] Numerous settlements depended almost entirely upon sea mammals. Some, strategically located for the purpose, depended upon whales as a major resource. Many communities maintained a balanced reliance upon land resources and sea resources; these people lived in substantial coastal villages, some of them also using more dispersed seasonal camps, often undistinguished by permanent habitations. Other people penetrated major watercourses—rivers such as the Yukon, the Kuskokwim, the Kobuk, the Nushagak, the Naknek—forming permanent inland river villages, although even here many of the people journeyed to the sea periodically to hunt. In the Brooks Range and elsewhere there developed a late specialization based upon caribou hunting, some of the hunters using crews modeled after those of the whaling villages; these hunters lived in less permanent houses or in tents. With the exception of the latter, the standard house of the horizon was some variation of that substantial semisubterranean structure of logs or whalebone with a sunken entrance

passage. In the south a central fireplace furnished light and heat. In
the north the fireplace was replaced by oil lamps. The same substantial
house was transferred across northern Canada to Greenland by people of
the Thule migration, but after the cooling period of approximately
A.D. 1200, the houses were abandoned in the Central Eskimo area as
Thule descendants returned to the more mobile pattern of their predecessors.

SUBSISTENCE. Heavy use of sea mammals at all seasons characterized the
coast. During the warm period of the tenth to eleventh centuries, retraction of the polar ice cap apparently resulted in some shift in the pattern
of migratory sea mammals, bringing on the migration of Thule open-
water sea mammal hunters across northern Canada (McGhee 1970). In
Alaska the use of resources became more varied and specialized through
time, with some people coming to rely almost entirely upon river products—especially migrating fish—and others almost entirely upon land
mammals—caribou in particular. All in Alaska, however, continued to
make heavy use of sea mammal oil, obtained either by seasonal hunting
trips or by trade. In northern Canada the deteriorating climate brought
on responses resulting in the migratory subsistence pattern of recent
Central Eskimos.

Summary of Eskimo Prehistory

The Arctic Small Tool horizon represents a generalized hunting people
adapted to life in the tundra, who spread across arctic North America to
Greenland by 2000 B.C. Subsistence was based on fishing, land mammal
hunting, and seasonal hunting of sea mammals on the coast, a way of life
that endured in Alaska for about a thousand years. In the east, the descendants of these people were those of Dorset culture. By the last centuries before the Christian era, the presumed descendants of the Alaskan
Small Tool people, those of the Norton horizon, were spread over coastal
Alaska from the Alaska Peninsula northward. Equipped with new techniques, more sedentary, more strongly adapted to life on the seacoast,
these people spread as far east along the Arctic coast as it was possible
for them to do and still maintain their customary life. At Bering Strait
these same people initiated a cultural florescence based upon the heavy
use of sea mammals, which resulted in the initiation of the pattern of
culture of the Thule horizon. Succeeding centuries saw an increasing

specialization in the use of sea mammals and subsidiary developments of the specialized use of other resources—of salmon and caribou in particular. Around the end of the first millennium A.D., when warmer weather resulted in a change in the path of sea mammal migration, the north Alaskan sea mammal hunters were induced to move eastward across northern Canada in their pursuit. This movement carried them as far as Greenland and resulted in the inundation of the Dorset people. Later, deteriorating conditions in northern Canada forced an abandonment there of the sedentary life based upon sea mammal hunting in open water, and a return to more nomadic conditions reminiscent of those of the Pre-Dorset predecessors.

A diagram indicating the extent of the three horizons appears in Figure 13.2.

Propositions and Hypotheses

The following propositions are expected to apply in the case presented here:

1. The relaxation of population control, the resultant population growth, and the attendant expansion of subsistence means may be expected to occur with the beginning of sedentary living.

2. Population growth and the expansion of subsistence are interrelated. In summarizing the prehistory of the Eskimo areas of Alaska, it was indicated that the Norton horizon marked a change from a relatively migratory existence toward sedentary living. As a rule Alaskan Eskimos were transhumant. But in most cases their home bases were far more permanent after 500 B.C., and in later times most of the travel away from home was by boat or dogsled, technologically sophisticated means that permitted the transportation of a sizable kit over substantial distances. Thus it is likely that technological developments in transportation permitted both increased sedentism and the aggregation of population into larger and larger settlements, as it became possible for people to control a larger territory from a single center. One would therefore expect the following:

1. During the Small Tool horizon there should be relatively little evidence of population growth—that is, increased density of settlement—or of intensification of subsistence.

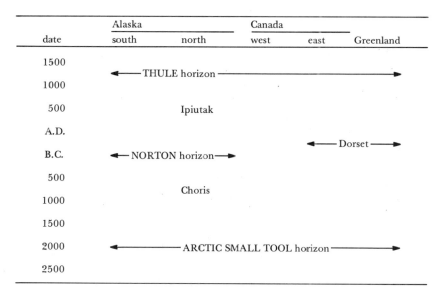

date	Alaska		Canada		Greenland
	south	north	west	east	
1500					
	◄——— THULE horizon ——————————————————►				
1000					
500		Ipiutak			
A.D.					
				◄——— Dorset ———►	
B.C.	◄— NORTON horizon —►				
500					
		Choris			
1000					
1500					
2000	◄——————— ARCTIC SMALL TOOL horizon ———————►				
2500					

Figure 13.2.   Extent of the three horizons.

2. Beginning with the Norton horizon, however, there should be direct evidence of both population growth—in increased density of settlement—and of the intensification of subsistence. According to the formulation presented in the preceding chapter, intensification of subsistence might consist of (a) increase in labor input, including the construction of more labor-expensive implements, (b) expansion into new territory, (c) some social reorganization directed toward subsistence, (d) adoption of new power resources, or (e) conquest to obtain new labor, land, or power sources. These hypotheses are examined in the following section.

Tests of Hypotheses

During the Arctic Small Tool horizon there was little population growth or intensification of subsistence.

One of the principal difficulties in dealing with the lengthy period covered by the Small Tool horizon is the apparent stability of material culture. Thus, in the Naknek drainage in southwestern Alaska the initial analysis suggested that the 800 to 1,000 years of Small Tool occupation could be divided into two cultural phases on the basis of changes in technology (Dumond 1963). Further research, with a quintupling of the sample, indicates very clearly that the original conception was based upon sampling error; if there was significant change in material culture during that period, present evidence is not sufficient to show it. The conclusion here is that the period was one of remarkable technological stability. And without some technological change to use for assistance in seriation, there is no feasible way to control for variations in population size through time.

At Cape Krusenstern, where Giddings (see Giddings 1967 for a summary) worked out a careful progression based upon a striking sequence of ocean beach ridges, he indicates he can discern two periods of development within the local Denbigh Flint complex, with the later implements displaying a deterioration of the fine technique known earlier. The sequence has not yet been published in sufficient detail to substantiate this, however, and there is no indication in information published thus far whether there is a variation in intensity of site use through time.

From no other area is there evidence sufficient to bear on this question. The conclusion on the basis of present evidence, therefore, is that once population growth was achieved sufficient to fill the area to which the people were adapted—by 2000 B.C. or shortly thereafter—there was no further increase in population density or intensification of subsistence means. Rather, the indication is of a population in sustained equilibrium with its subsistence resources.

Beginning with the Norton horizon and continuing through the Thule horizon, there was increased density of population and intensification of subsistence.

Density of Settlement
It is relatively easy to obtain impressionistic indications that the density has increased—that is, Thule horizon settlements are more obvious by far than those of earlier horizons. Thus Eskimo archaeology waited until 1939 and the discovery of the Ipiutak site at Point Hope for the first evidence in arctic Alaska of culture earlier than that of the Thule horizon. But the relatively higher visibility of later over earlier aboriginal occupation is familiar to archaeologists in many areas and may imply nothing regarding population density.

I am aware of only two more specific bits of prehistoric evidence. One is a concrete indication on St. Lawrence Island that Punuk settlements (of the end of the first millennium A.D.) significantly outnumber Old Bering Sea settlements (of the early first millennium A.D.) (Bandi 1969: 78; Ackerman 1961: 17, 181) although I am unable to present figures. The second consists of a recent attempt of my own to quantify settlement data from a portion of the Naknek drainage, which I now summarize.

Brooks River, the area from which these data are drawn, is a mile-and-a-half-long stream between two lakes in the Naknek River drainage system, an area that receives a substantial run of salmon from Bristol Bay and apparently has done so for several millennia. A chief drawback to archaeological research in the area is a deposit of volcanic ash nearly a foot thick, laid down in 1912 and now immediately under the sod. This layer effectively masks much surface evidence of prehistoric occupation. As a result, the only visible sign of aboriginal occupation, with the exception of one site that is being actively eroded by Brooks River, is the presence of surface depressions. Many of these are the remains of aboriginal habitations; others are simply roughened zones remaining in areas of aboriginal occupation; others are depressions of noncultural origin that have been used for campsites in prehistoric times; and a few are similar depressions that have not had the good fortune to be lived in by man.

In an attempt to determine the extent of prehistoric occupation, all depressions lying on the river terraces and adjacent lake terraces were counted (total 1,014). Based upon the clustering of depressions on river or lake terraces that seemed to promise a single date of geological origin, localities were defined that might provide the possibility of contemporaneous occupation. A carefully selected random sample of depressions was chosen to include a minimum of 5 percent and a maximum of 20 percent of the depressions in each locality, and these were tested by means of a small (sub-grave-sized) trench. The result permits an estimate of the number of depressions in each locality that may be expected to yield the remains of occupation—that is, a figure of "expected productive depressions per locality."

In six seasons of intensive excavations along the river (with site selection based in part on the testing program and in part on other criteria), it has been made abundantly clear that there is no one-to-one correlation between visible depressions and single aboriginal occupations. Rather, there are many more occupation floors—of all time levels—than there are visible depressions, and the depressions still visible may be the result of activity of any cultural phase in the last 4,000 years. Nevertheless, it is also clear that sites with heavier occupation exhibit more depressions regardless of the time period or the number of successive cultural phases. It has therefore been possible in every major locality but one to calculate for those areas intensively excavated a ratio of the number of separate single occupations (living floors, isolated hearths, etc.) per phase to the number of depressions visible in the area. The resulting ratio of occupations per depression was multiplied by the expected number of productive depressions in each locality, yielding a figure of the number of expected occupations per phase per locality. These were then summed, to give a total figure of "occupations expected per phase," and the results were divided by the number of centuries allotted to each phase. The final number, then, is "expected occupations per century," calculated for each separate phase and, it is hoped, adequate for the entire area of settlement along the river.[4] The only exception to this is the result of the fact that one of the major sites along the river—a single occupation site of the earlier of the Thule horizon phases—is now covered almost entirely by a sport fishing lodge operated by one of the Alaskan airlines. With most surface depressions eradicated and with the ability to excavate severely restricted, the loss of this site makes an estimate of occupation for that single phase infeasible.

In view of the sampling difficulties, of the strong possibility that "individual occupations" are not equivalent, of the fact that double projections—first of productive depressions and then of occupations per depression—are involved, I am hesitant to place strong reliance upon the resulting figures (I do not attempt to introduce confidence limits). But I can say that the results, given in Figure 13.3, are in accord with my own impressions: the occupation of the Arctic Small Tool horizon is substantial and is not approached in intensity until fairly late in the Norton horizon; but the intensity of occupation in both the Arctic Small Tool horizon and the Norton horizon is exceeded in the Thule horizon. Furthermore, during the period of Russian domination—a time later than that covered in Figure 13.3—there was an interior Eskimo settlement (Severnovsk) of about 150 inhabitants, centered some twenty miles farther up the drainage.[5] Year-round occupation at Brooks River itself is suggested by the nature of the habitations present during much of the time

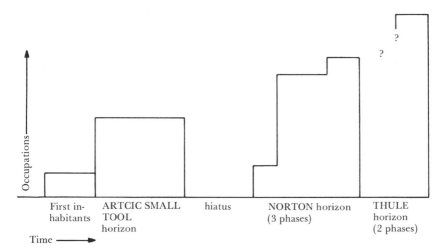

Figure 13.3. Relative prehistoric population density at Brooks River, in the Naknek drainage system, southwestern Alaska, as reflected in an estimate of single occupations of each phase. The "first inhabitants," believed to represent a non-Eskimo population, are not discussed. The absence of an estimate for the earlier of the two Thule horizon phases is explained in the text.

of the Thule horizon. I doubt that year-round occupation of the area was a feature of most of the Norton horizon.

In Alaska as a whole, one might take the expansion of people up the various river systems as evidence of population growth. But because in this essay expansion into new territory was considered a means of expanding subsistence, it will be considered as such in the following section.

Subsistence Expansion

In developing the hypothesis that is examined here, a number of ways in which subsistence might be expanded were indicated. These are examined separately.

1. Increase in labor input. This factor was certainly involved in the elaboration of technology noticeable in the Thule horizon, with increased specialization of tools, increased construction of boats, and so on. In all of these the labor input was in the direction of labor-intensive capital goods. Whether labor was increased in the subsistence quest directly is not certain, nor would any uniform answer to this question be likely throughout Alaska even if data were available.

2. Expansion to new territory (beyond that implied in the initial expansion to fill an ecological niche). Clearly this occurred. It seems implicit in the increased use of the Brooks River portion of the Naknek drainage mentioned earlier and shown in Figure 13.3. It is also suggested very strongly by the evidence from the Kobuk River (Giddings 1952), which appears to indicate that Eskimos moved upstream between A.D. 1200 and 1750. In both of these areas, which must be representative of many of the Alaskan river systems (see, for instance, Oswalt 1967: 241), the subsistence patterns required for permanent occupation would have been substantially different from that of the coast. Between A.D. 300 and 1000 there was an increasing press of Bering Sea people moving to the north Pacific (Dumond 1969a, 1971), where winter subsistence would have been strikingly different from that to the north. And it is around the end of the first millennium A.D. that Thule horizon people moved across northern Canada, although one may perhaps consider this movement to be the result of a climatic change that expanded the ecological niche, rather than a move to expand subsistence in the present sense.

3. Social reorganization for subsistence aims. This development is present in the organization of whaling crews and obviously must have followed upon the use of toggling harpoons and umiaks for whaling. The same crew organization was later used for caribou hunting in the Brooks Range (see Spencer 1959).

4. Adoption of new power resources. It is conceivable that the use of dog traction predated the time of the Norton horizon, but it seems very doubtful. Dog power was strongly in evidence in late Thule times and may be considered a power resource for subsistence. As with the use of domestic animals in agriculture mentioned by Boserup (1965: 35ff.), the addition of meat-eating animals to the household must have increased human labor requirements.

5. Conquest. It is difficult to know whether the Thule migration across Canada and the movement of people onto the north Pacific, both previously mentioned, fall best into the categories of expansion to new territory or of conquest. Certainly some conquest must have been involved in both areas; in both the result was linguistic acculturation of the previous inhabitants, so that Eastern Eskimo was spread to Greenland, and Western Eskimo was moved onto the north Pacific (see Dumond 1965a; 1969a).

Conclusion

Among the relatively nomadic people of the Arctic Small Tool horizon, there was in effect a systematic check on population growth, probably a direct result of the mobility requirement of the way of life. This check was relaxed with the increasingly sedentary life of the Norton and Thule horizons. The resulting population growth was closely related to changes in subsistence that involved the intensification of labor input through more complex hand technology, the organization of teams for specialized subsistence tasks, the development of dog traction, and the willful movement into new territory, some of which presented new subsistence requirements and some of which was already occupied by other people.

However, among *terrestrial* hunters and gatherers, I perceive few instances of improved technology that seem to relate directly to population pressure. For example, although the introduction of the horse to the plains was a very obvious case of a technological adaptation permitting improved use of resources, I do not see that one can relate it to population pressure. Rather it seems that once terrestrial hunters are well adapted to a territory, no continuing chain of technological improvement and population growth is normally to be found.

Along the Alaskan seacoast, on the other hand, the inferred population increase accompanied the rather steady evolution of a complicated technology for taking sea mammals and fish. For unlike game resources of the land, those in the sea tend to be invisible, and their possibilities are not so immediately perceptible. Consequently, there is the long-term opportunity for the development of better and better equipment. In that sense, then, resources of the seacoast are more apparently *expandable* to hunters than are resources of the land.

Agriculture, of course, is far more expandable yet, as both the techniques of husbandry and the crops themselves evolve. I suspect that most real expansion of subsistence techniques by terrestrial hunters and gatherers involves, not the perfection of existing land hunting techniques, but rather a shift either to seacoast or to agriculture. Such a shift, of course, may well itself be a response to a sense of impending population pressure.

In spite of this reservation, I conclude that the hypotheses developed in this paper are confirmed for the Alaskan situation by the evidence examined here and that the propositions presented in the previous chapter, from which these hypotheses were drawn, are validated to the extent that these particular hypotheses may serve that end.

Notes

1. This refers to the fact that the apparently post–Small Tool manifestation at Cape Krusenstern called "Old Whaling" has been radiocarbon dated to the early second millennium B.C. (Giddings 1967: 243, n. 1). A unique find, the materials may not now be related in any satisfactorily systematic fashion to the known archaeology of the Eskimo area; so I omit it here. To judge by tools and subsistence, the Old Whalers should be a group of Aleuts unaccountably lost on the shores of the Chukchi Sea.

2. J. V. Wright is responsible for this characterization.

3. Oswalt (1967) presents a summary of recent Alaskan subsistence and settlement patterns that is applicable to at least the later portion of the Thule horizon.

4. These varied from a low of 16 occupations per century ("first inhabitants" of Figure 13.3) to a high of 103 (second Thule-horizon phase). In view of the availability of migrating salmon in the river, I am inclined to suspect that all of these estimates are substantially lower than the actual aboriginal visitation.

5. There is additional information for the historical period. The vital statistics record of the Alaska Russian Church for the mission of Nushagak on Bristol Bay, during the period from 1878 to 1897 includes a total of 1,218 births and 983 deaths. For the shorter period from 1878 through 1890, a time that appears to have received the most consistently complete vital statistics reportage of any period covered by the records, there were 975 births and 812 deaths. Although there is no assurance that deaths of all very young (and unbaptized) children were recorded, or that deaths of all unbaptized older people were recorded, the 20 percent preponderance of births over deaths is interesting. Average age at death for the 812 individuals during the shorter, better-reported period was 35.3. Deaths among men were not chiefly by drowning or other violent means, even though a substantial proportion of these people were active hunters.

14 Population Growth and the Beginnings of Sedentary Life among the !Kung Bushmen

Richard B. Lee

Here we return to the central problem of Chapter 1. The latest evidence indicates that the beginning of agriculture in Southwest Asia was preceded by a fairly long period of semisedentary life based on the exploitation of wild cereal grains and riverine resources (Binford 1968; Flannery 1970). As population grew, the wild resources alone became insufficient to feed the increased numbers. This population pressure stimulated the first experiments with the improvement of wild grass seed, and these manipulations started the populations on the path that eventually led to the first systematic farming techniques.

This chapter examines further the demographic and economic bases of the beginning of agriculture in the ethnographic context of an African hunter-gatherer society—the !Kung Bushmen. The ethnographic method, of course, produces a whole range of data that are not available to the archaeologist. Particular attention is paid to the shift to sedentary life and a cereal diet and to the possible effects of these shifts on fertility and population growth.

Lee has been able to collect data to show what happens to the birthrate of this nonsedentary, hunter-gatherer society when its members settle and cultivate and to relate this finding to the requirements of the changing technologies. Thus, while the main part of his essay is concerned with an analysis of the range of factors that determine optimum birth spacing among the !Kung Bushmen, it has fascinating implications for the study of sedentarization at the dawn of the Neolithic.

The Dobe area !Kung Bushmen of Botswana are nomadic hunters and gatherers who during the 1950s and 1960s were observed in the process of settling down to a more sedentary life. The current situation among the !Kung, some of whom continue to hunt and gather while others have begun to adopt agriculture, offers a natural laboratory situation for generating and testing hypotheses about the origins of agriculture as a general process.[1]

The questions to be asked are three. First, what are the factors that regulate fertility of the Bushmen under traditional hunting and gathering conditions? Second, how is the balance of these factors altered by the shift from nomadic to sedentary life? And third, what are the possible causal mechanisms involved in the alterations in Bushmen fertility? The focus will be on the women, specifically on the intersection of their role in the economic system and their role in the reproductive system. In hunting and gathering groups there is a tight articulation between these two systems. This articulation enables the analyst to show how a shift in one of the variables in either system leads to adjustment in each of the other variables in the systems.

The Role of Women in the Bushman Economy

The subsistence economy of the Dobe area !Kung Bushmen has been described in (Lee 1968b, 1969a, and forthcoming). The hunting and gathering !Kung live in camps of ten to fifty individuals situated within a mile of a water hole. The camp serves as a home base for its members, some of whom leave it each day to seek food in the countryside lying within a 16-km radius. Camps are abandoned and new camps built every three months in winter and every two or three weeks in summer.

Woman's work—gathering wild vegetable foods—provides about two-thirds of all the food consumed by a Bushman camp. Men's hunting activities and gifts of food from other camps make up the remainder. Subsistence work occupies two or three days of work per week for each adult woman. On each workday a woman walks from 3 to 20 km (2 to 12 miles) round trip, and on the return leg she carries loads of 7 to 15 kg (15 to 33 lb) of vegetable foods—a combination of wild nuts, berries, fruits, leafy greens, and roots that varies according to season. Another one or two days a week are occupied in visiting other Bushman camps

situated from 2 to 16 km distant from the home camp. Small quantities
of food (1 to 5 kg) may be carried on both legs of the journey. When the
entire group moves camp or when families decide to visit distant camps,
the woman has to carry all her possessions—ostrich eggs, mortar, pestle,
and cooking utensils—for distances up to 100 km. Her possessions plus
the water carried on long trips weigh from 5 to 10 kg. Subsistence work,
visits, and group moves require an adult woman to walk about 2,400 km
(1,500 miles) during the course of an annual round. For at least half this
distance she carries substantial burdens of food, water, or material goods.

The major burden carried by women has yet to be mentioned. On most
gathering trips and on every visit and group move, a woman has to carry
with her each of her children under the age of four years. Infants and
young children have an extremely close relationship with their mothers.[2]
For the first few years of an infant's life mother and child are rarely separated by more than a few paces. Although solid foods are introduced at
the age of six months or earlier, breast feeding continues into the third or
fourth year of life. For the first year or two infants are carried on the
mother's back in a pouch made from the skin of small antelope. Then
from two to four they are carried straddling the mother's shoulder. For
the first two years of life a child is carried everywhere. In the third year
some baby sitting occurs, and this increases in the fourth year. At age
four, well after they have been weaned from the breast, they are weaned
from the back. For gathering trips the four-year-old may remain in camp
while his mother goes out alone or with his younger sibling. On visits and
group moves the child walks part of the way and for part of the way is
carried on his father's shoulder. By the age of six or seven, carrying
ceases entirely, and the child walks wherever the group goes. For each of
the first two years of life a child is carried by the mother for a distance
of 2,400 km; in the third year this decreases to about 1800 km; and in
the fourth year to about 1200 km. Over the four-year period of de-
pendency a Bushman mother will carry her child a total distance of
around 7,800 km (4,900 miles).

The Reproductive System[3]

The onset of puberty in Bushman girls is late, usually occurring between
the ages of fifteen and seventeen. First pregnancies are further delayed

for several years by post menstrual adolescent sterility. Thus a woman does not bear her first child until she is between eighteen and twenty-two years of age. The first pregnancy is followed by four to eight others spaced three to five years apart until menopause occurs after age forty. Fertility appears to be lower among the Bushmen than among other populations. The causes of this lower fertility are under study by Nancy Howell.

What is critical to the present analysis is not the overall fertility picture as expressed in birthrate but the frequency with which successive births occur to individual women—that is, the interval between births or birth spacing, expressed in months or years.

The Economic Consequences of Birth Spacing

Since every child has to be carried, it is fortunate that generally the birth interval among the Bushmen is as long as it is. The advantage of long birth spacing to hunter-gatherers is obvious. A mother can devote her full attention to caring for an offspring for a longer period, and the older the offspring is when his mother turns to the care of the subsequent young, the better are his chances for survival.

There is also the matter of the sheer weight of an infant to be carried by the mother. A woman whose children are spaced four years apart will have only one child to carry at any one time. By the time the next infant is born, the older child is mature enough to walk on his own. On the other hand, a woman whose births are spaced only two years apart will have to carry two children at once: a newborn to two-year-old on the back and a three- to four-year-old on the shoulder. No sooner is the older child "weaned" from the shoulder when yet another newborn arrives.

The !Kung Bushmen of the Dobe area recognize the plight of the woman with high fertility and express it in the saying "A woman who gives birth like an animal to one offspring after another has a permanent backache."

The actual work involved in raising young children in a hunting and gathering society is in large part a function of three variables: weight of children, the distance to be traveled, and the frequency with which children are born to a given woman. Fortunately each of these variables can be precisely quantified, and from their interaction a simple calculus can be developed to show more precisely the relationship between birth spacing and woman's work—that is, between the reproductive system and the economic system.

Women's Work

The Weights of Infants and Children

Bushman adults are small in stature and light in weight by Western standards. The men average 46 kg in weight and 157 cm in height, the women 41 kg and 147 cm (Bronte-Stewart et al. 1960). Birth weights and rates of infant growth for the first six months of life are comparable to Western standards. Thereafter Bushman children grow more slowly than Western children. The weights of the former at each age run about 75–80 percent of the latter. For example, a three-and-a-half-year-old American child weighs about 16.0 kg, while a Bushman child of about the same age weighs 12.5 kg.

The average weights of Bushman infants and children from birth to eight years are shown in Table 14.1. The figures are based on 164 observations on 40 Bushman children weighed during fieldwork in 1967–1969. The values vary from 6.0 kg in the first year of life to 17.6 kg in the eighth year. Note that these figures represent average weight during the year, and not the weight attained at the end of the year. Presenting the data in this form enables us to calculate the average burden to be carried by the mother during each year of the child's life.

In the first year children weigh from 3.1 kg at birth to a high of 8.7 kg

Table 14.1 Average Weight in Kilograms and Pounds by Age for Forty Bushman Children from Birth to Eight Years

Age in Years	Weight of Child				Observations on Individuals	
	kg	Range in kg	lb	Range in lb	No. of Observations	No. of Individuals
0–1	6.0	3.1–8.7	13.2	7–19	32	12
1–2	8.8	7.3–11.8	19.4	16–26	21	12
2–3	11.6	8.2–14.1	25.6	18–31	15	9
3–4	12.4	10.9–15.0	27.4	24–33	15	7
4–5	13.4	9.5–15.9	29.6	21–35	31	11
5–6	14.7	12.3–16.8	32.3	27–37	20	10
6–7	15.3	11.8–17.7	33.8	26–39	13	7
7–8	17.6	12.7–19.5	38.7	28–43	17	5

for an exceptionally fat older infant, with the average weight of infants being 6.0 kg. In the second year of life the mother's burden is 8.8 kg, with a range of 7.3 kg to 11.8 kg. By the fourth year this average has increased to 12.4 kg, with a range of 10.9 to as high as 15.0 kg.

The Distance to Be Traveled

I have estimated that a woman walks about 2,400 km during a year's activity. Apart from the food, water, and personal belongings, a woman will carry each of her children under the age of four for all or much of this distance. The weight she actually carries is determined by the age of the child and its rate of growth. Table 14.2 shows the different burdens of women with children of various ages. I introduce the useful, though somewhat cumbersome, measure of the "kilogram/kilometer," which is simply a product of weight times distance, that is, a load of 1 kg carried a distance of 1 km.

The Interval between Births

Given a mean birth interval among Bushmen of four years (for women of normal fertility), the work load of an average woman's reproductive career can be estimated. Her first baby is born in year one, her second baby in year five, her third in year nine, and so on. Each year she will have a variable weight of child to carry, depending on the age of the child. For a ten-year period her work effort will be as shown in Table 14.3.

Table 14.2 The Work Load of Women with Children of Various Ages

Child's Age in Years	Average Weight of Child		Average Annual Distance to Be Carried		Work Load for the Mother in kg/km
	kg	lb	km	miles	
0–1	6.0	(13.2)	2,400	1,500	14,400
1–2	8.8	(19.4)	2,400	1,500	21,120
2–3	11.6	(25.6)	1,800	1,125	20,880
3–4	12.4	(27.4)	1,200	750	14,880
4–5	13.4	(29.5)	—	—	—
5–6	14.7	(32.3)	—	—	—
6–7	15.3	(33.8)	—	—	—
7–8	17.6	(38.7)	—	—	—

Table 14.3 Average Daily Burden over a Ten-Year Period

	Year	Kilograms to Carry
First Baby	1	6.0
	2	8.8
	3	11.6
	4	12.7
Second Baby	5	6.0
	6	8.8
	7	11.6
	8	12.7
Third Baby	9	6.0
	10	8.8

During the ten-year period the average woman will raise three children and will have carried an average burden of 9.2 kg per day. Her burden will be least during the years when she is carrying a newborn (6.0 kg per day) and greatest when she is carrying a three-year-old (12.4 kg per day plus the burden of being pregnant at the same time). With shorter birth spacing, both the number of children and the weight of children to be carried will go up.

Table 14.4 shows the work load required of mothers with four different birth intervals: two, three, four, and five years. The table shows the number of babies and the weight in babies for each year of a ten-year period of the reproductive career.[4]

As one moves from longer to shorter birth spacing, the work required of the mother progressively increases. At one extreme, a mother with five-year spacing will at the end of ten years have raised two children and will have carried an average daily burden of only 7.8 kg (17.2 lb). At the other extreme, a woman with two-year spacing will after the same time period have five children, and her average daily burden will have been 17.0 kg (37.4 lbs), and for four of the ten years will have been as high as 21.2 kg (46.6 lb). Two-year birth spacing in fact represents a theoretical upper limit of birth frequency for Bushman women. We have no cases of the interval between successive live births as short as two years, although we have recorded several examples of actual birth intervals of as short as 30 to 36 months. The significance of these short intervals will be discussed in a later section of this paper.

Table 14.4 Effect of Different Birth Intervals on Work Effort of Mother

| Year | Birth Interval | | | | | | | |
| | 2 Years | | 3 Years | | 4 Years | | 5 Years | |
	Weight kg	Baby No.	Weight kg	Baby No.	Weight kg	Baby No.	Weight kg	Baby No.
1	6.0	1	6.0	1	6.0	1	6.0	1
2	8.8	1	8.8	1	8.8	1	8.8	1
3	17.6	1 & 2	11.6	1	11.6	1	11.6	1
4	21.2	1 & 2	18.4	1 & 2	12.4	1	12.4	1
5	17.6	2 & 3	8.8	2	6.0	2	—	—
6	21.2	2 & 3	11.6	2	8.8	2	6.0	2
7	17.6	3 & 4	18.4	2 & 3	11.6	2	8.8	2
8	21.2	3 & 4	8.8	3	12.4	2	11.6	2
9	17.6	4 & 5	11.6	3	6.0	3	12.4	2
10	21.2	4 & 5	18.4	3 & 4	8.8	3	—	—
No. of children at end of 10 years	5		4		3		2	
Average weight of baby per annum	17.0 kg (6–21.2)		12.2 kg (6–18.4)		9.2 kg (6–12)		7.8 kg (0–12)	
No. of years carrying 2 children	8		3		0		0	
No. of years carrying 1 or 0 children	2		7		10		10	

For the great majority of fertile women the intervals between live births varies between five and three years. Shortening the birth interval from five to four years adds a daily burden of 1.4 kg to a woman's work load. Shortening the interval further from four to three years more than doubles the increase in burden to 3.0 kg for a total weight of 12.2 kg.

We have noted how actual work for the mother is a product of weight carried times distance traveled. To carry a Bushman child for one year requires between 14,000 and 21,000 kg/km of effort by the mother. To carry one child for the full four years requires a total of 71,280 kg/km and the average per year of 17,820 kg/km.

Table 14.5 shows how the amount of work is affected by different lengths of birth spacing. The curve of increased work effort rises slowly as the birth interval shortens from five to four years; it rises more steeply as the birth interval reduces to three years and extremely sharply as the interval is further reduced to two years. This table indicates some of the

Table 14.5 Work per Mother per Year According to Birth Spacing (in kilogram/kilometer)

	Birth Interval			
	2 years	3 years	4 years	5 years
Average kg/km per year	32,064	22,824	17,808	14,256

"costs" in work effort of raising children under nomadic, hunting and gathering conditions, and it also shows the added costs of an increase in the birth rate.

A mother with five-year birth spacing will have two children at the end of ten years. To add a third child during the same period (by lowering the birth interval to four years) will add only 3,500 kg/km to a mother's work load. To add a fourth child (by further lowering the birth interval to three years) will "cost" 40 percent more than the cost of adding a third child—5,016 kg/km as opposed to 3,542 kg/km. And to add a fifth child (by lowering the birth interval even further to two years) would "cost" over two and one-half times as much per child as adding a third.

Given these "high costs" of short birth spacing, it is not surprising that under nomadic conditions the birth intervals average around four years, and this is maintained even in the absence of contraceptive measures; the !Kung practice post partum sex taboos but only during the first year of the baby's life. This long birth spacing is adaptive both at the individual level and at the level of population. The individual woman is better equipped to care for each of her children if births do not follow too closely one after another, and this long birth spacing lowers overall fertility so that the population does not grow so rapidly that it threatens the food supply. Long birth spacing alone is not sufficient to keep the population in long-term balance with resources, but the modest amount of excess fertility of the Bushmen is readily absorbed by infant mortality, occasional infanticide, and by outmigration.

In this context it is worth noting that the slow rates of growth of Bushman children are also adaptive. For people who have to walk a lot, small babies are easier to carry than large babies. Therefore the small size of Bushman children in comparison to Western "standards" is not necessarily due to inadequate nutrition.

Mobility, Birth Spacing, and Population Growth

I have examined the implications of higher and lower fertility levels for the economic adaptation of the hunting and gathering Bushmen. More babies and/or greater distances to travel mean more work for Bushman mothers. Similarly, work effort would decline with fewer babies and/or less walking. It is the latter possibility—less walking or reduction of mobility—that is of interest here. This is precisely what happens when hunters and gatherers shift to agriculture. Even partial agriculture allows more food to be grown closer to home, allowing the population to maintain the same level of nutrition with much less walking.

What are the consequences for a Bushman mother's work load of a partial shift to food sources closer to home? To raise one child to the point where he can walk by himself requires four years of carrying for an average annual work load of 17,820 kg/km. This average is based on 1,200–2,400 km per year of walking. If walking is reduced by a third—to 800–1,600 km per year— then the annual work load falls to 11,880 kg/km.

Table 14.6 sketches the implications of reduced work effort for birth spacing. Formerly the mother with five-year birth spacing had an annual work load of 14,256 kg/km. Under the more sedentary conditions this falls to 9,504 kg/km. A mother with four-year birth spacing used to work 17,808 kg/km per year. Now she works only 11,872 kg/km, which is less than that of a mother with five-year birth spacing under the nomadic conditions.

What this means in practical terms is that with reduced mobility a woman may shorten the interval between successive births and continue to give each child adequate care while keeping her work effort a constant.

Table 14.6 The Effect of Reduced Mobility on Fertility

	kg/km Work per Year for Women with Various Birth Intervals			
	2 years	3 years	4 years	5 years
Under nomadic conditions: 1,200–2,400 km per year	32,064	22,824	17,808	14,256
Under more sedentary conditions: 800–1,600 km per year	21,376	15,216	11,872	9,504

To put it another way, a mother can have more children with no increase in work effort. Table 14.6 shows how a mother may now have
babies every three years with slightly less work effort than having babies
every four years required under nomadic conditions (15,216 kg/km vs.
17,808 kg/km). Shortening the mean birth interval results in a general
rise in the level of fertility, which, in turn, leads to an upswing in the
rate of population growth.

I do not intend to imply that sedentarization alone causes population
growth. In the first instance reduction of mobility may produce a situation where the number of children remains the same but there is more
leisure time. In the concluding section of this paper a stricter causal
explanation is offered. What I am suggesting here is that *settling down
removes the adverse effects of high fertility on individual women.* Among hunters
and gatherers high natural fertility is maladaptive: women who gave
birth as frequently as every two years have not survived to contribute
this high fertility tendency to the current !Kung Bushman population.
Even with three-year birth spacing the mother's work load may be great
enough to endanger her own fitness and affect the survival chances of
her offspring. With sedentary life these restraints are removed, three-year
birth spacing becomes no more strenuous to the mother than was four-
year birth spacing to mothers under nomadic conditions.

Thus for the population as a whole sedentarization may lead to the
upsetting of the hunting-gathering low-fertility adaptation and trigger
population growth, even in the absence of any expansion in the food
supply. The cause of the sedentarization need not be the shift to agriculture, though such a shift is occurring among the !Kung Bushmen. It
is apparent that any change in the subsistence economy that allows reduced mobility may be sufficient to increase fertility. Such preagricultural examples of sedentarization as the exploitation of wild grains with
a milling technology or the exploitation of coastal and riverine resources
may have had a similar effect of increasing fertility by reducing mobility.

The relation between nomadism and long birth spacing has been
known at least since 1922, when Sir Alexander Carr-Saunders referred
to "the problem of transportation in nomadic societies." He pointed out
that the necessity of carrying children for the first few years of life sharply
limited the number of children a woman could successfully rear during
her reproductive span (Carr-Saunders 1922). And J. B. Birdsell speaks of

at least a three-year birth interval among Australian aboriginal women (Birdsell 1968: 236). To my knowledge the first person to pinpoint *birth spacing* as a key variable in the shift from hunting and gathering to sedentary life was Lewis R. Binford, as quoted by John Pfeiffer in "The Emergence of Man":

Binford suggests that one result [of a more reliable food supply at the end of the Pleistocene] may have been an increased trend toward year round settlements reducing the need to pack up and move on to new hunting grounds, and permitting an adjustment of primitive birth control measures. As long as mothers had to keep on the move, they were limited to one child every three or four years because that was all they could carry . . . [but birth control practices] could be relaxed in more settled times with fish and fowl to supplement basic supplies of reindeer meat [Pfeiffer 1969: 218].

Causality in the Relation between Fertility and Food Supply

Two final questions can now be raised. First, what are the mechanisms by which the long birth spacing is maintained under hunting and gathering conditions? And second, what factors could underlie the shortening of birth spacing when the shift to sedentary life is made?

Some of the !Kung Bushmen we are studying are undergoing a similar shift at this time, and the possible explanation suggested here is specific to the !Kung. This is not to say that the same mechanisms are at work in other populations of hunter-gatherers.

The answer to the first question is that long lactation suppresses ovulation in Bushman women. The mothers are observed to nurse their children for the first two and a half to three and a half years of life. During the latter half of this period her sexual life is active, yet conception does not occur. The long period of vigorous, continuous nursing suppresses ovulation in enough women enough of the time to produce a four-year average birth interval.

The data on the relation between lactation and ovulation in other populations are difficult to interpret. Careful studies of this phenomenon have demonstrated a suppressant effect in populations in India (Giosa 1955) and in Rwanda (Bonte and van Balen 1969), while in some urban western populations this suppressant effect has not been shown (see Guttmacher 1962). The Bushmen appear to show this effect to a *greater degree than other populations*, and the reason for this is that other populations

are not facing the kinds of nomadic work demands faced by the
Bushmen and other hunter-gatherers. What does not work in urban
North America may very well work in the Kalahari, where a clear
adaptive advantage is offered to the woman who has the physiological
makeup whereby ovulation is suppressed by continued lactation. For the
Bushman woman, the alternative to suppressed ovulation may be higher
infant mortality and/or the necessity for frequent infanticide.

Now let us turn to the second question. What factors underlie the
shortening of birth spacing when the shift to sedentary life is made?
Here I offer an explanation worked out by Nancy Howell (n.d.). One of
the practical reasons why lactation continues so long among the Bushmen
is the relative absence of soft, easily digestible foods in the wild diet that
are suitable supplements for infants and young children.

Agriculturalists and pastoralists have milk and mush on which to wean
their children. The Bushmen lack such alternatives; they have no domesticated animals, and apart from breast milk the infant diet consists of
nuts, berries, fibrous roots, and meat—all foods of low digestibility. Solid
foods are introduced around six months, but I suspect not in the same
quantities as among agricultural peoples.

A few of the Bushmen have settled down in recent years and started to
keep goats and plant maize, sorghum, and melons. There is some evidence of a lower birth interval—33 to 36 months—among the more
sedentary Bushmen. It is possible that the availability of softer foods
lessens the infant's dependence on breast milk and thus permits an earlier
resumption of the mother's ovulatory cycles, leading to earlier conception
date and a shorter birth interval.

The point is that these are not either-or propositions. When you have
a shift in a variable such as diet, it will affect different women differently.
In some women it may lead to earlier conception; in others it may not.
The net statistical effect, however, would be a shorter birth interval and
a rise in the birth rate.

These are hypotheses that are being tested with demographic data on
the Bushmen collected by Howell. For the present I can only sketch
out the implications in a preliminary way. The most recent thinking
about the origin of agriculture has a stage of sedentary life based on harvesting of wild grains *before* actual domestication of plants. At this stage
there is also some evidence for population growth without any possibility

of expansion of the food supply. This preagricultural period has puzzled researchers working in this area. Data on the !Kung (who are in one sense also on the threshold of the Neolithic) suggest that *sedentarization alone may trigger population growth, since women may have children more frequently without any increase in work on their part and without reducing their ability to provide for each one.*

Once population growth is initiated, pressure on resources may stimulate technological change in the direction of manipulation of and improvement of wild grains, a process that sets man on the road to agriculture. It is at this point that the processes of population growth in relation to agricultural change presented by Boserup take effect.

Notes

1. Fieldwork among the !Kung was carried out by the author in 1963–1965 and 1967–1969 for a total of 37 months. Financial support was provided by the National Science Foundation (U.S.), the National Institute of Mental Health (U.S.), and the Wenner-Gren Foundation for Anthropological Research.
2. Child-rearing practices and infant behavior have been studied by Patricia Draper and Melvin Konner, both of Harvard University, and by N. G. Blurton-Jones of the Institute of Child Health, University of London. I want to thank these colleagues and Nancy Howell for their useful suggestions on the model.
3. Bushman demography has been studied by Dr. Nancy Howell, Office of Population Research, Princeton University, during fieldwork in 1967–1969 supported by the National Institute of Mental Health (U.S.).
4. In this simple model of birth spacing and mother's work the effects of infant mortality have not been incorporated. Since between one-third and one-half of the children born to the Bushmen do not survive to maturity, only a proportion of children are carried the full four years. In order to consider infant mortality, it would be necessary to know, first, the age-specific death rates for infants; second, the effect of infant mortality on shortening the birth interval; and third, differential mortality in relation to family size. Data on these questions are being analyzed by Howell, and will be included in later versions of this model.

15

The Intensification of Social Life among the !Kung Bushmen

Richard B. Lee

In the preceding chapters we have been concerned with technological and political intensification in relation to population growth. We now turn briefly to what might be called social intensification to differentiate it from the political intensification discussed by Netting. Owing to the nature of the ethnographic method (on which data on social organization largely depend) it is particularly difficult to document examples of the effects of population growth on social organization. What Lee offers us here is an analysis of the comparative dynamics of small and large groups and the centrifugal and centripetal forces that make for each among the !Kung Bushmen.

The secular growth in world population has been accompanied by a parallel tendency for men to group themselves together in larger and larger communities. The effect of living in larger communities has been to stimulate a more intensive social life. When the size of the local group grows beyond the scale where everyone knows everyone else well, new modes of behavior and new forms of social organization must crystallize in order to regularize the added complexity. Such processes of group formation, especially in historical perspective, are still poorly understood. It may be useful to examine the phenomenon in a relatively simple context—among the hunting and gathering !Kung Bushmen of the Republic of Botswana.

Intensification of social life is not associated solely with population growth. Societies of hunter-gatherers exhibit this process cyclically during the course of an annual round. Here I describe what happens when more hunters gather in one place, delineate those factors that bring people together and those that keep people apart, and examine the shift of these factors in the light of recent political developments. Finally, the relative

weight of ecological and social forces in the intensification of Bushman
social life will be evaluated.

Traditional Society: The Public Life and the Private Life

In a now classic paper *Essai sur les variations saisonnières des sociétés eskimos*
(1906), Mauss and Beuchat discussed the various groupings formed by
the Central Eskimo at different times of the year. They distinguished two
phases in the annual cycle of the Eskimo, which they labeled the "public
life" and the "private life." The public life takes place in the winter sealing camps; up to 150 people get together in ten or twenty igloos for the
purpose of hunting seals through breathing holes in the offshore ice. It is
at this time of year that the winter ceremonials and shamanistic performances take place. In the spring the private life phase begins, when
the large winter camp splits up and the people disperse into smaller
domestic groups of one to several families, who move inland for caribou
hunting and for fishing. This phase lasts through the summer until the
next freeze-up, when the large winter camps are re-formed.

This division of the year into two phases, a period of concentration and
a period of dispersion, appears to be characteristic of not only the Central
Eskimo but most of the world's hunter-gatherers as well (Lee and DeVore,
1968).

Among the !Kung Bushmen of the Kalahari Desert, availability of
water was the key seasonal variable. During the winter dry season (May–
August) all the Bushmen were concentrated at one of several permanent
water points in groups of as many as 150 to 200 people. In the spring
(September–November) the rains created temporary pools of water all
over the desert, and the people went out to live at them. During the main
rains (December–April) the people were dispersed in groups varying in
size from 7 to 50 people, who ranged widely as the major food plants
came into season. After a brief autumn, when the summer waters had
dried up, the Bushmen again converged on the permanent water holes
to form the large winter camps.

Like the Eskimo and most other hunter-gatherers, the nature of the
ecology demanded flexibility in Bushman living arrangements. In drought
years the public life phase was extended because water was available at
only the few most reliable water holes. During years of higher rainfall,

the minor water points might hold water through the winter and into the next rainy season. Thus people could live there throughout the year and remain more widely dispersed than in years of drought, thereby extending the private life phase.

What Brought People Together

Although the winter camp, public life phase was dictated partly by the ecology, living together in large groups had many social benefits for the Bushmen. This was the period of the year when social life was more intense, a period of large-scale trance dancing and curing, initiations, trading, story telling, and marriage brokering.

The Bushman men's initiation camps or *choma* were held in the winter every four or five years. The *choma* brought together the largest aggregations of Bushmen. The reason for this is that at least seven boys of the correct age were needed to make it worthwhile to run the elaborate six-week-long initiation program, and one had to call in a large number of local groups to get together enough boys between the ages of fifteen and twenty. The families of the boys camped together and provided food for the initiation camp throughout the six-week period. When very large groups of twenty or more boys were initiated together, the numbers in the adjacent camps must have been well over 200.

Even in the years when *choma* camps were not formed, winter camps of 100 to 200 were common. The trance-dance curing ceremonies (Lee 1967, 1968a) brought together medicine men from far and wide. The curing medicine was thought to be especially effective when many performers entered a trance at the same dance. Since the big trance dances went on round-the-clock for twelve to thirty-six hours, subsistence had to be organized to provide support for the singers, dancers, and trance performers. This was difficult to do unless there were fifty or more adults in a camp, since to be effective the trance dance had to have at least fifteen to twenty adults participating at any one time.

A third activity of the public life phase was *hxaro* trading. *Hxaro* is the term applied by the Bushmen to their peculiar institution of long-distance exchange networks. Goods traveled for hundreds of miles across the Kalahari from one *hxaro* partner to another. Any individual would have dozens of partners, many of whom he or she would see less than once a

year. Fulfilling trading commitments and putting new goods into circulation were major activities at all Bushmen camps but especially the large
ones that brought together people who saw each other infrequently. The
peculiarity of Bushman *hxaro* trading was the inordinate length of time
separating the two halves of a transaction. Individual A gave B a trade
item—such as a spear, arrow, or ostrich eggshell-bead necklace—and
A and B would part. Months or years later they would come together
again, and B would give A an item in return.

Hxaro trading is a traditional form of exchange among the Bushmen,
but it has become particularly important as an avenue through which
novel items of Bantu and European manufacture have been disseminated
into the interior of the Kalahari.

Marriage brokering was another of the activities bringing together
large groups of Bushmen. Because of the small size of local groups and
the frequent disparities in sex ratios, parents had to look far afield in
arranging a spouse for their son or daughter. It was rare that an individual could find a spouse from within the home group or adjacent groups.
More frequently marriages brought together people from twenty-five to
fifty miles apart (H. Harpending, personal communication). The large
winter camps gave the local families the opportunity of casting a wider
net in seeking a spouse.

All of these activities—religious, medical, economic, and marital—
brought Bushmen together and contributed to the intensity of social life.
In general, the winter dry season camp was a period of higher social
velocity, during which more time was spent interacting with larger numbers of people. But life in large groups was not an unmixed blessing, and
there were many occasions when water and food resources were abundant,
but large groupings failed to materialize. The question can now be
raised: Given the obvious advantages of larger grouping, why didn't the
Bushmen spend more of their time together in one place?

What Kept People Apart

The major disadvantage of intense social life in larger groups is the increased frequency of conflict. Arguments and fights take place in Bushman
camps of all sizes and at all seasons, but the larger camps seem particularly plagued with disputes. For example, at /ai/ai, a water hole with

a large resident population (100 to 150), serious disputes broke out about once every two weeks during 1968–1969. The comparable rate for water holes like Dobe and Mahopa, with resident populations averaging between 40 and 60, was three or four times a year. In the past, the *choma* initiation camps often failed because of disputes on procedural matters. The big camps would split up, and the participants would disperse into smaller groupings in local areas.

Keeping very large groups together requires special efforts from individuals. They must maintain higher levels of cooperation and coordination of hunting and gathering activities than would be necessary in smaller domestic groupings. For this reason the largest aggregations of Bushmen and of other hunters such as the Pygmies (Turnbull 1965; 1968) were inherently unstable; fights were likely to break out and lead to the breakup of the group.

The largest groupings that the Bushmen could muster thus had an inherent dilemma. The people sought the stimulation of a more intense social life, but there was always the danger of serious conflict. The Bushmen annual round was structured to allow both kinds of social life—the intensity of the public life, with its inherent dangers, and the domestic tranquillity of smaller groupings in the private life.

The coalescing and splitting of hunter-gatherer local groups have often been considered as an adjustment to changing ecological conditions, and there is a great deal of validity to this view (Steward 1936; 1955). Given the annual and regional variability in water and food supply, it is highly adaptive for Bushmen to move frequently and to maintain flexibility in order to make the most effective use of their resources. But within the framework imposed by the ecology, conflict also plays a role in the rearrangement of groups. If people have a good enough reason for staying together—such as the performance of a ritual—they can do so but only if they are prepared to work harder at it. Bushman groups of over 100 people can be sustained for months but only at the cost of an increasingly high input of subsistence effort per capita. When conflicts break out and poison the atmosphere of the camp, the members may find it preferable to split up and seek greener pastures.

The combination of the factors of seasonal ecology and the disruptive effects of conflict worked out so that in the traditional hunting and gathering society an average of approximately three months out of the year was spent in the larger groups of the public life and the other nine months were spent in the private life.

Contemporary Society: Stabilizing the Public Life

Now I shall consider how this state of affairs has been affected by recent contact of the Bushmen with the outside world. About forty-five years ago, in the mid-1920s, the Bantu-speaking Herero pastoralists entered the Dobe area and set up their cattle posts at the large permanent water holes. The Bushmen built camps near the Herero and asked them for milk, tobacco, and trade goods. Gradually a pattern was established in which the Bushmen visited the cattle posts on a regular basis while continuing to depend on wild vegetable foods and game for the major part of their subsistence. As the herds of the Herero prospered, some Bushman families settled with the Herero to provide extra labor as cowboys and milkmaids. Their families acted as a conduit for funneling surplus milk to more isolated groups so that all Bushmen participated at least indirectly in the contact economy for periods varying from a few weeks each year to most of the year.

By the late 1960s for example, at the /ai/ai water hole (where I spent fourteen months in 1968–1969) there were 150 Bushmen resident in seven adjacent camps, along with 70 Hereros and over 500 head of cattle. This large semipermanent aggregation of Bushmen puzzled me. How could so many Bushmen stay together in one place for so long? Then I realized that what had happened was that the Bushmen of /ai/ai had achieved a permanent public life situation. Instead of spending nine months of the year dispersed and three months of the year together, they had reversed the ratio. Many Bushmen lived at /ai/ai for nine months in the winter and spring and dispersed only for a short period at the height of the fresh food season in late summer and early fall.

Two essential factors enabled the Bushmen to achieve this happy state of affairs. First their overall subsistence has been assisted by an input of Herero milk, meat, and agricultural produce. Wild vegetable food and game still provide over half of the total subsistence in calories, but these hunting and collecting activities still leave plenty of time free for socializing, resting, and dancing.

Without the Herero food, the /ai/ai aggregation would not be possible (or possible only at the expense of unprecedented subsistence effort by the Bushmen). But an additional element is necessary—namely the legal umbrella provided by the Hereros to maintain order among such a large number of feisty Bushmen.

Arguments are a frequent occurrence at /ai/ai, but whenever a dispute comes to blows or shows other signs of becoming nasty (as it did about once every two weeks during my fieldwork at /ai/ai), someone runs for the Herero. At this point one or more Hereros intervene to separate the combatants and mediate the dispute. Formerly, the Bushmen did their serious fighting with spears and poisoned arrows. The Bushmen have been deterred from doing this since the mid-1950s, when several Bushmen were brought to Maun, the tribal capital, to stand trial for homicides resulting from arrow fights. Thus the Bushmen can maintain an intensity of social life over long periods that would not have been possible under the traditional hunting and gathering conditions. Under the old order real conflict and the threat of conflict tended to work against the Bushmen's desire for a more intense social life. It is the presence of the Hereros as mediators, backed up by the legal sanctions of the Batawana Tribal Authority and, until 1966, by the British Colonial administration, that provides the umbrella that enables 150 Bushmen to live together in relative harmony for the greater part of the year (see Netting, Chapter 9, this volume).

This example illustrates nicely how economic-demographic factors on the one hand and sociological factors on the other dovetail in the analysis of the implications of population growth. If the !Kung Bushmen were more tightly organized, they could have maintained larger aggregations for longer periods. Instead, their relatively brief periods of intense social life were surrounded by much longer periods of relative isolation in small domestic groupings. The evidence of large gatherings being sustained in the face of quite unfavorable food situations demonstrated to me that the Bushmen *could* live in larger groups if they wanted to. Put another way, their mean group size and intensity of land utilization were measurably lower than the levels that could be supported by the resources. The gap between what could be supported and what was observed as being supported can be explained by the Bushmen's avoidance of conflict situations.

A *conflict* explanation should not be considered to be in some way opposed to an *economic* explanation of Bushman social arrangements. In fact, conflict may best be considered as a part of ecological explanation—that is, fear of conflict acts as a spacing mechanism to keep hunters and gatherers widely dispersed and thus to stabilize their population density well below the level that could be supported by available resources.

16

Biological Factors in Population Control

Solomon H. Katz

These last two chapters represent noncultural voices. Katz explains the mechanics of human fertility in the context of their interaction with cultural and ecological factors and argues for a holistic model of demographic change that would include biological, cultural, and ecological factors.

In anthropology the concept of the interaction of subsistence systems and population growth derives mainly from archaeology (Childe 1951) and cultural ecology (Steward 1955). However, if we discuss the relationship between agricultural surplus and population growth without taking the biological system into account, we must realize that this is essentially reducing biology to the level of a dependent variable On the other hand, it is true that for a long time human biologists have tended to play down the sociocultural factors in human adaptation, such as the cultural factors involved in assortative mating and migration. What we need are more holistic models of human ecology if we are to begin to understand the range of factors involved in demographic change. For example, it is clear from data derived from studies of human adaptation to diseases such as malaria and sickle-cell anemia or kuru that there is interplay between man's biology, sociocultural systems, ecology, and demography (see Figure 16.1) and that this interplay is evolutionary in both a biological and a cultural sense. This essay discusses the biological factors in fertility and demonstrates, wherever possible, the significance of these factors for an integrated model of demographic change.

The Demographic Problem

Human fertility can be considered on several biological levels: (1) the genetic level, where we can ask what kinds of genetic adaptations are present in the population that may enhance or inhibit rapid changes in population numbers; (2) the physiological level, where we can ask about (a) long-term adaptations over some significant proportion of the life

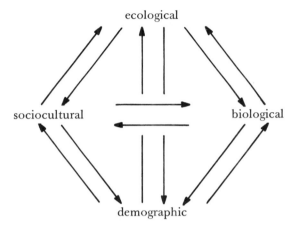

Figure 16.1. Relation between man's biology, sociocultural systems, ecology, and demography.

cycles of individuals, which are essentially irreversible, or (b) short-term acclimatizations, which are for the most part reversible; (3) the behavioral level, which concerns the interplay between the biological changes in fertility and the sociocultural factors that interact with these changes. It is important to keep each of these in mind throughout this discussion.

To cover each of these levels adequately would require a book-length discussion. My aim here is to demonstrate the physiological context of human fertility and discuss the significance of its function, development, and, wherever possible, the relevance of various environmental factors such as nutrition.

At the outset of this discussion it is important to point out some of the conceptual problems that are involved. First, the approach must be inclusive. It has to contain not only all the relevant internal endocrine factors but also the significant external factors such as disease, temperature, light, altitude, nutrition, and possibly others. These data must be meaningfully and logically organized. For example, the growth and development approach in physical anthropology allows for discussion of the time dimension and follows the actual human developmental sequence. The discussion must also be designed in such a way as to incorporate the sociocultural factors that promote and limit fertility at various behavioral and psychological levels. Finally, it is necessary to develop a conceptual definition of fertility that keeps the demographic variables continually in full perspective. One way of accomplishing this task is to discuss the physiology of the reproductive system first and then to indicate how various extrinsic factors, which are of importance to anthropological studies, may influence its function.

Reproductive Biology

The reproductive system is controlled by a complex neuroendocrine mechanism that is sensitive both to internal physiological and psychological factors and to external environmental factors. Each of these factors is important to our understanding of the function of the system. Thus, before going further, it is necessary to consider briefly the current status of our knowledge concerning its mechanism of physiological control. This is represented in Figure 16.2 and the accompanying note.

Puberty, Fertility, and Sexual Maturity

One of the most remarkable human growth and developmental phenomena of the last hundred years is a secular growth trend toward a marked increase in body size and an earlier onset of pubescence, leading to an earlier age of ovulation. Such a trend may be an important factor contributing to the population explosion. It could bring about (1) a decrease in the interval between successive generations; (2) an increase in viable births, since it is well known that there are more genetic defects in children born to older mothers; and (3) an increase in number of births for the mother if her expected life-span is less than the expected age at which fertility declines. However, it should be pointed out that the onset of puberty is not the same as the onset of full sexual maturity. In a study of German women, it has been suggested (Doring 1963) that although menstruation had begun much earlier, a large number of the menstrual cycles in women under twenty were anovulatory, as evidenced by a lack of the rise in the basal body temperature, which characterizes the second half of the menstrual cycle if ovulation has taken place. Although there are other studies of postpubescent sterility in females, it is obvious that further studies should be made on this important topic in order to clarify whether or not the highly significant reduction in the age of menarche

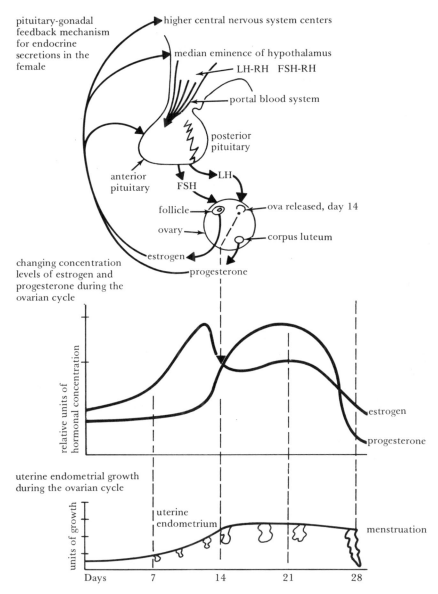

Figure 16.2. Timing and feedback mechanisms of endocrine secretions during the ovarian cycle.

Technical Note for Figure 16.2

The adenohypophysis (the anterior lobe of the pituitary gland) is directly connected to the median eminence region of the hypothalamus (within the brain) via a portal venous blood system. This system is capable of carrying blood and neurally secreted small molecular weight compounds (releasing hormones) to the adenohypophysis, where they control the release of the various anterior pituitary hormones, among which are the gonadotrophins (follicle-stimulating hormone, FSH, and luteinizing hormone, LH). These releasing factors are apparently secreted by the neurons of the median eminence region of the hypothalamus. There is evidence that the pituitary hormones themselves can move back up the portal system and influence the secretion of their respective releasing factors. This is called "short loop" feedback. Upon reaching the bloodstream, these pituitary hormones stimulate the gonads to produce various steroid hormones.

In the female, FSH stimulates the development of an egg-containing follicle in the ovary that slowly secretes increasing amounts of estrogen into circulation. At approximately fourteen days after the beginning of the menses, LH is secreted in large quantities and triggers the rupture of the follicle and the ejection of an egg, which is literally caught by the fimbriae of the fallopian tubes. It is then slowly transported down these tubes toward the uterus in preparation for fertilization. If fertilization does not occur, then the egg is lost along with the lining of the uterus some fourteen days after ovulation at the beginning of the menses.

At the level of the ovary the evacuated follicle forms after ovulation a corpus luteum stage, which for approximately fourteen days secretes a second hormone, progesterone, as well as estrogen. Both estrogen and progesterone feed back upon the adenohypophysis and hypothalamus to control its secretion of FSH and LH. In addition, both of these hormones appear also to influence behavioral functions at higher levels of the limbic system.

In the male, FSH stimulates the seminiferous tubules of the testes to produce growth and maturation of sperm, and LH stimulates the cells of Leydig to produce testosterone. The latter feeds back at pituitary, hypothalamic, and limbic sites—probably much like estrogen and progesterone—to control the secretion of the gonadotrophins and influence male behavior. In addition to effecting a feedback control upon the secretion of the gonadotrophins, these steroid hormones also act upon various tissues of the body to produce a variety of effects. Nearly all secondary sex characteristics in the male and female are produced by these hormones.

over the last several generations is concomitant with a decrease in age at onset of regular ovulatory cycles. If this is confirmed, any significant decline in the age at onset of full fertility in sociocultural contexts where early sexual intercourse is practiced will certainly result in a highly significant change in demographic structure.

In general, the factors that influence the onset of puberty are the same as those that influence fertility. Thus, while it is important to separate conceptually the onset of puberty from the onset of full sexual maturity in the female, it is desirable to avoid redundancy in any discussion of the effects of the same environmental factor once for puberty and another time for the sexually mature reproductive system. It is also quite important for the reader to realize that much of the evidence concerning the effects of environment and other factors on puberty is derived from studies with species other than man.

The gonads, adenohypophysis, and the hypothalamus are all part of a highly regulated system that markedly changes its function at puberty. Before puberty the whole system is functional as indicated by the presence of adenohypophyseal gonadotrophins and their significant but low-level secretion as shown in Figure 16.2. At puberty the gonads of both the male and female continue to secrete small amounts of estrogen and testosterone, and the hypothalamic control system remains highly sensitive to the inhibitory feedback effects of these sex steroids. But there is much evidence to indicate that the hypothalamic neurons sensitive to these hormones somehow lose their sensitivity at puberty. This loss of inhibition then means that the neurons become free to secrete their releasing factors into the hypophyseal blood portal system flowing into the adeno-hypophysis, where they activate a marked increase in the release of FSH and LH and therefore initiate pubertal gonadal activity. The latter results in the higher levels of estrogen and progesterone in the female and testosterone in the male.

While few investigators would challenge the concept of maturational changes in the sensitivity of certain hypothalamic neurons to prepubertal levels of steroid hormones, the significance of the various environmental factors that directly or indirectly influence the hypothalamus (in man) remain to be determined. However, many of these same environmental stimuli have been shown experimentally to be significant in animal studies of puberty.

Genetics

Before beginning any discussion of the environmental factors influencing puberty and fertility, it is first necessary to mention briefly the genetic question. Although there is evidence that there is a higher concordance between age of menarche in identical twins than in fraternal twins (Petri 1935), it is apparent from other studies (Melbin 1962; Tanner 1962) that the environmental component is a very significant factor in the timing of puberty. Of course, the latter statement has to be understood in the context of the concept that the growth and development phenomena leading to puberty are obviously regulated by the interaction of genes and environment.

Nutrition

Perhaps it is appropriate to begin the discussion of environmental factors that influence puberty with an examination of the effects of nutrition on the timing of puberty and upon fertility. Garn and Haskell (1960) have reported that obese children reach puberty earlier than lean children. They reported that this earlier onset of puberty is also accompanied by increases in height and skeletal age.

In rat studies the time of puberty can be significantly delayed under the influence of caloric malnutrition (Asdell and Crowell 1935). Other studies of large litters versus small litters, where presumably the small litters were better nourished, demonstrated significantly earlier puberty in rats from smaller litters (Widdowson and McLance 1960; Kennedy and Mitra 1963). In general, it is thought that the weight factor is extremely important in governing the timing of puberty in all mammals. For example, the data of Hartman (1931) indicate that in female macaques puberty was reached at approximately 3 kg and ability to conceive (full reproductive maturity) at 5 kg.

Data published on Negro girls in New York City indicated that menarche occurred ten months earlier than in southern Negro girls; however, the subjects of the study in New York City were of a higher socioeconomic status than the girls in the South (Michelson 1944). There are many other studies of this nature, indicating that city girls tend to reach menarche sooner than country girls (Ito 1942; Wilson and Sutherland 1953; Tanner 1962; Wolanski 1963). Whether or not this is an effect of better nutrition in the cities or some other factor, of course, remains to be determined.

The effects of nutrition on fertility are profound. Leathem (1958) reported that malnutrition has an adverse effect on reproductive organs of both sexes, and it appears that the effect is at the level of the hypothalamus. In general, protein deficiency, vitamin B deficiency, caloric deficiency, and deficiency of specific minerals, such as iodine, produce hypofunctional gonads. This effect appears to be an adaptation to survival under these conditions, since gonadal function is not necessary for the maintenance of the life of the individual. The mechanism by which malnutrition acts on the hypothalamus is not yet known except for certain cases such as severe iodine deficiency, where the resulting lowered thyroid activity has an adverse effect upon the synthesis of gonadotrophins in the adenohypophysis, this synthesis being essential for pubertal gonadal activity.

Thus it is clear that undernutrition of various kinds would adversely affect both the timing of the onset of puberty and fertility in sexually mature adults. It is interesting to note that this effect and low production of testosterone also has clear behavioral implications, as indicated by Keys (1949) in studies of voluntary human starvation where interest in sexual activity markedly declined as the starvation progressed. How these factors of infertility, delayed onset of puberty, and decreases in sexual behavior interact with the changes in nutrition provided by a shift in subsistence technology is very interesting. We can only speculate that a shift to a stable and possibly balanced nutritional base may eliminate many of the factors that inhibit population growth—factors that may be present when the day-to-day nutritional base is more variable, as it often is in a hunting-gathering subsistence pattern.

Temperature

It is not known if cold temperatures are a significant factor in the timing of puberty or the fertility of human populations, since studies to date indicate no significant differences in menarche in girls exposed to different environmental temperatures (Ellis 1950; Levine 1953). However, the fact that human clothing and dwellings tend to neutralize any cold temperature effect is important, because temperature does appear to have an effect on puberty in animal studies. This is demonstrated by the experiments of Barnett and Coleman (1959), where cold-exposed mice reached puberty later than room-temperature-exposed controls. Thus it is likely that inhibitory effects of cold temperatures upon the onset of puberty or upon fertility may have been mitigated long ago by the technological innovations leading to adequate clothing and dwellings in most human populations. Warm temperatures are also especially important in the sexually mature male. The testes must be approximately

1° C below core body temperature to produce viable sperm. In the human male this temperature is achieved by a rather elaborate anatomic mechanism that allows the testes to ascend and descend in the scrotum according to the activity of ambient scrotal temperature receptors. This mechanism is adequate under most environmental conditions with one notable exception. Restrictive clothing in the region of the scrotum can raise the testicular temperature to the level of core body temperature and significantly reduce sperm production. This means that the same technological innovations leading to protective clothing may also lead, if improperly designed, to a highly significant reduction in male fertility (see Ekvall, Chapter 11, this volume).

Altitude

Carlos Monge (1948) has traced the history of the influence of high Andean altitude upon the early Spanish settlers and upon the native populations. It was some fifty-three years after the establishment of the Spanish-founded city called "The Imperial City of Potosi," at 4,000 meters, that the *first* Spanish child was born. For this reason, and many others related to their problems with altitude adaptation, the capital city was finally moved to coastal Lima. In animal studies, Donayre (1966) reports that in rats subjected to hypoxia (effect of high altitudes), there was a cessation of the normal ovarian cycle marked by sustained estrus. Furthermore, Donayre (ibid.) reports that effects of high altitude reduce sperm counts and increase abnormally formed sperm in the human. On the other hand, it is clear from the studies of Hoff (1968) that fertility of Peruvian highlanders in Nuñoa was well within expected ratios of similar lowland populations.

In studies of adolescence, Baker (1969) and Frisancho and Baker (1970) have reported significant retardation in the timing and magnitude of the pubescent growth spurt in Nuñoa children in comparison with standards from U.S. white children and Peruvian lowlanders. What role altitude plays in setting limits on the reproductive system either in the form of fertility or at some later stage of embryonic or fetal development following conception remains to be determined. It is reasonable to assume that natural selection of certain advantageous genetic traits probably has taken place. What we must also assume is that certain behavioral adjustments such as culturally determined activity levels may be influential in enhancing fertility under these conditions.

Population Density and Psychological Factors

As human populations under urban conditions reach unprecedented numbers, the question arises as to whether or not the actual density of humans in a given area has an effect upon fertility or onset of puberty. In studies of crowding in mice, Christian and Davis (1964) have reported retardation of puberty and decreases in fertility (see also Coon 1961: 427–464). It is thought that the mechanism for this overcrowding effect is one of stress that increases adenohypophyseal ACTH secretion which in turn stimulates adrenal steroid output. This adrenal androgenic steroid fraction then adds to the sex steroids already in circulation to inhibit further FSH and LH secretion.

Rakoff (1963) has assembled evidence for this stress effect in human populations from studies of concentration camp and bombing victims where stress and fear were so excessive that a variety of menstrual disorders existed, all of which had the effect of lowering or eliminating fertility. In some forms of severe psychic disturbance in prepubescent children, there are also similar reports of a functional hypopituitarism that leads to a stunted growth pattern and delay of puberty. It is unquestionable that a variety of psychogenic stimuli have a profound effect upon hypothalamic and hence gonadal functions. What needs to be done is to document further the sources of this stress and determine how it interacts directly and indirectly with the demography, culture, and ecology of the population (see Stott 1962). We are at a point in anthropological investigations where we can evaluate carefully those social and cultural conditions that lead to an increase in stress for the individuals of a population. For example, what are the relationships between fertility and stress during the early stages of a revitalization movement? Do population numbers decline, and is there a catch-up phenomenon in terms of fertility if there is a successful outcome to the movement?

Another source of variation in crowding studies arises from olfactory stimuli. Marsden and Bronson (1964) demonstrated that the odor of female urine produced a cessation of estrus cycling in grouped female rats and that the mere presence of the odor (pheromones) of male urine reversed the inhibition on estrus cycling in the females. In humans, the "boarding-house amenorrhea" occasionally reported for all-girl boarding schools may be due to this kind of phenomenon. Additionally, we should take into account the significance of the use of certain odoriferous substances such as perfumes and deodorants that are used extensively under crowded conditions. Such technological inventions may have significance beyond their pleasant odor and may serve to mask certain human odors that may enhance or inhibit fertility and sexual behavior under urban conditions of high population density.

Pregnancy, Implantation, and Lactation

If conception occurs, then the fertilized ovum is transported down the fallopian tube to the uterus, where the ovum is implanted in the uterine wall. The corpus luteum left in the ovary continues to secrete progesterone under the presumed influence of the adenohypophyseal secretion of LH and possibly luteotrophic hormone (LTH) or prolactin. (Evidence for the function of this hormone in the ovarian cycle comes at present entirely from animal studies.) Following its implantation the trophoblast secretes human chorionic gonadotropin (HCG), which acts on the corpus luteum to maintain its production of progesterone and estrogen. Later in development the placenta forms its own steroid hormones, but initially the corpus luteum apparently is necessary for its maintenance. The high levels of estrogen and pregnanediol found in the urine of human females account for the continued inhibition of gonadotrophin secretion and together with prolactin aid in the development of the breast tissues. Following birth and loss of the placenta there is a rapid decline in circulating steroid hormones, but ovulation does not immediately return. Instead, the adenohypophysis continues to secrete LTH as long as impulses arising out of stimulation of the nipples during nursing continues. There is evidence first, that, unlike the other adenohypophyseal gonadotrophic hormones, prolactin has an inhibiting factor that controls its secretion. Second, it appears that there is a reciprocal relationship between the secretion of prolactin and LH. When LTH is secreted, LH is inhibited, and vice versa. Although it is not yet clear, it is possible that the releasing hormone for LH inhibits the secretion of LTH or stimulates the production of a separate prolactin inhibiting factor. Bruce (1961) has reported that among rats the suckling-stimulated inhibition of the gonadotrophins has two variables, the duration and the amount of nursing. He has found that mothers of large litters begin approximately one week later than ones with small litters and furthermore that the inhibition on fertility can be maintained by replacing the older litter with a younger one. Ford (1945) has listed a host of cross-cultural data that are important to the significance of this nursing inhibition of pregnancy. It is altogether possible that many interesting and significant demographic variables can be explained by shifts from breast nursing to bottle feeding and by other nursing practices such as wet nursing. Again we have an important biological factor interacting with the sociocultural system and its technology to produce demographic change.

Sociocultural Factors and Birth Control

Rather than discuss the myriad different cultural practices for the regulation of reproduction, it appears more valuable in this context to point out the various possibilities for the inhibition of increases in population at various stages (see Table 16.1) of the reproductive cycle.

Although clearly beyond the scope of this paper, questions concerning the effects of rapid increases in population size upon sociocultural organization and individual behavior are highly significant. This is particularly important in the present context because it leads us into archaeological questions concerning how various cultures have adjusted technologically to problems of population growth in the past (see Chapters 1–2 of this volume.) Among many variables that are important to the broader understanding of this problem, we consider only agricultural intensification. Data from the archaeological time perspective may also provide considerable insight into the kinds of adaptations necessary to the population explosion now proceeding in many large human populations.

Pathology and Disease

As Malthus originally pointed out, besides war and famine, disease has been a major check to human population growth. Many investigators (not including Boserup) attribute the world population explosion exclusively to the significant improvement in medicine. They reason that the

Table 16.1 Biology and Technology of Birth Control

A. Inhibition of sperm and ova production and transport

1. Temperature increase up to body temperature in male, which inhibits sperm production

2. Pharmacologic contraceptives mostly in females (synthetic estrogen and progesterone) preventing ovulation; few chemicals used in the male

3. Sterilization—in the male, vasectomy; in the female, removal of ovaries or tying fallopian tubes

4. Pregnancy and lactation (see earlier discussion)

B. Inhibition of fertilization

1. Mechanical methods—diaphragm (caps cervix of female); condom (sheath covering male penis)

2. Chemical—spermicides used by female

3. Abstinence

4. Coitus interruptus

5. Rhythm method—depends on abstinence at fertile period around time of ovulation

6. Immunological—possible use of antibodies against sperm following suitable immunization of the female

7. Anatomic—urethral fistula at the base of the penis

C. Inhibition of implantation of fertilized ovum

1. Mechanical intrauterine device (loop, ring, coil)

2. Pharmacologic—some contraceptives may also inhibit implantation if ovulation and fertilization do take place

3. Combinations of 1 and 2 (loop impregnated with pharmacologic agent and/or copper)

D. Embryonic or fetal interruption: abortion—surgically or pharmacologically induced (for example, prostaglandins)

E. Neonatal: infanticide

F. Puberty: possibility of delayed onset leading to delay in full sexual maturity

---

highly significant increase in longevity and consequent decrease in mortality lead to a total upset of earlier demographic equilibrium in many areas of the world. It is unquestionable that twentieth-century medicine, largely by means of antibiotics, vaccines, modern hospital technology, and parasite eradication programs (for example, malaria) have saved countless lives. However, examination of any graph of world population growth over the last thousand years obviously indicates that the exponential trend of population growth started well before modern developments in medicine. What did prevent disease from spreading, according to Cockburn (1967), was the development of sanitation systems (along with the recognition of the germ theory of disease)—in other words, a medically related technological development. Even when the plague struck in the Middle Ages, all indications are that there was a rapid recovery of population size, followed by a continuation of the exponential population growth rate (see Figure 6.2). This suggests that factors other than the modern concept of medicine led to this exponential trend of increasing population in the last thousand years. The population explosion of the twentieth century is the product of a variety of forces, among which are changes in fertility, decreases in mortality from infectious and noninfectious disease, improvements in nutrition, and significant changes in technology and social organization throughout the world probably influencing all of the aforementioned factors. Again, what we need is a comprehensive, multifaceted model that would enable us to examine the variables and their interrelationships (see Figure 16.1) in order to come closer to an understanding of the extreme changes in demographic structure over the last century.

A more specific discussion of the effects of pathology and disease upon the reproductive system is somewhat beyond the scope of this chapter. However, it is noteworthy that much of the evidence with regard to the neuroendocrinology of gonadotrophin control in man comes from various studies of lesions and particularly tumors in and around the region of the hypothalamus. Another important factor is the mode by which various diseases interact with the reproductive cycle. Infectious disease organisms can act upon the reproductive system itself (venereal diseases such as syphilis, gonorrhea, and cancer of the cervix) or upon the developing fetus as in the case of some of the aforementioned diseases and many other infectious and other pathological conditions, while other diseases strike as a result of some interaction with an infectious organism directly after birth. What is important again is the concept that we tie in the ecology of disease and pathological conditions with the demographic and sociocultural factors that interact with it over the full reproductive cycle.

Light-Dark Cycles

One of the most interesting and profound effects of the environment upon the reproductive cycle of a number of species involves responses to the various levels of illumination. In the nocturnal rat continuous light stimulates an earlier onset of puberty (Jöchle 1956). In the human being, blind girls who did not perceive light reached menarche earlier than girls with sight (Zacharias and Wurtman 1964). In sheep the breeding season starts earlier if the amount of light usually available in the spring decreases (Yeates 1949).

In an excellent review Wurtman, Axelrod, and Kelly (1968) suggest strongly that the effects of light upon the reproductive system are mediated through the pineal gland, an endocrine organ in the brain. The evidence so far indicates that the light receptor is associated with the retina of the eye. The neural pathway to the pineal gland follows a most unusual route. It courses from the eye into the preoptic region of the brain and passes down brain medulla and out the upper thoracic spinal cord to the superior cervical ganglian and from there as a postganglionic fiber back up into the brain to enervate the pineal gland.

Within the pineal gland, serotonin, a well-known brain amine, is synthesized and through the action of two enzymes becomes converted to melatonin. Melatonin has been demonstrated to inhibit ovulation in the same rats where the removal of the pineal gland accelerated the estrus cycle. Moreover, the pineal gland of the rat decreases its weight under the influence of continuous light. Further investigations of the enzymes responsible for converting serotonin to melatonin have indicated that the activity of one of the enzymes, HIOMT (hydroxyindole-O-methyl transferase), apparently is sensitive to the effects of light. In the rat the effect of continuous light depresses the activity of this enzyme, and darkness or blinding increases its activity. What this means is that when light is present and the enzyme is not active, melatonin is produced in small quantities, and its inhibitory effects upon the reproductive cycle are minimal. Decreasing the light raises HIOMT activity, increasing the synthesis of melatonin, which inhibits the ovarian cycle. Serotonin content of the pineal gland is also sensitive to light, but in a different manner from the HIOMT activity. In continuous darkness serotonin content in the rat continues to cycle, whereas in continuous light serotonin content increases.

Of course, the question here is whether or not such light-dark rhythms are of significance in human populations and, if they are, whether the development of artificial electric lighting over the last seventy years has had any effects upon natural light-dark cycles controlling fertility. To examine this hypothesis, approximately 2,000 north slope Alaskan Eskimo birth dates were plotted as a function of seasonal changes in light-dark cycles (see Figure 16.3). Study of this population gave us the opportunity to observe the maximum effects of light-dark cycles in human populations.

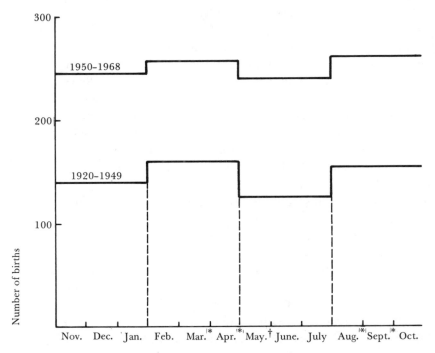

Figure 16.3. Seasonal changes in light and birth cycle of the north slope Eskimo
*Peak months   †Lowest month.

Although the results are preliminary, the data from 1920 to 1949 appear to indicate a significant biphasic curve of birthrate where conception (nine months previous) took place at either the maximum period of darkness or maximum light. At this time it is difficult to interpret fully the significance of such differences in terms of possible changes in human pineal activity or of some social factor that may have contributed to such a cyclical effect. However, it is clear that with the rapid change in technology marked by the introduction of electric lighting, closed-circuit television, and other devices interrupting the light-dark cycle in the fifties and sixties on the north slope, the biphasic birth cycle has practically disappeared.

Discussion and Conclusions

Although much of the discussion in this paper has focused on the interaction of biological and environmental factors that contribute to fertility, it is important to emphasize again that its implications do not stop at this level. Referring back to Figure 16.1, we see that the biological factors interact also with the sociocultural system and thus involve behavioral and psychological factors. Furthermore, through technology and material reorganization of the environment, the cultural system does interact with a variety of biological variables. Thus we should conceive of the possibility that these kinds of models may be operating under a variety of conditions and that the inclusion of the biological dimension may aid us substantially in the explanation of many phenomena at the demographic level.

I think at this juncture it is valid to ask: Just how significant are these biological factors? If the physiology connected with fertility is rather insensitive to the environmental inputs, then we could conceivably reduce the significance of the biological component to a constant factor that could be dealt with at a simple level. If, on the other hand, there are a number of environmental factors that enhance or inhibit fertility, as this paper already demonstrates, then we must integrate them into our conceptualizations of the demographic effects of technological change. For example, a shift in technology leading to agriculture often appears to yield increased nutrition for members of a group and helps to stabilize the possibility for continued increases in food production. This means more than just an increase in the number of people that can be fed, because the increased nutrition may influence fertility in such a way as to upset a vital balance that previously existed. Once the fertility and population growth begin to increase counter to social expectations, then a variety of social factors may need modification or redefinition in order to inhibit population growth further or to incorporate its growth into its value systems.

When we examine the environmental factors that influence the physiology of fertility, it is evident that there are others besides nutrition. How we integrate these factors in our discussion of technological change and shifts to agricultural subsistence patterns is also important. We could attempt to demonstrate that nutrition does not always account for demographic change. For example, a shift in technology over the last hundred years toward the use of artificial electric lighting fixtures might have led to the large-scale changes toward earlier menarche that are known to have occurred in many technologically advanced countries. On a biological level such changes may be quite independent from the effects of the changes in nutrition produced by an agricultural technology.

Another way of handling these fertility-influencing environmental factors is to determine what role certain environmental conditions play in facilitating or inhibiting population growth where agriculture is not practiced. In other words, is it possible to add to our explanation of how some populations have not grown by examining some environmental factor which inhibits fertility? In this context, it is interesting to note that, at least from a superficial point of view, many of the environmental factors that are known to inhibit fertility biologically appear to be absent in the so-called cradles of civilization where agricultural technology developed. This could lead us to ask if the ecological conditions that facilitated the development of agriculture also facilitated, or at least did not inhibit, possible increases in fertility. Conversely, we can ask, for example, if high altitude low in oxygen and/or volcanic soils devoid of iodine, such as in the Andes, and possibly other important minerals necessary for fertility, are additional factors that limit population growth. Thus the kinds of subsistence patterns that will be successful under the kinds of ecological conditions that limit fertility (and other biological functions) are quite different from those which result from a combination of increasing population pressure and the environmental conditions necessary to support agricultural intensification.

We must also account for the possibility of other kinds of variation that may influence the interaction of ecology with the biology of fertility. It is possible that the same technological change in two different populations will produce entirely different effects upon fertility as a result of either a genetic or an ecological difference. For example, if a shift toward artificial lighting was made in an equatorial population and in an Arctic population, the effects upon fertility might be greater in the Arctic population since the artificial light would provide an important source of illumination during the long Arctic winter darkness.

In summary, I have attempted to assemble evidence demonstrating that the biology of fertility and the reproductive cycle in general is indeed sensitive to ecological variables. Inasmuch as this evidence is valid, we must begin to integrate it with our concepts of how culture and ecology interact. In fact, this essay strongly supports the concept that we add the human biological dimension to our basic anthropological models of human ecology. In addition, the biological and hence demographic consequences of certain environmental factors that either preexist or are changed as a result of technological innovation have been presented.

As a general conclusion, it is important to realize that the interactions of the ecological, sociocultural, biological, and demographic variables are complex. This suggests that simplified explanations of technological change leading to changes in demographic parameters, or vice versa, are at best only partially valid. What we must do is develop holistic models capable of handling a multifactorial approach if we are ever to understand and explain explosive increases in human population and the evolution of subsistence technology in a comprehensive manner.

17

The Viewpoint of Historical Demography[1]

John D. Durand

This concluding chapter is a brief note to provide a demographic frame of reference for some of the earlier archaeological discussions. The presence of a professional demographer was of immense value to the colloquium, for few if any of the anthropological participants appreciated the actual demographic mechanics of population growth. It is worth noting, for instance, as Carneiro interjected at one point in the discussion, that if we start with a basal population of 100, a net annual rate of increase of 0.5 percent would at the end of 1,000 years yield a population of 14,800. However, if that average annual rate of increase were raised another 0.1 percent, which is only one extra person per decade, then the total population after 1,000 years is not 14,800 but 39,820 (see Carneiro and Hilse 1966). Thus, even a very small increase in the rate makes a very great incremental difference over a long period of time. Similarly, if women in one population have a certain number of children at the average of twenty, while women in a second population have the same number of children at the average age of thirty, then the rate of growth of the first population is 50 percent greater than that of the second.

A more significant point in our context lies, perhaps, in the logistical and psychological factors involved in the practice of infanticide. When Dumond's model (Chapter 12, this volume) was discussed, Boserup formulated the distinction between the "environmental limit" and the "family limit" to population growth.

A population reaches the environmental limit when the area is full up, in the sense that it is impossible for a larger population to produce more food in that area, so that the size of population must somehow be adapted to that limit. Malthus thought that popula-

tion would usually reach that limit, but in fact it is
very flexible, because increasing populations change
from food collection to agriculture, or otherwise
intensify their agricultural systems. Therefore, we
rarely see this limit being reached.

The family limit to population growth is related,
not to the total amount of food which can be produced
in an area if the labor force is large enough to permit
maximum intensity of land use, but to the amount of
food which can be produced per person. The family
limit is reached when output per man hour in food
production is so low that parents are unable to feed
more than a couple of children, even if they are working at maximum effort.

There are, of course, such cases, but we have many
more cases where family size is small although the
parents could easily feed more children. For example,
we have the situation described by Lee (Chapter 14,
this volume) where mothers can carry only a certain
number of children, but if they could carry more, they
could feed them. We have other cases where parents
do not want to work so hard as they would have to if
they were to have more children. I believe we might
find infanticide in communities where it would be
possible for the parents to feed more children, but
they just consider two children enough for them. In
our culture, there is a strong moral commandment
that mothers have to love their babies, and so we are
inclined to think that mothers would kill their newborn babies only if they really could not feed them.

Katz supported this by referring to the vast behavioral changes that follow directly on childbirth
in women because of the rapid change in hormonal
levels at that point. The capability of abnormal behavior right at that point is very high. Finally, Lee contributed the observation that among the Bushmen the
childbirth bed is very confidential. "The women go

off to the bush, and may be alone there with one or two other women. The men are not involved. So if the woman comes back and says the child was born dead, the men often say they do not believe it. But the women play their cards very close to their chests, and very few cases of infanticide are attested."

Dumond may want to classify such cases where the family limit is operating as examples of his "tendency to overpopulate" (Chapter 12, this volume). But there are many cases of low or negative rates of population growth in communities where parents would have no difficulty in feeding more children and are not deliberately limiting their numbers. In such cases an increase of productivity would not raise the rate of growth. This, obviously, is Ekvall's case (see Chapter 11, this volume) which is indeed interesting as an example of people who would like to have more children but nevertheless have a low birthrate for some special reason. Similarly, there are other cases where the population is stagnating owing to a high rate of mortality that has nothing to do with the availability of food. These are all important aspects of our problem, for which we need guidance by demographers.

I wish briefly to provide a demographic frame of reference for our discussion of the conditions of mortality, fertility, and natural increase that might have been typical of human population in the past and a view of the natural power of multiplication. In this volume less attention has been paid to mortality than to fertility, but the levels of mortality and their variations are of course also important terms in the demographic equations. In fact, the role of mortality variations may have been more important as a factor in the variations of population growth that have occurred in the world than in the variations of fertility, though I should not wish to suggest that the latter had not been significant.

Regarding the conditions of mortality in the remote past, we have the archaeological evidence. From the distributions of excavated skeletons by estimated age of death, it is possible to obtain rough estimates of rates of mortality in prehistoric and ancient populations. I have collected some of this material and used it for estimating rates of survival between successive age groups in such a way as to try to reduce as far as possible the biases—often serious—to which this kind of material is subject. The results have led me to think that an expectation of life at birth of the order of twenty years may have been fairly favorable for early agricultural societies and that lower levels may not have been unusual. It also appears to me that one can see in these data (though the material is not strong enough to warrant any very definite statements) some suggestion that the typical levels of expectation of life for hunter-gatherers could have been lower than those of early agricultural societies and that the typical levels were somewhat higher for populations like those of medieval Europe.

If such differences are typical and true, they might in themselves be enough to explain the variations in rates of population growth which appear to have been associated with the changes from one form of economy to another in the course of history, and for the general form of the long-range trend of the growth of human population in general, even if there had been no variations in fertility. In a situation in which the expectation of life at birth is twenty years, what level of fertility would be necessary to bring an increase in the population? For approximate answers to such questions, we can refer to demographic models, although they might not be strictly appropriate to the conditions of ancient and prehistoric populations, since they are based on observations of modern times. These models indicate that with a life expectation of twenty years at birth, a total fertility rate of six children would probably be required to keep the population stationary. Among the extraordinarily fertile Hutterites a total fertility rate of something in excess of eight has been observed, but the Hutterites are a very healthy population, and they have the benefit of modern medical health protection that was not available to human societies in the past. So far as one can judge from the available information about rates of sterility and of loss of reproductive power through subfecundity and fetal mortality in nonindustrial populations observed in recent times, it would appear that few of them would approximate this level of eight, that a total fertility rate of six would be quite good, and that the biologically achievable total fertility rate in many nonindustrial populations may fall considerably lower, even as low as four. So with the life expectation at birth of twenty years, a pretty vigorous fertility is needed to maintain the population. A total fertility rate of seven (which is very good indeed—very few populations observed in modern times have reached this level) would be enough, with an expectation of life of twenty years, to provide a natural increase at the modest rate of about three and a half per thousand per year. Of course, such a rate could be reached with lower fertility by increasing the expectation of life at birth. It might be that with a life expectancy of twenty-five years, a total fertility rate of six would be sufficient to bring a modest natural increase.

The implication is that it is not necessary to suppose as a general rule in human societies of the past that, if population failed to make a large growth over long periods of time, this was due necessarily to the imposition of severe restrictions on reproductive power—whether by infanticide, abortion, or other means of control. One can envisage that population might often have failed to make natural growth even with minimal restriction on procreation, in view of the conditions of mortality. On the other hand, when and where an expansion of population took place, we do not necessarily have to view it as a result of the relaxation of controls on fertility. In many cases, and perhaps in most cases, improved conditions of mortality may have been the main cause of demographic expansion.

Note

1. Since this chapter was written, an excellent study along similar lines has appeared by Acsádi and Nemeskéri (1970).

Bibliography

Aberle, D. F.
1966   *The peyote religion among the Navaho.* Viking Fund Publications in Anthropology 42. Chicago: Aldine Publishing Company.

Ackerman, R. E.
1961   *Archaeological investigations into the prehistory of St Lawrence Island, Alaska.* Ann Arbor: University Microfilms no. 61–3450.

Acsádi, Gy., and Nemeskéri, J.
1970   *History of human life span and mortality.* Budapest: Akadémiai Kiadó [Publishing House of the Hungarian Academy of Sciences].

Adams, Richard E. W.
1965   "The ceramic chronology of the southern Maya: First preliminary report." Manuscript.

Adams, Robert McC.
1960   "Early civilizations, subsistence and environment." In *City invincible, a symposium on urbanization and cultural development in the ancient Near East,* C. H. Kraeling and R. M. Adams, eds., pp. 269–295. Chicago: University of Chicago Press.

1961   "Changing patterns of territorial organization in the central highlands of Chiapas, Mexico." *American Antiquity* 26(3):341–360.

1962   "Agriculture and urban life in early southwestern Iran." *Science* 136 (3511):109–122.

1964   "The origins of agriculture." In *Horizons of anthropology,* Sol Tax, ed., pp. 120–131. Chicago: Aldine Publishing Company.

1965   *Land behind Baghdad.* Chicago: University of Chicago Press.

1966   *The evolution of urban society: Early Mesopotamia and Pre-hispanic Mexico.* Chicago: Aldine Publishing Company.

1969   "The study of ancient settlement patterns and the problem of urban origins." *Sumer* 25:111–124 [1970].

forthcoming   "Patterns of urbanization in early southern Mesopotamia." In *Settlement patterns and urbanization.* P. J. Ucko, ed. London:Gerald Duckworth.

Adams, Robert, and Nissen, H. J.
forthcoming   *The Uruk countryside.* Chicago: University of Chicago Press.

Allan, W.
1965   *The African husbandman.* New York: Barnes and Noble.

Allchin, B and R.
1968   *The birth of Indian civilization*. Baltimore: Penguin.

Anderson, E.
1967   *Plants, man and life*. Berkeley: University of California Press [1952].

Andrews, E. Wyllys
1965   "Archaeology and prehistory in the northern Maya lowlands."
In *Handbook of Middle American Indians*, vol. 2, part 1, pp. 288–330. Austin:
University of Texas Press.

Andrews, J. M.
1935   *Siam, 2nd rural economic survey* 1934–35. Bangkok: W. H. Mundie,
Bangkok Times Press.

Appelbaum, S.
1958   "Agriculture in Roman Britain." *Agricultural History Review* 6:66–86.

Arkell, A., and Ucko, P.
1965   "Review of predynastic development in the Nile valley." *Current
Anthropology* 6:145–166.

Asdell, S. A., and Crowell, M. F.
1935   "The effect of retarded growth upon the sexual development of
rats." *Journal of Nutrition* 10:13–24.

Bacon, E. E.
1958   *Obok*. Viking Fund Publications in Anthropology 25. New York:
Wenner-Gren Foundation for Anthropological Research.

Badawy, A.
1967   "The civic sense of pharaoh and urban development in ancient
Egypt." *Journal of the American Research Centre in Egypt* 6:103–109.

Baer, K.
1962   "The low price of land in ancient Egypt." *Journal of the American
Research Centre in Egypt* 1:25–45.

———
1963   "An eleventh dynasty farmer's letters to his family." *Journal of the
American Oriental Society* 83:1–19.

Baker, P.
1969   "Human adaptation to high altitude." *Science* 163:1149–1156.

Bandi, Hans-Georg
1969   *Eskimo prehistory*, A. Keep, trans. Studies of Northern Peoples 2.
College: University of Alaska Press.

Barker, P. A.
1969   "Hen Domen, Montgomery, Montgomeryshire." *Calendar of
excavations: Summaries* 1969, p. 17. London: Council for British
Archaeology.

Barnett, H. G.
1953   *Innovation: The basis of cultural change.* New York: McGraw-Hill Book Company.

Barnett, S. A., and Coleman, E. M.
1959   "The effect of low environmental temperature on the reproductive cycle of female mice." *Journal of Endocrinology* 19:232–240.

Barrau, Jacques
1958   *Subsistence agriculture in Melanesia.* Bernice P. Bishop Museum Bulletin 219.

Barth, F.
1960   "Nomadism in the mountain and plateau areas of southwest Asia." In *The problems of the arid zone,* pp. 341–355. New York: UNESCO.

———

1961   *Nomads of south Persia: The Basseri tribe of the Khamseh confederacy.* Oslo: University Press.

———

1967   "On the study of social change." *American Anthropologist* 69:661–669.

Bartlett, H. H.
1961   "The possible separate origins of the Ladang and Sawah types of tropical agriculture." In *Fire in relation to primitive agriculture and grazing in the tropics: An annotated bibliography,* H. H. Bartlett, ed., 3:55–59.

Beardsley, R. K.; Hall, J. W.; and Ward, R. E.
1959   *Village Japan.* Chicago: University of Chicago Press.

Beloch, K. J.
1899   "Die Bevölkerung Galliens zur Zeit Caesars." *Rheinisches Museum* 54:414–438.

Bender, D. R.
1969   "Population and the agricultural productivity of bush fallow systems in tropical forest habitats." A modified version of a paper presented at the 68th Annual Meeting of the American Anthropological Association, New Orleans.

Benet, F.
1960   "A study leading to action programmes for the modernization of peasant life and animal husbandry in the Zagros." Tehran: mimeographed.

Bernal, Ignacio
1965   "Archaeological synthesis of Oaxaca." In *Handbook of Middle American Indians,* vol. 3, part 2, pp. 788–813. Austin: University of Texas Press.

Biebuyck, D., ed.
1963   *African agrarian systems.* London: Oxford University Press for International African Institute.

Bietak, M.
1966   "Ausgrabungen in Sayala-Nubien 1961–1965; Denkmäler der C-Gruppe und der Pan-Gräber-Kultur." *Österreichische Akademie der Wissenschaften, philosophisch-historische Klasse Denkschriften,* vol. 92.

Binford, L. R.
1968   "Post-Pleistocene adaptations." In *New perspectives in archeology,* S. R. Binford and L. R. Binford, eds., pp. 313–341. Chicago: Aldine Publishing Company.

Birdsell, J. B .
1957   "Some population problems involving Pleistocene Man." *Population studies: animal ecology and demography.* Cold Spring Harbor Symposia in Quantitative Biology, 22:47–69.

1968   "Some predictions for the Pleistocene based on equilibrium systems among recent hunter-gatherers." In *Man the hunter,* R. B. Lee and I. DeVore, eds., pp. 229–240. Chicago: Aldine Publishing Company.

Blitz, R. C.
1967   Review of *The conditions of agricultural growth,* by Ester Boserup. *Journal of Political Economy* 75:212–213.

Bloch, M.
1966   *French rural history: An essay on its basic characteristics.* Berkeley: University of California Press [translation of 1931 original edition in French.]

Bohannan, Laura
1958   "Political aspects of Tiv social organization." In *Tribes without rulers.* John Middleton and David Tait, eds. London: Routledge and Kegan Paul.

Bohannan, Laura and Paul
1953   *The Tiv of central Nigeria.* London: International African Institute.

Bohannan, Paul
1954   "The migration and expansion of the Tiv." *Africa* 24:2–16.

1955   "A Tiv political and religious idea." *Southwestern Journal of Anthropology* 11:137–149.

1958   "Extra-processual events in Tiv political institutions." *American Anthropologist* 60:1–12.

Bohannan, Paul and Laura
1968   *Tiv economy.* Evanston, Ill.: Northwestern University Press.

Bonte, M., and van Balen, H.
1969   "Prolonged lactation and family spacing in Rwanda." *Journal of Biosocial Science* 1:97–100.

Borhegyi, Stephen
1965   "Archaeological synthesis of the Guatemalan highlands." In *Handbook of Middle American Indians*, vol. 2, part 1, pp. 3–58. Austin: University of Texas Press.

Boserup, Ester
1965   *The conditions of agricultural growth: The economics of agrarian change under population pressure*. Chicago: Aldine Publishing Company.

———
1970a   "Present and potential food production in developing countries." In *Geography and a crowding world: A symposium of population pressures upon physical and social resources in the developing lands*, Wilbur Zelinsky, Leszek A. Kosinski, and R. Mansell Prothero, eds., pp. 100–113. London: Oxford University Press.

———
1970b   *Woman's role in economic development*. New York: St. Martin's Press.

———
1970c   "Population growth and food supplies." In *Population control*, Anthony Allison, ed., pp. 152–164. Baltimore: Penguin Books.

Boston, J.
1962   "Notes on the origin of Igala kingship." *Journal of the Historical Society of Nigeria* 2:373–383.

Braidwood, R. J.
1952   *The Near East and the foundations for civilization: An essay in appraisal of the general evidence*. Condon Lectures. Eugene, Oregon: Oregon State System of Higher Education.

———
1967   *Prehistoric men*, 7th ed. Glenview, Ill.: Scott, Foresman and Company.

Braidwood, R. J.; Braidwood, Linda; Smith, James G.; Leslie, Charles
1952   "Matarrah. A southern variant of the Hassunan assemblage, excavated in 1948." *Journal of Near Eastern Studies* 11(1):2–75.

Braidwood, R. J., and Howe, B.
1960   *Prehistoric investigations in Iraqi Kurdistan*. Oriental Institute Studies in Ancient Oriental Civilization 31. Chicago: The Oriental Institute.

Braidwood, R. J.; Howe, B.; and Reed, C. A.
1961   "The Iranian prehistoric project." *Science* 133:2008–2010.

Braidwood, R. J., and Reed, C. A.
1957   "The achievement and early consequences of food-production: a consideration of the archaeological and natural-historical evidence." *Population studies: animal ecology and demography*. Cold Spring Harbor Symposia in Quantitative Biology, 22:19–31.

Braidwood, R. J., and Willey, G. R., eds.
1962   *Courses toward urban life: Archaeological considerations of some cultural alternatives*. Viking Fund Publications in Anthropology 32. Chicago: Aldine Publishing Company.

Brand, D. D.
1951   *Quiroga, a Mexican municipality*. Institute of Social Anthropology, Publ. 11. Washington, D. C.: Smithsonian Institution.

Bratanić, B.
1952   "On the antiquity of the one-sided plough in Europe, especially among the Slavic peoples." *Laos* 2:51–61.

Breasted, James H.
1906   *Ancient records of Egypt: Historical documents from the earliest times to the Persian conquest, collected, edited and translated with commentary*. Chicago: University of Chicago Press.

Bronson, Bennett
1966   "Roots and the subsistence of the ancient Maya." *Southwestern Journal of Anthropology* 22:251–279.

Bronte-Stewart, B.; Budtz-Olsen, O. E.; Hinckley, J. M.; and Brock, J. F.
1960   "The health and nutritional status of the Kung Bushmen of south west Africa." *South African Journal of Laboratory and Clinical Medicine* 6(4): 187–216.

Brookfield, H. C., and Brown, P.
1963   *Struggle for land: Agriculture and group territories among the Chimbu of the New Guinea highlands*. Melbourne: Oxford University Press.

Brookfield, H. C., and White, J. P.
1968   "Revolution or evolution in the prehistory of the New Guinea highlands." *Ethnology* 5:43–52.

Brothwell, D. R.
1963   *Digging up bones*. London: British Museum.

Brown, Paula
1951   "Patterns of authority in west Africa." *Africa* 21:261–277.

Bruce, H. M.
1961   "Observations on the suckling stimulus and lactation in the rat." *Journal of Reproduction and Fertility* 4:313–318.

Brunton, G.
1927   *Qau and Badari I, II*. London: British School of Archaeology in Egypt.

—————

1930   *Qau and Badari III*. London: British School of Archaeology in Egypt.

1937   *Mostagedda*. London: Bernard Quaritch.

1948   *Matmar*. London: Bernard Quaritch.

Brunton, G., and Caton-Thompson, G.
1928   *The Badarian civilisation and predynastic remains rear Badari*. London: British School of Archaeology in Egypt.

Buck, J. L.
1937   *Land utilization in China*. Chicago: University of Chicago Press.

Bullard, William R., Jr.
1960   "Maya settlement pattern in northeastern Petén, Guatemala." *American Antiquity* 25(3):355–372.

Buringh, P.
1957   "Living conditions in the lower Mesopotamian plain in ancient times." *Sumer* 13(1–2):30–46.

Butzer, K. W.
1959   *Die Naturlandschaft Ägyptens während der Vorgeschichte und der dynastischen Zeit*. Akademie der Wissenschaften und der Literatur in Mainz, Abhandlungen der mathematisch-naturwissenschaftlichen Klasse nr. 2.

1960   "Remarks on the geography of settlement in the Nile Valley during Hellenistic times." *Bulletin de la société de géographie d'Egypte* 23:5–36.

1961   "Archäologische Fundstellen Ober-und Mittelägyptens in ihrer geologischen Landschaft." *Mitteilungen des deutchen archäologischen Instituts, Abteilung Kairo* 17:54–68.

1964   *Environment and archaeology: An introduction to Pleistocene geography*. Chicago: Aldine Publishing Company.

1966   "Archaeology and geology in ancient Egypt." In *New roads to yesterday*, Joseph R. Caldwell, ed., pp. 210–227. New York: Basic Books.

1970   "Physical conditions in eastern Europe, western Asia, and Egypt before the period of agricultural and urban settlement." *Cambridge Ancient History*, 3rd ed., vol. I, part 1, chap. 2. Cambridge: Cambridge University Press [1965].

Carneiro, Robert L.
1958   "Agriculture and the beginning of civilization." *Ethnographisch-archäologische Forschungen* 4(1–2):22–27.

———
1960   "Slash-and-burn agriculture: A closer look at its implications for settlement patterns." In *Men and cultures*, A. F. C. Wallace, ed., pp. 229–234. Philadelphia: Selected Papers of the 5th International Congress of Anthropological and Ethnological Sciences, 1956.

———
1961   "Slash-and-burn cultivation among the Kuikuru and its implications for cultural development in the Amazon Basin." Reprinted in *Man in adaptation: The cultural present*, Yehudi A. Cohen, ed., pp. 131–145. Chicago: Aldine Publishing Company, 1968.

———
1967   "On the relationship between size of population and complexity of social organization." *Southwestern Journal of Anthropology* 23(3):234–243.

———
1970   "A theory of the origin of the state." *Science* 169:733–738.

Carneiro, Robert L., and Hilse, Daisy F.
1966   "On determining the probable rate of population growth during the Neolithic." *American Anthropologist* 68:177–181.

Carr-Saunders, Sir A. M.
1922   *The population problem: A study in human evolution.* Oxford: Clarendon Press.

Chagnon, Napoleon A.
1970   "The culture-ecology of shifting (pioneering) cultivation among the Yanomamö Indians." *Proceedings, 8th International Congress of Anthropological and Ethnological Sciences*, 1968, Tokyo and Kyoto. vol. 3, Ethnology and archaeology, pp. 249–255.

Chapple, E. D., and Coon, C. S.
1942   *Principles of anthropology.* New York: Henry Holt and Company.

Childe, V. Gordon
1935   "Changing methods and aims in prehistory." [Presidential address.] *Proceedings of the Prehistoric Society* (n.s.) 1:1–15.

———
1936   *Man makes himself.* London: Watts and Company.

———
1937   "A prehistorian's interpretation of diffusion." In *Independence, convergence and borrowing in institutions, thought and art*, pp. 3–21. Harvard Tercentenary Publications. Cambridge, Mass.: Harvard University Press.

———
1942   *What happened in history.* London: Penguin.

———
1950   "The urban revolution." *Town Planning Review* 21:3–17.

1951   *Social evolution*. London: Watts and Company.

1952   *New light on the most ancient East*. New York: Grove Press.

Chisholm, M.
1967   *Rural settlement and land use: An essay in location*. New York: Science Editions, John Wiley and Sons.

Christian, J. J., and Davis, D. E.
1964   "Endocrines, behavior, and population." *Science* 146:1550–1560.

Clark, C.
1963   "Agricultural productivity in relation to population." In *Man and his future*, G. Wolstenholme, ed., pp. 23–35. London and Boston: Little, Brown and Company.

1967   *Population growth and land use*. New York: St. Martin's Press.

Clark, C., and Haswell, M.
1967   *The economics of subsistence agriculture*, 3rd ed. New York: St. Martin's Press.

Clark, D. W.
1966   "Perspectives in the prehistory of Kodiak Island." *American Antiquity* 31:358–371.

Clark, F. E.; Zaumeyer, W. J.; and Presley, J. T.
1957   "Soilborne plant diseases." In *Yearbook of Agriculture* 1957, pp. 327–338. Washington, D.C.: United States Department of Agriculture.

Clark, J. G. D.
1952   *Prehistoric Europe: The economic basis*. New York: The Philosophical Library.

1961   *World prehistory: An outline*. Cambridge: Cambridge University Press.

1967   *The stone age hunters*. New York: McGraw-Hill Book Company.

Clarke, W. C.
1966   "From extensive to intensive shifting cultivation: A succession from New Guinea." *Ethnology* 5(4):347–359.

Clayton, W. D.
1963   "The vegetation of Katsina Province, Nigeria." *Journal of Tropical Ecology* 51(2):345–351.

Cockburn, A.
1967   *Infectious diseases*. Springfield, Ill.: Charles C Thomas Company.

Coe, Michael D., and Flannery, Kent V.
1967   *Early cultures and human ecology in south coastal Guatemala.* Smithsonian Contributions to Anthropology, vol. 3. Washington, D. C.: Smithsonian Institution Press.

Coe, William R.
1967   *Tikal, a handbook of the ancient Maya ruins.* Philadelphia: University Museum, University of Pennsylvania.

Cohen, Yehudi A.
1969   "Ends and means in political control." *American Anthropologist* 71: 658–687.

Collingwood, R. G.
1929   "Town and country in Roman Britain." *Antiquity* 3:261–276.

Collins, B. E., and Guetzkow, H.
1964   *A social psychology of group processes for decision-making.* New York: John Wiley and Sons.

Conklin, Harold C.
1957   *Hanunóo agriculture: A report on an integral system of shifting cultivation in the Philippines.* F.A.O. Forest Development Paper no .12. Rome: Food and Agriculture Organization of the United Nations.

———
1961   "The study of shifting cultivation." *Current Anthropology* 2(1):27–61.

Coon, Carleton S., ed.
1961   "Symposium on crowding, stress, and natural selection." *Proceedings of the National Academy of Sciences,* 47:427–464.

Cowgill, Ursula M.
1961   "Soil fertility and the ancient Maya." *Transactions of the Connecticut Academy of Arts and Sciences,* 42:1–56.. New Haven.

———
1970   "The people of York: 1538–1812." *Scientific American* 222(1):104–113.

Cowgill, Ursula M.; Goulden, Clyde E.; Hutchinson, G. Evelyn; Patrick, Ruth; Raček, A. A.; and Tsukada, Matsuo.
1966   "The history of Laguna de Petenxil." *Memoirs of the Connecticut Academy of Arts and Sciences,* vol. 17. New Haven.

Crocombe, R. G., and Hogbin, G. R.
1963   *Land, work and productivity at Inonda.* New Guinea Research Unit Bulletin no. 2. Canberra: Australian National University.

Curwen, E. C.
1938   *Air photography and the evolution of the corn-field.* Economic History Society Pamphlet no. 2. London: London School of Economics.

Damas, D., ed.
1969   *Contributions to anthropology: Ecological essays.* Ottawa: National Museums of Canada. Bulletin 230.

Darby, H. C.
1936   "The economic geography of England, A.D. 1000–1250." In *An historical geography of England before A.D. 1800*, H. C. Darby, ed., pp. 165–229. Cambridge: Cambridge University Press.

Davis, K.
1968   Review of *Population growth and land use*, by Colin Clark. *Scientific American* 218(4):133–138.

d'Azevedo, Warren L.
1962   "Some historical problems in the delineation of a central west African region." *Annals of the New York Academy of Sciences* 96:Art. 2:512–538.

Deevey, E. S., Jr.
1960   "The human population." *Scientific American* 203(3):194–204.

DeSchlippe, P.
1956   *Shifting cultivation in Africa: The Zande system of agriculture.* London: Routledge and Kegan Paul.

Dike, K. Onwuka
1956   *Trade and politics in the Niger delta.* London: Oxford University Press.

Dikov, N. N.
1965   "The Stone Age of Kamchatka and the Chukchi Peninsula in the light of new archaeological data." *Arctic Anthropology* 3(1):10–24.

Dillon, Richard
n.d.   "An analysis of Mbembe political organizations." Manuscript.

Dobyns, H. F.
1966   "Estimating aboriginal American population: An appraisal of techniques with a new hemispheric estimate." *Current Anthropology* 7(4):395–416.

Donayre, J.
1966   "Population growth and fertility at high altitude." *Life at high altitudes*; proceedings of the special session held during the fifth meeting of the Pan American Health Organization Advisory Committee on Medical Research, June 15, 1966. Pan American Health Organization Scientific Publication no. 140, pp. 74–79. Washington D.C.: Pan American Health Organization, Pan American Sanitary Bureau.

Doring, G. K.
1963   "Uber die Relative Sterilität in den Jahren nach der Menarche." *Geburtshilfe und Frauenheilkunde* 23:30–36.

Dovring, F.
1966 Review of *The conditions of agricultural growth*, by Ester Boserup. *Journal of Economic History* 26:380–381.

Drioton, E., and Vandier, J.
1962 *L'Egypt*. Paris: Presse Universitaire de France.

Duignan, M.
1944 "Irish agriculture in early historic times." *Journal of the Royal Society of Antiquaries of Ireland*, 74:124–145.

Dumond, D. E.
1961 "Swidden agriculture and the rise of Maya civilization." *Southwestern Journal of Anthropology* 17(4):301–316.

———

1963 "Two early phases from the Naknek drainage." *Arctic Anthropology* 1(2):93–104.

———

1965a "On Eskaleutian linguistics, archaeology, and prehistory." *American Anthropologist* 67:1231–1257.

———

1965b "Population growth and cultural change." *Southwestern Journal of Anthropology* 21(4):302–324.

———

1969a "Prehistoric cultural contacts in southwestern Alaska." *Science* 166:1108–1115.

———

1969b "The prehistoric pottery of southwestern Alaska." *Anthropological Papers of the University of Alaska* 14(2):18–42. College.

———

1970 "Competition, cooperation, and the folk society." *Southwestern Journal of Anthropology* 26:261–286.

———

1971 *A summary of archaeology in the Katmai region, southwestern Alaska.* University of Oregon Anthropological Papers, No. 2. Eugene: Department of Anthropology, University of Oregon.

Dyson, Robert H., Jr.
1965 "Archaeological Evidence of the Second Millennium B.C. on the Persian Plateau." *Cambridge Ancient History* Fasc. 66. Cambridge: Cambridge University Press.

———

1968 "Annotations and corrections of the relative chronology of Iran, 1968." *American Journal of Archaeology* 72(4):308–313.

Ekvall, Robert B.
1968 *Fields on the hoof: Nexus of Tibetan nomadic pastoralism.* New York: Holt, Rinehart and Winston.

Ellis, R. W. B.
1950 "Age of puberty in the tropics." *British Medical Journal* 1:85–89.

El-Wailly, F., and Abu es-Soof, B.
1965   "The excavations at Tell Es-Sawwan: First preliminary report (1964)." *Sumer* 21(1–2):17–32.

English, Paul Ward
1966   *City and village in Iran.* Madison: University of Wisconsin Press.

———
1968   "The origin and spread of qanats in the Old World." *Proceedings of the American Philosophical Society* 112(3):170–181.

Erasmus, C. J.
1965   "Monument building: Some field experiments." *Southwestern Journal of Anthropology* 21(4):277–301.

Evans, E. E.
1956   "The ecology of peasant life in western Europe." In *Man's role in changing the face of the earth*, W. L. Thomas, ed., pp. 217–239. Chicago: University of Chicago Press.

Evans-Pritchard, E. E.
1940   *The Nuer.* Oxford: Clarendon Press.

———
1948   *The divine kingship of the Shilluk of the Nilotic Sudan.* Cambridge: Cambridge University Press.

———
1962   "The divine kingship of the Shilluk of the Nilotic Sudan." Reprinted in *Essays in social anthropology*. London: Faber and Faber.

Eyre, S. R.
1963   *Vegetation and soils.* Chicago: Aldine Publishing Company.

Farmer, B. H.
1957   *Pioneer peasant colonization in Ceylon.* London: Oxford University Press.

Ferdon, E. N., Jr.
1959   "Agricultural potential and the development of cultures." *Southwestern Journal of Anthropology* 15(1):1–19.

Firth, Raymond
1936   *We, the Tikopia.* London: Allen and Unwin.

Fischer, H. G.
1968   *Dendera in the third millennium* B.C. Locust Valley, N.Y.: J. J. Augustin.

Fisher, W. B.
1950   *The Middle East: A physical, social and regional geography.* London: Methuen and Company.

Fisk, E. K.
1962   "Planning in a primitive economy: Special problems of Papua-New Guinea." *The Economic Record* 38(84):462–478.

Fitzpatrick, J. F. J.
1910   "Some notes on the Kwalla district and its tribes." *Journal of the African Society* 10:16–52, 213–221.

Flannery, Kent V.
1965   "The ecology of early food production in Mesopotamia." *Science* 147(3663):1247–1256.

———
1968   "The Olmec and the valley of Oaxaca: A model for inter-regional interaction in formative times." *Dumbarton Oakes Conference on the Olmec, October 28–29, 1967,* Elizabeth P. Benson, ed., pp. 79–117. Washington, D.C.: Dumbarton Oakes Research Library and Collection, Trustees for Harvard University.

———
1969   "Origins and ecological effects of early domestication in Iran and the Near East." In *The domestication and exploitation of plants and animals,* P. J. Ucko and G. W. Dimbleby, eds. pp. 73–100. Chicago: Aldine Publishing Company.

Flannery, Kent V., and Coe, Michael D.
1968   "Social and economic systems in formative Mesoamerica." In *New perspectives in archeology,* S. R. and L. R. Binford, eds. pp .267–284. Chicago: Aldine Publishing Company.

Flannery, Kent V., and Wheeler, J.
1967   "Animal bones from Tell as-Sawwan." *Sumer* 23:179–182.

Flannery, Kent V.; Kirkby, Anne V. T. and Michael J.; Williams, Aubrey W., Jr.
1967   "Farming systems and political growth in ancient Oaxaca." *Science* 158(3800):445–454.

Ford, C. S.
1945   *A comparative study of human reproduction.* Yale University Publications in Anthropology 32. New Haven: Yale University Press.

Forde, C. D.
1937   "Land and labor in a cross river village in southern Nigeria." *The Geographical Journal* 40:24–51.

Fortes, Meyer
1953   "The structure of unilineal descent groups." *American Anthropologist* 55:17–41.

Fortes, Meyer, and Evans-Pritchard, E. E.
1940   *African political systems.* London: Oxford University Press.

Fowler, Melvin L.
1968   *Un sistema preclásico de distribución de agua en la zona arqueológica de Amalucan, Puebla.* Puebla, Mexico: Instituto poblano de antropología e historia.

1969   "Middle Mississippian agricultural fields." *American Antiquity* 34(1):365–375.

Fowler, P. J.
1966   "Romano-British settlements in Dorset and Wiltshire, part 2: The distribution of settlement." In *Rural settlement in Roman Britain*, A. C. Thomas, ed., pp. 54–67. London: Research Report 7 of the Council for British Archaeology.

Fowler, P. J., and Thomas, A. C.
1962   "Arable fields of the pre-Norman period at Grithian." *Cornish Archaeology* 1:61–84.

Fox, Sir Cyril
1959   *Personality of Britain*, 4th ed. Cardiff: National Museum of Wales.

Freeman, J. D.
1955   *Iban agriculture, a report on the shifting cultivation of hill rice by the Iban of Sarawak*. London: Her Majesty's Stationery Office.

Fried, M. H.
1967   *The evolution of political society: An essay in political anthropology*. New York: Random House.

Frisancho, R., and Baker, P.
1970   "Altitude and growth." In *Symposium on human adaptation*, S. Katz, ed. *American Journal of Physical Anthropology* 32:279–291.

Gardiner, A.
1941   "Ramesside texts relating to the taxation and transport of corn." *Journal of Egyptian archaeology* 27:19–73.

1947   *Ancient Egyptian onomastica*, vols. 1 and 2. London: Oxford University Press.

1961   *Egypt of the Pharaohs*. Oxford: Clarendon Press.

Garn, S. M., and Haskell, J. A.
1960   "Fat thickness and developmental status in childhood and adolescence." *American Journal of Diseases of Children* 99:746–751.

Gazetteer of Persia
ca. 1900   British government of India.

Geddes, W. R.
1954   *The Land Dyaks of Sarawak*. London: Her Majesty's Stationery Office.

Geertz, Clifford
1963   *Agricultural involution: The process of ecological change in Indonesia*. Berkeley: University of California Press.

Ghirshman, R.
1938   *Fouilles de Sialk, prés de Kashan*, vol. 1. Paris: Musée du Louvre.

Giddings, J. L.
1952   *The Arctic woodland culture of the Kobuk River.* Philadelphia: University of Pennsylvania Press.

———
1967   *Ancient men of the Arctic.* New York: Alfred A. Knopf.

Gilbert, E. W.
1936   "The human geography of Roman Britain." In *An historical geography of England before A.D. 1800*, H. C. Darby, ed., pp. 30–87. Cambridge: Cambridge University Press.

Giosa, A. R.
1955   "Incidence of pregnancy during lactation in 500 cases." *American Journal of Obstetrics and Gynecology* 70:61–75.

Gluckman, Max
1941   *Economy of the central Barotse Plain.* Rhodes-Livingstone Papers 7. London: Oxford University Press.

———
1965   *Politics, law and ritual in tribal society.* Chicago: Aldine Publishing Company.

Gordon, B. L.
1969   "Anthropogeography and rainforest ecology in the Bocas del Toro Province, Panama." Unpublished report on fieldwork. Berkeley: Department of Geography.

Gourou, P.
1956   "The quality of land use of tropical cultivators. In *Man's role in changing the face of the earth*, W. L Thomas, ed , pp 336–349. Chicago: University of Chicago Press.

Gow, A. S. F.
1914   "The ancient plough." *Journal of Hellenic Studies* 34:249–275.

Gray, H. L.
1915   *English field systems.* Cambridge, Mass.: Harvard University Press.

Gray, Robert F.
1963   *The Sonjo of Tanganyika.* London: Oxford University Press.

Grove, David C.
1968   "The pre-classic Olmec in central Mexico: Site distribution and inferences." *Dumbarton Oaks Conference on the Olmec, October 28–29, 1967*, Elizabeth P. Benson, ed., pp. 178–185. Washington, D.C.: Dumbarton Oaks Research Library and Collection Trustees for Harvard University.

Guttmacher, A. F.
1962   *Pregnancy and birth: A book for expectant parents.* New York: Viking Press.

Haarnagel, W.
1961   "Zur Grabung auf der Feddersen Wierde 1955–1959." *Germania* 39:42–69.

Haddon, A. C.
1912   "Horticulture." In *Reports of the Cambridge anthropological expedition to Torres Straits,* vol. 4, A. C. Haddon, ed., pp. 144–151. Cambridge: Cambridge University Press.

Hamblin, R. L.
1958   "Leadership and crises." *Sociometry* 21: 322–335.

Harlan, J. R.
1967   "A wild wheat harvest in Turkey." *Archaeology* 20:197–201.

Harlan, J. R., and Zohary, D.
1966   "Distribution of wild wheats and barley." *Science* 153(3740):1074–1080

Harris, D. R.
1969   "Agricultural systems, ecosystems and the origin of agriculture." In *The domestication and exploitation of plants and animals,* P. J. Ucko and G. W. Dimbleby, eds., pp. 3–16. London: Gerald Duckworth.

Harris, M.
1959   "The economy has no surplus?" *American Anthropologist* 61(2):185–199.

Harris, Rosemary
1965   *The political organization of the Mbembe, Nigeria.* London: Her Majesty's Stationery Office.

Hartman, C. G.
1931   "On the relative sterility of the adolescent organism." *Science* 74:226–227

Hartmann, F.
1923   *L'agriculture dans l'ancienne Égypte.* Paris: Librairies-imprimeries réunies.

Haviland, William A.
1966   *Maya settlement patterns: A critical review.* Middle American Research Institute. New Orleans: Tulane University

————
1967   "Stature at Tikal, Guatemala: Implications for classic Maya demography and social organization." *American Antiquity* 32:316–325.

————
1969   "A new population estimate for Tikal, Guatemala." *American Antiquity* 34:429–433.

Hayes, W.
1970   "The middle kingdom in Egypt." *Cambridge Ancient History,* 3rd ed., vol. 1, part 2, chap. 20 [1964].

Hayes, W.; Rowton, M.; and Stubbings, F.
1970   *Chronology: Egypt, western Asia, and the Aegean Bronze Age.*Cambridge Ancient History, vol. 1, part 1, chap. 6 [1962].

Hedin, Sven
1910   *Overland to India*, 2 vols. London: Macmillan.

Helbaek, Hans
1964   "Early Hassunan vegetable food at Es-Sewwan." *Sumer* 20(2):45–48.

——

1969   "Plant collecting, dry farming, and irrigation agriculture in prehistoric Deh Luran." In *Prehistory and human ecology of the Deh Luran Plain*, Frank Hole, Kent V. Flannery, and J. A. Neely, eds. Ann Arbor: Memoirs of the Museum of Anthropology, University of Michigan, no. 1.

Herskovits, Melville
1952   *Economic anthropology: A study in comparative economics.* New York: Alfred A. Knopf.

Hickerson, H.
1965   "The Virginia deer and intertribal buffer zones in the upper Mississippi valley." In *Man, culture and animals: The role of animals in human ecological adjustments*, A. Leeds and A. P. Vayda, eds., pp. 43–65. Washington, D C.: American Association for the Advancement of Science, pub. no. 78.

Higham, C. F. W.
1968   "Trends in prehistoric European caprobovine husbandry." *Man* (n.s.) 3:64–75.

——

1969   "Towards an economic prehistory of Europe." *Current Anthropology* 10(2–3):139–150.

Ho, P-.T.
1959   *Studies on the population of China, 1368–1953.* Cambridge: Harvard University Press.

Hoff, C. J.
1968   *Demography and research with high altitude population.* Occasional Papers in Anthropology, 1:65–84. University Park, Pa.: Pennsylvania State University.

Hole, F.
1966   "Investigating the origins of Mesopotamian civilization." *Science* 153(3736):605–611.

Hole, F., and Flannery, Kent V.
1967   "The prehistory of southwestern Iran: A preliminary report." *Proceedings of the Prehistoric Society* 33:147–206.

Hole, F.; Flannery, Kent V.; and Neely, J. A.
1969   *Prehistory and human ecology of the Deh Luran Plain: An early village sequence from Khuzistan, Iran.* Ann Arbor: Memoirs of the Museum of Anthropology University of Michigan, no. 1.

Hollingsworth, T.
1969   *Historical demography.* Ithaca, N.Y.: Cornell University Press.

Howell, N.
n.d.   *!Kung Bushman demographic studies: A preliminary report.* Princeton, N.J.: Office of Population Research.

Ito, P. K.
1942   "Comparative biometrical study of physique of Japanese women born and reared under different environments." *Human Biology* 14:279–351.

Jacobsen, T., and Adams, R. M.
1958   "Salt and silt in ancient Mesopotamian agriculture." *Science* 128 (3334):1251–1258.

Janlekha, K. O.
1955   *A study of the economy of a rice growing village in central Thailand.* Bangkok: Division of Agricultural Economics, Ministry of Agriculture.

Jaquet-Gordon, H.
1962   *Les noms des domains funéraires sous l'ancien empire égyptien.* Bibliothèque d'Étude,34. Le Caire: Institut français d'Archéologie orientale.

Jöchle, W.
1956   "Über den Einfluss des Lichtes auf Sexualentwicklung und Sexualperiodik bei Säugetieren." *Endokrinologie* 33:129–138.

Jones, W. O.
1967   Review of *The conditions of agricultural growth*, by Ester Boserup. *American Economic Review* 57:679–680.

Kaiser, W.
1961   "Bericht uber eine archäologisch-geologische Felduntersuchung in Ober und Mittelägypten." *Mitteilungen des Deutschen archäologischen Instituts.* Abteilung Kairo 17:1–53.

Kees, H.
1961   *Ancient Egypt: A cultural topography*, T. G. H. James, ed.; Ian F. D. Morrow, trans. Chicago: University of Chicago Press.

Keesing, Roger
1967   "Statistical models and decision models of social structure: The Kwaio case." *Ethnology* 6:1–16.

Kelley, I., and Palerm, A.
1952   *The tajin Totonac, part* 1. Institute of Social Anthropology, publ. 13. Washington, D. C.: Smithsonian Institution.

Kennedy, G. C., and Mitra, J.
1963 "Body weight and food intake as initiating factors for puberty in the rat." *Journal of Physiology* 166:408–418.

Kenyon, K. M.
1959 "Some observations on the beginnings of settlement in the Near East." *Journal of the Royal Anthropological Institute* 89(1): 35–43.

Keys, A.
1949 "The physiology of the individual as an approach to a more quantitative biology of man." *Federal Proceedings* 8:523–529.

Kirchhoff, P.
1955 "The principle of clanship in human society." *Davidson Journal of Anthropology* 1:1–10.

Kopytoff, Igor
1967 "Labor allocation among the Suku." Unpublished paper presented at the Conference on Competing Demands of Labor in Traditional African Societies, Holly Knoll, Virginia.

Kramer, F. L.
1967 "Eduard Hahn and the end of the 'three stages of man'." *Geographical Review* 57(1):73–89.

Kroeber, Alfred L.
1939 *Cultural and natural areas of native North America.* University of California Publications in American Archaeology and Ethnology 38. Berkeley: University of California Press.

———

1948 *Anthropology.* New York: Harcourt Brace Jovanovich.

Lambton, A. K. S.
1954 *Landlord and peasant in Iran.* London: Oxford University Press.

———

1967 "The evolution of the Iqta^c in mediaeval Iran." *Iran* 5:41–50.

Lange, Frederick W.
1969 "Marine resources: A viable subsistence alternative for the prehistoric lowland Maya." Manuscript.

Larsen, H.
1968 "Near Ipiutak and Uwelen-Okvik." *Folk* 10:81–90.

Laughlin, R. M.
1969 "The Tzotzil." In *Handbook of Middle American Indians*, vol. 7, part 1, R. Wauchope and E. Z. Vogt, eds., pp. 152–194. Austin: University of Texas Press.

Leach, Edmund R.
1959 "Some economic advantages to shifting agriculture." *Proceedings the 9th Pacific Science Congress (1957)* 7: 64–66. Bangkok.

1965   *Political systems of highland Burma.* Boston: Beacon Press. [Originally published 1954.]

Leathem, J. H.
1958   "Hormones and protein nutrition." *Recent Progress in Hormone Research* 14:141–155.

Lebar, F. M.; Hickey, G. C.; and Musgrave, J. K.
1964   *Ethnic groups of southeast Asia.* New Haven: Human Relations Area Files Press.

Lee, R. B.
1967   "Trance cure of the !Kung Bushmen." *Natural History* 76:30–37.

1968a   "Sociology of !Kung Bushman trance performances." In *Trance and possession states*, R. H. Prince, ed., pp. 35–54. Montreal: R. M. Bucke Memorial Society.

1968b   "What hunters do for a living, or, how to make out on scarce resources." In *Man the hunter*, R. B. Lee and I. DeVore, eds., pp. 30–48. Chicago: Aldine Publishing Company.

1969a   "!Kung Bushman subsistence: An input-output analysis." In *Ecological essays,* D. Damas, ed , pp. 73–94. Ottawa: National Museums of Canada Bulletin 230.

1969b   "!Kung Bushman violence." Paper presented at the Annual Meeting of the American Anthropological Association, New Orleans.

forthcoming "The !Kung Bushmen of Botswana." In *Simple societies*, M. Bicchieri, ed. New York: Holt, Rinehart and Winston.

Lee, R. B., and DeVore, I. eds.
1968   *Man the hunter.* Chicago: Aldine Publishing Company.

Lees, G. M., and Falcon, N. L.
1952   "The geographical history of the Mesopotamian plain." *Geographical Journal* 113:24–39.

Le Strange, Guy
1930   *Lands of the eastern caliphate.* Cambridge: Cambridge University Press.

Levine, L. D.
1969   "Contributions to the historical geography of the Zagros in the Neo-Assyrian period." Doctoral dissertation. Philadelphia: University of Pennsylvania.

Levine, V. E.
1953   "Studies in physiological anthropology, III. The age of onset of menstruation of the Alaskan Eskimo." *American Journal of Physical Anthropology* (n.s.) 11:262.

Lévi-Strauss, Claude
1963   "The use of wild plants in tropical South America." In *Handbook of South American Indians*, vol. 6, J. H. Steward, ed., pp. 465–486. Washington, D.C.: U.S. Government Printing Office.

Lewis, H. S.
1966   "The origins of African kingdoms." *Cahiers Études Africaines* 6(23): 402–407.

Livingstone, F. B.
1967   "The ecology of warfare in the human species." *Natural History* 76(10):61–65.

Lloyd, Peter C.
1954   "The traditional political system of the Yoruba." *Southwestern Journal of Anthropology* 10:366–384.

————
1965a   "The political structure of African kingdoms." In *Political systems and the distribution of power*. Association of Social Anthropologists Monographs 2. London: Tavistock Publications.

————
1965b   "The Yoruba of Nigeria." In *Peoples of Africa*, James Gibbs, ed., pp. 549–582. New York: Holt, Rinehart and Winston.

Lloyd, S.
1938   "Some ancient sites in the Sinjar District." *Iraq* 5:123–142.

Lloyd, S., and Safar, F.
1945   "Tell Hassuna: Excavations by the Iraq government directorate general of antiquities in 1943 and 1944." *Journal of Near Eastern Studies* 2(2):255–289.

————
1947   "Eridu: A preliminary communciation on the first season's excavations." *Sumer* 3:84–111.

Lowe, Gareth W., and Mason, J. Alden
1965   "Archaeological survey of the Chiapas Coast, highlands, and upper Grijalva Basin." In *Handbook of Middle American Indians*, vol. 2, part 1, pp. 195–236. Austin: University of Texas Press.

Lundell, Cyrus Longworth
1937   *The vegetation of the Petén*. Carnegie Institution of Washington Contribution 478. Washington, D.C.: Carnegie Institution.

McCracken, Robert D.
1971   "Lactase deficiency: An example of dietary evolution." *Current Anthropology*, October–December 1971: 479–517.

McGhee, R. J.
1970   "Speculations on climatic change and Thule culture development." *Folk* 11–12:173–184.

McLoughlin, Peter F. M., ed.
1970   *African food production systems: Cases and theory.* Baltimore: Johns Hopkins Press.

MacNeish, Richard S.
1964   "Ancient Mesoamerican civilization." *Science* 143(3606):531–537.

Marsden, B., and Bronson, G.
1964   "Estrous synchrony in mice: Alteration by exposure to male urine." *Science* 144:1469.

Marshall, Carter L.; Brown, Roy E.; and Goodrich, Charles H.
1971   "Nutrition and public health as determinants of world population growth." *Clinical Pediatrics* 10(7):363–368.

Maruyama, M.
1963   "The second cybernetics: Deviation-amplifying mutual causal processes." *American Scientist* 51:164–179.

Mauss, Marcel
1954   *The gift.* London: Cohen and West.

Mauss, Marcel, and Beuchat, H.
1906   "Essai sur les variations saisonnières des sociétés eskimos." *L'Année Sociologique.* (1904–1905), pp. 39–132.

Meade, C. G.
1968   "Luristan in the first half of the first millennium B.C." *Iran* 6:105–134.

Meek, C. K.
1931a   *Tribal studies in northern Nigeria.* London: Oxford University Press.

———
1931b   *A Sudanese kingdom.* London: Kegan Paul.

———
1949   *Land, law, and custom in the colonies.* London: Oxford University Press.

Megard, R. O.
1967   "Late-quaternary *Cladocera* of Lake Zeribar, western Iran." *Ecology* 48(2):179–189.

Megaw, J. V. S.; Thomas, A. C.; and Wailes, B.
1961   "The Bronze Age settlement at Gwithian, Cornwall: Preliminary report on the evidence for early agriculture." *Proceedings of the West Cornwall Field Club* 2(5):200–215.

Melbin, T.
1962   "The children of Swedish nomad Lapps: A study of their health, growth, and development." *Acta Paediatrica* 51(supp. 131):1–97.

Meldgaard, J.; Mortensen, P.; and Thrane, H.
1964   *Excavations at Tepe Guran, Luristan.* Copenhagen: Ejnar Munksgaard.

Merrill, R. S.
1968   "Technology: The study of technology." In *International Encyclopedia of the Social Sciences* 15:576–589. New York: Macmillan Company and Free Press.

Michelson, N.
1944   "Studies in the physical development of Negroes, IV. Onset of puberty." *American Journal of Physical Anthropology* (n.s.) 2:151–166.

Middleton, John, and Tait, David
1958   *Tribes without rulers.* London: Routledge and Kegan Paul.

Miles, S. W.
1957   "The sixteenth century pokom—Maya: A documentary analysis of social structure and archaeological setting " *Transactions of the American Philosophical Society* (n.s.) 47(part 4):733–781.

Millar, E. G.
1926   *English illuminated manuscripts from the tenth to the thirteenth century.* Paris and Brussels: G. van Oest.

Millon, René
1962   *Variations in response to the practice of irrigation agriculture.* University of Utah, Cultivation in Arid Lands, Anthropological Papers, no. 62. Salt Lake City.

_____
1966   "Extensión y población de la ciudad de Teotihuacán en sus diferentes periodos: un calculo provisional." *Teotihuacán, Onceava Mesa Redonda.* Mexico City: Sociedad Mexicana de Antropologia.

_____
1967   "Teotihuacán." *Scientific American* 216(6):38–63.

_____
1969   "Urbanization at Teotihuacán: The Teotihuacán mapping project." *El proceso de urbanización en America desde sus origines hasta nuestros dias,* E. Hardoy and R. Schaedel, eds. Buenos Aires: Editorial del Instituto.

Miracle, M.
1967   *Agriculture in the Congo Basin.* Madison: University of Wisconsin Press.

Moerman, M.
1968   *Agricultural change and peasant choice in a Thai village.* Berkeley: University of California Press.

Monge Medrano, Carlos
1948   *Acclimatization in the Andes—historical confirmation of "climatic aggression" in the development of Andean man.* Baltimore: Johns Hopkins Press.

1968   "Man: Climate and changes of altitude." In *Man in adaptation: The biosocial background*, vol. 1, Yehudi A. Cohen, ed., pp. 176–185. Chicago: Aldine Publishing Company.

Montet, P.
1961   *Géographie de l'Égypte ancienne*, part 2. Paris Imprimerie Nationale.

Morgan, Lewis H.
1877   *Ancient society*. New York: Henry Holt and Company.

Morgan, W. B.
1955   *The change from shifting agriculture to fixed settlement in southern Nigeria.* Department of Geography Research Notes, no. 7. Ibadan: University College of Ibadan.

Mortensen, P.
1964   "Additional remarks on the chronology of early village-farming communities in the Zagros area." *Sumer* 20(1–2):28–36.

Müller-Wille, M.
1965   *Eisenzeitliche Fluren in den festländischen Nordseegebieten*. Münster: Geographische Kommission.

Murdock, George Peter
1964   "Cultural correlates of the regulation of premarital sex behavior." In *Process and pattern in culture: Essays in honor of Julian Steward*, R. A. Manners, ed., pp. 399–410. Chicago: Aldine Publishing Company.

Murra, J. V.
1958   "On Inca political structure." In *Systems of political control and bureaucracy in human affairs*. V. F. Ray, ed., pp. 30–41. Seattle: University of Washington Press.

Nash, R. J.
1969   *The Arctic small tool tradition in Manitoba*. Winnipeg: University of Manitoba Press.

Netting, Robert M.
1964   "Beer as a locus of value among the west African Kofyar." *American Anthropologist* 66:375–384.

1968   *Hill farmers of Nigeria: Cultural ecology of the Kofyar of the Jos Plateau.* Seattle: University of Washington Press.

1969a   "Women's weapons: The politics of domesticity among the Kofyar." *American Anthropologist* 71:1037–1046.

1969b   "Ecosystems in process: A comparative study of change in two west African societies." In *Contributions to anthropology: Ecological essays*, D. Damas, ed., pp. 102–112. Ottawa: National Museum of Canada Bulletin 230.

Nightingale, M.
1953   "Ploughing and field shape." *Antiquity* 27: 20–26.

Nims, C.
1965   *Thebes of the pharaohs.* New York: Stein and Day.

Nye, P. H., and Greenland, D. J.
1960   *The soil under shifting cultivation.* Technical Communication no. 51. Commonwealth Bureau of Soils. Farnham Royal, Berks: Commonwealth Agricultural Bureaux.

Oates, D.
1968   *Studies in the ancient history of Iraq.* London: Oxford University Press.

Oates, Joan
1968   "Prehistoric investigations near Mandali, Iraq." *Iraq* 30(1):1–20.

————
1969   "Choga Mami 1967–68: A preliminary report." *Iraq* 31:115–152.

Oberg, K.
1955   "Types of social structure among the lowland tribes of South and Central America." *American Anthropologist* 57:472–487.

————
1965   "The marginal peasant in rural Brazil." *American Anthropologist* 67:1417–1427.

Orans, M.
1966   "Surplus." *Human Organization* 25(1):24–32.

Orwin, C. S. and C. S.
1954   *The open fields,* 2nd ed. Oxford: Clarendon Press.

Oswalt, W. H.
1967   *Alaskan Eskimos.* San Francisco: Chandler.

Ottenberg, Simon
1958   "Ibo oracles and intergroup relations." *Southwestern Journal of Anthropology* 14:295–317.

————
1968   "The development of credit associations in the changing economy of the Afikpo Igbo." *Africa* 38:237–251.

Palerm, Angel
1961   "Sistemas de regadío en Teotihuacán y en el Pedregal: La agricultura y el desarrollo de la civilización." *Revista Interamericana de Ciencias Sociales* 1(1).

————
1967   "Agricultural systems and food patterns." In *Handbook of Middle American Indians,* vol. 6, R. Wauchope and M. Nash, eds., pp. 26–52. Austin: University of Texas Press.

Parsons, Jeffrey R.
1968   "Teotihuacán, Mexico, and its impact on regional demography."
Science 162:872–877.

———
1970   "Prehistoric settlement patterns in the Texcoco region, Mexico."
Manuscript.

Parsons, Jeffrey R., and Blanton, Richard E.
1969   "Prehispanic demography in the eastern valley of Mexico: The
Texcoco, Ixtapalapa, and Chalco areas." Manuscript.

Parsons, Talcott
1964   *The Social system.* Glencoe, Ill.: Free Press [1952].

Payne, F. G.
1947   "The plough in early Britain." *Archaeological Journal* 104:82–111.

———
1957   "The British plough: Some stages in its development." *Agricultural
History Review* 5:74–84.

Pelzer, K. J.
1945   *Pioneer settlement in the Asiatic tropics.* American Geographical Society Special Publication, no. 29. New York.

Perkins, A. L.
1949   *The comparative archaeology of early Mesopotamia* Chicago: University of Chicago Press.

Perkins, D., Jr.
1969   "Fauna of Catal Hüyük: Evidence for early cattle domestication
in Anatolia " *Science* 164:177–179.

Perkins, D. H.
1969   *Agricultural development in China 1368–1968.* Chicago: Aldine Publishing Company.

Peters, D. U.
1950   *Land usage in the Serenje district.* Rhodes-Livingstone papers, no. 19.
London: Oxford University Press.

Peters, E. L.
1963   "Aspects of rank and status among Muslims in a Lebanese village."
In *Mediterranean countrymen*, J. Pitt-Rivers, ed. The Hague: Mouton.

Petri, E.
1935   "Untersuchungen zur Erbbedingtheit der Menarche." *Zeitschrift
für Morphologie und Anthropologie* 33:43–48.

Petrie, W.
1930   *Antaeopolis.* London: British School of Archaeology in Egypt.

Pfeiffer, J. E.
1969   *The emergence of man.* New York: Harper and Row.

Piggott, Stuart
1965　*Ancient Europe*. Chicago: Aldine Publishing Company.

Pirenne, H.
1956　*Medieval cities: Their origins and the revival of trade*, F. D. Halsey, trans. New York: Doubleday and Company.

Polanyi, K.; Arensberg, C. M.; and Pearson, H. W., eds.
1957　*Trade and markets in the early empires*. Glencoe, Ill.: Free Press.

Porada, Edith
1965—"The relative chronology of Mesopotamia. Part 1: Seals and trade (6000–1600 B.C.)." In *Chronologies in Old World archaeology*, Robert W. Ehrich, ed., pp. 133–200. Chicago: University of Chicago Press.

Porter, B., and Moss, R.
1937　*Topographical bibliography of ancient Egyptian hieroglyphic texts, reliefs, and paintings*, vol. 5. Oxford: Clarendon Press.

Pospisil, L.
1963　*Kapauku Papuan economy*. Yale University Publications in Anthropology 67. New Haven: Yale University Press.

Poyck, A. P. G.
1962　"Farm studies in Iraq." *Mededelingen van de Landbouwhogeschool te Wageningen, Netherlands* 62(1):1–99.

Pugh, T. F.; Jeorath, B. K.; Schmidt, W. M.; and Reed, R. B.
1963　"Rates of mental disease related to childbearing." *New England Journal of Medicine* 268:1224–1228.

Puleston, D. E.
1968　"Brosimium alicastrum as a subsistence alternative for the classic Maya of the central southern lowlands." Unpublished Master's thesis, University of Pennsylvania, Department of Anthropology, Philadelphia.

Rakoff, A. E.
1963　"Human neuroendocrinology: Discussion." In *Advances in neuroendocrinology*, A. V. Nalbandov, ed., pp. 500–510. Urbana: University of Illinois Press.

Randall, H. J.
1930　"Population and agriculture in Roman Britain." *Antiquity* 4:80–90.

Rappaport, R. A.
1967　*Pigs for the ancestors*. New Haven: Yale University Press.

———
1969　"Population dispersal and land distribution among the Maring of New Guinea." In *Contributions to anthropology: Ecological essays*, D. Damas, ed., pp. 113–126. Ottawa: National Museums of Canada Bulletin 230.

Redfield, Robert
1953　*The primitive world and its transformations*. Ithaca, N.Y.: Cornell University Press.

Richards, A. I.
1939   *Land, labour and diet in northern Rhodesia.* London: Oxford University Press.

Rostovtzeff, M.
1953   *The social and economic history of the Hellenistic world*, 2nd ed., rev. by P. M. Fraser. Oxford: Clarendon Press.

Roys, R. L.
1943   *The Indian background of colonial Yucatan.* Carnegie Institution of Washington Publication 548. Washington, D.C.: Carnegie Institution.

Russell, J. C.
1948   "Demographic pattern in history." *Population Studies* 1:388–404.

1958   *Late ancient and medieval populations.* Transactions of the American Philosophical Society, New Series, vol. 48, part 3.

1966   "The population of medieval Egypt." *Journal of the American Research Centre in Egypt* 5:69–82.

Sahlins, Marshall D.
1958   *Social stratification in Polynesia.* Seattle: University of Washington Press.

1960   "Political power and the economy in primitive society." In *Essays in the science of culture*, G. E. Dole and R. L. Carneiro, eds., pp. 390–415. New York: Thomas Y. Crowell.

1963   "Poor man, rich man, big man, chief: Political types in Melanesia and Polynesia." *Comparative Studies in Society and History* 5:285–303.

1965   "On the sociology of primitive exchange." In *The relevance of models for social anthropology.* Association of Social Anthropologists Monographs 1: 139–236. London: Tavistock Publications.

1968   *Tribesmen.* Englewood Cliffs, N.J.: Prentice-Hall.

Salzman, P. C.
1969   "Multiple resource nomadism in Iranian Baluchistan." Paper delivered at the American Anthropological Association Meetings, November 1969. New Orleans.

Sanders, William T.
1960   "Prehistoric ceramics and settlement patterns in Quintana Roo, Mexico." Report no. 60. *Contributions to American Anthropology and History*, vol. 12, pp. 155–264. Washington, D.C.: Carnegie Institution.

―――――
1965 *Cultural ecology of the Teotihuacán Valley*. University Park: Pennsylvania State University, Department of Sociology and Anthropology.

―――――
1969 "The agricultural history of the Teotihuacán Valley." Paper given at the American Association for the Advancement of Science Meetings, December 1969. Boston.

Sanders, William T., and Michels, Joseph W.
1969 *The Pennsylvania State University Kaminaljuyu project: 1968 season*, part 1, "The excavations." Occasional Papers in Anthropology 2. University Park: Pennsylvania State University, Department of Anthropology.

Sanders, William T., and Price, B. J.
1968 *Mesoamerica: The evolution of a civilization*. Random House Studies in Anthropology. New York: Random House.

Sauer, Carl O.
1948 "Environment and culture during the last deglaciation." *Proceedings of the American Philosophical Society* 92(1):65–77.

―――――
1952 *Agricultural origins and dispersals*. New York: The American Geographical Society.

―――――
1956 "The agency of man on the earth." In *Man's role in changing the face of the earth*, W. L. Thomas, ed., pp. 49–69. Chicago: University of Chicago Press.

Säve-Söderbergh, T.
1941 *Ägypten und Nubien*. Lund: Håkan Ohlssons Boktryckeri.

Schlott, Adelheid
1969 "Die Ausmasse Ägyptens nach altägyptischen Texten." Doctoral dissertation, Eberhard-Karl University, Tübingen, Darmstadt.

Scudder, T.
1962 *The ecology of the Gwembe Tonga*. Kariba Studies, vol. 2. Manchester: Manchester University Press.

Service, Elman R.
1962 *Primitive social organization*. New York: Random House.

Shakapba, W. D.
1967 *Tibet: A political history*. New Haven: Yale University Press.

Shook, Edwin
1952 "Lugares arqeológicas del altiplano meridional central de Guatemala." *Antropologia e historia de Guatemala* 4(2). Ministirio de Educación Pública, Guatemala.

1965   "Archaeological survey of the Pacific coast of Guatemala." *Handbook of Middle American Indians*, vo . 2, part 1, pp. 180–194. Austin: University of Texas Press.

Siroux, M.
1959   *Les caravansérails de l'Iran.* Cairo: Institut Dominican d'Etudes Orientales.

Slicher Van Bath, B. H.
1963   *The agrarian history of western Europe* A.D. 500–1850, O. Ordish, trans. London: Edward Arnold.

Slotkin, J. S., ed.
1965   *Readings in early anthropology.* Viking Fund Publications in Anthropology 40. Chicago: Aldine Publishing Company.

Smith, Adam
1954   *The wealth of nations,* vol. 1. London: E. P. Dutton and Co.

Smith, A. Ledyard
1955   *Archaeological reconnaissance in central Guatemala.* Carnegie Institution of Washington, Publication 608. Washington, D.C.: Carnegie Institution.

Smith, A. Ledyard, and Kidder, Alfred V.
1951   *Excavations at Nebaj.* Carnegie Institution of Washington, Publication 594. Washington, D.C.: Carnegie Institution.

Smith, P. E. L.
1968   "Survey of excavations in Iran during 1966–67. Excavation reports, Ganj Dareh Tepe." *Iran* 6:158–160.

1970   "Ganj Dareh Tepe." *Iran* 8:174–176.

Smith, R. J.
1956   "Kurusu." In *Two Japanese villages,* J. B. Cornell and R. J. Smith, eds., pp. 1–112. Ann Arbor: University of Michigan Press.

Smock, David R.
1968   "Changing political processes among the Abaja Ibo." *Africa* 38:281–292.

Snow, Dean R.
1969   "Ceramic sequence and settlement location in pre-Hispanic Tlaxcala." *American Antiquity* 34(2):131–145.

Solecki, Ralph S.
1963   "Prehistory in Shanidar Valley, northern Iraq." *Science* 139(1551): 179–193.

Solecki, Rose L.
1964   "Zawi Chemi Shanidar, a post-Pleistocene village site in northern Iraq." *Report of the 6th International Congress on Quaternary* 4:405–412.

Southall, Aidan W.
1953   *Alur society.* Cambridge: Heffer and Sons.

Spencer, Herbert
1890   *First principles,* 4th ed. New York: D. Appleton and Company.

Spencer, J. E.
1966   *Shifting cultivation in southeast Asia.* University of California Publications in Geography, vol. 19. Berkeley: University of California Press.

Spencer, R. F.
1959   *North Alaskan Eskimo.* Bureau of American Ethnology, Bulletin 171. Washington, D.C.: Bureau of American Ethnology.

Spiro, M. E.
1965   "A typology of social structure and the patterning of social institutions: A cross-cultural study." *American Anthropologist* 67:1097–1119.

Spooner, Brian
1963   "The function of religion in Persian society." *Iran* 1:83–96.

———

1965a   "Arghiyān." *Iran* 3:97–108.

———

1965b   "Kinship and marriage in eastern Persia." *Sociologus,* 15(1):22–31.

———

1969a   "Politics, kinship and ecology in southeast Persia." *Ethnology* 8(2):139–152.

———

1969b   "Musavvada jihat-i bar-rasi-i jami' az kavir-ha va biyaban-ha-i vasat-i filat-i Iran." ["Outline for a comprehensive study of the deserts of the Central Iranian Plateau."] In *Yadnama-i Irani-i Minorsky,* Iraj Afshar and Mojtaba Minovi, eds., pp. 1–13. Teheran: University of Teheran.

———

1970   "South-west Khurasan." *Iran* 8:200.

———

1971a   "Notes on the toponymy of the Persian Makran." In *Iran and Islam,* C. E. Bosworth, ed., pp. 517–534. Edinburgh: Edinburgh University Press.

———

1971b   "Continuity and change in rural Iran: The eastern deserts." In *Iran: Continuity and variety,* Peter J. Chelkowski, ed. Fourth annual New York University Near Eastern Round Table 1970–1971. New York: The Center for Near Eastern Studies and the Center for International Studies, New York University.

1972a   "The status of nomadism as a cultural phenomenon." *International Studies in Sociology and Social Anthropology.* Leiden: Brill 12:122–131.

1972b   *Nomadism.* Addison Wesley Modular Publications (forthcoming).

Spores, Ronald
1969   "Settlement, farming technology and environment in the Nochixtlan Valley." *Science* 166(3905):557–569.

Stadelman, R.
1940   "Maize cultivation in northwest Guatemala.' *Carnegie Institution Contributions to American Anthropology and History 6.* Report no. 33, pp. 83–263.

Stamp, L. D., ed.
1937–1947   *The Land of Britain: The final report of the Land Utilization Survey of Britain,* 9 vols. London: Geographical Publications.

1938   "Land utilization and soil erosion in Nigeria." *Geographical Review* 28:32–45.

1969   *Man and the land,* 3rd. ed. London: William Collins, Sons and Company.

Stanford, D. J.
1969   "Recent excavations near Point Barrow, Alaska." Paper read at the 34th Annual Meeting of the Society for American Archaeology. Milwaukee.

Steckeweh, H., and Steindorff, G.
1936   *Die Fürstengraber von Qaw.* Leipzig: J. C. Hinrichs.

Steensberg, A.
1936   "North-west European plough-types of prehistoric times and the middle ages." *Acta archaeologia* 7:244–280.

1957   "Some recent Danish experiments in Neolithic agriculture." *The Agricultural History Review* 5(1):66–73.

Steggarda, Morris
1941   *Maya Indians of Yucatan.* Carnegie Institution of Washington, Publication 531. Washington, D.C.: Carnegie Institution.

Stevenson, R. F.
1968   *Population and political systems in tropical Africa.* New York: Columbia University Press.

Steward, Julian H.
1929   *Irrigation without agriculture*. Papers of the Michigan Academy of Sciences, Arts, and Letters 12:149–156.

_____
1936   "The economic and social basis of primitive bands." In *Essays in anthropology presented to A. L. Kroeber*. R. Lowie, ed. Berkeley: University of California Press, pp. 331–345.

_____
1955a   *Theory of culture change*. Urbana: University of Illinois Press.

_____
1955b   "Introduction" to *Irrigation civilizations: A comparative study*. Social Science Monographs, Pan-American Union. Washington, D.C.: Social science section, Department of cultural affairs.

Stewart, O. C.
1956   "Fire as the first great force employed by man " In *Man's role in changing the face of the earth*, W. L. Thomas, ed., pp. 115–129. Chicago: University of Chicago Press.

Stoecklin, J.; Eftekhar-nezhad, J.; and Hushmand-zadeh, A.
1965   *Geology of the Shotori Range*. Geological Survey of Iran, Report no. 3. Teheran: Ministry of Economy.

Stott, D. H.
1962   "Cultural and natural checks on population growth." In *Culture and the evolution of man*, M. F. Ashley Montague, ed., pp. 355–376. New York: Oxford University Press.

Struever, S.
1968   "Woodland subsistence—settlement systems in the lower Illinois valley." In *New perspectives in archaeology*, S. R. and L. R. Binford, eds., pp. 285–312. Chicago: Aldine Publishing Company.

Swartz, Marc J.; Turner, Victor W.; and Tuden, Arthur, eds.
1966   *Political anthropology*. Chicago: Aldine Publishing Company.

Swidler, W. W.
1969   "Some demographic factors regulating the formation of flocks and camps among the Brahui." Paper delivered at the American Anthropological Association Meetings, November 1969. New Orleans.

Tallgren, A. M.
1937   "The method of prehistoric archaeology." *Antiquity* 11:152–161.

Tanner, J. M.
1962   *Growth at adolescence*, 2nd ed. London: Basil Blackwell.

Tauber, H.
1962   "Copenhagen radiocarbon dates V." *Radiocarbon* 4:27–34.

Terra, G. J. A.
1954   "Mixed garden horticulture in Java." *Journal of Tropical Geography*
3:34–43.

Tobler, A. J.
1950   *Excavations at Tepe Gawra*, vol. 2. Philadelphia: The University
Museum.

Tolstoy, Paul, and Paradis, Louise
1970   "Early and middle preclassic culture in the basin of Mexico."
Science 167:344–351.

Toynbee, Arnold J.
1934   *A study of history*, vol. 3. London: Oxford University Press.

Trigger, B. G.
1965   *History and settlement in Lower Nubia*. New Haven: Department of
Anthropology, Yale University.

Tschol, Peter
1966   "Informe sobre el estado de los Trabajos arqueológicos (proyecto
areal interdisciplinario Puebla-Tlaxcala)." Manuscript.

Tuden, Arthur
1966   "Leadership and decision-making process." In *Political anthropology*,
M. J. Swartz, V. W. Turner, and A. Tuden, eds., pp. 275–283. Chicago:
Aldine Publishing Company.

Turnbull, C. M.
1965   *Wayward servants: The two worlds of the African pygmies*. Garden
City, N.Y.: Natural History Press.

1968   "The importance of flux in two hunting societies." In *Man the
hunter*, R. B. Lee and I. DeVore, eds., pp. 132–137. Chicago: Aldine Publishing Company.

Union Research Institute
1968   *Tibet 1950–1967*. Hong Kong: Union Press.

Vandier, J.
1936   *La famine dans l'Égypte ancienne*. Le Caire: Institut français d'archéologie orientale.

Van Liere, W. J., and deContenson, H.
1964   "Holocene environment and early settlement in the Levant."
Annales Archéologiques de Syrie 14:125–128.

Vansina, J. L.
1962   "A comparison of African kingdoms." *Africa* 32:324–335.

Van Zeist, W.
1967   "Late Quaternary vegetation history of western Iran." *Review of
Palaeobotany and Palynology* 2:301–311.

1969   "Reflections on prehistoric environments in the Near East." In *The domestication and exploitation of plants and animals*, P. J. Ucko and G. W. Dimbleby, eds., pp. 35–46. Chicago: Aldine Publishing Company.

Vyda, A. P.
1961   "Expansion and warfare among swidden agriculturalists." *American Anthropologist* 63(2):346–358.

Villa Rojas, A.
1945   *The Maya of east central Quintana Roo*. Carnegie Institution of Washington, Publication 559. Washington, D.C.: The Carnegie Institution.

Vogt, Evon Z.
1964   "Summary and appraisal." *Desarrollo cultural de los Mayas*. Seminario de la Cultura Maya, Universidad Autónoma Nacional de Mexico.

Wagley, C.
1951   "Cultural influences on population: A comparison of two Tupi tribes." *Revista do Museu Paulista* (n.s.) 5:95–104. [Reprinted in *Environment and cultural behavior: Ecological studies in cultural anthropology*, A. P. Vayda, ed., pp. 268–279. New York: Natural History Press, 1969.

Wailes, Bernard
1970   "The origins of settled farming in Temperate Europe." *Indo-European and Indo-Europeans*, George Cardona, Henry M. Hoenigswald, and Alfred Senn, eds., pp. 279–306. Philadelphia: University of Pennsylvania Press.

Wallace, Anthony F. C.
1966   *Religion: An anthropological view*. New York: Random House.

Wasylikowa, K.
1967   "Late Quaternary plant macrofossils from Lake Zeribar, western Iran." *Review of Palaeobotany and Palynology* 2:313–318.

Watson, J. B.
1965   "From hunting to horticulture in the New Guinea highlands." *Ethnology* 4(3):295–309.

Watters, R. F.
1960   "The nature of shifting cultivation: A review of recent research." *Pacific Viewpoint* 1:59–99.

Wertime, Theodore A.
1964   "Man's first encounters with metallurgy " *Science* 146(3649):1257–1267.

1967   "A metallurgical expedition through the Persian Desert." In *Investigations at Tal-i-Iblis*. J. R. Caldwell, ed. Illinois State Museum Preliminary Reports no. 9. [Reprinted in *Science* 159(3818), 1968.]

Wheatley, Paul
1971   *The pivot of the four quarters.* Chicago: Aldine.

Wheeler, R. E. M.
1930   "Mr. Collingwood and Mr. Randall." *Antiquity* 4:91–95.

White, Leslie A.
1959   *The evolution of culture: The development of civilization to the fall of Rome.* New York: McGraw-Hill Book Company.

White, Lynn, Jr.
1962   *Medieval technology and social change.* Oxford: Clarendon Press.

1969   "The expansion of technology 500–1500." *The Fontana Economic History of Europe,* C. M. Cipolla, ed., vol. 1, chap. 4. London: Fontana.

Whyte, R. O.
1961   "Evolution of land use in south-western Asia." In *A history of land use in arid regions,* L. Dudley Stamp, ed., pp. 57–118. Arid Zone Research 17. Paris: UNESCO.

Widdowson, E. M., and McLance, R. A.
1960   "Some effects of accelerating growth: 1. General somatic development" *Proceedings of the Royal Society* B 152:186–286.

Willey, Gordon R., and Smith, A. Ledyard
1969   *The ruins of Altar de Sacrificios, Department of Petén, Guatemala: An introduction.* Papers of the Peabody Museum of Archaeology and Ethnology 62(1). Harvard University, Cambridge.

Willey, Gordon R.; Bullard, William R., Jr.; Glass, John B.; and Gifford, James C.
1965   *Prehistoric Maya settlements in the Belize Valley.* Papers of the Peabody Museum of Archaeology and Ethnology, vol. 54. Harvard University, Cambridge.

Wilson, D. C., and Sutherland, I.
1953   "The age of the menarche in the tropics." *British Medical Journal* 2:607–608.

Wilson, J.
1955   "Buto and Hierakonpolis in the geography of Egypt." *Journal of Near Eastern Studies* 14:209–236.

Wittfogel, K. A.
1957   *Oriental despotism: A comparative study of total power.* New Haven: Yale University Press.

Witthoft, John
1967   "Glazed polish on flint tools." *American Antiquity* 32(3):383–388.

Wolanski, N.
1965 "Environmental modification of human form and function." In *Symposium on the biology of human variation*, J. Brozek, ed., pp. 826–840. Annals of the New York Academy of Science, vol. 134.

Wolf, Eric R.
1966 *Peasants*. Englewood Cliffs, N. J.: Prentice-Hall.

Wolf, Eric R., and Palerm, Angel
1955 "Irrigation in the old Acolhua domain, Mexico." *Southwestern Journal of Anthropology* 11(3): 265–281.

Wooldridge, S. W.
1936 "The Anglo-Saxon settlement." In *An historical geography of England before* A.D. *1800*, H. C. Darby, ed., Chap. 3. Cambridge: Cambridge University Press.

Wooldridge, S. W., and Linton, D. L.
1933 "The loam-terrains of southeast England and their relation to its early history." *Antiquity* 7:297–310.

Worsley, Peter M.
1957 "Millenarian movements in Melanesia." *Rhodes-Livingstone Institute Journal* 21:18–31.

Wright, H. E., Jr.
1960 "Climate and prehistoric man in the eastern Mediterranean." In *Prehistoric investigations in Iraqi Kurdistan*, R. J. Braidwood and B. Howe, eds., pp. 71–97. Chicago: Oriental Institute, Studies in Ancient Oriental Civilization 31.

———
1968 "Natural environment of early food production north of Mesopotamia." *Science* 161:334–339.

Wright, H. E.; McAndrews, J. H.; and Zeist, W. van
1967 "Modern pollen rain in western Iran and its relation to plant geography and quaternary vegetational history." *Journal of Ecology* 55: 415–443.

Wurtman, R.; Axelrod, A.; and Kelly, E.
1968 *The pineal*. New York: Academic Press.

Yeates, N. T. M.
1949 "The breeding season of the sheep with particular reference to its modification by artificial means using white light." *Journal of Agricultural Science* 39:1–16.

Young, Michael W.
1966 "The divine kingship of the Jukun: A re-evaluation of some theories." *Africa* 36:135–152.

Young, T. C., Jr.
1962   "Taking the history of the Hasanlu area back another five thousand years: Sixth and fifth millennium settlements in Solduz Valley, Persia." *Illustrated London News* 241:707–709.

————
1966   "Survey in western Iran, 1961." *Journal of Near Eastern Studies* 25:228–239.

Young, T. C., Jr., and Smith, P. E. L.
1966   "Research in the prehistory of central western Iran." *Science* 153:(3734):386–391.

Zacharias, H., and Wurtman, R.
1964   "Blindness: Its relation to age of menarche." *Science* 144:1154–1155.

Znaniecki, F.
1934   *The method of sociology.* New York: Farrar and Rinehart.

Zohary, D.
1969   "The progenitors of wheat and barley in relation to domestication and agricultural dispersal in the Old World." In *The domestication and exploitation of plants and animals*, P. J. Ucko and G. W. Dimbleby, eds., pp. 47–66. London: Gerald Duckworth.

Zohary, M.
1963   *On the geobotanical structure of Iran.* Bulletin of the Research Council of Israel, section D, Botany. 11D, Supp.

Index